Right to Development and Illicit Financial Flows from Africa

Africa: Past, Present & Prospects

Series Editors: Toyin Falola, The University of Texas, Austin; and Olajumoke Yacob-Haliso, Brandeis University, Waltham, MA

This series collates and curates studies of Africa in its multivalent local, regional, and global contexts. It aims fundamentally to capture in one series historical, contemporary and multidisciplinary studies which analyze the dynamics of the African predicament from deeply theoretical perspectives while marshalling empirical data to describe, explain, and predict trends in continuities and change in Africa and in African studies.

The books published in this series represents the multiplicity of voices, local and global in relation to African futures. It not only represents diversity, but also provides a platform for convergence of outstanding research that will enliven debates about the future of Africa, while also advancing theory and informing policy making. Preference is given to studies that deliberately link the past with the present and advances knowledge about various African nations by extending the range, breadth, depth, types and sources of data and information existing and emerging about these countries.

Recent and Forthcoming Titles

Right to Development and Illicit Financial Flows from Africa: Dynamics, Perspectives, and Prospects edited by Gerard Emmanuel Kamdem Kamga, Serges Djoyou Kamga, and Arnold Kwesiga

Social and Ethical Issues of Global Pandemics: A Southern African Perspective edited by Masake Pilisano Harris and Richard Obinna Iroanya

African Perspectives on Global Pandemics and the Challenges of Peace and Security edited by Masake Pilisano Harris and Richard Obinna Iroanya

African Political Economy in the Twenty-First Century: Theories, Perspectives, and Issues edited by Emeka C. Iloh, Ernest T. Aniche, and Stephen N. Azom

Citizenship and the Diaspora in the Digital Age: Farooq Kperogi and the Virtual Community, by Toyin Falola

Right to Development and Illicit Financial Flows from Africa

Dynamics, Perspectives, and Prospects

Edited by
Gerard Emmanuel Kamdem Kamga,
Serges Djoyou Kamga, and Arnold Kwesiga

LEXINGTON BOOKS
Lanham • Boulder • New York • London

Published by Lexington Books
An imprint of The Rowman & Littlefield Publishing Group, Inc.
4501 Forbes Boulevard, Suite 200, Lanham, Maryland 20706
www.rowman.com

86-90 Paul Street, London EC2A 4NE

British Library Cataloguing in Publication Information Available

Library of Congress Cataloging-in-Publication Data

Names: Kamga, Gerard Emmanuel Kamdem, editor, author. | Kamga, Serges Djoyou (Serges Alain Djoyou), editor, author. | Kwesiga, Arnold, editor, author.
Title: Right to development and illicit financial flows from Africa: dynamics, perspectives, and prospects / edited by Gerard Emmanuel Kamdem Kamga, Serges Djoyou Kamga and Arnold Kwesiga.
Other titles: Africa: past, present & prospects.
Description: Lanham: Lexington Books, 2024. | Series: Africa: past, present & prospects | Includes bibliographical references and index. | Summary: "Right to Development and Illicit Financial Flows from Africa: Dynamics, Perspectives, and Prospects discusses illicit financial flows and the right to development in Africa. The contributors examine recent examples of illicit financial flows and the impact that these have had on the African continent"—Provided by publisher.
Identifiers: LCCN 2023046332 (print) | LCCN 2023046333 (ebook) | ISBN 9781666932300 (cloth) | ISBN 9781666932317 (ebook)
Subjects: LCSH: Economic development—Africa. | Human rights—Economic aspects—Africa. | Flow of funds—Corrupt practices—Africa. | Commercial crimes—Africa. | Corruption—Africa. | Africa—Economic Conditions—21st century. | Africa—Social conditions—21st century.
Classification: LCC HC800.Z9 R544 2024 (print) | LCC HC800.Z9 (ebook) | DDC 332.0424096—dc23/eng/20231004
LC record available at https://lccn.loc.gov/2023046332
LC ebook record available at https://lccn.loc.gov/2023046333

Contents

Acknowledgements

This book is the product of continuous and persistent effort of many people.

We would like to acknowledge all the partners working on the right to development and whose concerted efforts paved the way for this book to become a reality. Our special gratitude goes to the Free State Centre for Human Rights, University of the Free State, the Centre for Human Rights, University of Pretoria and the Thabo Mbeki African School of Public & International Affairs.

We would like to thank all the reviewers and colleagues who have been working behind the scenes to make sure that this book aligns with the highest standard possible.

Finally, we want to thank all the contributors who, despite their busy schedule, agreed to be part of this project. We also want to thank them for their patience and understanding during the process that led to the publication of volume.

Gerard Emmanuel Kamdem Kamga
Serges Djoyou Kamga
Arnold Kwesiga

Introduction

Gerard Emmanuel Kamdem Kamga,
Serges Djoyou Kamga, and Arnold Kwesiga

RIGHT TO DEVELOPMENT AND ILLICIT FINANCIAL FLOWS FROM AFRICA: DYNAMICS, PERSPECTIVES, AND PROSPECTS

The first section of the United Nations Declaration on the Right to Development of 1986 provides that the right to development is an inalienable human right by virtue of which every human person and all peoples are entitled to participate in, contribute to, and enjoy economic, social, cultural, and political development, in which all human rights and fundamental freedoms can be fully realised. Even though this right has been subject to controversies, the current state of human rights and development in Africa following decades of colonisation and exploitation put back into context the approach that considers the right to development to be 'the alpha and the omega of human rights, the first and last human rights, the beginning and the end, the means and the goal of human rights'. It is in 1977 that the United Nations Commission on Human Rights adopted, for the first time, a resolution that formally recognised the RTD as a human right. At the international level, the right to development is recognised mostly by a series of soft laws including the Declaration on the Right to Development adopted in 1986 by the United Nations and the Vienna Declaration and Programme of Action of 1993. Regarding its binding force, the right to development is said to be part of customary international law and part of the norm of *jus cogens*, the latter being a key principle in international law that binds all states and does not provide exceptions. If at the global level, the right to development remains subject to a process of custom-formation, at the regional level, this right is legally binding under the African Charter on Human and Peoples' Rights adopted in

1981 and entered into force in 1986. Section 22 of this instrument provides further clarifications on the meaning of the right to development, that is, 'all peoples have the right to their economic, social and cultural development with due regard to their freedom and identity and in the equal enjoyment of the common heritage of mankind. States shall have the duty, individually and collectively, to ensure the exercise of the right to development'. The case of *SERAC & Another v. Nigeria* where two nongovernmental organisations on the basis of Section 22 of the African Charter on Human and Peoples' Rights filed a complaint against the government of Nigeria before the African Commission remains one of the few instances where the RTD as a core human right was reaffirmed at the continental level.

The realisation of the right to development in Africa is fundamentally linked to economic performances and the extent to which the state can deliver. For the past years, the economic performance of the African continent has been featuring among the top economies in the world. One would have expected this performance to bring about social-economic change, allowing people to achieve their human potential inherent to the idea of development but this has not been the case. Development is a broad concept, for not only does it include sound economic performance and fair distribution of benefits, but it also requires the improvement of the living conditions of individual citizens through the provision of quality, accessible and affordable healthcare services, housing, infrastructure, and education – key areas for human capital development. The gap between recent economic achievements on the continent and its state of generalised underdevelopment coupled with rampant poverty, corruption, prolonged economic crisis, and political instabilities signals an issue with resource allocations and inequities in distribution. How to understand that despite such economic performance and being endowed with a variety of natural resources and raw materials that the rest of the world is longing for, Africa remains one of the poorest continents in the planet, with one-third of its population undernourished and millions with no access to clean water, electricity, education, healthcare, and infrastructure? The continent currently sits at the bottom of the most major development indices. The 2021/2022 Human Development Report shows that in several African countries less than 3 per cent of the population living in the bottom 40 per cent of the income distribution is expected to rely on support from governments or nongovernmental organisations – and the rest were most likely to rely on family and friends. This situation is exacerbated by the fact that the Global Human Development Index value has declined two years in a row, erasing the gains of the preceding five years. A combination of factors is at the origin of such a situation, including among others, weak state institutions, poor governance, lack of transformative leadership, and more importantly the proliferation of illicit financial flows.

Illicit Financial Flows are defined as money illegally earned, transferred, or used. These occur when the funds involved are proceeds from illegal transactions and when the transfer of such funds failed to comply with legal prescriptions, namely transparency, accountability, and tax deduction. What characterises illicit financial flows is that the 'flows of money are in violation of laws in their origin, or during their movement or use, and are therefore considered illicit'. Recent research shows that the phenomenon of illicit financial flows constitutes a key disabler of development in general and the Right to Development in particular. In 2015, a report by the High Level Panel on Illicit Financial Flows from Africa headed by former South African president Thabo Mbeki, showed that the continent loses an average of $50 billion yearly through illicit financial flows. The United Nations Conference on Trade and Development held in 2020 revealed that this number has since increased to the amount of $89 billion yearly; an amount that is equivalent to 3.7 percent of Africa's Gross Domestic Product. As previously mentioned, the right to development is an inalienable human right by virtue of which every human person and all peoples are entitled to participate in, contribute to, and enjoy economic, social, cultural, and political development, in which all human rights and fundamental freedoms can be fully realised. In essence, the failure to counter illicit financial flows and recover stolen assets is a denial of access to basic health care, education, safe water and sanitation, adequate housing, and infrastructure, all of which are basic conditions for the enjoyment of human rights in general and the right development in particular. So far, the common practice has been to bring in so-called development aid and loans with unbearable interest rate to the detriment of the continent and its population. Yet, it is axiomatic that the right to development in Africa cannot be achieved as long as numerous countries remain trapped within the paradigm of relying on 'generous' development aid and foreign loans. This probably explains why the continent is currently among the most indebted around the globe. According to some predictions and projections, some countries are in the impossibility of paying back their debt for, such debt has reached unprecedented levels.

The proliferation of IFFs fuelled by some multinational corporations and other criminal networks has compelled Africa to contract foreign loans and agreements with leonine clauses to the detriment of their natural resources, sovereignty, and populations. Recent estimates depict the extent to which a staggering sum of money is drained out of the continent year in, year out to pay not the capital, but the interests. Another way of understanding the link between illicit financial flows and human rights is to examine the link between the availability of resources and the capacity of states to address extreme poverty, which is generally considered a human rights concern. Illicit financial flows not only impede the development agenda of the African continent but also question the very nature of development as a human right. These preoccupations are at the heart of the upcoming developments and insights provided by different contributors from a variety of perspectives.

OVERVIEW OF THE BOOK

The book is organised in two parts. The first part is dedicated to digging for development, dynamic, and perspectives in curbing illicit financial flows, whereas the second part focuses on illicit financial flows, multinational corporations, and natural resource exploitation in Africa. In the first chapter of the book entitled 'Agenda 2063: Illicit Financial Flows and Africa's Right to Development' Toyin Falola sets the scene by referring to the dire need for an all-round development across the fifty-four African countries. As he puts it, while everyone agrees on this, the matter lies with how to realise this robust development, for over the years, different policies – municipal, country-wide, and regional – have attempted to tackle it. Despite such initiatives, the results have often fallen short of expectations due to long-standing problems like illicit financial flows affecting core developments in Africa.

In chapter 2, Gerard Emmanuel Kamdem Kamga makes 'An Appraisal of the Architecture to Curb Illicit Financial Flows from South Africa and Their Impact on the Right to Development'. Given the sound economic performance of South Africa and the wealth from its mining sector, one would have expected an improvement of the living conditions of its populations, but the situation is otherwise and simply mirrors what is going on across the continent. The reason for this setback is that despite the astounding economic performance, the country is subject to weak state institutions and more importantly to the theft of its resources by individual and criminal networks as well as multinational corporations through illicit financial flows.

The argument differs from that of chapter 3 dedicated to 'Ethiopia: Illicit Financial Flows' Consequences Exacerbating Conflict in the Northern Corridor' where the author T. K. Seife is of the view that Illicit financial flows have become a significant development and security impediment in Africa, particularly in least developed countries such as Ethiopia. According to him, Ethiopia has been harmed for the last three decades owing to illicit financial flows orchestrated by the Tigray People's Liberation Front (TPLF) a leftist ethnic nationalist secessionist paramilitary force which was a critical component of Ethiopia's leadership.

This narrative is far from that which is put forward by Arnold Kwesiga and Linah Aduda who review 'Tax Cooperation in Curbing Illicit Financial Flows from Africa' in chapter 4. As articulated by these authors, the Addis Ababa Agenda for Action 2015 portrays how the elimination of illicit financial flows will ensure that resources lost through this plague are redirected to development. Africa loses $88.6 billion to illicit financial flows, and if these resources were channelled to their right destination, the continent's dependency on donor aid would also be heavily reduced.

In chapter 5 entitled 'State Complicity in Impairing Its Development Rights: Salient Lessons from the Nigerian Halliburton Bribery Scandal', Marie-Louise Fehun Aren reiterates the urgency of initiating relevant steps towards a genuine realisation of the right to development. The author observes that the ability of states to effectively realise their development goals has been severely impaired by their own complicity in undermining their development rights through corporate illicit financial movement from multinational corporations via bribery, money laundering, corruption, and legislative passivity in formulating/implementing long-term pro-development rights and laws. Yet, recent studies further indicate that eliminating illicit financial flows could significantly reduce the $200 billion financing gap African countries face in achieving its Sustainable Development Goals targets.

In chapter 6 dedicated to 'Advocating for a Human Rights-Based Approach to Combatting Illicit Financial Flows' Annelie De Man suggests a human rights-based approach to curb illicit financial flows: an approach based on the notion that the realisation of human rights should be at the heart of development. As she puts it, this approach calls for implementing entrenched human rights principles (i.e. non-discrimination, participation, empowerment, and accountability) to ensure fair and sustainable programming that fulfils the values recognised in the Declaration on the Right to Development.

This argument is not far from the one raised by Marianne Séverin who, in chapter 7, analysed the situation in 'South African Banks, State Capture, Illicit Financial Flows, and Violation of the Right to Development'. African countries signed and ratified the African Charter, and so the right to development through article 22. Nevertheless, African states are far from complying with the realisation of this right, the issue being a combination of weak state institutions, poor governance, lack of democracy, corruption, and illicit financial flows.

The South African Banking Sector is once again scrutinised in the subsequent chapter by Isaac Shai and Felix Dube. When focusing on 'Neoliberal Legality, Illicit Financial Flows, and the Complicity of the South African Banking Sector' both authors are of the opinion that the deliberate 'looking away' by banks makes not only banks complicit but also participants in illicit financial flows. Their argument is grounded on the premises according to which the ability of banks to 'look away' is made possible by neoliberal legality that has entrenched itself in laws regulating banking in South Africa. They went on to suggest that despite the limitations of law as an instrument to combat the deleterious effects of neoliberalism, there is an opportunity to reorient the laws regulating banking with the purpose of addressing rampant illicit financial flows.

This perspective on illicit financial flows and the right development is different from that articulated by Olayinka Oluwakemi Adeniyi and John Oluwadamilare Olawuyi who analyse the 'Gendered Impact of Illicit Financial Flows: Women's Participation and Contribution in Curbing Illicit Financial Flows from Africa with Focus on Nigeria and South Africa' in chapter 9. The authors argue that the issue of illicit transfer of funds in Africa is akin to a parasite that has come to stay but true to its parasitic nature cannot but prove itself by underlying the stagnancy or underdevelopment of the continent for many years. According to them while the acts of illicit fund transfer may camouflage its effect on the individual citizens of the countries, they affect women differently than men with the obvious impact on socio-economic rights.

This chapter serves as a transition into the second part of the book where a set of chapters are dedicated to illicit financial flows, multinational corporations, and natural resource exploitation in Africa.

Chapter 10 is the first chapter of the second part of the book entitled 'Digging for Development: The Impact of Illicit Financial Flows on the Realisation of the Right to Development in Africa's Mineral and Petroleum Exploration Industries' by Rita Ozoemena and Chané Henney. The authors begin by observing that the mining sector is not only one of Africa's most lucrative industries bringing in revenue through business transactions and investments but also an industry that is vulnerable to corruption. They proceed by reviewing how illicit financial flows in the mining industry hinders the realisation of the inalienable right to development in Nigeria, South Africa, and Zimbabwe, countries with significant natural resources that contribute immensely to their Gross Domestic Product.

In chapter 11 entitled 'Manufacturing Underdevelopment: Coins Trafficking as Illicit Financial Flows in Disguise within the Central Africa Economic and Monetary Cooperation' Gerard Emmanuel Kamdem Kamga provides insight into the phenomenon of scarcity of coins in the CEMAC region. The phenomenon derives from a unique kind of traffic through which coins are taken out of the region and exported to China where they are melted and turned into jewellery for more profit. This results in devastating consequences for the economy and the right to development in the region.

A topic in line with the exportation of raw materials to China devoted to resource financed infrastructure under SICOMINES agreement as an impediment to achieving the right to development in the Democratic Republic of Congo is presented in chapter 12 by Tumba Tuseku Dieudonne and Muyamba Mangu. Both authors enlighten the readers about the government of the Democratic Republic of Congo's attempt to realise the right to development through an agreement, a resource financed infrastructure with a group of Chinese companies to build public infrastructures such as hospitals, roads and railways, and airports in the country. Such infrastructures are said to be funded by a $ 6.5 billion loan from a Chinese bank named Exim. The contributors further observe that rather than being a conduit for development, the agreement appears to have facilitated the exportation of raw mineral resources from the DRC to China.

The matter is different when it comes to tax justice which is the focus of chapter 13 on 'Taxation, Tax Injustice and the Right to Development in Africa' by Serges Djoyou Kamga who explores the significance of tax injustices or tax abuses on the enjoyment of the right to development in Africa. In his view, tax injustice takes place in the form of tax evasion and tax avoidance with the ultimate objective to siphon funds away from the national treasury, a practice that is at the heart of the violation of the right to development in Africa.

In the quest for a genuine solution to the problem of illicit financial flows, in chapter 14 entitled 'Haemorrhaging: The Impacts of Illicit Financial Flows on the Realisation of the Right to Development in Africa: A Case for Uganda', Nampwera Chrispus and Kirunga Joyce consider this phenomenon as a concern given Africa's inadequate growth and high poverty levels, translating into limited access to a range of social services, infrastructure, and investments. According to them realising the right to development and all the other rights enshrined in the African Charter requires adequate resources.

Part 1

DIGGING FOR DEVELOPMENT

DYNAMIC AND PERSPECTIVES IN CURBING ILLICIT FINANCIAL FLOWS FROM AFRICA

Chapter 1

Agenda 2063

Illicit Financial Flows and Africa's Right to Development

Toyin Falola

INTRODUCTION

There is no doubt about the fact that there is a dire need for an all-round development across the fifty-four African countries. While everyone agrees on this, how to realise this robust development is usually where the problem is. Over the years, different policies – municipal, country-wide, and regional – have attempted to tackle these problems. Still, the results have often fallen short of expectations due to long-standing problems like IFFs affecting core developments in Africa. In a bid to renew the efforts towards the development of Africa, the Agenda 2063 developmental plan was reached in 2013. This chapter provides insight into how the implementation of this 50-years plan would deliver the development it needs. This is why I will be discussing what Africa stands to gain by embarking on the pursuit of the goals and aspirations of this Agenda, particularly the importance of stakeholders coming together to ensure that the development that is promised by the Agenda 2063 comes to fruition. In so doing, I will first consider the 'Right to Development' in Africa, its prospects, and how, among other things, IFFs from Africa are mounting a stumbling block to proper development.

DEVELOPMENT IN AFRICA: THE PAST AND PRESENT REALITIES

For more than half a century that Africa has attained political independence, the state of development in the continent has witnessed a snail-paced movement.[1] Of course, there have been some levels of development recorded in different aspects in Africa.[2] However, if these developments are juxtaposed with the expected level of development that a continent like Africa – with its enormous resources – should have, the reality of stack underdevelopment is made more explicit.[3] In fact, countries in Africa, more than any other continent, make the list of the least developed countries in the world.[4] This is the heartbreaking reality of the continent.

The state of underdevelopment in Africa has different facets and is expressed in diverse ways. For decades, though having enormous resources, the continent has not gone beyond surface development in areas that hardly translate to betterment in the lives of the African people. The World Bank, in a recent report, estimated that with the surge of the COVID-19 pandemic and the contraption in the economy of African states, about 40 million people are expected to be pushed into extreme poverty.[5] This is different from the calamitous effects the pandemic would have on development across the continent.

AFRICA'S RIGHT TO DEVELOPMENT

The fight for human rights globally has primarily focused on enacting and entrenching personal, political, civil, and sociocultural freedoms. It seemed in the past that all the human person needed to live an ordinary life was access to fundamental rights to life, freedom of movement, free expression, proper enfranchisement, among others. However, times have changed. While these sets of rights are still vastly important, a vital component of the debate on rights that was left out is economics.

As unfolding circumstances have proven, for the recognition of rights to be wholesome, much attention must be paid to economics, and this means that the focus of human rights should be much more developmental rather than political. The reason for this is firmly entrenched in the reasoning that humans and the rights they wish to exercise would flourish better in an environment that furthers development rather than an entire focus on the pursuit of political ideology.

Regrettably, however, the focus on politics instead of development is much more prevalent on the African continent. This gets reflected in Africa's relationship with international diplomacy. Diplomatic interests in Africa have primarily been about alliances along ideological lines and usually forced subservience to world powers. As a result, if they ever existed, foreign investments in economic development have more often than not been subjected to the back burner.[6] The slightest instances of efforts around helping Africa to develop economically usually involved monetary aid, which has only constantly delivered suboptimal returns.[7]

The direct impact of the erstwhile status quo is palpable. For instance, the continent is regarded as the poorest region on the planet, with a great majority of its population living below minimum and reasonably acceptable poverty lines.[8] Sadly, Africa features nine of the ten countries with the lowest gross domestic product (GDP) per capita, and out of the bottom fifty, it features an overwhelming majority of 33, per World Bank data.[9] Africa has an outsized representation on the United Nations' list of least-developed countries[10] and is heavily featured on the *Heavily Indebted Poor Countries* (HIPC) Initiative created by the IMF and the World Bank.[11] The effect of Africa's ubiquitous poverty is translated to dilapidating infrastructure,[12] gross economic inequality,[13] and a poor showing across human development parameters, especially in education and health.[14]

The preceding all point to the fact that Africa must set in motion imminent sporadic economic development. However, for this to happen, the continent must be able to experience what has come to be described in international relations parlance as 'The Right to Development'.

The Right to Development is conceived as a sacrosanct right through which a person can access overall development. Following the United Nations conception of the Right, the Right to Development could be regarded as a 'right of rights' as it aims to realise all other human rights and freedoms. A vital element of the Right to Development is its multifaceted and varied approach to the idea of development. It incorporates such areas that will not have traditionally been regarded as components of development.

In the past, across the globe, development was never seen as a human rights issue. Basically, governments in various regions viewed developmental issues as fundamental problems that had to do with fiscal and monetary policy and that fiscal and monetary policies could proffer solutions to developmental problems. The results of this then-prevalent school of thought included persistent poverty and inequality. While financial policies made by central banks and finance ministries were instrumental, they failed to deliver broad-based development because development could not be tackled from that sole viewpoint. Today, conceptualising development will entail looking at such ideas as education, culture, neocolonialism, international relations, and diplomacy.

The Right to Development is quite unique in that it is a collective right as much as it is an individual right. On the micro-level, it grants the individual the Right to attain their desired economic aims and sets frameworks to aid this attainment. On the macro level, it grants groups of persons the collective power to be liberated from factors that militate against the attainment of economic freedoms. A central theme of this collective power is the abhorrence of domination of a people's local economy by foreign interests and entities. The resultant state of affairs is that locals have more say and sway in the prevailing circumstances of their economies. It also encourages the notion of globalisation as it helps players from all countries play vital roles in the global economy.

The concept of collectivity in granting the Right to Development introduces the impact of international diplomacy on the attainment of the Right. While sovereign states are tasked with formulating policies to help empower their citizens with this Right, the collective power to attain their economic aims might be hampered by foreign domination and stunt their contribution to globalisation. This is the African experience. Apparently, as a result of colonial legacies, many African countries still have their economies being heavily influenced by the interests of their once colonial powers to the detriment of Africans. Breaking these holds is one of the central elements of entrenching the Right to Development.

The origins of the Right to Development are said to be the United Nations, but facts show that African regional legal frameworks had introduced this Right before it became a part of international law. However, there started to be a shift in international thinking from the mid-sixties culminating in enacting documents such as the International Covenant on Economic, Social and Cultural Rights 1966, which recognised socio-economic and cultural rights as fundamental human rights.[15] This was further consolidated with the signing of the Declaration on the Right to Development 1986.[16] This supposedly marked a departure in the conception of human rights.

Going forward, stakeholders started to acknowledge the importance of these developmental rights (economic, social, cultural) to attain what can be referred to as "traditional" fundamental human rights. Conversely, granting fundamental human rights was also sacrosanct to attaining sociocultural and economic rights. In essence, these sets of rights were symbiotic and never exclusive. Subsequent efforts such as the unveiling of the Minimum Development Goals (MDGs)[17] and the consequent Sustainable Development Goals (SDGs)[18] were furtherance of this prevailing conception. However, the push for what is now known as the Right to Development did not start with the 1986 Declaration. Years earlier, the *African Charter on Human and People's Rights 1981* clearly states that 'civil and political rights' are not dissociable from economic and social rights and that the satisfaction of socio-economic rights helps guarantee civil and political rights.[19]

PROSPECTS OF THE RIGHT TO DEVELOPMENT IN AFRICA

The full realisation of the Right to Development in Africa can unleash well-rounded development in all ramifications on the continent. The perceptible effects in alleviating inequality, broadening access to elementary services, and improving human development will be nothing short of remarkable. Some of the prospects that the Right to Development is perceived to have include:

REDUCING INEQUALITY

While Africa does not feature on the list of wealthiest regions on the planet, it still suffers from debilitating economic inequality.[20] The gap between the upper class and those at the bottom of the economic ladder is one of the widest in the world.[21] Several factors can be adduced for this state of affairs, ranging from colonial-era economic policies that have persisted to date to stunted and unequal economic growth. However, one of the central elements actively eviscerating the chances of reversing the course of things is an absence of welfare policies that can assist the poor to move up the economic ladder. The attainment of developmental rights, with the multi-sectoral approach it brings to development issues, will spur the introduction of societal safety nets that will provide critical assistance to the desperately poor.

This will, in turn, improve a vital but flagrantly absent modicum of development which is social mobility. Moreover, cushioning the effects of extreme poverty can enable the poor to engage in productive ventures that have the potential to enable them to escape the proverbial poverty trap.[22] With the proper achievement of the Right to Development, Africa might as well just be closing the wide gap of inequality prevalent in the continent.

BROAD ACCESS TO BASIC SERVICES

Basic amenities of life are as good as non-existent in most places on the continent. Nevertheless, from education to health, infrastructure, and security, many states seemingly lack essential services to afford decent human living. Due to the government's failure, many of these amenities have to be provided by the largely profit-oriented private sector. The resultant effect is that these conveniences that are fundamental to the survival of humans everywhere are offered at the steepest prices. However, the problem is not entirely that of the exorbitant costs, but that a tiny portion of the population was impoverished and therefore are flagrantly unable to bear the expenses. The corollary repercussion is that the middle class spends a tremendous amount of their income to address primitive needs while the poor (in their large numbers) can afford them. The entrenchment of the Right to Development will unleash welfare services that will address inequality in access to basic amenities, offering the opportunity to the so-called ordinary citizens.

IMPROVEMENT IN HUMAN DEVELOPMENT PARAMETERS

It has been established that one of the tenets of the Right to Development is that it offers varied techniques to how development is conceived and achieved. Thus, economic development merely stops reducing the unemployment rate or increasing overall GDP by specific percentage points. Social, cultural, and political factors are also considered in gauging development. This translates to the fact that human development issues will be accorded some priority. Africa's extant human development indicators from health to education report poor performance across the fifty-plus countries in the region.[23] With increasing emphasis on societal safety nets and welfare, the critical parameters of education and health are poised to receive heavy economic, legal, and other investments.

All these and many more are the prospects that the rights to development in Africa will achieve. However, while the prospects of the Right to Development are praiseworthy and enviable as they help to bolster genuine development across Africa, it is crucial to understand that there are still extant problems in Africa that can create bottlenecks for the achievement of these rights. One of such problems that has existed in Africa as long as the political and socio-economic history of the continent is concerned is IFFs.

IFFS AS A CLOG IN THE WHEEL OF THE RIGHT TO DEVELOPMENT IN AFRICA

Suppose the developmental goals of attaining equality, improving human development parameters, and broadening access to social amenities and resources must be expended. In that case, the educational infrastructure and the health facilities that will boost human development and the various social security and welfare programmes have to be paid for using public resources. This underscores the need for driving an increase in financial inflows, especially to government coffers. Unfortunately, however, this is not the case, leaving Africa's development quest grossly underfunded. Several factors can be cited for this status quo, but principal among them is corruption, typified by what is known as IFFs.

The term 'illicit financial flows' is quite challenging to define as it can mean several things. Nevertheless, it essentially entails the illegal movement of funds or monetary assets across national borders in a manner and under circumstances that violate national or international protocols.[24] These illicit movements of money happen for various reasons. A popular one is dishonest financial gains; another is to avoid legal and contractual financial responsibilities and regulations, especially tax and other governmental charges.

IFFs manifest in two major types. First, Illicit Capital Outflows are those financial resources that are siphoned out of a country or region. The manners through which these are carried out include multinationals evading taxes in countries where they conduct business and repatriating the funds to their home countries. Second, on the other hand, Illicit Financial Inflows involve the inflow of funds that contravene the law.

Nonetheless, both types tend to wreak havoc in similar way, and even then the differentiation might not be necessary. This is because Illicit outflows out of a country almost always translate into illicit inflows into another. Hence the general term, illicit financial flows. It is essential, too, however, to note that in the case of Africa, illicit capital outflows seem to have a more debilitating impact.

MANNERS OF IFFS

The seeming popular conception of 'IFFs' is that public officials almost entirely siphon them through blatant embezzlement. While this carries a great degree of veracity, the fact is, in terms of volume, IFFs in Africa are commercial. About 65 per cent of the value of IFFs making their way out of the continent per annum are said to be by corporations, an overwhelming majority of which are foreign-owned.[25] The scenarios under which IFFs happen in commercial dealings are multifarious. For example, an importer may utilise misinvoicing tactics to avoid paying customs duties, among other taxes such as Value-added Tax.

Another conception is that the illegal flows are conducted through so-called underground channels or outside proper legal banking frameworks, but that is not the case. Instead, perfectly crafted licit transactions might be designed to facilitate funds using the proper banking channels out of a country. These, in fact, are the most difficult to detect and forestall. As such, acts that constitute IFFs tend to fall into several categories.[26] These include:

- Grossly Illegal Acts, a more familiar instance of IFFs, is the movement of funds for illegal purposes, including evading tax by corporations or embezzlement by public officials. Funds Resulting from Illegal Acts are orchestrated through several illegal activities conducted outside the state's purview but generate income.
- Overseas transactions resulting from these fall into the domain of illegal financial flows. These include smuggling commodities, trafficking in people or drugs, armed robbery, among others.

- Transactions to Fund Illegal Activities include inflows or outflows targeted at funding illegal activities such as organised crime.

All these shows are that regardless of the forms or types of IFFs carried out, there are impacts in some aspects that Africa feels, especially on its level of development, which consequently affect the attainment of development rights.

IMPACTS OF IFFS

The negative impact of IFFs on the developmental strides of the continent runs deep and cuts across all phases of the continent's development. While the impact is diverse, the significant implication is that it deprives the continent of desperately needed financial resources to fund its development. IFFs have deprived the continent of at least $1 trillion over the past three decades.[27] Unfortunately, the tide does not seem to be abating; about $89 billion is being siphoned on a continuous annual basis, according to UN estimates.[28] The effects could not be more appalling. The continent is said to have a gaping average of $80 billion in infrastructure financing every year.[29] Essentially, a sweeping majority of the continent's infrastructure needs could be funded by the sums it loses to illicit flows.

Sadly, rather than tackle IFFs, block the loopholes and leakages, and divert the money to funding infrastructures, the continent has resorted to funding infrastructure projects through crippling debt to national and international entities. This has left the country susceptible to foreign domination[30] and geopolitical politicking.[31] Governments of countries such as Nigeria already expend almost all of their income on servicing these infrastructure loans;[32] the channels to repayment are not even clear.[33] It, therefore, is a source of concern that funds that could alleviate this quagmire are illegally extracted from the continent.

It is important to note that the government concentrating its revenue on debt servicing means that it cannot afford to fund infrastructure among other social investment and welfare programmes, which in turn delay the attainment of the goals of the Right to Development. Therefore, it is clear that without addressing and eradicating IFFs in Africa, attaining the Right to Development might as well be a long-time mirage for the present generation and the generation to come.

ADDRESSING IFFS AS A WAY TO ACHIEVING THE RIGHT TO DEVELOPMENT

It is no gainsaying that IFFs are a time bomb that can eviscerate all the continent's chances to achieve its developmental objectives. Thus, there is the need to drastically reduce, if not eradicate, them by plugging the loopholes through which funds find their way out of the continent. In the past, there have been efforts across various lines targeted at this problem. It is believed that those strategies can be pretty effective if implemented correctly. Some of the suggested ways to tackle these IFFs are:

BUILDING INSTITUTIONS

Institutions on the African continent are weak, and this includes the fiscal ones.[34] This weakness, however, stems from several factors. For one, officials in various capacities may not be versed in prevalent happenings in their industries of oversight. For instance, companies might have invented novel phoney transactions to facilitate the movement of funds without the regulator being aware of the latest tricks. By the time the regulator discovers, vast amounts of funds would have been moved. Even if laws are not allowed to be retroactive, the guilty corporations will not face sanctions.

As such, capacity building should be one of the central goals of institution building. Officials, especially those in charge of tax, should be trained appropriately in fraud detection and prevention, alongside empowerment with requisite tools. Legislations and regulations may also be developed that will increase the oversight powers of the concerned agencies to strengthen their capabilities to detect potential flows.

FACILITATING INTERNATIONAL COOPERATION

IFFs are not carried out in isolation. They require the involvement of several parties, usually across two or more countries. Frequently, the country out of which the funds flow may not detect the transactions initially. However, the recipient countries may be able to flag the inflows. Thus, there is a need to strengthen international cooperation in information sharing and IFF detection. The Bank of International Settlement that helps facilitate large international financial transactions may also take it upon itself to check IFF transactions. In all, there is an urgent need for the international community to proffer ways out of the concept of tax havens and the states that offer such services, considering the outsized role they play in the growth of IFFs.[35]

MASSIVE DATA COLLECTION DRIVE

African countries can only be aware that they have been cheated via IFFs if they know those transactions existed. Therefore, the onus is on governments to embark on a drive to collect data on transactions around trade and customs, international payments (especially significant ones) and multinational companies' operations, among others. These data can clearly show the number of transactions undertaken against those reported for taxation by the government. The insights can then be utilised to develop regulations, systems, technologies, and other strategies to stem the tide of Illicit international flows.

International cooperation can also be utilised in data gathering as information on companies can be extracted from the countries' authorities where they are headquartered. The Right to Development can transform Africa's developmental landscape and put it on course to achieving the 2063 Agenda, even earlier than planned. However, IFFs have been a clog in the wheel, which has to be removed from actual development to flourish.

AGENDA 2063: 'THE AFRICA WE WANT'

In 2013, African leaders gathered at the African Union Summit and unanimously adopted the Agenda 2063 to serve as a blueprint for delivering Africa We Want through genuine economic and sustainable growth across all countries in the continent.[36] The Agenda 2063 – Africa We Want – would later be interpreted as the unwavering support and affirmation by African political leaders and governments towards the robust transformation of Africa into a competitive global powerhouse.[37]

The Agenda 2063 came after the 50 years existence of the Organization of African Union in 2013. With the mindset of having a renewed and refocused sustainable plan for Africa for the next fifty years, the Agenda was adopted to serve as a master plan for development in Africa. The fifty-year plan is to progress with fifteen flagship projects to help fast-track the development throughout Africa.[38] These flagship projects cut across different infrastructural projects that would lift the developmental face of Africa in different ramifications. Highlights of these projects include a high-speed train network that connects commercial centres and capitals in all African countries, the establishment of the Africa free trade zone, establishment of a pan-African digital data network, fostering peace and stability and unity in Africa, and advancing Pan-Africanism among other things.

Without a doubt, if achieved, all these flagship projects would deliver real-time development across Africa. They will touch on economic development and real-time infrastructure in the continent, significantly affecting poverty eradication, creating jobs, and achieving better living conditions for Africans.

What makes the Agenda 2063 plan stand out is that, unlike the past developmental plans for countries, regions, or the continent, for this one, there is a feasible implementation plan that African heads of states and governments have adopted. Furthermore, this implementation plan is to be monitored, and its progress is reported every ten years. It is expected that this progress report will help African countries evaluate the continuous feasibility of implementing the developmental projects and plans of the Agenda and better position the continent for achieving the African We Want.[39]

Agenda 2063 also has aspirations that, if achieved, are believed to bring Africa closer to achieving actual development across all levels by the target year of 2063. The aspirations which cover expectations of different developmental projects and actions across Africa, according to the AU, are reflective of the desire of African leaders and citizens for shared development across different quarters. The seven aspirations are as relevant as the developmental plans and projects outlined to be carried out across all African countries in Agenda 2063. These aspirations are also to serve as prospective guidelines and watchwords towards achieving the developmental plans of Agenda 2063. The strengths of Agenda 2063 are reflected in different facets. One of which is the basis for which it was initially formulated. The Agenda, through its content, is set out to position African countries for real growth by leveraging on the experiences of the past and adequately utilising the resources, expertise, and strategies of the present. Accordingly, it first takes cognisance of the necessity for a shift in the method and ways things are being done and refocus attention to a new perspective of achieving genuine growth in Africa.

Besides this, the Agenda recognising the developmental pace in the continent is seeking a faster way to ensure that all hands are on deck to accelerate Africa's development. This is why the Agenda is seeking solidarity and sacrifice from key stakeholders and Africans at large alongside the plans and programmes. The readiness for solidarity is first reflected in the build-up stages to the formation of the Agenda 2063, where consultation was sought from think tanks, youth, the private sector, women, civil society organisations, faith-based organisations, Africa in diaspora, past and present government officials and many more others. The reason for all that is to ensure that all concerned views are represented in the Agenda and to create an attachment or ownership of the Agenda by Africans from different walks of life.

While all of these are commendable, it is important to still bear in mind that the contents and aspirations of the Agenda will only become attainable if those who are supposed to play their roles in the implementation of the plans are not lagging or not missing in action. This is why, as much as everyone gets excited by the boldness and developmental propensity of the Agenda, attention must also be drawn to the roles of stakeholders in bringing those aspirations to fruition.

THE ROLE OF AFRICAN STAKEHOLDERS IN ACHIEVING THE 'AFRICA WE WANT'

This is not the first time Africa will be ambitious about a developmental plan.[40] In the past, there have been plans that sought to achieve sustainable development and key into the realities of the time, but today, different indications show that the success they have achieved is not enough to deliver the ambitions they had, in the beginning, set out to achieve.[41] In many of these cases that occurred in the past, the problems have often been a lack of consolidation of efforts from the people, institutions, government, and quarters that matter to the fulfilment of those plans and projects.[42]

True, Agenda 2063 is ambitious enough to pass the message that the goals and ambitions it seeks to achieve are unlike the experience of the past. Indeed, many have said that with the Agenda 2063 in place, development in Africa is not business as usual.[43] While this is commendable, Africa must go beyond this. The theoretical ambitions and goals of the Agenda will not be achieved if there is no display of genuine efforts to implement them. In this light, different stakeholders have to come together to achieve robust implementation of the Agenda. Unlike what was experienced in the past with other regional and continental developmental plans with willingness at the central level, but the regional and national government differed significantly on the purpose, goals, or process of achieving the developmental plans. Therefore, this time around, particular focus has to be given to the implementation plan to ensure that it is not just at the centre of the AU that the plans are accepted and attested to but that each government takes the developmental message of Agenda 2063 down to the national level and begins robust implementation of the plans.

The truth is that where the governments of African countries are torn apart on implementing the plans of the Agenda, it would be impossible for there to be any reasonable success recorded. This is why, beyond the ambitions of the Agenda 2063, there have to be clear indications that all hands are on deck for achieving the Africa We Want.

The AU, too, has a critical role in the journey towards delivering the Africa We Want. There should be little worry that the African Union founded on Pan-Africanism would pull its total weight behind the struggle to achieve the aspirations in Agenda 2063. As a union championing the struggle towards fulfilling the seven aspirations of the Agenda, its roles must necessarily be integral to the fulfilment of these aspirations leading towards Africa We Want.

The consolidated efforts of the private sectors are also needed in achieving the Africa We Want. The private sector has always been known to command the respect of required resources in Africa. The government might develop the plans and be willing to implement them, but if there are no resources to pursue these implementations, there would be little to no success recorded. Given that the private sector often has the financial muscle to pursue humongous projects that would help deliver some of the goals of Agenda 2063, their efforts must be secured in the journey towards delivering an Africa We Want. For instance, with the financial muscle of the private sector, the government can enter a private-public partnership agreement for delivering developmental infrastructure in Africa.[44] This would ensure that the transformation that Africa needs is handled with the coveted expertise of the private sector, but it would also mean that there would be a rapid fulfilment of these plans because of the readiness of the private sector to support its resources and expertise.[45]

The non-governmental organisations in Africa have a critical role in ensuring that Agenda 2063 are met and a sustainable Africa for everyone is delivered before or by the end of 2063. Therefore, the place of NGOs in Africa is crucial to achieving Africa We Want. For decades, NGOs have proven to have a strong niche of holding the government accountable for their promises and filing the lacuna left by the government in achieving their various developmental plans.[46] The NGOs can help follow up, critically, what the government of different countries are working towards on the plans and programmes of the Agenda 2063. This is important because it is often through this that Africans are most assured of a non-partisan assessment of the progress of the plans of the Agenda 2063.

If there is one thing that would make an ambitious and bold plan like the Agenda 2063 work, it is the understanding that the people for which it is made are solidly behind it. To focus on all other aspects of achieving the Africa We Want without considering the critical stake of the people will amount to little or nothing. Africa was built and continues to strive on the strength of her people. This means that there has to be a special place for the people in all situations through the journey of delivering the Africa We Want.

On the part of the people, there has to be a renewed level of commitment to achieving these aspirations and getting to achieve an Africa with sustainable development. Like never before, the people of Africa need to make plans and projects for Agenda 2063 on their own. There is no better watchdog for the plans than the people of Africa. This is why the solid support and commitment of the people is a sine qua non to the achievement of the Africa We Want. Nevertheless, though the African people have always been known as supportive of their own thing, the level of distrust in the past decades may have hampered the level of commitment that might be given to the achievement of the Agenda 2063.

Therefore, it is essential not to turn a blind eye to the damage public distrust between the people and the government in many African countries has caused. While it makes sense to support every developmental plan projected by the government of African countries, the lethargic experience of the past coupled with the unaccountability of the government has cast a strong signal of doubts on the trust that would typically have existed between the government and the people. This, however, should not be the end of the road for the plan. Of course, the distrust has created some bottlenecks, but these can still be handled pragmatically.

What appears to be the way forward is for the government to show a renewed level of commitment to the people it has pledged to serve. True, the ambitions of the Agenda 2063 are robust enough to secure people's belief in its capability to transform Africa, but these are mere ambitions on paper. They need the influence and interventions of stakeholders and the government to bring them to fruition. For this to happen, the government does not only need to sit tight with the highest level of commitment but also needs to show the people that genuine efforts are being taken to ensure that there is the fulfilment of the content of Agenda 2063. Only when this is done can there be a willingness on the part of the people to give their unwavering commitment to the government and support the plans of achieving Africa We Want.

Aside from this, another way to secure the people's commitment is to put them at the centre of the plans and ambitions of Agenda 2063. The culture and experience of the African people have shown that more outstanding commitment is often given when there is an understanding that the ownership of a thing, programme, or policy belongs to them. When there is a belief that the ownership of the plans and policies of the Agenda 2063 belongs to the people, a strong message is sent to everyone that the success and failure of the programmes are tied to them. As such, more focus is given to it because no true African wants to be associated with the failure of a policy or programme that has been committed to his hands. For this reason, the process of implementing the policies and programmes of Agenda 2063 must be made to reflect a strong connection with the people – a message that without the people, there is little to nothing that can be achieved.

Also, there has to be a deep involvement in achieving the policies and plans of the Agenda 2063 with the people. It is not enough that the programmes reflect a continental Agenda. Genuine attempts must be made to ensure that the programmes and fulfilment of Agenda 2063 are regionally and nationally domesticated. For a robust plan, proximity to the people in terms of the process of achieving it matters a lot. So much difference can be made if the people are made to understand that the programmes are a reflection of Africa they have all yearned for, especially if the achievement of the programmes are domesticated and made to reflect the norms of the people. It is believed that if this is done, there would be less restraint in fulfilling the ambitions of Agenda 2063.

In all, as there are efforts to achieve a robust fulfilment of the plans and programmes of Agenda 2063, it is crucial to bear in mind that a large proportion of the help, resources, expertise, and leverage that Africa needs resides in the continent. There has to be a shift from the past perspective that help will come from messianic Western powers. This time around, Africa has to look critically inwards of what it can offer the world and use the resources it has to trigger genuine development across the continent. True, there might be instances where help would have to come from outside the continent, but total reliance should not be placed on this because, as experience has shown, this help often comes with the underlying purpose of serving the interest of the Western world and slowing the pace of the development of Africa. At a time like this, this is not what Africa wants. The need for sustainable development in the continent is too dire that there should be detour by foreign debt or interest in the journey towards development in Africa.

IDENTIFYING AND ADDRESSING POSSIBLE PROBLEMS TOWARDS ACHIEVING "AFRICA WE WANT"

For a developmental plan seeking to deliver sustainable development and create the Africa We Want, it is unlikely there would be challenges that would debilitate its fruition in Africa. This becomes clearer if one considers the current state of Africa and the torrents of political and economic problems it is facing. For this reason, attention should be drawn to some of the challenges that might be awaiting the plans to achieve Africa We Want by 2063. Once these problems are identified, stakeholders would gear up and robustly tackle them before they metamorphose into unconquerable continental problems.

No doubt, the Agenda 2063 is a bold and ambitious move for Africa, but there are still extant problems that have not been resolved which might create bottlenecks for the success of the Agenda's implementation. Two of these core problems are discussed in this chapter.

FINANCES

True, Africa has enormous resources – tapped and untapped – but over time, these resources have not been translating to financial sufficiency, let alone stability for the continent. There is still a lot to be achieved with finances in Africa. All of the infrastructures that have been outlined to be constructed to develop Africa all require a lot of capital to achieve. With the absence of such funds in Africa, it becomes a problem to pursue this infrastructure to a reasonable end.

Like before, Africa might be compelled to leverage the dangling opportunities of loans from international financial institutions, but these opportunities should be taken with caution if at all they would be taken. Experience of past years has shown that many of these loans have alternate interests they are serving, which are rarely to the benefit of Africa. To achieve success with the plans and programmes of Agenda 2063, Africa must be ready to look inwards and leverage the resources it has by exploiting them and putting them to proper use. Also, like the other parts of this paper has mentioned, the problem of IFFs would also need to be eradicated, or at least brought to its minimal level. There's no doubt that when the loopholes of IFFs are blocked, the money recovered, stopped from the transfer, and those retained in the continent can be diverted into developmental projects that align with the goals and aspirations of Agenda 2063.

POLITICAL INSTABILITY

The core of achieving all of the goals and aspirations of Agenda 2063 relies on political willingness in the continent, but this willingness cannot be achieved with series of political instability within the continent. Africa is currently besieged by instances of political instability, which seems to be rapidly spreading across different countries. The problem, therefore, arises that if there is a need for the governments of all countries to work together to deliver on the promises of the Agenda, but they are being held down and distracted by political instability, how then will they be able to focus on the aspirations of the Agenda?

Though one of the goals of the Agenda is to ensure stability in government across countries in Africa, how this will be done with the current state of instability is still yet to be seen. It is, however, hoped that actual intervention from the AU and the relatively stable African countries will be taken to bring peace to different aspects of Africa. It is when this is done that the much-coveted devotion and solidarity that the Agenda needs can be given by all the concerned stakeholders in the continent. It therefore appears that Africa must first address the problems of political instability and problem of financial inadequacy before there can be a reasonable pursuit of the fulfilment of the goals and aspirations of the Agenda 2063.

CONCLUSION

So far, this chapter has shown that there is a dire need for overall development across the fifty-four countries in Africa. It has shown that though everyone realises this, the reason the continent seems stagnant, especially regarding attaining the Right to Development, is owed to long-standing problems like IFFs. It has also shown that the Right to Development in Africa might never be achieved if the problem of IFFs is not first tackled. Conceding that IFFs are a problem in Africa, the way to address it has also been examined. Consequently, this chapter has addressed Agenda 2063 and the implementation of this 50-years plan. It has considered the impacts of the fulfilment of the Agenda on Africa's development, recognised the role of stakeholders in achieving these developments, and identified the problems that might debilitate the success of the goals and aspirations of the Agenda.

In all, the whole essence of all these still tilts towards the call of urgency for all stakeholders in Africa to consciously attend to the issues of Africa's development, look inward, and consolidate on the relevant efforts channelled towards achieving Africa We Want. This development for Africa has long been overdue, and it is high time everyone got to work. If we all pledge our commitment to seeing Africa grow and develop to the continent we want, then we can all forge forward to attaining the rights to development, stopping IFFs, and achieving the goals and aspirations of the Agenda 2063.

NOTES

1. J. D. Sachs and A. M. Warner, "Sources of slow growth in African economies," *Journal of African economies* 6, no. 3 (1997): 335–376.
2. World Bank, "Sub-Saharan Africa," 2015.
3. M. A. Ikenna, "Understanding the crisis of development in Africa: Reflections on Bedford Umezs analysis," *African Journal of Political Science and International Relations* 3, no. 9 (2009): 354–359.
4. World Population Review, "Least Developed Countries 2021," World Population Review, retrieved on September 20, 2021, via https://worldpopulationreview.com/country-rankings/least-developed-countries
5. The World Bank, "Driven by the economic fallout of the COVID-19 pandemic, growth in Sub-Saharan Africa is predicted to fall to –3.3% in 2020, pushing the region into its first recession in 25 years," June 2, 2021, https://www.worldbank.org/en/region/afr/overview.
6. L. Mangi, "Us diplomatic interests in Africa: An overview," *Pakistan Horizon* 39, no. 2 (1986): 22–37.
7. K. Gyimah-Brempong, "Aid and economic growth in LDCS: Evidence from Sub-Saharan Africa," *The Review of Black Political Economy* 20, no. 3 (1992): 31–52.
8. Poverty Rate, OECD, Retrieved 10/09/21 via https://data.oecd.org/inequality/poverty-rate.htm.
9. GDP per capita (current US$) World, World Bank, retrieved 10/09/21 via https://data.worldbank.org/indicator/NY.GDP.PCAP.CD?most_recent_value_desc=false&start=2020.

10. UN list of least developed countries, *UNCTAD*, retrieved 10/09/21 via https://unctad.org/topic/least-developed-countries/list.

11. Heavily Indebted Poor Countries (HIPC) Initiative, *World Bank,* retrieved 10/09/21 via https://www.worldbank.org/en/topic/debt/brief/hipc.

12. A. Jerome, *Infrastructure in Africa: The record*, African Development Bank, 1999.

13. K. Gyimah-Brempong, "Corruption, economic growth, and income inequality in Africa," *Economics of Governance* 3, no. 3 (2002): 183–209.

14. B. Arimah, "Poverty reduction and human development in Africa," *Journal of Human Development* 5, no. 3 (2004): 399–415.

15. The International Covenant on Economic, Social and Cultural Rights 1966, *UN OHCHR,* retrieved 10/09/21 via https://www.ohchr.org/en/professionalinterest/pages/cescr.aspx.

16. United Nations Declaration on the Right to Development, 1986, *UN OHCHR,* retrieved 10/09/21 via https://www.ohchr.org/en/professionalinterest/pages/righttodevelopment.aspx.

17. United Nations Minimum Development Goals, *UN.org,* retrieved 10/09/21 via https://www.un.org/millenniumgoals/.

18. United Nations Sustainable Development Goals, 2015.

19. The African Charter on Human and Peoples Rights 1981, African Commission on Human and Peoples' Rights, retrieved 10/09/21 via https://www.achpr.org/legalinstruments/detail?id=49.

20. K. Gyimah-Brempong, "Corruption, economic growth, and income inequality in Africa."

21. E. W. Nafziger and W. Nafziger, *Inequality in Africa: Political elites, proletariat, peasants and the poor*, CUP Archive, 1988.

22. J. Sachs, J. W. McArthur, et al., "Ending Africa's poverty trap," *Brookings Papers on Economic Activity* 2004, no. 1 (2004): 117–240.

23. United Nations Development Programme Human Development Reports, *UNDP.org*, retrieved 10/09/21 via http://hdr.undp.org/en/africa.

24. OECD, Policy Coherence for Sustainable Development (PCSD), Thematic module on illicit financial flows, Workshop, 2015, pg. 3.

25. Africa could gain $89 billion annually by curbing illicit financial flows, *UNCTAD*, retrieved 10/09/21 via https://unctad.org/news/africa-could-gain-89-billion-annually-curbing-illicit-financial-flows.

26. Illicit Financial Flows, World Bank, retrieved 10/09/21 via http://www.worldbank.org/en/topic/financialmarketintegrity/brief/illicitfinancialflowsiffs.

27. S. Landry, M. Sow, and P. Madden, Illicit financial flows in Africa: Drivers, destinations and policy options, *Africa Growth Initiative,* Brookings Institution, 2020.

28. Africa could gain $89 billion annually by curbing illicit financial flows, *UNCTAD*, retrieved 10/09/21 via https://unctad.org/news/africa-could-gain-89-billion-annually-curbing-illicit-financial-flows.

29. H. Leo and C. Heitzig, Figures of the week: Africa's infrastructure paradox, Africa in Focus, Brookings, 2021, retrieved 10/09/21 via https://www.brookings.edu/blog/africa-in-focus/2021/02/24/figures-of-the-week-africas-infrastructure-paradox/.

30. R. Southall and H. Melber, *A new scramble for Africa?: Imperialism, investment and development*, Scottsville: University of KwaZulu-Natal Press, 2009.

31. M. Power and G. Mohan, "Towards a critical geopolitics of China's engagement with African development," *Geopolitics* 15, no. 3 (2010): 462–495.

32. A. Everest, T. Jaiyeola, et al., Debt servicing rises, gulps 72% of FG revenues, *Punch Nigeria Newspapers*, 2021, retrieved 10/09/21 via https://punchng.com/debt-servicing-rises-gulps-72-of-fg-revenues/.

33. A. Isaac, IMF slams FG says Nigeria cannot repay loans, 2018, *The Sun Newspapers,* retrieved 10/09/21 via https://www.sunnewsonline.com/imf-slams-fg-says-nigeria-cant-repay-loans/.

34. A. Diop, G. Dufrénot, and G. Sanon, "Is per capita growth in Africa hampered by poor governance and weak institutions? An empirical study on the ECOWAS countries," *African Development Review* 22, no. 2 (2010): 265–275.

35. J. Christensen, "The looting continues tax havens and corruption," Critical perspectives on international business (2011).

36. African Union Commission, *Agenda 2063*, The African Union Commission, 2015.

37. African Union Commission, *Agenda 2063*, The African Union Commission, 2015.

38. V. Ndizera and H. Muzee, "A critical review of Agenda 2063: Business as usual?" *African Journal of Political Science and International Relations* 12, no. 8 (2018): 142–154.

39. V. Ndizera and H. Muzee, "A critical review of Agenda 2063: Business as usual?".

40. T. Mkandawire, "Thinking about developmental states in Africa," *Cambridge Journal of Economics* 25, no. 3 (2001): 289–314.

41. C. Ake, *Democracy and development in Africa*, Brookings Institution Press, Washington DC, 2001.

42. J. Herbst, *States and power in Africa*, Princeton University Press, New Jersey, 2014.

43. V. Ndizera, and H. Muzee, "A critical review of Agenda 2063: Business as usual?".

44. K. Boyfield, "Private sector funding of public sector infrastructure," *Public Money & Management* 12, no. 2 (1992): 41–46.

45. K. Boyfield, "Private sector funding of public sector infrastructure."

46. A. Fowler, "The role of NGOs in changing state-society relations: Perspectives from Eastern and Southern Africa," *Development Policy Review* 9, no. 1 (1991): 53–84.

BIBLIOGRAPHY

A. Diop, G. Dufrénot, and G. Sanon, "Is per capita growth in Africa hampered by poor governance and weak institutions? An empirical study on the ECOWAS countries," *African Development Review* 22, no. 2 (2010): 265–275.

A. Everest, T. Jaiyeola, et al., Debt servicing rises, gulps 72% of FG revenues, *Punch Nigeria Newspapers*, 2021. Retrieved 10/09/21 via https://punchng.com/debt-servicing-rises-gulps-72-of-fg-revenues/

A. Fowler, "The role of NGOs in changing state-society relations: Perspectives from Eastern and Southern Africa," *Development Policy Review* 9, no. 1 (1991): 53–84.

A. Isaac, IMF slams FG says Nigeria cannot repay loans, 2018, *The Sun Newspapers.* Retrieved 10/09/21 via https://www.sunnewsonline.com/imf-slams-fg-says-nigeria-cant-repay-loans/

A. Jerome, *Infrastructure in Africa: The record.* African Development Bank, 1999.

Africa could gain $89 billion annually by curbing illicit financial flows, *UNCTAD.* Retrieved 10/09/21 via https://unctad.org/news/africa-could-gain-89-billion-annually-curbing-illicit-financial-flows

African Union Commission, *Agenda 2063*, The African Union Commission, 2015.

B. Arimah, "Poverty reduction and human development in Africa," *Journal of Human Development* 5, no. 3 (2004): 399–415.

C. Ake, *Democracy and development in Africa*, Brookings Institution Press, Washington, DC, 2001.

E. W. Nafziger and W. Nafziger, *Inequality in Africa: Political elites, proletariat, peasants and the poor*, CUP Archive, 1988.

GDP per capita (current US$) World, World Bank. Retrieved 10/09/21 via https://data.worldbank.org/indicator/NY.GDP.PCAP.CD?most_recent_value_desc=false&start=2020

H. Leo and C. Heitzig, Figures of the week: Africa's infrastructure paradox. Africa in Focus, Brookings, 2021. Retrieved 10/09/21 via https://www.brookings.edu/blog/africa-in-focus/2021/02/24/figures-of-the-week-africas-infrastructure-paradox/

Heavily Indebted Poor Countries (HIPC) Initiative, *World Bank.* Retrieved 10/09/21 via https://www.worldbank.org/en/topic/debt/brief/hipc

Illicit Financial Flows, *World Bank.* Retrieved 10/09/21 via http://www.worldbank.org/en/topic/financialmarketintegrity/brief/illicitfinancialflowsiffs

J. Christensen, "The looting continues tax havens and corruption," *Critical Perspectives on International Business* 7, no. 2 (2011): 177.

J. D. Sachs and A. M. Warner, "Sources of slow growth in African economies," *Journal of African Economies* 6, no. 3 (1997): 335–376.

J. Herbst, *States and power in Africa*, Princeton University Press, New Jersey, 2014.

J. Sachs, J. W. McArthur, et al., "Ending Africa's poverty trap," *Brookings Papers on Economic Activity* 2004, no. 1 (2004): 117–240.

K. Boyfield, "Private sector funding of public sector infrastructure," *Public Money & Management* 12, no. 2 (1992): 41–46.

K. Gyimah-Brempong, "Aid and economic growth in LDCS: Evidence from Sub-Saharan Africa," *The Review of Black Political Economy* 20, no. 3 (1992): 31–52.

M. A. Ikenna, "Understanding the crisis of development in Africa: Reflections on Bedford Umezs analysis," *African Journal of Political Science and International Relations* 3, no. 9 (2009): 354–359.

M. Power and G. Mohan, "Towards a critical geopolitics of China's engagement with African development," *Geopolitics* 15, no. 3 (2010): 462–495.

OECD, Policy Coherence for Sustainable Development (PCSD), Thematic module on illicit financial flows, Workshop, 2015, pg. 3.

Poverty Rate, OECD. Retrieved 10/09/21 via https://data.oecd.org/inequality/poverty-rate.htm

R. Southall and H. Melber, *A new scramble for Africa?: Imperialism, investment and development*, University of KwaZulu-Natal Press, Scottsville, 2009.

S. Landry, M. Sow, and P. Madden, Illicit financial flows in Africa: Drivers, destinations and policy options, *Africa Growth Initiative.* Brookings Institution, 2020.

T. Mkandawire, "Thinking about developmental states in Africa," *Cambridge Journal of Economics* 25, no. 3 (2001): 289–314.

The African Charter on Human and Peoples Rights 1981, African Commission on Human and Peoples' Rights. Retrieved 10/09/21 via https://www.achpr.org/legalinstruments/detail?id=49

The International Covenant on Economic, Social and Cultural Rights 1966, *UN OHCHR.* Retrieved 10/09/21 via https://www.ohchr.org/en/professionalinterest/pages/cescr.aspx

The World Bank, "Driven by the Economic Fallout of the COVID-19 Pandemic, Growth in Sub-Saharan Africa Is Predicted to Fall to −3.3% in 2020, Pushing the Region into Its First Recession in 25 Years," June 2, 2021. https://www.worldbank.org/en/region/afr/overview

UN list of least developed countries, *UNCTAD.* Retrieved 10/09/21 via https://unctad.org/topic/least-developed-countries/list

United Nations Declaration on the Right to Development, 1986, *UN OHCHR.* Retrieved 10/09/21 via https://www.ohchr.org/en/professionalinterest/pages/righttodevelopment.aspx

United Nations Development Programme Human Development Reports, *UNDP.org.* Retrieved 10/09/21 via http://hdr.undp.org/en/africa

United Nations Minimum Development Goals, *UN.org.* Retrieved 10/09/21 via https://www.un.org/millenniumgoals/

United Nations Sustainable Development Goals, 2015.

V. Ndizera and H. Muzee, "A critical review of Agenda 2063: Business as usual?" *African Journal of Political Science and International Relations* 12, no. 8 (2018): 142–154.

World Population Review, "Least Developed Countries 2021," World Population Review. Retrieved 20/09/21 via https://worldpopulationreview.com/country-rankings/least-developed-countries

Chapter 2

An Appraisal of the Architecture to Curb Illicit Financial Flows from South Africa and Their Impact on the Right to Development

Gerard Emmanuel Kamdem Kamga

INTRODUCTION

My aim in this chapter is to review the architecture to curb illicit financial flows (IFFs) from South Africa and their impact on the Right to Development. The concept of IFFs is defined by the High Level Panel on Illicit Financial Flows from Africa, as 'money illegally earned, transferred or used'.[1] Put differently, IFFs amount to the funds that are proceeds from illegal transactions, escaped from legal constraints and are characterised by their opaque nature, origin and hidden from public officials. It is further observed that 'these flows of money are in violation of laws in their origin, or during their movement or use, and are therefore considered illicit'.[2] Another characterisation of IFFs was put forward by the United Nations Office on Drugs and Crime (UNODC) that considers this phenomenon as being generated by methods, practices, and crimes aiming to transfer financial capital in contravention of national or international laws.[3] Prior to further elucidation, it is crucial to outline the contextual framework of this chapter. For the past several years, the African continent has been performing well economically and achieving one of the highest growths around the globe. South Africa, which ranks as the second largest economy in Africa after Nigeria, is nonetheless struggling to address poverty issues, education, housing, and the delivery of infrastructure and other basic services. Yet with the sound economic performance, one would have expected the situation to be otherwise. The reason for this setback is that despite this astounding performance the country is subject to weak state institutions and more importantly to the theft of its resources by individual and criminal networks as well as multinational corporations through IFFs. According to the finding by the HLP, several methods are used by criminal entrepreneurs to illegally move and transfer money and assets around. This can be done in three different ways, namely commercial activities, criminal activities, and corruption. Regarding commercial activities, the report of the HLP observes that IFFs originating from commercial activities have several purposes, including hiding wealth, evading, or aggressively avoiding tax, and dodging customs duties and domestic levies. Some of these activities, especially those linked to taxation, are described from a more technical perspective as 'base erosion and profit shifting' especially within the ambit of the OECD.[4] For example, back in April 2019, the South Africa Revenue Service (SARS) announced the preliminary revenue outcome for the financial year 2018–19. What transpired at the time was that for the financial year that ended on 31 March 2019, SARS collected an amount of R1 287.6 billion, against the 2019 Budget estimate of R1 302.2 billion. As one can notice there was a deficit of R14.6 billion, an amount that is equivalent to −1.1 per cent. This loss has been a general trend across the entire African continent for decades. Back in 2015 a report by the above High Level Panel on Illicit Financial showed that Africa loses an average of $50 billion annually through IFFs. This figure has since increased substantially given that during the United Nations Conference on Trade and Development in 2020, it was revealed that the continent was now losing $ 88.6 billion annually through the same phenomenon. The amount is equivalent to 3.7 per cent of Africa's Gross Domestic Product (GDP).[5] This staggering loss has been consistent over the years across all regions of the continent. When it comes to South Africa, Global Financial Integrity (GFI) noted with concern that between 2004 and 2013, the country's cumulative IFFs amounted to $209,220 million in nominal value. During this period, the organisation ranked South Africa seventh place globally among the top ten source economies for IFFs. Like many countries that rely on natural resources and for their development and the realisation of the Right to Development, South Africa will further move backwards if nothing is done to prevent the proliferation of IFFs along with their criminal networks and obscure chain of command. The consequences on the Right to Development are devastating as IFFs constitute one of the key obstacles to the realisation of such right. It is within this framework that the first section of the Declaration on the Right to Development of 1986 provides that the Right to Development is an inalienable human right by virtue of which every human person and all peoples are entitled to participate in, contribute to, and enjoy economic, social, cultural, and political development, in which all human rights and fundamental freedoms can be fully realised. It is also within this context that an architecture to address IFFs has been established in a bid to curb this phenomenon in South Africa and around the globe. Relevant steps must be taken to assess the efficiency of such architecture. How much efficient is the current architecture and to what extent can it contribute to prevent the proliferation of IFFs? This preoccupation is at the heart of the upcoming developments.

THE PROLIFERATION OF IFFS FROM SOUTH AFRICA

In terms of IFFs there are three main categories, namely commercial activities, criminal activities, and corruption. These constitute the main channels through which criminal networks use to move and transfer money across borders in an illegal manner. This typology of IFFs was confirmed by a report by GFI reviewing trade-related IFFs from 135 developing countries between 2008 and 2017. Detailed developments about these channels are available somewhere else.[6] IFFs through the channel of commercial activities have the potential to facilitate the illicit outflows of funds. In fact, the development of international commerce, new technologies, digital economy, means of transports, communication, and globalisation have contributed to literally collapsed the borders and undermined states' capacity of oversight, monitoring, and control. It is said that even though globalisation enables global trade, it is nonetheless described as a 'blessing in disguise'. On the one hand, it has brought economic opportunities in terms of businesses, employment, and poverty reduction.[7] On the other hand, it has contributed to expose economies to intense competition and regulatory challenges.[8] As a result, corruption, bribery, and money laundering have flourished and facilitated the rise of various traffics across the African continent and the rest of the globe. It is within this framework that South Africa and the rest of the Africa continent became one of the main roads for international traffic of illicit goods and products. The point is that in terms of regulations, it is not evident to separate between what is legal and what is not. The regulations framing commercial activities sometimes contain grey areas that do not necessarily frame every occurrence. In this context the HLP points out that the business sector has relative strengths in interpreting laws and rules and being able to avoid compliance with these laws and rules because of the legal, accounting, and financial assistance that it can draw upon.[9] This probably explains why abusive transfer pricing, trade mispricing, misinvoicing of services, the use of unequal contracts, aggressive tax avoidance, and illegal export of foreign exchange are the main channels used by criminal networks in the country.[10] In this section, I will focus on two particular practices that appear to be a serious concern within the context of South Africa, namely trade misinvoicing and trade mispricing.[11] Trade misinvoicing is used by multinational corporations established in various states with different fiscal policies. There are genuine concerns regarding this practice as confirmed by a report by GFI in 2018.

The report sheds light on a practice that has been going on for decades especially in the mining industry. Then one learns that for much of the twentieth century, diamonds went out of South Africa with no export data reported. In addition, there was no government statistics regarding the value or weight of stones mined locally and shipped overseas.[12] It is evident through this recurrent practice that multinational companies operating in the mining sector have contributed to destroying the layers of the South African economy and they impoverish the country further. This practice led to budget deficit resulting in state not being able to comply with its commitments to deliver in terms of job creation, healthcare, education, housing, and infrastructures. In its report of 2018 GFI further observed that trade misinvoicing is the most frequently utilised mechanism facilitating measurable IFFS. In its report on South Africa, GFI further emphasises how misstating import and export values has become normalised in much of commercial trade, and the same facilitating shadow financial system being used to move money of criminal and corrupt origin. The report also reveals the techniques behind trade misinvoicing that happens in various ways notably through under-invoicing of imports or exports and over-invoicing of imports or exports. In practice, trade misinvoicing occurs when importers and exporters deliberately falsify the stated prices on the invoices for the goods they are importing or exporting as a way to illicitly transfer value across international borders, evade tax and/or customs duties, launder the proceeds of criminal activity, circumvent currency controls, and hide profits offshore.[13] Previous research already noted that between 1995 and 2006, the South African mining sector cumulative trade misinvoicing outflows amounted to about $167.19 million and peaked at as much as $31.7 million in the year 2006.[14] Estimates from the abovementioned report by GFI similarly depict the extent to which important funds have unduly been taken out of the country's economy for decades, which seriously contributed to the current socioeconomic turmoil. Then researches on trade misinvoicing in South Africa between 2010 and 2014 show that the potential loss of revenue to the government is $7.4 billion annually or a total of $37 billion during that period. In the same vein, it is demonstrated that the average portion of revenue lost due to import misinvoicing each year is $4.8 billion. This value can be further be divided into its component parts: uncollected VAT tax ($2.1 billion), customs duties ($596 million), and corporate income tax ($2.1 billion). Lost revenue due to misinvoiced exports was $2.6 billion on average each year which is related to lower-than-expected corporate income and royalties.[15] GFI's very conservatively estimated US$37 billion in lost revenues over the last five years of available data represents resources that could have made an immense difference in housing, education, and health services and could have gone far in easing poverty and inequality and accompanying social strains.[16] South Africa being deprived of resources from the mining industry at the heart of its economy, little can be done by authorities especially regarding their obligations to deliver in terms of basic social services, education, housing, health care, and so on.

Transfer pricing occurred through commercial activities like trade misinvoicing and amounts to IFFs as well. Multinational corporations use this process to move money across borders. It is a process by which companies that operate in more than one state fraudulently increase their expenses in states with a high taxation system and increase their revenues in states with a low taxation system. A joint report compiled by the African Development Bank and GFI shows that trade mispricing outflows have two components namely, export under-invoicing and import over-invoicing.[17] The process works as follows: with export under-invoicing, exporters understate their export revenues on their invoices and request their trading partners to deposit the balance in a foreign account. With import over-invoicing, importers overstate import expenditures, overpaying foreign exporters and asking them to divert the excess funds to a tax haven or a bank in an advanced country.[18] This report also points out that the proceeds of commercial tax evasion perpetrated through trade mispricing account for an average of 54.7 per cent of cumulative illicit flows from developing countries. By highlighting this information, the report portrays the extent to which multinational corporations rely on obscure practices and unorthodox methods to deprive governments of staggering sum of money. Therefore, authorities find themselves in a difficult situation when it comes to poverty alleviation and the improvement of the living conditions of the most vulnerable. The consequence of this practice on the realisation of the Right to Development is concerning. It is within this framework that the following observation was made:

> [i]n spite of the weakness of the regime of business and human rights, the emerging view is that business can no longer be indifferent to human rights violations caused by their operations. This in itself is a legal and even moral argument in which the human rights and RTD obligations of TNCS [transnational corporations] is based.[19]

After reviewing the proliferation of IFFs from South Africa especially trade misinvoicing and transfer mispricing, it is axiomatic that the situation has reached a critical point in the country. What occurs in South Africa derives from the global trend. With the environment of IFFs it is important to note that Africa is the most vulnerable as Western countries remain the main cause and the biggest beneficiaries. Indeed, findings show that the United Kingdom through its overseas territories and crown dependencies is responsible for 29 per cent of the global corporate tax losses.[20] In the same vein, a recent joint report by Tax Justice Network, Public Service International and Global Alliance for Tax Justice confirm that 98 per cent of all the global tax loss are caused by developed nations whereas developing countries contribute to 2 per cent to such loss.[21] Yet there is an interesting architecture to curb IFFs in place. My purpose in the next section is to assess such architecture.

ASSESSING THE ARCHITECTURE TO CURB IFFS FROM SOUTH AFRICA

In this section, I review the architecture in place designed to curb IFFs from South Africa. First, given that IFFs is a phenomenon that involves more than one state, the measures in place were designed to be implemented at the global and regional levels. As per the provisions of section 4(1) of the Declaration on the Right to Development, states have the duty to take steps, individually and collectively, to formulate international development policies with a view to facilitating the full realisation of the Right to Development. At the international level, one of the key documents to curb IFFs is the United Nations Convention against Corruption (UNCAC) adopted by the United Nations General Assembly in 2003 that went into force in 2005. The idea of UNCAC emerged from the discussions pertaining to another key instrument, that is, the United Nations Convention against Transnational Organised Crime (UNCTOC) that was adopted in 2000 and went into force in 2003. The issue of corruption was integrated into UNCTOC, but given its complexity, it became evident that corruption necessitated an entire treaty of its own. In 2001, the General Assembly reiterated the necessity of 'an effective international legal instrument against corruption, independent of the United Nations Convention against Transnational Organized Crime'.[22] Therefore the UNCAC came into being and was to play a crucial role in the fight against corruption at the global level. The late Kofi Annan, the then UN Secretary General pointed out the following in the foreword of this important instrument:

> The Convention introduces a comprehensive set of standards, measures and rules that all countries can apply in order to strengthen their legal and regulatory regimes to fight corruption. It calls for preventive measures and the criminalization of the most prevalent forms of corruption in both public and private sectors. And it makes a major breakthrough by requiring Member States to return assets obtained through corruption to the country from which they were stolen.

This quote provides a clear overview and the relevance of the UNCAC in its initiative to fight corruption. If implemented properly, the UNCAC could contribute to curbing IFFs and allow for the possibility of the realisation of the Right to Development. Section 1 of the UNCAC proposes an aim that is threefold:

(a) To promote and strengthen measures to prevent and combat corruption more efficiently and effectively;
(b) To promote, facilitate and support international cooperation and technical assistance in the prevention of and fight against corruption, including in asset recovery;
(c) To promote integrity, accountability and proper management of public affairs and public property.

From the reading of the above section, it appears that the UNCAC provides a common international framework where corruption can be dealt with through a uniform set of guidelines. Any state including South Africa, experiencing the impacts of IFFs can rely on the principles embedded in the UNCAC to tackle this phenomenon. In order to cope with corruption and then IFFs in an efficient manner, the UNCAC prescribes not only relevant preventive steps but also more importantly investigative and retaliatory actions to initiate against the culprits. The scope of the treaty is articulated in the provision of article 3(1) as follows:

> This Convention shall apply, in accordance with its terms, to the prevention, investigation and prosecution of corruption and to the freezing, seizure, confiscation and return of the proceeds of offences established in accordance with this Convention.

Broadly speaking, the UNCAC is structured around four pillars dealing with the issue of corruption. These pillars are divided into chapters, each dedicated to preventive measures, criminalisation, international cooperation and asset recovery. The UNCAC targets major activities and settings where corruption is highly likely to occur. When emphasising the case of 'Bribery of foreign public officials and officials of public international organizations' section 16 prescribes steps to be initiated against corruption in public sector. In the same vein, when referring to 'Bribery in the private sector', section 21 provides for measures to be initiated in such instances. The prohibition of international commercial bribery in both private and public sectors by the UNCAC (sections 16 and 21) is instrumental given that commercial activities are among the main channels of the proliferation of IFFs including corruption. The late Kofi Annan coined that corruption is a key element in economic underperformance and a major obstacle to poverty alleviation and development. According to him corruption hurts the poor disproportionately by diverting funds intended for development, undermining a government's ability to provide basic services, feeding inequality and injustice and discouraging foreign aid and investment.[23] It is worth mentioning that member states who ratified the convention must comply with its recommendations in addressing corruption. In so doing, state compliance is assessed following a peer review mechanism coupled with a periodic report to the Conference of the State Parties about the manner and extent to which the UNCAC is implemented. This is a key process to step up the fight against IFFs and allow for the possibility to realise the Right to Development in South Africa and in particular and Africa in general. Despite the presence of IFFs as a global phenomenon, one must keep in mind that developing countries remain the most affected.

Another key feature at the global level to counter IFFs is the Sustainable Development Goals 2030. The document clearly considers the phenomenon of IFFs as a key disabler of development. On this account, IFFs was listed as target 16 of the framework of the Sustainable Development Goals (SDG) in the following way:

> 16.4 By 2030, significantly reduce illicit financial and arms flows, strengthen the recovery and return of stolen assets and combat all forms of organised crime
> 16.5 Substantially reduce corruption and bribery in all their forms
> 16.6 Develop effective, accountable and transparent institutions at all levels
> 16.7 Ensure responsive, inclusive, participatory and representative decision-making at all levels
> 16.8 Broaden and strengthen the participation of developing countries in the institutions of global governance.

The above SDG provisions designed to curb IFFs in South Africa but across the globe pave the way to take initiatives not only in terms of preventative measures but also as remedies. In so doing, the SDG outlines the practices at the origin of IFFs including among other corruption, bribery, lack of transparency, and accountability. Target 16 also prescribes measures as how as how to improve governance, the management of public affairs to bring about sustainable development.

At the regional level, there are instruments that are parts of the architecture to curb IFFs from South Africa. One of the key instruments in this matter is the African Union Convention on Preventing and Combating Corruption (CPCC). This instrument was adopted in 2003 during the 2nd Ordinary Session of the Assembly of the African Union in Mozambique. It is the first instrument at the regional level to fight corruption. From its preamble, the anti-corruption convention expresses its concern 'about the effects of corruption and impunity on the political, economic, social and cultural stability of African states and devastating effects on the economic and social development of the African people'. Following the provisions of section 2, the goals of the CPCC are the promotion and strengthening of development in Africa, the promotion, and regulations of cooperation among member states, the coordination and harmonisation of the policies and legislation between member states and the promotion of socioeconomic development, transparency, and accountability in the management of public affairs. The key driver of IFFs on the continent remains corruption and this explains why the CPCC is a key instrument at the regional level. The purpose of this instrument is to address the dire consequences of corruption in Africa and enhances the possibility to realise the RTD. It is within this framework that the HLP recommends that Article 22 of the CPCC concerning the functions of the AU Advisory Board on corruption should be extended to 'develop methodologies for analysing the nature and extent of IFFs from Africa and disseminate information and sensitise the public on the negative effects of IFFs from Africa'.[24]

At the regional level, the United Nations Addis Ababa Action Agenda (the Agenda) is another crucial initiative to curb IFFs. The Agenda is dedicated to the financing for development with the fight against IFFs at its heart. Given the gravity of the problem, the Agenda appears as a platform of concertation where states initiated measures in a bid to prevent the recurrence of IFFs. The Agenda committed to promote peaceful and inclusive societies through good governance, rule of law, human rights, fundamental freedoms, equal access to fair justice systems and measures to combat corruption and curb IFFs.[25] In its paragraph 23, the document reaffirms what was already mentioned in target 16.4 of the SDG by emphasising the necessity to scale up the efforts to reduce IFFs by 2030, with a view to eventually eliminating them, strengthening national regulation and increasing international cooperation through the insertion of anti-abuse clauses in all tax treaties.

Despite the relevant plan of the Agenda, the landmark initiative in terms of addressing illicit outflows of capitals at the regional level was the establishment of the HLP on IFFs from Africa in February 2012. The HLP Report on IFFs was adopted as a declaration during the twenty-fourth African Union Summit. Historically, this initiative emerged from the fourth Joint African Union Commission/United Nations Economic Commission for Africa (AUC/ECA) Conference of African Ministers of Finance, Planning and Economic Development held in 2011. At the time, the negative impacts of IFFs were critical not only economically but also in every other aspect of people's life. As a result of these negative impacts, the African continent failed to meet the Millennium Development Goals during the target period ending in 2015. The

2011 Conference went on to mandate the Economic Commission for Africa to setup the HLP on IFFs from Africa with the following missions:

- Develop a realistic and accurate assessment of the volumes and sources of these outflows;
- Gain concrete understanding of how these outflows occur in Africa, based on case studies of a sample of African countries and;
- Ensure that we make specific recommendations of practical, realistic, short- to medium-term actions that should be taken both by Africa and by the rest of the world to effectively confront what is in fact a global challenge.[26]

The report of the HLP is available to the public and confirms the premise according to which IFFs is disabler of the RTD on the continent. The recommendations outlined by this body remain one of the most efficient measures to curb the phenomenon of IFFs from Africa and enhance the realisation of the RTD. When it comes to the commercial component of IFFs, the HLP recommends African countries to have clear and concise legislation that make it illegal to state the price, quantity, quality, or other aspect of trade intentionally, incorrectly, or inaccurately in goods and services to move capital or profits to another jurisdiction or to manipulate, evade, or avoid any form of taxation. In the same vein, the Panel calls on national and multilateral agencies to make fully and freely available, and in a timely manner, data on pricing of goods and services in international transactions, according to accepted coding categories. A key recommendation is the strengthening of global and regional cooperation through which an automatic exchange of tax information among states and among them and the rest of the world should take place.[27] Concerning the corrupt component of IFFs, the HLP recommends that this phenomenon should be integrated as a specific component in the CPCC and that actions should be initiated at a global level. The Panel went on to request the global community in all of its institutions, including parliaments to take all necessary steps to eliminate secrecy jurisdictions and introduce transparency in financial transfers and crack down on money laundering. The Panel also calls for stronger collaboration and consistent engagement between Africa and global players such as the United States, the European Union, the G8 and G20 to help ensure greater transparency in the international banking system, with banks being required to ascertain the identity, source of wealth and country of origin of their depositors and their deposits.[28] The Panel came up with a strategic recommendations thereby advising African states to adopt a normative instrument in the form of a declaration to commit to combating IFFs and urging similar actions at the global level.

At the domestic level, the fight against IFFs requires the establishment of specific institutions to deal with this matter. The HLP urges African states to set up or strengthen independent institutions and agencies of government such as for instance intelligence units, anti-fraud agencies, customs and border agencies, revenue agencies, anti-corruption agencies and financial crime agencies, all responsible for preventing IFFs.[29] Such agencies should provide regular reports on their activities and findings to national legislatures.

The above review of the architecture to curb IFFs from South Africa in particular and from Africa in general shows that there is genuine will to break with the past. It has become axiomatic that the continent will not make progress in terms of improving the living conditions of its population, in terms of poverty alleviation, the delivery of education, housing, healthcare, infrastructure, and critical social services. The Independent Expert on the effects of foreign debt and other related international financial obligations of states on the full enjoyment of all human rights, particularly economic, social, and cultural rights outline the following:

> There is a clear link between illicit financial flows in that such flows diminish the resources available to States for investment in programmes that contribute to the realization of human rights, particularly economic, social and cultural rights. In essence, the failure to counter illicit financial flows and recover stolen assets is a denial of access to basic health care, education, safe water and sanitation, adequate housing and infrastructure, all of which are basic conditions for the enjoyment of human rights.[30]

The above quote is relevant, and this probably explains why in addition to the current architecture to curb IFFs, some African states have made further commitment to address this situation. The Yaounde Declaration signed by thirty-four African states in 2017 has paved the way towards a common will to initiate relevant steps to combat IFFs through international cooperation. The Declaration 'encourage all African countries and the Regional Economic Communities to strengthen their efforts in the fight against international tax evasion through tax cooperation and transparency and work towards more regional coordination'.[31]

The proliferation of IFFs fuelled by some multinational corporations has compelled South Africa and numerous states on the continent to contract foreign loans and agreements with leonine clauses to the detriment of their countries and populations. Such loan conditions generally come with a high interest rate, pushing countries to sometimes surrender their natural resources and relevant sections of their sovereignty at the expense of present and future generations. Recent estimates depict the extent to which staggering sum of money is drained out of Africa year in, year out to pay not the debt itself, but interests. Back in 2015 for example, a number of African states received $32.8 billion in loans and spent half of that money, that is, $18 billion in debt interest and principal payments, with the overall level of debt rising rapidly.[32] It is therefore crucial to keep in mind that the measures in place to combat IFFs can work only if such they are implemented in concert with other nations across the globe. An urgent implementation becomes necessary owing to the fact that, the consequences and damages resulting from IFFs may not be reversible. The UNDOC observes that even if portions of the illicit funds are reinvested within the economy this may not prevent the already critical situation from worsening:

> Criminal funds, even if invested in the legal economy, may create a number of problems, from distortions of the resource allocation, to 'crowding out' licit sectors and undermining the reputation of local institutions, which, in turn, can hamper investment and economic growth. The situation is less clear-cut for financial centres receiving illicit funds, but the long-term consequences may be negative if they do not actively fight money laundering.[33]

As already mentioned, IFFs occur across borders and necessarily involve a multiplicity of actors and one or more several states. This means that the robust instruments and initiatives to address IFFs that will not be sufficient by themselves. This will require a strong commitment and will from all parties to really implement such architecture. It was observed that to succeed, IFFs generally require trespassing borders and involving more than one state because 'long-term neglect of this problem means that the world now faces highly developed criminal organizations that undermine the rule of law, international security and the world economy and which, if they are allowed to continue unimpeded, could threaten the concept of the nation-state'.[34] By relying on these sophisticated mechanics to divert important funds and assets from authorities, transnational corporations escape not only from their professional responsibilities but also from their ethical obligations of honesty and integrity due to their host countries. It is worth nothing that a certain number of multinational corporations are at the heart of the proliferation of IFFs and by doing so, they deprive their host country of staggering amount of money. Their role in IFFs financial environment strongly contributes to dismantle the layers of the economy, the governance structure and contribute to violate human rights in general and the Right to Development in particular. Some reports show that multinational corporations are responsible for shifting approximately $1.38 trillion profits into tax havens each year resulting in $245 billion lost in taxes. Within this context, Africa loses about $25.7 billion to offshore tax havens.[35] Yet it is recognised that even though they may not be parties to human rights instruments, multinational corporations have nonetheless the obligation to comply with such rights. Concerning the realisation of the Right to Development, it was rightly observed that in spite of the weakness of the regime of business and human rights, the emerging view is that business can no longer be indifferent to human rights violations caused by their operations. This in itself is a legal and moral argument in which the human rights and the Right to Development obligations of multinational national corporations is based.[36] The impacts of IFFs affect more the poorest and more vulnerable section of the population of the population than any other one. Despite the good economic performance recorded by the continent for the past few years, the gap between the rich and the poor has been increasing. The United Nations estimates show that from 1990 through 2010 the number of people living on less than $1.25 a day in Africa nearly doubled from 219 million to 414 million. One can only hope that the robust architecture to curb IFFs will receive a global support and will be implemented frankly and honestly.

CONCLUSION

My purpose in this chapter was to review the architecture to curb IFFs from South Africa and assess the extent to which they could impact on the Right to Development. I have shown that there is serious proliferation of IFFs from South Africa with devastating consequences not only on the economy but more importantly on human rights and the realisation of the Right to Development. In so doing, I depicted how trade misinvoicing and trade mispricing are used by some multinational corporations and other criminal networks to divert important sum of money from the South African treasury. This reinforces my conviction that South Africa in particular and Africa in general are underdeveloped not because of poor resources but owing of the misappropriation of available resources by criminal entrepreneurs and obscure networks that sabotage every development initiative by taking advantages of weak state institutions and poor governance structures. To break with the past, a robust architecture to prevent IFFs from South Africa and around the world has been established decades ago. There are key instruments at the global level such as the UNCAC and other at the African regional level notably the African Union CPCC. These documents provide relevant steps and initiatives to prevent the continued proliferation of IFFs and abuse of human rights. However, one has to keep in mind that no matter how good and relevant they are, instruments do not have the ability to implement themselves and require humans to so. The challenge is that within the environment of IFFs, African states remain the most affected victims whereas some developing countries profit from this practice. The point is therefore to convince the latter to give up on these profits by putting forward their unethical nature and emphasising the devastating consequences these cause to an entire continent and the threat it can cause to world peace.

NOTES

1. Addis Ababa Action Agenda United Nations General Assembly August 2015, UN document A/RES/69/313, available at https://sustainabledevelopment.un.org/index.php?page=view&type=400&nr=2051&menu=35.

2. Addis Ababa Action Agenda United Nations General Assembly August 2015, UN document A/RES/69/313, available at https://sustainabledevelopment.un.org/index.php?page=view&type=400&nr=2051&menu=35.

3. Sustainable Development Goals, Compilation of Metadata for the Proposed Global Indicators for the Review of the 2030 Agenda for Sustainable Development, available at https://unstats.un.org/sdgs/iaeg-sdgs/metadata-compilation/.

4. Marie-Louise Gumuchian, Security Woes Hit Libya Oil and Gas as Guards become Menace, Reuters, 7 March 2013, available at <https://www.reuters.com/article/libya-oil-militia/securitywoes-hit-libya-oil-and-gas-as-guards-become-menace-idUSL6N0BY5DS20130307>.

5. United Nations Conference on Trade and Development, Africa could Gain $89 billion Annually by Curbing Illicit Financial Flows, 28 September 2020, available at https://unctad.org/news/africa-could-gain-89-billion-annually-curbing-illicit-financial-flows.

6. Trade-Related Illicit Financial Flows in 135 Developing Countries: 2008–2017, Global Financial Integrity 2020, available at https://gfintegrity.org/report/trade-related-illicit-financial-flows-in-135-developing-countries-2008-2017/.

7. Rahim, H. L., et al., Globalization and its Effect on World Poverty and Inequality, *Global Journal of Management and Business*, 1(2), 2014.

8. Mrak, M., Report of Globalization: Trends, Challenges and Opportunities, 2000.

9. Gumuchian, Marie-Louise, Security Woes Hit Libya Oil and Gas as Guards become Menace, Reuters, 7 March 2013, available at <https://www.reuters.com/article/libya-oil-militia/securitywoes-hit-libya-oil-and-gas-as-guards-become-menace-idUSL6N0BY5DS20130307>.

10. Gumuchian, Marie-Louise, Security Woes Hit Libya Oil and Gas as Guards become Menace, Reuters, 7 March 2013, available at <https://www.reuters.com/article/libya-oil-militia/securitywoes-hit-libya-oil-and-gas-as-guards-become-menace-idUSL6N0BY5DS20130307>.

11. See for instance GE Kamdem Kamga, Linkages between Illicit Financial Flows and the Non-realisation of the Right to Development in Africa, *Comparative and International Law of Southern Africa*, 52(2 and 3), 2019, UNISA Press.

12. South Africa: Potential Revenue Losses Associated with Trade Misinvoicing, Global Financial Integrity 2018, available at https://gfintegrity.org/report/south-africa-potential-revenue-losses-associated-with-trade-misinvoicing/.

13. Illicit Financial Flows and the Problem of Net Resource Transfers from Africa: 1980–2009, Global Financial Integrity and African Development Bank 2013, http://www.gfintegrity.org/storage/gfip/documents/reports/AfricaNetResourse.

14. Ashman, S., Fine, B., and Newman, S., Amnesty International? The Nature, Scale and Impact of *Southern African Studies*, 37(1), 2011.

15. South Africa: Potential Revenue Losses Associated with Trade Misinvoicing, Global Financial Integrity 2018, available at https://gfintegrity.org/report/south-africa-potential-revenue-losses-associated-with-trade-misinvoicing/.

16. South Africa: Potential Revenue Losses Associated with Trade Misinvoicing, Global Financial Integrity 2018, available at https://gfintegrity.org/report/south-africa-potential-revenue-losses-associated-with-trade-misinvoicing/.

17. African Development Bank and Global Financial Integrity, Illicit Financial Flows and the Problem of Net Resource Transfers from Africa: 1980–2009, Global Financial Integrity and African Development Bank 2013, available at http://www.gfintegrity.org/storage/gfip/documents/reports/AfricaNetResourse.

18. High Level Panel on Illicit Flows from Africa, Track It! Stop It! Get It! Report of the High Level Panel on Illicit Financial Flows from Africa, Addis Ababa: Commissioned by the AU/ECA Conference of Ministers of Finance, Planning and Economic Development, 2015.

19. Kamga, Serges Djoyou, *The Right to Development in the African Human Rights System*, Routledge, 2018.

20. Tax Justice Network, Public Service International & Global Alliance for Tax Justice, The State of Tax Justice 2020: Tax Justice Network in the Time of COVID-19, 2020.

21. As above.

22. Vlassis Dimitri, The United Nations Convention Against Corruption Origins and Negotiation Process, UNAFEI, *Resource Material Series,* 66, 2002, 126–131 at 126.

23. United Nations Convention Against Corruption, United Nations New York, 2004, iii.

24. High Level Panel (n 2) at 84.

25. Addis Ababa Action Agenda United Nations General Assembly August 2015, UN document A/RES/69/313, available at <https://sustainabledevelopment.un.org/index.php?page=view&type=400&nr=2051&menu=35>.

26. High Level Panel (n 2) at 2.

27. High Level Panel (n 2) at 80.

28. High Level Panel (n 2) at 85.

29. High Level Panel (n 2) at 82.

30. The Negative Impact of the Non-repatriation of Funds of Illicit Origin on the Enjoyment of Human Rights, Final Report of the Independent Expert on the Effects of Foreign Debt and Other Related International Financial Obligations of States on the Full Enjoyment of all Human Rights, Particularly Economic, Social and Cultural Rights, Cephas Lumina, available at https://digitallibrary.un.org/record/768139?ln=en.

31. The Yaoundé Declaration – Fighting Illicit Financial Flows in Africa, available at https://www.oecd.org/tax/transparency/what-we-do/technical-assistance/the-yaounde-declaration.htm.

32. How the World Profits from Africa's Wealth, Honest Accounts? 2017, available at https://www.healthpovertyaction.org/wp-content/uploads/2018/12/Honest-Accounts-2017-1.pdf.

33. Estimating Illicit Financial Flows Resulting from Drug Trafficking and Other Transnational Organized Crimes Research Report, United Nations Office on Drugs and Crime 2011, 8.

34. Louise Shelley, Transnational Organized Crime: An Imminent Threat to the Nation-State? *Journal of International Affairs*, 48(2), 1995, 464–465.
35. As above.
36. Djoyou Kamga (n 5) 70.

BIBLIOGRAPHY

Addis Ababa Action Agenda United Nations General Assembly August 2015, UN document A/RES/69/313, available at https://sustainabledevelopment.un.org/index.php?page=view&type=400&nr=2051&menu=35.

African Development Bank and Global Financial Integrity, Illicit Financial Flows and the and African Development Bank 2013, available at <http://www.gfintegrity.org/storage/gfip/documents/.

Ashman, S., Fine, B., and Newman, S., Amnesty International? The Nature, Scale and Impact of *Southern African Studies*, 37(1), 2011, 7–25.

Estimating Illicit Financial Flows Resulting from Drug Trafficking and Other Transnational Organized Crimes Research Report, United Nations Office on Drugs and Crime, 2011, 8.

Gumuchian, Marie-Louise, Security Woes Hit Libya Oil and Gas as Guards become Menace, Reuters, 7 March 2013, available at <https://www.reuters.com/article/libya-oil-militia/securitywoes-hit-libya-oil-and-gas-as-guards-become-menace-idUSL6N0BY5DS20130307>.

High Level Panel on Illicit Flows from Africa, Track It! Stop It! Get It! Report of the High Level Panel on Illicit Financial Flows from Africa, Addis Ababa: Commissioned by the AU/ECA Conference of Ministers of Finance, Planning and Economic Development, 2015.

How the World Profits from Africa's Wealth, Honest Accounts? 2017, https://www.healthpovertyaction.org/wp-content/uploads/2018/12/Honest-Accounts-2017-1.pdf.

Illicit Financial Flows and the Problem of Net Resource Transfers from Africa: 1980–2009, Global Financial Integrity and African Development Bank 2013, http://www.gfintegrity.org/storage/gfip/documents/reports/AfricaNetResourse.

Kamga, G.E. Kamdem, Linkages between Illicit Financial Flows and the Non-realisation of the Right to Development in Africa, *Comparative and International Law of Southern Africa*, 52(2 and 3), 2019, UNISA Press.

Kamga, Serges Djoyou, *The Right to Development in the African Human Rights System*, Routledge, 2018.

Mrak, M., Report of Globalization: Trends, Challenges and Opportunities, 2000.

Rahim, H. L., et al., Globalization and its Effect on World Poverty and Inequality, *Global Journal of Management and Business*, 1(2), 2014, 8–13.

Shelley, Louise, Transnational Organized Crime: An Imminent Threat to the Nation-State? *Journal of International Affairs*, 48(2), 1995, 464–465.

South Africa: Potential Revenue Losses Associated with Trade Misinvoicing, Global Financial Integrity, 2018, available at https://gfintegrity.org/report/south-africa-potential-revenue-losses-associated-with-trade-misinvoicing/.

Sustainable Development Goals, Compilation of Metadata for the Proposed Global Indicators for the Review of the 2030 Agenda for Sustainable Development, available at https://unstats.un.org/sdgs/iaeg-sdgs/metadata-compilation/.

Tax Justice Network, Public Service International & Global Alliance for Tax Justice, The State of Tax Justice 2020: Tax Justice Network in the Time of COVID-19, 2020.

The Negative Impact of the Non-repatriation of Funds of Illicit Origin on the Enjoyment of Human Rights, Final Report of the Independent Expert on the Effects of Foreign Debt and Other Related International Financial Obligations of States on the Full Enjoyment of all Human Rights, Particularly Economic, Social and Cultural Rights, Cephas Lumina. https://digitallibrary.un.org/record/768139?ln=en.

The Yaoundé Declaration – Fighting Illicit Financial Flows in Africa, https://www.oecd.org/tax/transparency/what-we-do/technical-assistance/the-yaounde-declaration.htm.

Trade-Related Illicit Financial Flows in 135 Developing Countries: 2008–2017, Global Financial Integrity 2020, available at https://gfintegrity.org/report/trade-related-illicit-financial-flows-in-135-developing-countries-2008-2017/.

United Nations Conference on Trade and Development, Africa could Gain $89 billion Annually by Curbing Illicit Financial Flows, 28 September 2020, available at https://unctad.org/news/africa-could-gain-89-billion-annually-curbing-illicit-financial-flows.

United Nations Convention Against Corruption, United Nations New York, 2004, iii.

Vlassis Dimitri, The United Nations Convention Against Corruption Origins and Negotiation Process, UNAFEI, *Resource Material Series*, 66, 2002, 126–131 at 126.

Chapter 3

Ethiopia

Illicit Financial Flows' Consequences Exacerbating Conflict in the Northern Corridor

T. K. Seife

INTRODUCTION

Numerous studies demonstrate that Africa has developed into a transit point for billions of dollars in aid and investment via illicit financial flows (IFFs).[1] The primary reason is that IFFs have depleted developing nations' finite financial resources for development and poverty alleviation, eroding the effectiveness of foreign aid significantly. Attempts by developing countries to rein in illegal financial outflows have been unsuccessful due to the existence of numerous institutions that are not merely willing but actively seeking to absorb these IFFs. Africa will thus need to consider not only how aid should be spent inside the continent but also how it finances its development goals and lowers its reliance on official development assistance.[2] Besides, illicit finance flows have acted as a roadblock to development, impeding the desired outcome. Numerous factors contribute to a lack of accountability among a select few, including corruption, ineffective government, political instability, a lack of the rule of law, and a deficiency in regulatory monitoring.[3]

Capital flight from Africa needs to be researched, and a method to identify sources of such illegal behaviour is crucial for policy formulation. Additionally, it is critical to consider the destinations' interests and policy gaps when addressing illicit finance flows. While the international development community pays close attention to the amount of aid and investment that comes in Africa, the funds that leave the region are generally overlooked.[4] What exacerbates the complexity of illicit finance flows is the actors' anonymity and multiplicity. Signé stated that cash smuggling, remittance transfers, trade finance, and shell corporations are simply a few of the ways that money is transferred between nations. A wide range of policies and activities are required to tackle IFFs because of their complex nature and cross-sectoral nature.[5] Thus, examining how IFFs emanating from Africa have developed into a security risk to development. It is necessary to evaluate the source and destination of illicit finance flows in order to make policy recommendations for combating illicit capital flight. The policy advice should be grounded in reality and take African countries' implementation capacities into account.

Africa's poverty is not due to a scarcity of natural resources, market access, or technical expertise; rather lack authentic leadership, an adaptive policy framework that is responsive to local conditions, and equitable and robust institutions. The question that needs to be answered is, 'Why is Africa so horribly poor?' Greg Mills made some compelling arguments about the inherent character of poverty, and I concur with several of his points. I also want to know whether illicit finance flows are the outcome of maladministration or a symptom of institutional weakness; these are questions that need to be answered in order to offer some feasible solutions. According to the Economic Development in Africa Report 2020 by the United Nations Conference on Trade and Development (UNCTAD), Africa loses approximately US$88.6 billion, or 3.7 per cent of its GDP each year. Illicit finance flows out of Africa have long been a cause of concern due to their volume and adverse impact on the continent's development and governance goals.[6] Unfortunately, the majority of African financial institutions were established to protect colonial interests, and without institutional ownership and regulatory framework adjustments, only a limited amount of progress can be made. According to Mills, colonial powers' top-down imposition of states and borders on Africa's diverse ethnic and sectarian fabric established inadequate governance institutions.[7] Mills also hinted that African states were made and kept going not through higher taxes and the provision of public services, like in Europe, but through colonial fiat. However, during the last fifty years, the Organization of African Unity and the African Union have been vehemently opposed to modifying Africa's colonial borders and weak financial institutions, which they could not allow to happen due to the powerful Western countries.[8]

The fundamental reason for this is because IFFs have depleted developing nations' scant financial resources for development and poverty reduction while also significantly hurting the effectiveness of foreign development assistance. Institutions such as the African Union and the agencies of the United Nations are not just willing but actively attempting to block IFFs. Despite the fact that emerging countries have attempted to do so numerous times without success. Actions in developed countries must complement developing countries' economic and governance efforts to make it more difficult for illicit funds to enter their economy.[9] Natural resources abound on the African continent; practising a lack of sound resource management could help Africa finance a large chunk of its own development. In addition, the composition of these outflows' challenges long-held notions about illegal money transfers.

Numerous explanations for Africa's slow development have been advanced, including a lack of human and government capacity, inadequate infrastructure and trade access, the consequences of insufficient or excessive foreign aid, the legacy of arbitrary colonial boundaries, low productivity, the Cold War and geography, financial sector mismanagement, and poor governance in various parts of the continent.[10] IFFs squander resources that could be used to boost the continent's development. IFFs syphon resources away from the continent's development; as a result, reducing IFFs has the potential to reduce aid dependence by enhancing domestic resource availability.[11] There are two ways to analyse the link between IFFs and poverty reduction in Africa: directly through reduced government spending for programmes like health and education or indirectly through the impact of low investment on earnings.

Examining IFFs through the lens of national and regional security is critical; the UN-ECA studies indicate a correlation between national security threats and unlawful money transfers. Aside from budgetary deficits, IFFs directly impact the provision of public services such as schools and clinics, sanitation; national security; health and social protection; and the ability to provide these services.[12] To date, the majority of research and policy efforts have been focused on establishing a link between IFFs and a detrimental effect on national security, which is defined as a country's capacity to avoid insecurity at the individual, communal, and governmental levels. While additional research is necessary to ascertain the relative strength and significance of the numerous connections in various contexts, the overarching message is clear: governments concerned with peace and security should also be concerned with IFFs and vice versa. Concerning Africa specifically, authorities should consider the extent to which financial secrecy is required to promote IFFs, at both the national and regional levels and worldwide, in terms of how it affects the continent's economies.[13]

According to the 2014 Tana High-Level Forum on Security in Africa, an estimated $946.8 billion was removed from developing nations in 2011, with a total of $5.9 trillion in illegal financial outflows between 2002 and 2011. This further supports the idea that illicit financial flows are the most severe economic problem affecting today's global South.[14] The most concerning finding of the report are that IFFs are expanding at an alarming rate, especially in the global South. In the last decade, there has been a growth in the amount of IFFs that are leaving developing nations. This is thought to be one of the causes of commodity markets and monetary inflation. However, there is a lack of cohesive effort at the national and regional levels to recognise the catastrophic nature of the issue, without which all development measures will fail.

Among the top ten illicit flow emitters, nine countries attribute a substantial portion of total exports to natural resources: mining products in South Africa, the Democratic Republic of the Congo; Botswana; and Zambia; and oil and gas in Nigeria, Angola, Sudan, and Cameroon.[15] Signé said that South Africa, the Democratic Republic of the Congo, Ethiopia, and Nigeria are the top four illicit flow emitters, accounting for almost 50 per cent of all IFFs from Africa. Throughout the years, illicit money flows from Africa have shifted away from developed nations and towards developing economies; this change can be related to the decline in commerce with the industrialised regions. Non-oil exporting countries such as South Africa, Morocco, Côte d'Ivoire, and Ethiopia also had substantial IFFs levels from 1970 to 2008; in Ethiopia, IFFs have resulted in an average loss of 2.2 per cent in GDP growth every year.[16]

The TPLF's looting system has had a catastrophic effect on Ethiopia's economy. According to Kukutschka analysis, the TPLF is a mafia organisation that has amassed more than $32 billion in ill-gotten gains by playing the Ethiopian government's ethnic card. The TPLF leadership and its associates have perpetrated financial sabotage against Ethiopia's impoverished society, specifically the Tigray people.[17] As outlined by Gebregziabher in his article soldiers in business: the hazards of METEC's initiatives within the context of Ethiopia's civil–military relations, one of the indications is the party-led business corporations that are profoundly involved in corruption.[18] The organisation has been involved in high-level corruption, state capture, and IFFs that have aided criminal enterprises' success. The Endowment Fund for the Rehabilitation of Tigray (EFFORT) played a vital role in the maintenance and functioning of the oligarchy that was the TPLF.[19] This conglomerate of EFFORT commerce and industries has established a presence throughout Ethiopia not only by manipulating local politicians and plundering economic sectors but also by employing financial muscle to penetrate and dominate all key business sectors.

THE DISRUPTIVE EFFECTS OF IFFS ON A COUNTRY'S DEVELOPMENT

The most direct effect of IFFs is a decrease in domestic spending and investment, both public and private. This results in fewer healthcare facilities and schools, decreased national security and a lack of infrastructure development such as roads and bridges. The main reason for this is that illegitimate financial flows have severely hampered the efficiency of international development aid and robbed poor countries of much-needed funds for development and poverty reduction. Because there are numerous institutions that are not merely willing but actively seeking to absorb these IFFs, efforts by developing countries to reduce illicit financial flows have failed.[20] IFFs pose a severe danger to global political and economic stability, particularly in developing countries; they result in decreased domestic spending and investment, as well as a loss in foreign direct investment. A consensus among multilateral financial institutions has emerged that most developing nations are unable to raise sufficient domestic investment capital to sustain long-term economic growth as a result of IFFs.[21]

Developing countries' economic and governance strategies must be supported by measures in affluent countries to make illicit funds more challenging to acquire. Regulations and oversight to promote greater transparency and accountability must be equally applied to offshore centres and banks if they have been complicit in absorbing illegal monies.[22] Because of these factors, evaluating IFFs' social and political dimensions is critical. Social and political transformation are not ending results but essential features of growth. Policymakers and researchers should pay attention to how IFFs affect society and the political system. Economic growth could be negatively affected as well by the social and political effects of IFFs. One of the biggest obstacles facing global attempts to help developing countries overcome hunger, endemic illness, and other development issues is the massive outflow of illicit funds.[23] Capital flight from Africa is not a new problem. Furthermore, data suggests that the situation is becoming worse.

Some types of IFFs, such as the revenues of bribery and the trafficking of narcotics, people, and firearms, are by their very nature secretive and hence impossible to measure accurately. As a result, the amount of money lost by Africa each year due to IFFs is likely to exceed US$88.6 billion by a large margin.[24] This should be of the utmost concern in light of the developing nation's lacklustre economic growth and the extreme levels of poverty. The other obstacle is the expectations of the donor country in terms of resources, as well as the shifting focus away from direct development assistance and towards combating global climate change. Despite the fact that African economies have grown at an average pace of roughly 5 per cent per year since the turn of the century, this rate is regarded as positive but insufficient by many.[25] IFFs are a significant constraint to development financing in Africa. IFFs drain resources that may be used for the development of the continent; hence, a reduction in IFFs has the potential to result in a comparable reduction in assistance dependence by boosting the availability of local resources.[26]

Regardless of the conceptual concerns, numerous international organisations regard IFFs as a hindrance to development; the most immediate effect of IFFs is a decrease in domestic spending and investment, both public and private.[27] IFFs are a major barrier to development investment in Africa, but it's hard to determine their link. And poverty reduction because this link manifests through reduced government financing for poverty reduction programmes like health and education, or through indirect routes like the detrimental effect of low investment on incomes. As a global governance issue, IFFs are more than just an African problem; they call for a wide range of responses, including those at the international financial architecture.[28]

IMPACT OF CAPITAL FLIGHT ON POVERTY ALLEVIATION

As a result of capital flight, the strength of the economy and the government are reduced, which has a detrimental influence on poverty alleviation. As a direct consequence of this, the purchasing power of the populace is diminished, and the value of vital assets in the nation that is being affected may deteriorate. The developing nations have an obligation to demonstrate that they are willing to battle IFFs at whatever cost. Instead of being misappropriated by persons in positions of power within their respective nations, the stolen cash could have been put towards alleviating poverty and accomplishing other development goals.[29]

African governments might grant time-limited amnesty to anyone who is willing to return illicit assets without fear of being punished, replicating the successful experiences of nations that have experienced capital flight repatriation in the past. Chile is often recognised as the most successful illustration of capital repatriation used to finance economic investments.[30] Alternatively, countries should reserve the authority to prosecute any of their citizens who are accused of owning assets in a foreign country that were illegally transferred from their home countries, regardless of their citizenship. The question of why we need to know where IFFs are initially absorbed is an important one to consider. Should we be concerned that these flows are being routed through offshore financial hubs or non-offshore developed country banks? There are a large number of institutions that are not just willing but actively eager to absorb these illicit outflows, despite the fact that emerging countries have made numerous attempts to do so with little success.

Actions in prosperous countries must support economic and governance strategies in developing nations to make it more difficult for illicit funds to be absorbed into their economies.[31] Even if sizeable international assistance inflows have almost likely discouraged many African governments from reforming their economies, Africa's poverty is not primarily a result of inadequate infrastructure or commercial access. Despite receiving privileged access to foreign markets, such as through the African Growth and

Opportunity Act (AGOA), from the United States, Africa has lagged behind other, less fortunate competitors. However, such opportunities do not come without strings attached; Africa would be better off if it created and utilised its own market opportunity with more than 1.2 billion people.

Poverty reduction in Africa relies on strong and sustained economic growth. In recent years, a substantial amount of research has been devoted to understanding how to reduce poverty in Africa, as well as its prerequisites and alternative economic policies. However, IFFs are an essential source of domestic resource leakage, reducing foreign exchange reserves, tax collections, foreign investment, and poverty in the world's poorest developing countries. Most unrecorded private IFFs involving capital that is illegally produced, transferred, or utilised, often used by residents to accumulate overseas assets in contravention of existing capital restrictions and regulatory frameworks are referred to as IFFs.[32] Even if the transaction is genuine, such as the profits of a respectable corporation, their transfer abroad in contravention of exchange control restrictions or corporate tax laws will deem the capital illegal.

Low and falling public investment in Africa's economy is causing the continent's economies to stagnate. In contrast to economists who have focused primarily on private investment, research suggests that low and declining state investment may be a more pressing concern for African countries. Academic research showed that IFFs make it much harder for African economies to grow and get out of poverty.[33] IFFs is one of the main issues African nations face is their failure to sustain high growth rates long enough to reduce poverty significantly.

As a result, the primary growth challenges continue to be increasing growth, broadening the growth base, and sustaining growth for an extended period.[34] In spite of the fact that many African countries have had long-standing and even growing investment-saving inequalities, Africa as a whole is characterised by a stunning contradiction. This contradiction is brought about by the fact that many African countries have had investment-saving inequalities. It is essential to keep in mind, despite this, that the continent is also a major source of IFFs that are not documented, occurring within the continent from one African nation to the next.

ILLEGAL MONEY LAUNDERING TECHNIQUES AS THE STANDARD OF IFFS

According to the extant research on IFFs, these flows are often the result of money laundering, corporate bribery, tax evasion, and trade mispricing/misinvoicing, to name but a few. Additionally, corruption, grand corruption, and state capture accounted for just a small percentage of IFFs, particularly when it comes to money laundering. Trade misinvoicing is a frequently used strategy for unlawfully transferring money from one jurisdiction to another. Importers overstate the value of their imports and exports in order to avoid paying customs tariffs and trade restrictions, and exporters understate the value of their exports to avoid paying customs duties and trade restrictions. Tax havens at international destinations are the primary conduit for illicit funds today, according to Thabo Mbeki Foundation, an NGO founded by the former South African president to promote Africa's resurgence.[35] An anti-corruption foundation claims that 'secrecy jurisdictions' run millions of 'disguised corporations' (i.e. companies that exist only on paper).[36] Anonymous trust accounts and bogus charitable foundations specialising in money laundering and trade over invoicing are also operated by these jurisdictions.

Trade misinvoicing and other forms of tax evasion are prevalent in developing countries where multinational corporations operate. When exporters or importers intentionally misreport the value, quantity, or nature of products and services in order to evade taxes, exploit tax advantages, dodge capital controls, or launder money, this is a form of trade misinvoicing.[37] Excessive use of illegitimate financing methods avoiding taxes by exploiting a loophole or exception to tax legislation or adopting an unanticipated interpretation of the law is referred to as 'tax avoidance' Anti-avoidance measures can be used to stop such practices, but IFFs can be a substantial source of tax evasion if such rules are not in place or are not effective. It is referred to as tax avoidance when a taxpayer takes measures in order to avoid a tax obligation by omitting or disguising the income from which the tax burden has arisen. Criminal or civil consequences may result from tax evasion as a component of IFFs. Although these numbers are large, the most worrisome takeaway from the investigation is precisely how fast IFFs are rising and have different mechanisms that are untraceable.

When inflation is considered, the average annual growth rate of illegal money transfers out of developing countries was more than 10 per cent.[38] Commercial tax evasion, trade misinvoicing, and predatory transfer pricing are among the methods used to obtain this money. In addition, certain legal definitions, such as residence, subsidiaries, affiliates, beneficial ownership, debt servicing, permanent installations, and the use of an international corporate structure, make it feasible to move throughout the globe within the confines of the law. Confusing and opaque legal principles make it difficult to understand.[39] Other methods include criminal activity such as drug trafficking, human trafficking, illegal arms selling, and contraband smuggling; bribery and theft by corrupt government officials; and commercial tax evasion, trade misinvoicing, and predatory transfer pricing. If nothing is done, these numbers will continue to rise indefinitely. Some critical reports will awaken international leaders to the need to address IFFs and act quickly. Annual estimates from our research indicate that criminals, smugglers, and corrupt officials smuggle millions of cash out of developing countries each year.[40]

The expansion of secrecy jurisdictions, safe havens, and tax havens, which give options for the transfer and concealment of IFFs, has made it easier for African countries to experience capital flight from their respective countries. Profits from natural resource export embezzlement, tax evasion, corruption, transfer pricing, and outright smuggling of capital out of African countries are examples of what is considered illicit. Because of this, any examination of the issue of capital flight must give substantial consideration to the role played by tax havens.[41] I suggest five approaches for tackling the problem of capital flight from Africa:

- Preventing illegal export of legally acquired capital.
- Addressing trade-related capital flight and tax evasion.
- Recovering and repatriating stolen assets.
- Combating the 'revolving door' and 'odious debt'.
- Enforcing banking transparency and tax compliance.

The strategy to combat capital flight must be organised along these dimensions.

In particular, banking secrecy has made it difficult to monitor and supervise private banking activity, even in countries with strict laws against domestic money laundering. This is true even in nations with strict laws against domestic money laundering. Even in high-profile situations (such as former African dictators and kings Mobutu, Sani Abacha, and King Haile/ Selassie), many nations have been unable to recover their stolen property. Capital flight was brought to public attention in 1999 when the Bank of New York assisted in the transfer of at least US$7 billion in ill-gotten gains from the Russian Federation into private bank accounts in the United States and other Western countries. However, the scandal, in this case, arose because the stolen funds were believed to have originated from the pockets of US taxpaying citizens through contributions to the IMF, which was, in fact, a falsehood.[42] For an accurate evaluation of the economic impact of IFFs from poor nations, it is possible to track whether or not they are timely. Partially monitoring and evaluating a nation's receipt of IMF/World Bank funds and expenditures on a particular project or total expenditures is possible. However, it has been proven that they have a significant impact, not merely a negative one. Because of IFFs, impacted nations lose out on considerable investment money that could otherwise be utilised to encourage economic growth and serve as a valuable complement to foreign loans and aid payments in the financing of public sector expenditures, among other reasons.

THE IMPACT OF ILLEGAL FINANCIAL ACTIVITIES ON NATIONAL SECURITY THREATS

How can IFFs threaten national security; what are the mechanisms, and how does the government protect its citizens? Within the context of IFFs, the issue at hand is crucial and must be addressed. Everything that has an impact on the physical well-being of a population, as well as the stability of a nation's economy or institutions, is considered a threat to national security. IFFs can be used to weaken the government's security apparatus by partnering with disgruntled members of society or foreign operations. Among many national security threats, the followings are critical: Local and foreign terrorism, organised crime, money laundering, foreign power-sponsored or locally coordinated activities, coup d'état; espionage; economic sabotage; targeting national infrastructure; collaboration with foreign agents; engagement with lobbyist groups seeking to remove African leaders from power; hiring mercenaries to fight against the central government, and so on.

My argument that few researches have studied the relationship between IFFs and national security challenges and how nations might prevent personal, social, and political levels of insecurity. There is, however, a paucity of data indicating the necessary connections and how they work. The initial repercussions of IFFs, which are caused mainly by illegal capital transactions, will be utilised for activities such as internal conflict. On the other side, conflicts weaken the institutions that can rein in IFFs and increase the risk that rent-seeking behaviour will exceed long-term economic investments. In addition, a state-controlled economy is characterised by illicit capital flight and attendant criminality and corruption. On the connections between IFFs and issues about the ability of states to prevent or get rid of insecurity at the personal, community, environmental, and political levels; more specifically, the ability and willingness of states to act to reduce the risk of violence against the person. There is a chance of being unsafe because of fights between groups, the environment getting worse, and political rights being violated.[43]

It is critical to understand the link between terrorism and the financing of terrorism and organised crime and the economic ramifications of terrorism and the fight against terrorism. Illegal money fosters the growth of terrorist and organised crime organisations; it is critical to combat terrorism by limiting terrorists' financial options, hence limiting the basis for their operations.[44] Due to the necessity of reviewing financial transactions, national security intelligence officials and law enforcement agents will be forced to work with accountants, banking and financial experts, and other financial experts if they wish to trace the money trail. Each nation faces a variety of national security threats on a different level; however, things become more complicated when agents attempt to manipulate and divert the national economy against its population and government. These threats can be social in nature, such as aggression from within the nation by individuals seeking political power in a neighbouring country, infiltration by a terrorist group, or global economic trends that jeopardise the nation's welfare; or they can be political, such as any other threat that undermines a nation's power and destabilises its well-being.

IFFs-related literature says that 'state capture' is a type of systemic political corruption in which corporate interests have a lot of power over how a state or a branch of a state makes decisions. In other words, private interests have considerable influence over a state's decision-making processes for their own gain. African governments are a victim of state capture in numerous ways. There is tremendous interest in containing IFFs, mainly by getting other actors' collaboration, compliance, and commitment.[45] African authorities strive to halt IFFs in order to maximise tax revenues, retain investable resources within their countries, avoid state capture, and thwart criminal and corrupt activities.

IFFs and state capture have always been inextricably linked in some form; corruption and cronyism in South Africa are considered incomplete without addressing private-sector economic crime.[46] Particularly the issue of IFFs; business in South Africa condemns corrupt public sector practices, while private-sector misbehaviour has been equally clear. One primary source of concern is that the business sector has been increasingly deafeningly silent on matters such as corruption in the country, as well as financial and economic crimes, in recent years. Because of its dominance and guidance, the corporate sector emerged as a prominent player in democratic debates towards the end of apartheid. While state capture poses an enormous, systematic threat to South Africa's democracy on a scale similar to a coup, it must be recognised as a political ambition cloaked in the guise of radical economic reform.[47] Corruption and tax evasion are entwined with state capture. For a variety of reasons, any examination of capital flight from African countries must consider the role of tax havens, safe havens, secrecy jurisdictions, and offshore financial centres (OFCs).[48] To begin, secrecy jurisdictions facilitate the transfer and concealment of capital, especially illicitly acquired funds through state capture, because the services provided to capital holders.

Illicit finances threaten global security and economic stability from organised crime, corruption, and tax evasion, which cross borders and negatively impact underdeveloped countries. Even wealthy nations, who have been the target of cyber-related crime for decades and have previously invested significantly in building capacity to combat technology-related crime and promoting a culture of cybersecurity, have numerous challenges in this field.[49] African authorities can address IFFs on a home level with immediate security gains. These steps can considerably strengthen African officials' ability to ensure that global agreements reflect African interests.[50] As a result, African countries and their inhabitants will bear the long-term consequences if African leaders fail to take decisive action. In this study, I will examine the relationship between IFFs and national security via the lens of a continuous conflict in Ethiopia's northern corridor, which began in 1974 and has been intensified since 2018.

IN THE ETHIOPIAN CASE STUDY, THE USE OF UNLAWFUL FINANCIAL ACCESS INSTRUMENTS

Ethiopia is one of the African countries that has been impacted by IFFs, which have had a considerable negative influence on the country's progress. Ethiopia's recent efforts should be supplemented by a more thorough investigation of questionable financial transactions involving the country's political system in order to avert IFFs. IFFs continue to cost Ethiopia billions of dollars each year, according to Global Financial Integrity (GFI) data from 2004 to 2013.[51] Further indicated that it has been IFFs out of Ethiopia and into countries including the United States and Europe, as well as the Middle East and the Far East. According to GFI, there are several sorts of financial crimes, but trade misinvoicing accounts for around 80 per cent of losses from IFFs.[52] Ethiopia is a country undergoing a quiet crisis as a result of a political system that has favoured a few elites operating under the guise of ethnic minorities to control the economic and political structures. Ethiopia's TPLF-led government is briefly discussed, as is IFF's role in grand corruption, state capture, money laundering, and the hiring of lobbyists and mercenaries to overthrow the central government.

Due to the complexity of IFFs in Ethiopia, a number of actors are involved. Unlike in any other country, government employees were the prominent actors in state takeover in Ethiopia. Regional favouritism and distributive politics are not novel concepts in Ethiopia; nonetheless, studies indicate that they have gotten worse since 1991, when the Tigray Peoples Liberation Front (TPLF) took over both regional and national governments.[53] The TPLF rebel group had no intention of governing Ethiopia, as its manifesto stated that they intended to secede from the start. However, sad circumstances have compelled them to lead a country they despise.[54] Through its financial umbrella organisation, the Relief Society of Tigray (REST), the TPLF amassed vast wealth off of famine-relief charity money. This was accomplished through widespread fraud, robbery, theft, and awful violence. The TPLF mercilessly transformed aid money into cash and military equipment.[55] The TPLF leadership and its sympathisers have committed theft and IFFs from Ethiopia's underprivileged society. The organisation has been involved in grand corruption, state capture, and IFFs that contributed to the success of criminal activities.[56,57]

The TPLF rose to power through open deception and thievery; while in reign, they stole public funds, and after being disposed of power, they began fighting back with Ethiopia's stolen funds. the TPLF established 'endowed' conglomerates through the use of stolen wealth (EFFORT).[58] As the Front preyed on 'donors', the EFFORT preyed on Ethiopians with the assistance of TPLF officials who wield economic dominance in Ethiopia. Throughout its history, the TPLF has operated under a corrupt and ruthless system. As a result, the TPLF is corrupt as a dominant faction. The TPLF leaders' deliberate fostering of ravenous corruption appears to be reaping fruit in the form of mounting regime resentment. Ethiopia's predatory system is collapsing as a result of the TPLF's/struggle with EPRDF's to keep power. The TPLF's kleptocratic system may outlive its founders. The EFFORT's extensive reach now encompasses all of Ethiopia's strategic economic sectors: agriculture, manufacturing, imports-exports, construction and urban land development, insurance, mining and exploration, banking and microfinance, pharmaceuticals, transportation, printing and publishing, broadcasting and consulting.[59]

With an understanding of the patterns and mechanics of organised crime on a broader scale, it is not difficult to pin down the TPLF's immoral behaviour in stealing and hoarding public resources; while they were a rebel organisation battling the central government, at the same time, they were a rebel organisation fighting the central government. However, some have established the foundations of mega empires through reports, surveys, and admissions of former TPLF leaders who became top government officials, corporate executives, and dissidents. The humanitarian assistance was supposed to save the lives of ordinary people, but the TPLF's unceasing theft of public riches began with.[60] Additionally, the legislation establishes that Western governments and international aid organisations were complicit in the plundering. The TPLF funded their guerrilla operations by diverting foreign humanitarian assistance, capturing privately owned enterprises, robbing government financial systems, and taxes on peasants.[61]

The TPLF developed the Endowment Fund for the Rehabilitation of Tigray as part of its economic repression campaign (EFFORT). The business firm was founded with a dual objective in mind: first, to exert control over the Ethiopian economy, and second, to suppress already established businesses in a manner similar to that of Economic Hit Man. EFFORT began its business thirty years ago with a US$3 billion paid capital investment, establishing the business enterprise as a large conglomerate in Ethiopia. Ethiopians considered the TPLF and its business arm EFFORT allowed Tigray to prosper while ensuring the rest of Ethiopia bled'.[62]

John Perkins's *Confessions of an Economic Hit Man* revealed how colonial interests imposed themselves on developing countries. It emphasised the cycle of financial sector manipulation and foreign entities such as the Bretton Woods institutions and USAID's widespread use of fiscal policy.[63]

> Economic hit men (EHMs) are highly paid professionals who cheat countries around the globe out of trillions of dollars. They funnel money from the World Bank, the U.S. Agency for International Development (USAID), and other foreign 'aid' organisations into the coffers of huge corporations and the pockets of a few wealthy families who control the planet's natural resources. Their tools include fraudulent financial reports, rigged elections, payoffs, extortion, sex, and murder. They play a game as old as an empire, but one that has taken on new and terrifying dimensions during this time of globalisation. I should know; I was an EHM.[64]

However, EFFORT does not possess the sophistication of an economic hit man's institutional capacity; however, they have attempted and succeeded in controlling and profiting from the Ethiopian economy on a modest scale. One of the most powerful parastatals in the country, EFFORT is frequently polluted by favouritism and corruption. It was established in such a way that it could exert control over the economy by investing in strategically important businesses. In order to maintain and expand its monopoly, the EFFORT corporation is systemically undermining and appropriating the entrepreneurial ideas of private capitalists. In a similar vein, the organisation is used to facilitate the transfer of illicit financial capital out of nation. Tax avoidance and evasion are accomplished by the use of the nature of the firm as an endowment. EFFORT was a tightly controlled organisation by the TPLF senior leadership, which included the party chairman as its leader, and only three people have been in charge of the organisation for three decades: Sebhat Nega, Zenawi himself, and his wife Azeb Mesfin.[65]

It is interesting to note that ('the late Meles Zenawi') the secretary-general of the TPLF and prime minister of Ethiopia has never openly condemned the 'Republic of Greater Tigray' or repudiated its secessionist objectives.[66] Even former prime minister Zenawi confessed in mid-2011 that US$2 billion had been stolen, and the cash was extradited to foreign banks economic sabotage, including Sir Geldof and co.'s Band-Aid fundraising campaign for the Tigray famine. He added that the PM was aware of how and where the funds were placed, but as was customary, his government never pursued the case and prosecuted the 'thieves', as he used to refer to them. A close friend of the late prime minister Zenawi describes the corruption phenomena in the country as follows: 'The reality is that (ethnic-based) patronage politics, or patron-client relationships have consumed Ethiopian government institutions at the municipal, regional, and federal levels.'

The EFFORT was dominated by a few TPLF figures, such as Sbhate Nega and Prime Minister Meles Zenawi's wife for three decades.[67] TPLF was enjoying unchecked political power under the Meles Zenawi dictatorship. The late Zenawi reversed his decision after finding out that his own regional-party-owned company, Guna Trading and his wife (Azeb Mesfin) might have been involved in the disappearance of the 'lost' 10,000 tons of coffee. Mr Sibhat Nega, one of the founders of the TPLF and veteran leader of the ruling party, most of which is obtained through obscene corruption and leveraging state resources and unfair trade practices. To construct their empire in the name of the Tigrayan people, Meles and Sibhat Nega regarded famine opportunists and utilised it as a criminal tool.[68] Mr Nega previously informed in various platforms that the TPLF is Africa's, if not the world's, wealthiest political party.[69] Mr Nega's audacious admissions reaffirm what the public already knows: the TPLF controls an enormous amount of political and economic power. There is no political dictatorship in the world that has made a farce of the privatisation programme that the IMF, the World Bank, and Western nations envisioned and campaigned for, and then exploited it to expand its economic empire through its corrupt para-NGOs except for TPLF.

EFFORT is born with the new law's letter rather than the spirit, and the TPLF-funded firms were transferred to the newly founded EFFORT in mid-1995. In accordance with the Ethiopian Civil Code of 1960, individual shareholdings in existing share firms were 'irrevocably donated' to EFFORT.[70] EFFORT is one of four Charities recognised by Ethiopian law: charitable endowments, charitable institutions, charitable trusts, and charitable societies. Additionally, to strengthen the IFFs, Addis Engineering and the Africa Insurance Company were created in Addis Ababa in the early 1990s, as was Senay Trading Company, afterwards Tower Trading Company, in London. Numerous of these organisations have since been dissolved or moved to new ownership. Meanwhile, Mega Communications has always been outside the scope of endowment funds.

The companies that facilitate IFFs were set up on offshore companies by EFFORT.[71] Tower Trading Tower Trading Company (Senay Trading till 1995) was founded in London in September 1993 with a £300,000 share capital. The company ceased trading several years ago, and it was closed down. The firm is listed because its shareholders are described as 'the trustees of EFFORT' by UK Companies House.[72] At least two former directors were Ethiopian diplomats in London. The latest records indicate annual earnings of £125,000 in 2006 and £102,000 in 2007 on a turnover of £1m-£1.2m.[73] EFFORT and its enterprises are part of a network of businesses in Tigray with close ties to the ruling party. TPLF military effort against previous administration produced some of them. EFFORT companies work with each of them:

- The Relief Society of Tigray (REST);
- The Tigray Development Association (TDA);
- The Tigray Veterans' Association;
- Farmers', Womens' and Youth Associations;
- Co-operatives;
- Dedebit Credit and Savings Institution Share Company (DECSI).[74]

ECONOMIC MANIPULATION TECHNIQUES AND THE LESSON TO BE LEARNED

By employing case studies, an attempt to identify the forces and reasons behind the push and pull factors in IFFs is crucial for giving empirical evidence. It is critical to examine the core techniques that are applied to unidentified illegal financial transactions. In this context, it is vital to mention tax evasion through the use of civil society platforms such as non-governmental organisations (NGOs), endowments, and foundations. Likewise, evaluating international criminal operations through the lens of financial manipulation, corruption, and state capture is critical. EFFORT/TPLF commercial empire, according to Woldesenbet,[75] has a long-term advantage in controlling the central government, which is the driving force for the establishment of the business empire. Following the TPLF's seizure of government control, all of the organisation's operations were registered under the civil society code or as an endowment, among other ways. EFFORT businesses were operating and competing legally with other companies throughout the country with little or no oversight or management for more than three decades are known as business empires. The TPLF political elite was in charge of the organisation.

The EFFORT ownership of the business organisational structure will continue to be a source of contention and perplexity for many concerned parties. That means the organisation was running by invisible hands with no accountability, and there was a conducive environment for IFFs. The complex web of looting mechanisms and local and foreign actors' affiliations is mesmerising, hinted that one of the financial umbrella organisations that were established in 1978, namely the Relief Society of Tigray (REST).[76] The TPLF cruelly converted aid money into cash and military weapons through a Band-Aid fundraising campaign that was illegal financial activities started. Financial sector manipulation served as a motivating factor or (pulling factor) for the TPLF/EFFORT, as there was no government structure in place to address financial irregularity. And the driving element (or pushing factor) was their belief that long-term economic dominance would result in political manipulation and central government control.

Initially, the EFFORT supported business-related activities were funded through REST and unrestricted borrowing from Ethiopia's state-owned banks, the latter of which was later written off as bad debt.[77] The premise is comparable to 'robbing Peter to pay Paul' similarly robbing Ethiopia and building the TPLF empire was done by design. The question remains unsolved as to whether shared financial secrets within TPLF high-ranking officials; yet, the company continues to play a vital part in the country's economy; the dilemma is who will own the company and on what grounds. It is unclear who will administer this vast corporation, how and who will refund the unlawfully obtained funds, or who would be the legal trustee after the TPLF era has terminated. Because they are convinced that controlling the economic sphere will reflect and aid in manipulating the political one, the TPLF has built a sizeable corporate empire. Mistakes were made, but winning over the public's affections was not among them. In any case, the economic dynasty that benefited from a manipulative and structured approach was not designed to trickle down the benefits to the public rather than the political elites.

CONCLUSION AND POLICY RECOMMENDATIONS

Ethiopia is used as an example in this chapter to highlight that capital flight has significant repercussions for African countries. As a result of the need to increase and maintain growth as a condition for alleviating poverty, IFFs is a threat to national security and a significant impediment to domestic investment. Africa's economic emancipation and prosperity must prioritise two crucial areas: removing internal and external obstacles for economic self-sufficiency and ensuring that economic development cannot occur without economic advancement. Africa financial and internal governance structural problems need to be replaced through indigenous knowledge systems capable of comprehending the African farmworker sociocultural structure's dilemma. On the other hand, the external component deserves close analysis and scrutiny, particularly those so-called international financial organisations that impede economic development. Thus, Africa's public intellectuals, academics, and government should devise a strategy for exiting Bretton Woods institutions such as the World Bank, the International Monetary Fund (IMF), and, indirectly, the European Union Partnership Agreement (EPA). As we all know, these institutions are designed in such a way that the wealthy continue to prosper while the impoverished continue to suffer.

The Western world has a Marshall plan for restoring countries, and any who oppose will face Marshall blows. Thus, to put an end to the 'central' and 'periphery' tragedies, Africans must unite and be vigilant to avoid economic disaster and instability on the continent. They have nothing to offer; everything they have stolen from Africans and the rest of the developing world is what they are giving us.

Illicit outflows cost African countries money required for public services, infrastructure, and economic development and are likely to exceed development funding. It is impossible to define 'IFFs' due to a lack of clarity in the idea. The issue of capital flight from Africa must be tackled at all levels. These include preventing the illegal export of properly acquired capital, resolving trade-related capital flight and tax evasion, recovering stolen assets and enforcing financial transparency and tax compliance in safe havens. Since most capital flight originates in the industrialised world, African countries must work closely with their counterparts. Global financial transparency benefits emerging and developed countries alike.

African countries, particularly Ethiopia, should revise their commercial and civil society registration codes to eliminate distinctions between party-owned and state-owned businesses and develop a monitoring framework. A firm stance against informal transfer systems, continual asset freeze, and a commitment to international legal cooperation should be the first steps taken by governments. This strategy should incorporate the following components: Create a global index of countries' susceptibility to terrorist financing in order to strengthen the international community's capacity to monitor and control terrorist financiers' preferred safe havens. Africa should reconsider the establishment of a central financial monitoring entity, with a particular emphasis on strengthening law enforcement institutions. Additionally, empowering citizens is vital in forbidding unlawful operations at the national level; empowering women and youth is crucial in the fight against the illegal financial flow.

NOTES

1. Kar et al. "The absorption of illicit financial flows from developing countries: 2002–2006." (2010).

2. "United Nations. Economic Commission for Africa (2015)." Illicit financial flows: Report of the high level panel on illicit financial flows from Africa. Addis Ababa. © UN.ECA.

3. T. K. Seife. "Educational system obstruction consequence in the political volatility: Comparative assessments Somalia and Djibouti." *The Education Systems of Africa* (2020): 1–27.

4. Signé et al. "Illicit financial flows in Africa: Drivers, destinations, and policy options." (2020).

5. R. M. B. Kukutschka. "Illicit financial flows in Ethiopia" (2018). Transparency International, September 2018.
6. "United Nations. Economic Commission for Africa (2015)". Illicit financial flows (n 2 above).
7. G. Mills. "Why is Africa poor?." *Culture & Civilization*, Routledge, 2018, 40–50.
8. S. T. Kidane. "The structural impediments to African Reintegration: A comparative analysis of EAC, ECOWAS and SADC." 2018.
9. Kar et al. *Illicit Financial Flows from Developing Countries: 2002–2011*. Washington, DC: Global Financial Integrity, 2013.
10. Mills (n 7 above).
11. Signé et al. (n 4 above).
12. "United Nations. Economic Commission for Africa (2015)". Illicit financial flows (n 2 above).
13. A. Cobham. "The impacts of illicit financial flows on peace and security in Africa." Tana High-Level Forum on Security in Africa, 2014.
14. Kar et al. (n 8 above).
15. Signé et al. (n 4 above).
16. Kukutschka (n 5 above).
17. Z. A. Ayele (2017).
18. T. N. Gebregziabher (2019).
19. M. J. McCracken. "Abusing self-determination and democracy: How the TPLF is looting Ethiopia." *Case Western Reserve Journal of International Law* 36 (2004): 183.
20. Kar et al. (n1 above).
21. M. Herkenrath. "Illicit financial flows and their developmental impacts: An overview." *International Development Policy| Revue internationale de politique de développement* 5, no. 3 (2014).
22. Kar et al. (n1 above).
23. L. Ndikumana. "Capital flight and tax havens: Impact on investment and growth in Africa." *Revue d'economie du developpement* 22(HS02) (2014): 99–124.
24. "United Nations. Economic Commission for Africa (2015)". Illicit financial flows (n 2 above).
25. "United Nations. Economic Commission for Africa (2015)". Illicit financial flows (n 2 above).
26. Signé et al. (n 4 above).
27. Kukutschka (n 5 above).
28. "United Nations. Economic Commission for Africa (2015)". Illicit financial flows (n 2 above).
29. J. D. Nkurunziza. "Illicit financial flows: A constraint on poverty reduction in Africa." *ACAS Bulletin* 87 (2012): 15–21.
30. H. Fofack and L. Ndikumana. "Capital flight repatriation: Investigation of its potential gains for sub-Saharan African countries." *African Development Review* 22, no. 1 (2010): 4–22.
31. Kar et al. (n1 above).

32. Kar and LeBlanc. *Illicit Financial Flows from Developing Countries: 2002–2011*. Washington, DC: Global Financial Integrity, 2013.

33. "United Nations. Economic Commission for Africa (2015)". Illicit financial flows (n 2 above).

34. Ndikumana (n 20 above).

35. "United Nations. Economic Commission for Africa (2015)". Illicit financial flows: Report of the High-Level Panel on illicit financial flows from Africa. Addis Ababa. © UN.ECA.

36. M. Tafirenyika. "Illicit Financial Flows from Africa: Track it, stop it, get it." *Africa Renewal* 27, no. 3 (2013): 14.

37. Ndikumana (n 20 above).

38. Kar and LeBlanc (n 28 above).

39. L. Latif. "Position paper and a common list of demands for representatives of the civil society from Africa to propose a reform of international corporate taxation in the fight against Illicit Financial Flows." (2018).

40. Kar and LeBlanc (n 28 above).

41. Ndikumana (n 20 above).

42. Kar et al. (n1 above).

43. A. Cobham (n 12 above).

44. F. Schneider. "The (Hidden) financial flows of terrorist and organized crime organizations: A literature review and some preliminary empirical results." 2010.

45. "United Nations. Economic Commission for Africa (2015)". Illicit financial flows (n 2 above).

46. Mulaudzi and Masenya. Coup D'état on South African Government: Is state capture a threat to democracy?. International Conference on Public Administration and Development Alternatives (IPADA), 2018.

47. Mulaudzi and Masenya (n 41 above).

48. Ndikumana (n 20 above).

49. T. Tropina. Do digital technologies facilitate illicit financial flows? (2016).

50. A. Cobham (n 12 above).

51. Kar and Spanjers. "Illicit financial flows from developing countries: 2004–2013." *Global Financial Integrity* (2015): 1–10.

52. Kar and Spanjers (n 49 above).

53. A. Adugna. "Regional economic favoritism and redistributive politics as a public good: The case of Tigray region in northern Ethiopia." *Journal of Geography and Geology* 11, no. 1 (2019): 1–12.

54. McCracken (n 12 above).

55. S. Y. Hassan. "Corruption, state capture, and the effectiveness of anticorruption agency in post-communist Ethiopia." *Economic and Political Studies* 6, no. 4 (2018): 368–416.

56. McCracken (n 12 above).

57. B. Abegaz. Political parties in business. The College of William and Mary, Department of Economics, Working Paper (113), 2011.

58. McCracken (n 12 above).

59. Hassan (n 48 above).

60. McCracken (n 12 above).

61. S. Y. Hassan. "The state capture onset in Ethiopia: Humanitarian aid and corruption," 2013.

62. Adugna (n 47 above).

63. J. Perkins. *Confessions of an Economic Hit Man.* Berrett-Koehler Publishers, 2004.

64. Ibid (Perkins, 2004).

65. B. Abegaz. "Political parties in business: Rent seekers, developmentalists, or both?." *Journal of Development Studies* 49, no. 11 (2013): 1467–1483.

66. McCracken (n 12 above).

67. Hassan (n 48 above).

68. A. Berhe. "The politics of famine, media activism, and donor aid in the horn." 2018.

69. Abegaz (n 58 above).

70. Vaughan and Gebremichael. "Rethinking business and politics in Ethiopia." Africa Power and Politics, UK Aid, Irish Aid. 2011.

71. Hassan (n 54 above).

72. Vaughan and Gebremichael (n 63 above).

73. Vaughan and Gebremichael (n 63 above).

74. Vaughan and Gebremichael (n 63 above).

75. W. G. Woldesenbet. "The tragedies of a state dominated political economy: Shared vices among the imperial, Derg, and EPRDF regimes of Ethiopia." *Development Studies Research* 7, no. 1 (2020): 72–82.

76. Constantine & Enterprise. "Exclusive: How Bill Casey's CIA ripped off the 1985 live aid concert to arm right-wing Ethiopian rebels and left thousands to starve to death."

77. McCracken (n 12 above).

BIBLIOGRAPHY

Abegaz, Berhanu. "Political parties in business." *College of William and Mary, Department of Economics* (2011): 1–67, Working Paper Number 113.

Abegaz, Berhanu. "Political parties in business: Rent seekers, developmentalists, or both?." *Journal of Development Studies* 49, no. 11 (2013): 1467–83.

Adugna, Aynalem. "Regional economic favoritism and redistributive politics as a public good: The case of Tigray region in northern Ethiopia." *Journal of Geography and Geology* 11, no. 1 (2019): 1–12.

Ayele, Zemelak Ayitenew. "Corruption in Ethiopia: A merely technical problem or a major constitutional crisis." 2017. In Conference paper https://www.researchgate.net/publication.

Berhe, Aregawi. "The politics of famine, media activism, and donor aid in the horn."

Cobham, Alex. "The impacts of illicit financial flows on peace and security in Africa." Tana High-Level Forum on Security in Africa, 2014.

Constantine, Alex, and Free Enterprise. "Exclusive: How Bill Casey's CIA ripped off the 1985 live aid concert to arm right-wing Ethiopian rebels and left thousands to starve to death."

Fofack, Hippolyte, and Leonce Ndikumana. "Capital flight repatriation: Investigation of its potential gains for sub-Saharan African countries." *African Development Review* 22, no. 1 (2010): 4–22.

Gebregziabher, Tefera Negash. "Soldiers in business: The pitfalls of METEC's projects in the context of Ethiopia's civil–military relations." *Review of African Political Economy* 46, no. 160 (2019): 261–278.

Hassan, Seid Y. "The state capture onset in Ethiopia: Humanitarian aid and corruption." Available at SSRN 2303692 (2013).

Hassan, Seid Y. "Corruption, state capture, and the effectiveness of anticorruption agency in post-communist Ethiopia." *Economic and Political Studies* 6, no. 4 (2018): 368–416.

Marc Herkenrath, "Illicit Financial Flows and their Developmental Impacts: An Overview", International Development Policy | Revue internationale de politique de développement [Online], 5.3 | 2014, Online since 26 January 2015, connection on 20 November 2023. URL: http://journals.openedition.org/poldev/1863; DOI: https://doi.org/10.4000/poldev.1863

Herkenrath, Marc. "Illicit financial flows and their developmental impacts: An overview." *International Development Policy| Revue internationale de politique de développement* 5, no. 3 (2014).

Kar, Dev, and Brian LeBlanc. *Illicit Financial Flows from Developing Countries: 2002–2011*. Washington, DC: Global Financial Integrity, 2013.

Kar, Dev, and Joseph Spanjers. "Illicit financial flows from developing countries: 2004–2013." *Global Financial Integrity* (2015): 1–10. https://gfintegrity.org/wp-content/uploads/2015/12/IFF-Update_2015-Final-1.pdf

Kar, Dev, Devon Cartwright-Smith, and Ann Hollingshead. "The absorption of illicit financial flows from developing countries: 2002–2006." Available at SSRN 2335028 (2010).

Kidane, Seife Tadelle. "The structural impediments to African Reintegration: A comparative analysis of EAC, ECOWAS and SADC." PhD diss., University of Pretoria, 2018.

Kukutschka, Roberto Martinez B. "Illicit financial flows in Ethiopia." (2018).

Latif, Lyla. "Position paper and a common list of demands for representatives of the civil society from Africa to propose a reform of international corporate taxation in the fight against Illicit Financial Flows." Available at SSRN 3386630 (2018).

McCracken, Matthew J. "Abusing self-determination and democracy: How the TPLF is looting Ethiopia." *Case Western Reserve Journal of International Law* 36 (2004): 183.

Mills, Greg. "Why is Africa poor?" In *Culture and Civilization Volume 4, Religion in the Shadows of Modernity*, edited by Irving Horowitz, 40–50. Routledge, 2012.

Mulaudzi, K. M., and M. J. Masenya. "Coup D'état on South African Government: Is state capture a threat to democracy?." International Conference on Public Administration and Development Alternatives (IPADA), 2018.

Ndikumana, Leonce. "Capital flight and tax havens: Impact on investment and growth in Africa." *Revue d'economie du developpement* 22, no. HS02 (2014): 99–124.

Nkurunziza, Janvier D. "Illicit financial flows: A constraint on poverty reduction in Africa." *ACAS Bulletin* 87 (2012): 15–21.

Perkins, John. *Confessions of an Economic Hit Man.* Berrett-Koehler Publishers, 2004.

Schneider, Friedrich. "The (Hidden) financial flows of terrorist and organized crime organizations: A literature review and some preliminary empirical results." (2010).

Seife, T. K. "Educational System Obstruction Consequence in the Political Volatility." In *The Education Systems of Africa. Global Education Systems*, edited by K. S. Adeyemo. Cham: Springer, 2021. https://doi.org/10.1007/978-3-030-44217-0_31.

Signé, Landry, Mariama Sow, and Payce Madden. "Illicit financial flows in Africa: Drivers, destinations, and policy options." (2020).

Tafirenyika, Masimba. "Illicit Financial Flows from Africa: Track it, stop it, get it." *Africa Renewal* 27, no. 3 (2013): 14.

Tropina, Tatiana. "Do digital technologies facilitate illicit financial flows?." (2016).

United Nations. Economic Commission for Africa. "Illicit financial flow: Report of the High Level Panel on illicit financial flows from Africa." (2015).

Vaughan, Sarah, and Mesfin Gebremichael. "Rethinking business and politics in Ethiopia." *Africa Power and Politics, UK Aid, Irish Aid* (2011).

Woldesenbet, Wassihun Gebreegizaber. "The tragedies of a state dominated political economy: Shared vices among the imperial, Derg, and EPRDF regimes of Ethiopia." *Development Studies Research* 7, no. 1 (2020): 72–82.

Chapter 4

Tax Cooperation in Curbing Illicit Financial Flows from Africa

Arnold Kwesiga and Linah Aduda

INTRODUCTION

The African Union Agenda 2063, which is a framework for sustainable development of Africa, notes that for development to be realised there is a need for increased domestic resource mobilisation, which can be made possible when concerns such as illicit financial flows (IFFs) are addressed.[1] Similarly, the 2015 Addis Ababa Agenda for Action stipulates that to increase domestic financing for development, the reduction in IFFs remains one of the most critical measures to be undertaken by states.[2] More so, the United Nations 2030 Agenda for Sustainable Development (UN 2030 Agenda) also recognises that the reduction of IFFs and recovery of stolen assets are integral in the promotion of peace and an inclusive society in sustainable development efforts.[3] It is without a doubt that African states need to increase resource mobilisation and allocation to finance their development agenda. The monies lost in IFFs, coupled with the skewed priorities around resource allocation to key development sectors, have a huge effect on sustainable development including the continent's human capital development.

According to Mukhisa Kituyi, secretary-general of the United Nations Conference on Trade and Development, 'Illicit financial flows and corruption are inhibiting African development by draining foreign exchange, reducing domestic resources, stifling trade and macroeconomic stability and worsening poverty and inequality.'[4] He further adds that faced with high capital flight, tax avoidance, and a marked dependence on corporate income taxes, African Governments face significant constraints to widening their tax base,[5] notwithstanding the fact that the large financing gap for the Sustainable Development Goals (SDGs) on the continent cannot be closed solely through government revenues.[6]

Development in Africa is pegged to the availability of funding to finance all key sectors relevant to the achievement of the SDGs. It is estimated that the yearly funding required for the SDGs is 200 billion USD,[7] yet through IFFs Africa loses 88.6 billion USD in capital flight every year – an equivalent of 3.7 per cent of the continent's gross domestic product.[8] This money, if retained, can be rerouted into developmental purposes and financing key projects and sectors that enhance economic and human capital development.

Furthermore, as part of assistance for development purposes, official development assistance (ODA) from developed donor countries remains one key source of funding that is directed into the economies of developing countries, most notably in Africa. It is interesting to note that the average amount of ODA directed to Africa yearly is estimated at 48 billion USD,[9] which is way less than the 88.6 billion USD lost through IFFs. Tackling IFFs will definitely lead to decline in dependency on ODA, as the domestic available financial resources will contribute to the developmental agenda of a developing or least developed country.[10] In this regard, the importance of curbing IFFs through cooperation between states becomes more apparent. Most of the financial outflows through IFFs are safely tucked in tax havens in order to escape taxation by the domestic tax systems. Tax havens have been defined as 'any jurisdiction that uses the promise of secrecy for overseas territories to compete for financial flows, as well as a low-tax regime, or special rules that allow foreigners to slash their liabilities.'[11] A tax haven often has a network of lawyers and accountants who help the wealthy shield assets from their home country's tax authorities.[12]

To ensure that the domestic tax systems recover taxes due to them, countries have a duty to cooperate in monitoring and dissemination of information on foreign financial accounts in their territories. The exchange of information can be on request or automatic, and detailed discussion of these two different standards will follow in the subsequent sections.

The aim of development as enshrined in the 2030 Agenda for Sustainable Development is among others, the eradication of poverty – which heavily relies on strengthening access to social services and increasing household income especially for marginalised and vulnerable groups. Nkurunziza argues that while a direct causal link between IFFs and poverty reduction cannot be established, there is no doubt that finances lost through IFFs can ultimately lead to a considerable reduction in the rate of poverty in Africa.[13] Hence, if well regulated, and managed, the financial resources lost through IFFs can be rerouted to financing this eradication, by mitigating the root causes and structural inequities that exacerbate poverty within marginalised and vulnerable communities. Coupled with the need to address high corruption levels, the fight against IFFs, and recovery of lost capital, if well directed into national development agendas, would ultimately enhance human capital and sustainable development. This can be achieved through strengthening access to affordable social services like education, health, and water among others, which all contribute to heavy out-of-pocket costs for the most vulnerable communities.

In conclusion, IFFs remain a deep impediment in resource collection, allocation, and utilisation, towards poverty eradication and sustainable development. The amount of money lost in Africa annually can go a long way in addressing key challenges in sectors driving socioeconomic transformation and sustainable development. ODA towards social and economic sectors cannot alone be relied upon to support these sectors – where the continent continues to lose double the sums of money that come in the form of aid. It is critical that the continent reassesses its priorities both at national and at continental level and develop strong cooperation measures and mechanisms to tackle IFFs in all its forms and structures.

THE NATURE AND SCOPE OF IFFS

What Are IFFs?

There is not a single universally accepted definition of IFFs. The World Bank defines IFFs to mean 'money illegally earned, transferred or utilized that crosses borders'.[14] The illegality of the money obtained can be attributed to activities such as drug trafficking, embezzlement of funds, tax and tariffs evasion, proceeds from crimes and corruption and money laundering among others.[15] Most organisations such as the United Nations (UN) have embraced the illegality of activities as being the cornerstone of IFFs. In a 2019 UN Resolution, the UN General Assembly identified tax evasion, corruption, and transnational organised crimes as being the impediments to development in developing countries and in their efforts of financing the SDGs.[16] However, the World Bank also considers cross-border movement of finances to be only illicit when they are connected to criminal activities in a local jurisdiction.[17] Expounding on this, SDG indicator 16.4.1 of the UN Agenda 2030 defines IFFs as 'financial flows that are illicit in origin, transfer or use, that reflect an exchange of value and that cross country borders'.[18] Indicator 16.4.1 further lays out the key features of IFFs to include[19];

a. *Illicit in origin, transfer or use*. A flow of value is considered illicit if it is illicitly generated (e.g. originates from criminal activities or tax evasion), illicitly transferred (e.g. violating currency controls) or illicitly used (e.g. for financing terrorism). The flow can be generated, transferred or used, but it must be illicit in at least one of these aspects. Some flows that are not illegal may fall within the definition of IFFs for statistical purposes, for example, cross-border aggressive tax avoidance which erodes the tax base of a country where that income was generated.

b. *Exchange of value*, rather than purely financial transfers. Exchange of value includes exchange of goods and services, and financial and non-financial assets. For instance, illicit cross-border bartering, meaning the illicit exchange of goods and services for other goods and services, is a common practice in illegal markets, and it is considered as IFFs.
c. IFFs measure *a flow of value over a given time*—as opposed to a stock measure, which would be the accumulation of value.
d. *Flows that cross a border.* This includes assets that cross borders and assets where the ownership changes from a resident of a country to a non-resident, even if the assets remain in the same jurisdiction.

Similarly, some scholars including Landry et.al define IFFs as not necessarily money gained through illegal activities but also those gained through activities that are 'undesirable, immoral, or unacceptable to the public'.[20] Tax avoidance whereas not necessarily illegal, is illustrative of such an activity. In its Economic Development Report of 2020, the United Nations Conference on Trade and Development (UNCTAD) defines tax avoidance as the exploitation of tax rules, both national and international, in order to gain advantages that were not envisioned by the involved countries when the tax rules were being adopted.[21] In most of these developing countries, corporate actors including multinationals and transnational corporations heavily rely on leading law and audit firms to navigate domestic tax regimes and avoid paying some taxes. Although not aligned as illegal practices, these methods designed to and perfected to manipulate weak tax rules have resulted in huge resources lost by countries which if curbed would ultimately support individual country's development agendas.

The SDG indicators, as discussed earlier, expand the definition of IFFs beyond mere criminal activities but cover various features that may not be criminal but morally wrong and undesirable, such as tax avoidance. To this end, this chapter stresses on tax IFFs, which are primarily tax avoidance and tax evasion. Further, the focus on tax cooperation in later sections of this chapter is on recovery of funds that are hidden in tax havens for purposes of defeating taxing from their domestic jurisdiction.

Developing countries heavily rely on revenue collections to finance their development agendas and when gaps in tax rules are manipulated to evade and avoid taxes, they find it hard to allocate necessary resources to key sectors that advance economic growth and human capital development. It is for this same purpose that developing countries find themselves heavily indebted as they often turn to constant borrowing to raise needed capital—notwithstanding the fact that the money lost in capital flight is more than what they receive in ODA and other foreign aid for the same sector financing.

It is thus imperative that the correlation between IFFs and the Right to Development is interrogated further. The importance of cooperation to curb illicit flow of capital is critical to retain much-needed revenue required for sustainable development. The recovery of these funds can be rerouted to developmental projects; and if well managed, they have a resultant effect of ensuring that the Right to Development is realised.

TAXATION AND THE RIGHT TO DEVELOPMENT

Generally, states carry the responsibility for mobilising and allocating resources necessary for the realisation of the Right to Development including the implementation of their international obligation to promote, protect, and fulfil human rights.[22] The fulfilment of these obligations – which are all key to the realisation of the Right to Development are all dependent on collection of taxes. Over the last few years, there has been increased foreign direct and local investments in key sectors in Africa. These include infrastructural development, natural resource exploitation, manufacturing and production, and agribusiness among others—which if well managed would ultimately increase domestic resource mobilisation through collection of taxes essential for the realisation of the Right to Development. However, most national development agendas are anchored around creating conducive environments for private actors to do business.[23]

Globalisation has meant that equitable taxation is not merely a matter of domestic concern, as the rush and competition for foreign investments has 'driven states to engage in a "race to the bottom", competing to offer the lowest taxes and most attractive tax incentives for business'.[24] Similarly, many business enterprises including Transnational Corporations (TNCs) and Multinational Corporations (MNCs) have been associated with the exploitation of tax codes, avoiding paying their fair share of taxes and tax evasion. If not curbed, this tax avoidance and evasion affect government's revenue collection measures, essential in the fulfilment of human rights and realisation of the Right to Development.

Tax Avoidance

Over the years, corporate entities have mastered the skill of avoiding paying for some taxes. With the help of leading law firms, accountants and audit firms, corporations especially Multinationals and Transnationals harness skills and procedures of bending tax system rules to try and gain a tax advantage that the drafters of the tax codes never intended. A 2015 Report of the High-Level Panel on Illicit Financial Flows from Africa defines tax avoidance as the legal practice of taking advantage of a loophole in tax regulations of a country and lawfully minimising any liability of payment of taxes.[25] The report acknowledges that tax avoidance is in fact a major component of IFFs.[26] MNCs are the greatest utilisers of tax avoidance mechanisms and the African continent loses so much of corporate revenue through this practice. Data illustrates that from the continent's aggregate government revenue,[27] corporate taxation amounts to one-sixth of total which translates to around 67 billion USD. On the other hand, revenue lost due to tax avoidance by MNCs amounts to a tenth of the total aggregate government revenue.[28] The statistics are indicative of the amount of corporate tax lost that can be redirected to development in the domestic taxing systems.

Globalisation has enabled MNCs to shift their profits to low-tax jurisdictions[29] and avoiding the payment of taxes from primarily where the corporation is physically based. In order to address tax avoidance by MNCs, the OECD Inclusive Framework on Base Erosion and Profit Sharing was established to enable countries to cooperate in sealing loopholes in taxing systems that the MNCs take advantage of.[30] The OECD framework is one mechanism that developing countries may utilise to assist their governments in strengthening their tax regimes and develop domestic frameworks that raise much-needed capital to finance their development agenda.

Tax Evasion

Tax evasion refers to actions that a taxpayer takes in order to escape a tax liability by concealing taxable income from the domestic taxing authorities.[31] It is thus an illegal undertaking that involves breaking the law.[32] Tax evasion facilitates the outflow of resources that could otherwise be rerouted to development and this eventually affects the budgets of states forcing governments to rely on scarce budget allocations.[33] In Africa, tax evasion not only affects the resources allocated to provision of 'basic public services but also limits efforts to address urgent institutional reforms'.[34] Tax evasion ultimately affects development prospects as allocation of government funds have to prioritise some areas over the others due to budgetary constraints.

To realise the Right to Development, it is paramount that efforts aimed at curbing the loss of resources through tax evasion should be addressed. To address tax evasion as a form of IFF, cooperation between states is fundamental, in exchanging financial accounts information where resources have been lost through tax evasion.

Tax Havens

Tax havens are the 'main channel for laundering the proceeds of tax evasion and routing funds to avoid payment of taxes'.[35] Tax havens are jurisdictions which have very low or zero tax rates for accounts held by non-residents, foreign persons or MNCs. Further to this, there is the likelihood of non-existence of mechanisms that allow for exchange of financial information with other countries and also the tax haven may also not require proof of any substantial activity by a MNCs or a foreign in its jurisdiction before qualifying for tax residency.[36]

In 2022, the European Union published a list of nine countries that it views as tax havens or what it terms as the non-cooperative jurisdictions for tax purposes and these include; American Samoa; Fiji; Guam; Palau; Panama; Samoa; Trinidad and Tobago; US Virgin Islands and Vanuatu.[37] Lénártováthe[38] writes that the mere existence of these tax havens destroys national economies. She argues that the countries of origin where the monies flow from have been met with economic consequences such as:

> Decrease in revenues to the domestic budgets; the lack of funds to finance the needs of the state—for education, health, (hospitals, prevention of diseases and epidemics, fight against pandemics); the lack of funds for the public sector, environmental protection, development programs, support for science, research and development, business support and job creation.

As reiterated earlier, it is through resources that states can fulfil their responsibility of allocating the required resources to realise the Right to Development. However, with constant resources being lost in capital flight to tax havens, the Right to Development cannot be realised without reliance on foreign aid and debts. More importantly, without cooperation from all states including those classified as tax havens, recovery of these resources remains a daunting task.

While cooperation with tax havens is nearly impossible given the likelihood of non-existence of mechanisms that allow exchange of financial information, Lénártováthe writes that through persuasion, which in itself is not enough, many tax havens usually agree to cooperate in exchanging financial information about accounts.[39] Through continued cooperation and persuasion with tax havens, exchange of information of financial accounts can be possible and monies recovered will be redirected to developmental projects in the countries of origin. As emphasised in previous texts, Africa loses 88.6 billion USD yearly to IFFs which are tucked away in tax havens; and within the principle of solidarity, persuasion, the possibility of cooperation with the tax havens, these resources can be recovered and rerouted into the national development agendas.

All in all, it is important to be reminded that businesses operate internationally and hence the effects of tax avoidance and evasion are global and as such, governments, including those that run tax havens, must act in solidarity to tackle tax avoidance and evasion and restore trust in domestic and international tax systems.[40]

LINKAGES BETWEEN THE RIGHT TO DEVELOPMENT AND IFFS

Domestic mobilisation and allocation of resources is crucial to the realisation of sustainable development in Africa. Most national development agenda rely heavily on foreign aid and ODA, which amounts are way lower than the finances that the continent unfortunately loses through IFFs. IFFs are a major impediment to development as they affect funding of key sectors, thus the over reliance on external aid to fund essential development areas.

For example, WHO Global Health Expenditure Database of 2022[41] and 2021[42] reveal that African countries are still heavily reliant on external aid to finance their health sector, and 17 billion USD was used in 2021 as external aid for health financing. On the other hand, World Bank's and UNESCO's Education Finance Watch 2022 report shed light on external aid for education that was extended to developing countries in 2020 at the onset of the COVID-19 pandemic. The report indicated that the aid extended was 18.1 billion USD.[43]

The revenue that Africa loses to IFFs is enough to stop its reliance on external aid for financing sectors, such as health and education, which are key areas of the economy. The 88.6 billion USD that Africa loses yearly if recovered can address the funding gaps for key sectors, ultimately realising development without reliance on external aid.

The UN Declaration on the Right to Development, 1986, recognises the Right to Development as a human right that entitles every person to enjoy 'economic, social, cultural and political development, in which all human rights and fundamental freedoms can be fully realized'.[44] In essence, the Right to Development can only be fully realised when all the fundamental human rights laid out in the different international instruments are also fulfilled. It is the duty of states to ensure that they formulate and adopt national development policies aimed at improving the welfare of their citizens.[45] The implementation of development policies in a country definitely require the availability of adequate resources to finance each development sector of the economy. According to Kamga, the context of finances being fundamental in realisation of the RTD is implied from Article 8 (1) of the Declaration on the Right to Development which states that:[46]

> States should undertake, at the national level, all necessary measures for the realization of the right to development and shall ensure, inter alia, equality of opportunity for all in their access to basic resources, education, health services, food, housing, employment and the fair distribution of income.

The practicality of ensuring that these basic services are equally available, affordable, and accessible to all is through ensuring mobilisation and allocation of necessary resources to key sectors. The recovery of funds lost through IFFs could adequately fund development initiatives.[47] While there is no guarantee that recovery of the funds would automatically be redirected to development priorities, there have been instances where assets recovered have been redirected to developmental projects that have been beneficial to the citizens thus underscoring the importance of recovering resources lost through IFFs. In a 2014 World Bank and OECD report, it was noted that through enforcement of a cooperation agreement between Angola and Switzerland in 2004 and 2012, assets worth 64 million USD belonging to officials from Angola were frozen and Switzerland subsequently returned them to Angola where they were tapped into development projects.[48] Similarly, in 2004, 21 million USD was recovered and directed to clearance of land mines and supporting agricultural projects; while 34 million USD recovered in 2012 was 'allocated for development needs that included establishment of a hospital infrastructure, water supply, and local capacity building for reintegration of displaced persons'.[49]

The underdevelopment of the continent and poverty levels has forced countries to resort to foreign debts and over dependence on foreign aid which is always issued with stringent conditionalities.[50] Some of these conditions are not anchored within a human rights-based approach to development and ultimately impede sustainable development. Many countries find themselves heavily indebted and rigorous annual debt financing undertakings affect their development agendas. For instance, in its 2022 annual report, the International Monetary Fund (IMF) indicated that 60 per cent of low-income developing countries were at high risk of debt distress; and with the end of debt relief service programme by the IMF and World Bank, it was expected that there would be an increase in the borrowing costs and interest rates that would strain national budgets of developing countries, hence the possibility that debts would not be serviced.[51]

The RTD will not be achieved if African countries continue to be trapped in the cycle of aid dependency and accepting loans that come with huge interest rates and heavy repayment plans that affect needed financing to key sectors, essential for development. Over the years, it has become highly unlikely that some of these debts would ever be paid to their entirety.[52] The resources that these countries constantly lose can certainly be used to address development concerns such as socio-economic transformation, poverty alleviation, and enhance access to basic social services.

A 2022 Initiative for Social and Economic Rights (ISER) report on IFFs in the Ugandan context highlighted that increased debt and debt serving expenses constrained public resources that ought to have been used in the provision of quality services and realisation of economic, social, and developmental rights. The report further notes that in the 2020/2021 fiscal year, Uganda spent 12.76 trillion Uganda Shillings (an estimate of 3.4 billion USD) on payment of debt interests, an amount that was 'more than the equivalent combined budget that the government allocated for public services including education, health, water and social protection.'[53] In the same year, Uganda lost 382.8 million USD on tax abuse,[54] which if injected to the economy would ensure that the country is not crippled by payment of loan interests. The same resources would also ensure provision, availability, and accessibility to basic services which are all essential in the realisation of national and human capital development. In essence, combating IFFs should evidently be a top global agenda to facilitate recovery of lost resources that can in turn be utilised in the provision of essential public services.

To achieve the RTD, mechanisms such as recovery of the tax-related IFFs hidden in different jurisdictions can be adopted to ensure that revenue lost can be rerouted back to the economies of African countries thus adequately addressing developmental agendas. Such recovery however banks on cooperation between countries. Given the global nature of IFFs and the involvement of different jurisdictions, emphasis on international tax cooperation becomes a matter of urgency.

The next section focuses on legal and institutional framework that encourages international tax cooperation as a mechanism through which IFFs can be curtailed and addressed; ultimately ensuring that the realisation of the RTD is achieved.

ANALYSIS OF LEGAL AND INSTITUTIONAL FRAMEWORK FOR TAX COOPERATION

IFFs generally and particularly tax evasion and tax avoidance are matters of global concern and as such, cooperation of states remains one viable strategy in combating the vice.[55] There is no doubt that the existence of tax havens critically hinders and has greatly impeded transfer of financial information from such jurisdictions in the fight against IFFs. This has mainly been due to the fact that most of these tax haven states are not party to any tax cooperation instruments or in other instances, they totally disregard their obligations under international law. It is for these same reasons that they remain attractive to many MNCs looking for safe havens to hide their financial loot. As such without strengthening domestic tax policies and regulatory frameworks and harmonising regional and international tax cooperation instruments, IFFs will continue to cripple many developing nations tax regimes and revenue collection mechanisms. It is important to reiterate that cooperation among states remains a critical area for states, especially developing ones in Africa and other regions to combat tax avoidance and evasion and redirect the recovered funds to national and regional development agendas.

In tax matters, globalisation and international financial systems have meant that evasion and avoidance of paying taxes remain a common occurrence with the sole purpose of defeating or taking advantage of gaps in the domestic tax systems. Statistics show that a majority of IFFs from Africa are hosted in Europe, Central or East Asia, and the Pacific regions.[56] It is without a doubt that through cooperation, particularly in the exchange of information and enforcement of international tax rules that recovery of the funds can be possible.

According to Landry, it is through international cooperation that IFFs can be halted and thus, there is a need for the global community to unite in the creation of initiatives that prevent the flight of money from a given jurisdiction.[57] In its ten-year anniversary report, the Global Forum on Transparency and Exchange of Information for Tax Purposes stated that cooperation has enabled the lifting of the veil of secrecy that had shielded tax evaders in hiding their assets offshore.[58] There are different international institutional and legal frameworks that stress on the need for international cooperation through among others, exchange of information. The African Tax Administration Forum provides a well-articulated analysis of the importance of cooperation stating that

> Taxpayers operate globally, while revenue administrations remain confined to their respective jurisdictions. Policy makers globally have worked tirelessly to address this imbalance through implementing programs to curtail harmful tax practices by focusing on improved transparency and co-operation between tax authorities. Countries have increasingly resorted to improved and broadened co-operation in tax matters. In a broader context, the efficient functioning of tax co-operation helps to ensure that taxpayers who have access to cross-border transactions do not also have access to greater tax evasion and avoidance possibilities than taxpayers operating only in their domestic market. The continued viability of an open world economy depends on international cooperation, including co-operation in tax matters. A key element of international co-operation in tax matters is exchange of information.[59]

This section thus analyses the different institutional and legal framework, both international and regional, that focus on exchange of information of financial transactions to enable recovery of funds that can be tapped back into realisation of the RTD on the continent.

INTERNATIONAL AND REGIONAL FRAMEWORKS

Global Forum on Transparency and Exchange of Information for Tax Purposes

The Global Forum on Transparency and Exchange of Information for Tax Purposes (the Global Forum) is the leading global multilateral body whose work is hinged around ensuring that there is effective transparency and exchange of information for tax purposes.[60] Its membership consists of OECD countries and developing countries, including thirty-three African states. As of April 2023, the overall membership of the Global Forum was 167 members.[61] Originally, the membership only consisted of OECD countries, but it was later expanded to also accommodate developing countries.[62]

The focus of the Global Forum is on two internationally recognised standards of exchange of information on request (EOIR) and automatic exchange of financial account information (AEOI).[63] EOIR refers to a 'situation where the designated tax authority of one jurisdiction asks for particular information from the authority of another jurisdiction in connection with a tax inquiry or investigation'.[64] All members of the Global Forum have committed to implementing the EOIR standard, and between 2009 and 2021, an estimated 11.5 trillion USD had been retrieved as additional tax revenue through the exchange of information.[65]

On the other hand, 'AEOI refers to a situation where jurisdictions obtain information from their financial institutions on financial accounts held by non-residents and exchange that information with the jurisdictions of residence of the account holders, every year, without being preceded by a specific request.'[66] Once a country commits to AEOI standards, the country is required to enact a legislation that will allow exchange of information automatically with any other state party that would be interested. An agreement on the details of the exchanges should also be contained in the legislation that is enacted. The transmission of information is through the Common Transmission System, which was developed by the OECD and is managed by the Global Forum.[67]

Through its subsidiary working bodies, the Global Forum is tasked with the responsibility of assisting its members to implement AEOI and EOIR standards. The assistance includes peer-to-peer learning and peer review. Peer-to-peer learning consists of regional training and seminars focused on teachings on the practice of exchange of information and solutions for their implementation; while peer review refers to a process where the implementation of a country's obligations is monitored by an examination analysis of its law and its practical implementation.[68] Between 2009 and 2020, the peer review mechanism had conducted peer review assessments of 126 jurisdictions' compliance with international standards of EOIR as well as through training and technical assistance activities.[69] This peer review is a great mechanism that has forced some countries to amend their legislation on a timely and effective process of exchange—helping in addressing major challenges around tax evasion. Section 2 of the Handbook for Peer Review lays out the standard of transparency and EOIR for tax purposes stipulating that

> Exchange of information for tax purposes is effective when reliable information foreseeably relevant to the tax requirements of a requesting jurisdiction is available, or can be made available, in a timely manner and there are legal mechanisms that enable the information to be obtained and exchanged.[70]

To ensure availability, transparency, and effective exchange of information, it is important that key institutions across jurisdictions cooperate as some of the information needed to combat IFFs, especially tax evasion may be in the hands of private financial institutions, accountancy and audit firms, and law firms. As such the need to strengthen domestic, regional, and international cooperation tax policies and rules can go a long way in combating tax evasion and IFFs in general.

Africa Initiative, 2014

In 2014, African members of the Global Forum Transparency and Exchange of Information for Tax Purposes decided to create an African-focused programme—the Africa Initiative.[71] The objective of the Africa Initiative was to focus more on challenges that are unique to Africa and to ensure that African countries were equipped to participate in EOIRs within the African countries and also on automatic exchange of information, so as to tackle tax evasion in Africa. This regional focus helps in ensuring that strategies and solutions are tailored in line with problems that are specific to the continent.[72] Similarly, this initiative work fits into broader agendas, as previously noted, 'tax transparency is an opportunity to stem illicit financial flows and increase domestic resource mobilization, which are central to the African Union Agenda 2063 and the SDGs'.[73]

The initiative is open to all African countries as signatories and its membership as of April 2023 was thirty-six countries.[74] The members meet every year to reflect on the progress in the African countries and any challenges faced. In its 2022 progress report, the Africa Initiative noted that African countries were increasingly using the EOIR platform and the increase use of the platform generated additional tax revenue for the countries. For instance, three African countries identified USD 38.9 million as a result of the requests they sent in 2021.[75]

In 2020, of requests sent by African countries, Uganda was able to identify and recover an estimated 34.7 million euros as additional tax,[76] the highest recovery for a single country in that year. It is not quite clear whether the recovered funds were used for development projects or provisions of services to the public which underpin the core elements of the RTD. However, this chapter proceeds with a strong assumption that upon recovery, Uganda's taxing authorities redirected the funds to either ongoing developmental projects beneficial to the citizens or the funds were included in the budgets of public and governmental institutions that provide services to the public. The ultimate objective is ensuring that the RTD, that encompasses among other economic and social rights, is achieved.

Generally, from 2014 to 2021, EOIR mechanism enabled nine African countries to identify over USD 244 million in additional revenue.[77] It is thus critical for African countries to continue utilising the EOIR platform, since through requests sent, recovery of additional revenues ensures provision of needed resources for national development agendas.

The Yaoundé Declaration, 2017

Preceding from the 2014 Africa Initiative, in 2017, the African members of the Global Forum, through the Yaoundé Declaration called on the Africa Union to begin a discussion on IFFs and tax cooperation in Africa.[78] The Declaration was premised on the fact that despite advancement in tax cooperation measures, African countries were still not taking advantage of tax cooperation yet they needed the domestic resources being lost through IFFs.[79]

At the inception, the Declaration only had a total of four members: Cameroon, Benin, Uganda, and Liberia. Other members would later join and as of March 2022 the membership totalled to thirty-four members: thirty-three countries and the African Union Commission.[80]

The Declaration noted that only a few African countries were benefitting fully from the transparent tax environment, stating that 'only 5 African countries are committed to automatic exchange of financial accounts information (AEOI), and a large number of African countries continue to have a small EOI network, gaps in their domestic legislation and administrative capacity constraints that hamper efforts to tackle international tax evasion'.[81]

The implementation of AEOI standard in Africa is yet to pick up pace. It is only five (5) African countries (Ghana, Mauritius, Nigeria, Seychelles, and South Africa) that have started the implementation of AEOI standard. Kenya and Morocco committed to start in 2022, Uganda in 2023, and Rwanda in 2024.[82]

As the use of AEOI is yet to pick up pace in the continent, it is highly likely that if its implementation is fastened then countries can automatically exchange information in a bid to re-route resources lost through IFFs. Recovered resources can successfully be used in projects beneficial to the citizens as shown in different reports, and the successful implementation and adoption of AEOI by African Countries will ensure a subsequent increase in the recovery of resources that can be tapped in developmental projects.

The slow pace of implementation can be pegged on lack of sufficient knowledge by taxing authorities on how to use the AEOI data.[83] Once collection of the data is facilitated, it is imperative that the data is used in the most effective way by the recipient country, and the lack of sufficient knowledge by taxing authorities on how to effectively use the data is a hindrance to the AEOI implementation.

Multilateral Convention on Mutual Administrative Assistance in Tax Matters (ETS No. 127)

The Multilateral Convention on Mutual Administrative Assistance in Tax Matters (Multilateral Convention No.127) was developed in 1988 by the OECD and the Council of Europe and amended by a Protocol in 2010.[84] The membership at the time was restricted to only OECD members. However, in 2010 following a G20 resolution in their 2009 summit, a resolution was passed which opened up the Convention to non-OECD member states. The rationale for expanding its membership was to assist developing countries to benefit from a cooperative tax environment where offshore tax evasion is adequately addressed.[85]

The Multilateral Convention No.127 is the most comprehensive multilateral instrument available for all forms of tax cooperation to tackle tax evasion and avoidance. It provides for administrative assistance between state parties, including the exchange of information on tax files of particular persons and transactions.[86] Article 5 provides for EOIR and is to the effect that a state may request for financial information, and in the instance that the information the requested state has is not complete, it is mandated to take all steps necessary to obtain the same and comply with the request. On automatic exchange of information, the convention stipulates that when states have a mutual agreement on terms, they both have agreed on, they can have automatic exchange of information and should cooperate in that regard.[87]

State Parties to the Convention rely on it to provide a legal foundation and backing that allows the exchange of information, whether automatically or on request.[88] As of March 2023, the Convention had 147 signatories, and this was inclusive of 22 African countries.[89] Once states ratify the Convention, a relationship is created among themselves, and this widens the pool that a country can source financial information of different accounts from. A wider pool translates to the possibility of recovery of revenue that has been hidden from taxing authorities in Africa. As emphasised in previous texts, the generation of additional revenue is integral to the realisation of the RTA, as the funds are rerouted to projects that are beneficial to citizens.

The Inclusive Framework on Base Erosion and Profit Sharing

In the current global development agenda, the Inclusive Framework on Base Erosion and Profit Sharing (Inclusive Framework) is a key component of the architecture for international tax and global development issues.[90] As of December 2022, the Inclusive Framework had a total of 142 members, with 27 being from Africa, collaborating on the implementation of the framework. However, only 96 have signed onto the multilateral instrument on Base Erosion and Profit Sharing (BEPS).[91] These all work on equal footing to monitor the implementation of measures to combat BEPS and the ongoing development of consensus-based, anti-BEPS solutions to strengthen the international tax system.[92]

BEPS refers to 'tax planning strategies used by multinational enterprises that exploit gaps and mismatches in tax rules to avoid paying tax'.[93] The Inclusive Framework is thus focused on ensuring that loopholes in existence that can be exploited through tax avoidance by MNCs are sealed. The Inclusive Framework successfully responds to the Addis Ababa Action Agenda on Financing for Development commitment to 'scale up international tax co-operation' and underlines 'the importance of inclusive cooperation and dialogue among national tax authorities on international tax matters'.[94]

It is without a doubt that international taxation issues are of critical importance to most developing countries—since most are more reliant on corporate income taxes and foreign direct investment.[95] As such, according to the OECD, this higher reliance on corporate income tax means they suffer from BEPS disproportionately as BEPS practices annually cost countries USD 100–240 billion in lost revenue.[96] The sole purpose of the Inclusive Framework is to help countries identify loopholes in their tax systems and laws that the MNCs always take advantage of. Developing countries, under the framework work alongside OECD/G20 to develop framework mechanisms of addressing tax avoidance.

However, Brown writes that the framework offers very little support for Africa, a continent which needs enhanced support in building the required administrative infrastructure and capacity to enforce anti-avoidance laws. The framework, at its inception, was focused on special tax concerns of high-income countries that MNCs had exploited, and its design left out African countries. Therefore, even with the enactment of tax laws aimed at curbing tax avoidance by MNCs, there is still a lack of capacity and expertise to enforce the laws in Africa.[97]

Given that Africa is more susceptible to disproportionate effects of BEPS due to its high reliance on corporate income tax, it is critical that high-income countries assist in development of the continent's institutional tax capacity in enforcing anti-avoidance laws. Assistance can be in the form of development of a fund, by the high-income countries, to 'train, recruit and effectively employ a solid tax administration'.[98] Building capacity of tax officials shall increase revenue collected through enforcement of laws meant to seal loopholes, and the revenue collected shall be directed to key projects and developments that advance the RTD of African countries.

United Nations Committee of Experts on International Cooperation in Tax Matters (UN Tax Committee)

In 2004, through resolution 2004/69 of the UN Economic and Social Council (ECOSOC), the 'Ad Hoc Group of Experts on International Cooperation in Tax Matters' was renamed to the 'Committee of Experts on International Cooperation in Tax Matters'. The committee is composed of twenty-five members with expertise on tax policy and administration, and who are nominated by their governments and appointed by the UN Secretary-General. The committee members represent the different regions in the world equally and their term of office is four years. The mandate of the committee of experts is among others to provide a dialogue framework for promotion of international tax cooperation between countries and also to advance recommendations on emerging issues that possibly affect international tax cooperation. In the 2021–2025 term period, six of the experts are from African countries represented by Angola, Mauritania, Zambia, Ghana, Malawi, and Nigeria.[99]

The committee keeps up with tax related contemporary trends, and it recognised the emerging digital economies that could possibly defeat taxing regimes and contribute to IFFs. As such, in 2021, in its 23rd Session, the UN Tax Committee agreed to the insertion of a new article provision in the UN Model Double Taxation Convention between developed and developing countries that would ensure taxation of digital economies.[100] Since it is a work in progress a subcommittee was formed that would unpack the salient tax matters that affect and emerge in the digital economy and also address areas of necessary cooperation.[101]

Evolution of business models which are now purely digital without any physical presence has posed new challenges to the taxing systems of countries.[102]These models have contributed to tax related IFFs, and it is only through exchange of information, automatic or on request, that countries can effectively tax them through corporate income and ensure that they do not escape liabilities.[103] Since digital economies is still an emerging area, the RTD can certainly use additional resources that are hidden or rerouted through digital economies in a bid to defeating taxing systems of African countries. Any digital mechanism through which IFFs are embodied should definitely be addressed to ensure that the RTD is realised in the continent.

CONCLUSION AND RECOMMENDATIONS

Conclusion

IFFs are an impediment to development, and their curtailment will ensure that the much-needed resources on the continent are seized and redirected to development. However, despite the available legal and institutional infrastructure for exchange of information, most African countries are yet to ratify most of the agreements and for the countries that have already ratified, the utilisation of the provisions is still wanting. This reluctance by the African countries to ratify the frameworks facilitates the outflow of the IFFs and ultimately impedes the fight against the illicit flow of capital from Africa. It is critical that there is cooperation through ratification of existing frameworks and exchange of information on IFFs, which will ultimately help in the recovery of lost resources further enhancing the realisation of the RTD.

While cooperation in exchange of information between countries is stressed this ought to be preceded by the ratification of the available instruments. Furthermore, peer-to-peer learning on how to implement provisions of the instruments is also necessitated and the Africa Initiative, among others, needs to educate the tax administrators on how to implement these provisions. For the continent to realise the RTD and subsequently the SDGs, resources that are lost through IFFs need to be rerouted to national strategies and budgets on development. The duty to cooperate in international law as discussed offers the best mechanism in curbing IFFs.

Recommendations

Peer Learning and Capacity Building of Tax Administrators

There is a need for constant peer learning and capacity building among tax administrators in Africa. With emerging areas such as digital economies, learning from themselves on how to navigate IFFs related to the digital world. Additionally, there is also the need for learning about the advantages of AEOI rather than still relying on sending requests through EOIR. The Africa Initiative's mandate of 2021–2023 is, among others, a continued drive to encourage more African countries to utilise the AEOI platform and infrastructure.[104]

The realisation that diverse sectors of a country's economy can be financed by resources lost through IFFs, it becomes imperative for tax administrators to be educated on the importance of cooperation in exchange of information. Exchange of information leads to recovery of resources that are hidden from domestic taxing authorities and learning about that infrastructure is crucial in realisation of the RTD.

Ratification of Instruments

Several African countries have not ratified some of the agreements, and the result is that they cannot access information from most jurisdictions. Most importantly, the Africa Initiative also notes that 'a narrow network of EOI instruments' is also an obstacle that prevents access to information for most taxing authorities.[105] Ratification of the instruments will ensure that exchange of information leads to recovery of resources that are hidden from the taxing authorities and as constantly stressed, the resources could be key in financing development projects and improving provision of basic services that are embodied in the RTD.

Political Goodwill

The implementation of the AEOI and EOIR standards is dependent on leadership of a country. Through political goodwill implementation of these standards will definitely be realised and cooperating with other countries in tackling tax-related IFFs will be facilitated and enabled. As the UN Declaration on the Right to Development stipulates, it is the duty of states to ensure that they formulate and adopt national development policies aimed at improving the welfare of their citizens.[106] Bearing this in mind, international cooperation that requires the implementation of instruments to facilitate exchange of information should be a priority for the governments of African countries. Acknowledging that recovered resources are crucial financial instruments that can be tapped into realisation of the RTD, implementation of instruments that will enable such recovery should thus be a top agenda.

Public Sensitisation and Awareness Creation

Reliance on laws alone is not enough to curb IFFs when the general public is unaware of what IFFs are. Sensitisation of the public about what IFFs are and the negative impacts that they have on development is thus crucial. Detailing the sectoral developments that are affected by the revenue lost will ensure that the public minimises their role in IFFs in the instance that they are involved, and also, it will ensure that suspected cases of IFFs are reported to the relevant authorities.[107]

NOTES

1. Africa Union Commission, 'Agenda 2063: Popular Version', 2015, 18, https://au.int/sites/default/files/documents/36204-doc-agenda2063_popular_version_en.pdf (accessed April 15, 2022).

2. Addis Ababa Action Agenda of the Third International Conference on Financing on Development, 2015; paras 23, 25, https://sustainabledevelopment.un.org/content/documents/2051AAAA_Outcome.pdf (accessed April 15, 2022).

3. Transforming Our World: The 2030 Agenda for Sustainable Development, A/RES/70/1, 2015, Target 16.4, https://sustainabledevelopment.un.org/content/documents/21252030%20Agenda%20for%20Sustainable%20Development%20web.pdf (accessed April 20, 2022).

4. UNCTAD, *Tackling Illicit Financial Flows.*

5. *Ibid.*

6. *Ibid.*

7. *Ibid.*, 17.

8. *Ibid.*, 13.

9. Africa Union, "Briefing for the Ministers on Illicit Financial Flows," 2020, 2 https://au.int/sites/default/files/newsevents/workingdocuments/39572-wdbriefing_paper_on_stemming_iffs_for_1st_extraordinary_stc.pdf (accessed April 16, 2022).

10. Landry Signé, Mariama Sow, and Payce Madden, "Illicit Financial Flows in Africa- Drivers, Destinations, and Policy Options," *Africa Policy Initiative Policy Brief* (2020): 4, https://www.brookings.edu/wp-content/uploads/2020/02/Illicit-financial-flows-in-Africa.pdf (accessed April 18, 2022).

11. UNCTAD, *Tackling Illicit Financial Flows*, 87.

12. *Ibid.*

13. Janvier Nkurunziza, "Illicit Financial Flows: A Constraint on Poverty Reduction in Africa," (2012): 15–19, https://citeseerx.ist.psu.edu/viewdoc/download?doi=10.1.1.361.667&rep=rep1&type=pdf (accessed April 19, 2022).

14. World Bank, *The World Bank Group's Response to Illicit Financial Flows: A Stocktaking*, 2016, 1, https://documents1.worldbank.org/curated/en/502341468179035132/pdf/104568-BR-SecM2016-0112-IDASecM2016-0071-IFC-SecM2016-00423-MIGA-SecM2016-0044-Box394878B-PUBLIC-disclosed-4-5-16.pdf (accessed April 24, 2022).

15. Signe, *Illicit Financial Flows in Africa.*

16. UN General Assembly, *Resolution on Promotion of International Cooperation to Combat Illicit Financial Flows and Strengthen Good Practices on Assets Return to Foster Sustainable Development*, A/RES/74/206, 2019.

17. World Bank, *The World Bank Group's Response to Illicit Financial Flows*, 2.

18. UN Sustainable Development Goals, *SDG Indicators, Metadata Repository*, https://unstats.un.org/sdgs/metadata/?Text=&Goal=&Target=16.4 (accessed April 21, 2022).

19. *Ibid.*

20. Signe, *Illicit Financial Flows in Africa*, 5.

21. UNCTAD, *Tackling Illicit Financial Flows*, 5.

22. UN, Office of the High Commissioner for Human Rights, *The Right to development and Taxation*, https://www.ohchr.org/sites/default/files/Documents/Issues/RtD/InfoNote_Taxation.pdf (accessed April 21, 2022).

23. *Ibid.*

24. *Ibid.*

25. Illicit Financial Flows, "Report of the High-Level Panel on Illicit Financial Flows from Africa," 2015:10, https://www.unodc.org/documents/NGO/AU_ECA_Illicit_Financial_Flows_report_EN.pdf (accessed April 21, 2022).

26. *Ibid.*

27. UNCTAD, *Tackling Illicit Financial Flows*, 21–22.

28. *Ibid.*, 21.

29. Gabriel Zucman, "Taxing across Borders: Tracking Personal Wealth and Corporate Profits," *Journal of Economic Perspectives* 28 (2014): 121, https://gabriel-zucman.eu/files/Zucman2014JEP.pdf (accessed April 20, 2022).

30. OECD, *Statement on a Two-Pillar Solution to Address the Tax Challenges arising from the Digitalisation of the Economy*, 2021, https://www.oecd.org/tax/beps/statement-on-a-two-pillar-solution-to-address-the-tax-challenges-arising-from-the-digitalisation-of-the-economy-october-2021.pdf (accessed April 19, 2022).

31. Illicit Financial Flows, "Report of the High-Level Panel," 10.

32. UNCTAD, *Tackling Illicit Financial Flows*, 5.

33. *Ibid.*, 124.

34. *Ibid.*, 168.

35. *Ibid.*

36. *Ibid.*

37. Conseil de l'Union européenne, https://www.consilium.europa.eu/media/54471/council-conclusions-24-february-2022.pdf (accessed April 20, 2022).

38. Gizela Lénártová, "The Economic and Social Consequences of Tax Havens in the World," 5 https://www.shs-conferences.org/articles/shsconf/pdf/2020/11/shsconf_appsconf2020_01041.pdf (accessed April 21, 2022).

39. *Ibid.*, 6.

40. OECD, *International Collaboration to End Tax Avoidance*, https://www.oecd.org/tax/beps/ (accessed April 20, 2022).

41. World Health Organization, "Global Spending on Health: Rising to the Pandemics Challenges," Global Report (2022) 11, https://apps.who.int/iris/bitstream/handle/10665/365133/9789240064911-eng.pdf (accessed April 27, 2023).

42. World Health Organization, "Global Spending on Health: Rising to the Pandemics Challenges," Global Report (2021) 2, https://apps.who.int/iris/bitstream/handle/10665/350560/9789240041219-eng.pdf?sequence=1&isAllowed=y (accessed April 27, 2023).

43. UNESCO and World Bank, Education Finance Watch, (2022), 7–8, https://thedocs.worldbank.org/en/doc/e52f55322528903b27f1b7e61238e416-0200022022/related/EFW-2022-Jul1.pdf (accessed April 26, 2023).

44. United Nations Declaration on the Right to Development, 1986, art 1.

45. *Ibid.,* art 2(3).

46. Serges Kamga, "Illicit Financial Flows, Asset Recovery, the Power Game and the Right to Development in Africa," *Comparative and International Law Journal of Southern Africa* 52 (2019): 209.

47. *Ibid.,* 208–209.

48. World Bank and the OECD, *Few and Far, The Hard Facts on Stolen Asset Recovery: Stolen Asset Recovery Series* (2014), 5.

49. *Ibid.*

50. Gerard Kamga, "Linkages between Illicit Financial Flows and the Non-Realization of the Right to Development in Africa," *Comparative and International Law Journal of Southern Africa* 52 (2019): 172.

51. IMF Annual Report, "Crisis Upon Crisis" (2022) 19, https://www.imf.org/external/pubs/ft/ar/2022/downloads/imf-annual-report-2022-english.pdf (accessed April 26, 2023).

52. Kamga, "Linkages between Illicit Financial Flows and the Non-Realization of the Right to Development in Africa," 173–74.

53. Initiative for Social and Economic Rights, *Curb Illicit Financial Flows to Fund Quality Public Social Services in Uganda: 2022 Report*, 3, https://iser-uganda.org/publication/curb-illicit-financial-flows-to-fund-quality-public-social-services-in-uganda/ (accessed April 22, 2022).

54. *Ibid.*, 4.

55. UNCTAD, *Tackling Illicit Financial Flows*, 113.

56. Signe, *Illicit Financial Flows in Africa*, 9.

57. *Ibid.*, 2.

58. Global Forum on Transparency and Exchange of Information for Tax Purposes, *Transparency and Exchange of Information for Tax Purposes, Multilateral Cooperation Changing the World: 10th Anniversary Report: 3*, https://www.oecd.org/tax/transparency/global-forum-10-years-report.pdf (accessed April 19, 2022).

59. African Tax Administration Forum, https://www.ataftax.org/Exchange-of-information (accessed April 22, 2022).

60. Global Forum on Transparency and Exchange of Information for Tax Purposes, https://www.un.org/esa/ffd/wp-content/uploads/sites/3/2017/05/Global-Forum_-info-sheet-2017.pdf (accessed April 22, 2022).

61. Global Forum on Transparency and Exchange of Information for Tax Purposes, *Global Forum Members*, https://www.oecd.org/tax/transparency/who-we-are/members/ (accessed April 27, 2023).

62. Signe, *Illicit Financial Flows in Africa*, 13.

63. Global Forum on Transparency and Exchange of Information for Tax Purposes, *Information Sheet*, https://www.un.org/esa/ffd/wp-content/uploads/sites/3/2017/05/Global-Forum_-info-sheet-2017.pdf (accessed April 22, 2022).

64. *Ibid.*

65. OECD and Global Forum on Transparency and Exchange of Information for Tax Purposes, *Tax Transparency in Africa 2022: Africa Initiative Progress Report,* 18, https://www.oecd.org/tax/transparency/documents/tax-transparency-in-africa-2022.pdf (accessed April 25, 2023).

66. Global Forum, *Information Sheet.*

67. Global Forum on Transparency and Exchange of Information for Tax Purposes, *Toolkit for the Implementation of the Standard for Automatic Exchange of Financial Account Information*, 14–16, https://www.oecd.org/tax/transparency/documents/aeoi-implementation-toolkit_en.pdf (accessed April 17, 2022).

68. OECD, *Putting an End to Offshore Tax Evasion.*

69. OECD, Global Forum, *Exchange of Information on Request: Handbook for Peer Reviews 2016–2020, 2016 Terms of Reference*, https://www.oecd.org/tax/transparency/documents/terms-of-reference.pdf (accessed April 19, 2022).

70. *Ibid.*

71. OECD and Africa Initiative, https://www.oecd.org/tax/transparency/what-we-do/technical-assistance/africa-initiative.htm (accessed April 19, 2022).

72. *Ibid.*

73. *Ibid.*

74. OECD, *Africa Initiative*, https://www.oecd.org/tax/transparency/what-we-do/technical-assistance/africainitiative.htm#:~:text=The%20Africa%20Initiative%20is%20currently,currently%20counts%2036%20member%20jurisdictions (accessed April 26, 2023).

75. OECD and Global Forum, *Tax Transparency in Africa 2022*, 15.

76. OECD and Global Forum on Transparency and Exchange of Information for Tax Purposes, *Tax Transparency in Africa 2021: Africa Initiative Progress Report*, 48, https://www.oecd.org/tax/transparency/documents/tax-transparency-in-africa-2021.htm (accessed April 19, 2022).

77. OECD and Global Forum, *Tax Transparency in Africa 2022*, 15.

78. Yaounde Declaration, 2017, https://www.oecd.org/tax/transparency/what-we-do/technical-assistance/Yaounde-Declaration-with-Signatories.pdf (accessed April 19, 2022).

79. *Ibid.*

80. *Ibid.*, 4–5.

81. *Ibid.*

82. OECD and Global Forum, *Tax Transparency in Africa 2022*, 15.

83. OECD and Global Forum, *Tax Transparency in Africa 2021*, 54–65.

84. Multilateral Convention on Mutual Administrative Assistance in Tax Matters, (1988): para 7, https://www.oecd.org/tax/exchange-of-tax-information/convention-on-mutual-administrative-assistance-in-tax-matters.htm (accessed April 19, 2022).

85. OECD, https://www.oecd.org/ctp/exchange-of-tax-information/theconventiononmutualadministrativeassistanceintaxmatters-background.htm (accessed April 21, 2022).

86. Multilateral Convention 1988, art 4.

87. *Ibid.*, art 6.

88. Global Forum, *Toolkit for the Implementation of the Standard for Automatic Exchange of Financial Account Information*, 53.

89. OECD, Jurisdictions Participating in the Convention on Mutual Administratiev Assistance in Tax Matters, 2023, https://www.oecd.org/tax/exchange-of-tax-information/Status_of_convention.pdf (accessed April 24, 2023).

90. OECD, *Developing Countries and the OECD/G20 Inclusive Framework on BEPS*, October 2021, https://www.oecd.org/tax/beps/developing-countries-and-the-oecd-g20-inclusive-framework-on-beps.pdf (accessed April 21, 2022).

91. OECD, *Members of the OECD/G20 Inclusive Framework on BEPS*, December 2022, https://www.oecd.org/tax/beps/inclusive-framework-on-beps-composition.pdf (accessed April 26, 2023).

92. OECD, *Developing Countries and the OECD/G20 Inclusive Framework on BEPS*.

93. OECD, *Inclusive Framework on Base Erosion and Profit Shifting*, https://www.oecd.org/tax/beps/about/ (accessed April 21, 2022).

94. OECD, *Developing Countries and the OECD/G20 Inclusive Framework on BEPS*.

95. *Ibid.*

96. *Ibid.*

97. Karen Brown, 'Tax Initiatives and Sub-Saharan Africa', *Pepperdine Law Review* 48 (2021): 1013–18.

98. *Ibid.*, 1018.

99. UN, https://www.un.org/press/en/2021/sga2051.doc.htm (accessed April 20, 2022).

100. UN Committee of Experts on International Cooperation in Tax Matters, *Report on the Twenty-Third Session*, 2021:11–12, https://www.un.org/development/desa/financing/sites/www.un.org.development.desa.financing/files/2022-02/N2140002E.pdf (accessed April 22, 2022).

101. *Ibid.*

102. UNCTAD, *Tackling Illicit Financial Flows*, 112.

103. *Ibid.*

104. OECD, *Tax Transparency in Africa 2021,* 46.

105. *Ibid.,* 38.

106. United Nations Declaration on the Right to Development, 1986.

107. Advocacy Manual for Lawyers' Associations in the Global South, *A Toolkit on Illicit Financial Flows: Module III* (2020) 24, https://www.cbgaindia.org/wp-content/uploads/2020/03/Module-3_Advocacy-Manual-for-Lawyers-Associations-in-the-Global-South.pdf (accessed April 24, 2023).

BIBLIOGRAPHY

Advocacy Manual for Lawyers' Associations in the Global South. *A Toolkit on Illicit Financial Flows: Module III*, 2020. https://www.cbgaindia.org/wp-content/uploads/2020/03/Module-3_Advocacy-Manual-for-Lawyers-Associations-in-the-Global-South.pdf (accessed April 24, 2023)

Africa Union. "Briefing for the Ministers on Illicit Financial Flows," 2020. https://au.int/sites/default/files/newsevents/workingdocuments/39572-wdbriefing_paper_on_stemming_iffs_for_1st_extraordinary_stc.pdf (accessed April 16, 2022)

Africa Union Commission. "Agenda 2063: Popular Version," 2015. https://au.int/sites/default/files/documents/36204-doc-agenda2063_popular_version_en.pdf (accessed April 15, 2022)

African Tax Administration Forum. https://www.ataftax.org/Exchange-of-information (accessed April 22, 2022)

Conseil de l'Union européenne. https://www.consilium.europa.eu/media/54471/council-conclusions-24-february-2022.pdf (accessed April 20, 2022)

Council of Europe. "Chart of Signatures and ratifications of Treaty 127," https://www.coe.int/en/web/conventions/full-list?module=signatures-by-treaty&treatynum=127 (accessed April 21, 2022)

Global Forum on Transparency and Exchange of Information for Tax Purposes. https://www.un.org/esa/ffd/wp-content/uploads/sites/3/2017/05/Global-Forum_-info-sheet-2017.pdf (accessed April 22, 2022)

Global Forum on Transparency and Exchange of Information for Tax Purposes. "Putting an End to Offshore Tax Evasion," https://www.oecd.org/tax/transparency/ (accessed April 22, 2022)

Global Forum on Transparency and Exchange of Information for Tax Purposes. "Toolkit for the Implementation of the Standard for Automatic Exchange of Financial Account Information," https://www.oecd.org/tax/transparency/documents/aeoi-implementation-toolkit_en.pdf (accessed April 17, 2022)

Global Forum on Transparency and Exchange of Information for Tax Purposes. "Transparency and Exchange of Information for Tax Purposes, Multilateral Cooperation Changing the World: 10th Anniversary Report," https://www.oecd.org/tax/transparency/global-forum-10-years-report.pdf (accessed April 19, 2022)

Illicit Financial Flows. "Report of the High-Level Panel on Illicit Financial Flows from Africa," 2015. https://www.unodc.org/documents/NGO/AU_ECA_Illicit_Financial_Flows_report_EN.pdf (accessed April 21, 2022)

IMF Annual Report. "Crisis Upon Crisis," 2022. https://www.imf.org/external/pubs/ft/ar/2022/downloads/imf-annual-report-2022-english.pdf (accessed April 26, 2023)

Initiative for Social and Economic Rights. "Curb Illicit Financial Flows to Fund Quality Public Social Services in Uganda: 2022 Report," https://iser-uganda.org/publication/curb-illicit-financial-flows-to-fund-quality-public-social-services-in-uganda/ (accessed April 22, 2022)

Karen Brown. "Tax Initiatives and Sub-Saharan Africa," *Pepperdine Law Review* 48, 2021: 995–1022.

Kamga Gerard. "Linkages between Illicit Financial Flows and the Non-Realization of the Right to Development in Africa," *Comparative and International Law Journal of Southern Africa* 52, 2019: 169–92.

Kamga Serges. "Illicit Financial Flows, Asset Recovery, the Power Game and the Right to Development in Africa," *Comparative and International Law Journal of Southern Africa* 52, 2019: 193–214.

Lénártová Gizela. "The Economic and Social Consequences of Tax Havens in the World," https://www.shs-conferences.org/articles/shsconf/pdf/2020/11/shsconf_appsconf2020_01041.pdf (accessed April 21, 2022)

Nkurunziza Janvier. "Illicit Financial Flows: A Constraint on Poverty Reduction in Africa," 2012. https://citeseerx.ist.psu.edu/viewdoc/download?doi=10.1.1.361.667&rep=rep1&type=pdf (accessed April 19, 2022)

OECD. *Africa Initiative*. https://www.oecd.org/tax/transparency/what-we-do/technical-assistance/africainitiative.htm#:~:text=The%20Africa%20Initiative%20is%20currently,currently%20counts%2036%20member%20jurisdictions (accessed April 26, 2023)

OECD. *Automatic Exchange Portal*. https://www.oecd.org/tax/automatic-exchange/ (accessed April 20, 2022)

OECD. *Developing Countries and the OECD/G20 Inclusive Framework on BEPS*, October 2021. https://www.oecd.org/tax/beps/developing-countries-and-the-oecd-g20-inclusive-framework-on-beps.pdf (accessed April 21, 2022)

OECD. *Jurisdictions Participating in the Convention on Mutual Administrative Assistance in Tax Matters*, 2023. https://www.oecd.org/tax/exchange-of-tax-information/Status_of_convention.pdf (accessed April 24, 2023)

OECD. https://www.oecd.org/ctp/exchange-of-tax-information/theconventiononmutualadministrativeassistanceintaxmatters-background.htm (accessed April 21, 2022)

OECD. https://www.oecd.org/tax/transparency/ (accessed April 19, 2022)

OECD. *Inclusive Framework on Base Erosion and Profit Shifting*. https://www.oecd.org/tax/beps/about/ (accessed April 21, 2022)

OECD. *International Collaboration to End Tax Avoidance*. https://www.oecd.org/tax/beps/ (accessed April 20, 2022)

OECD. *Members of the OECD/G20 Inclusive Framework on BEPS*, December 2022. https://www.oecd.org/tax/beps/inclusive-framework-on-beps-composition.pdf (accessed April 26, 2023)

OECD. *Peer Review of the Automatic Exchange of Financial Account Information*, 2020. https://www.oecd-ilibrary.org/sites/175eeff4-en/index.html?itemId=/content/publication/175eeff4-en (accessed April 19, 2022)

OECD. *Statement on a Two-Pillar Solution to Address the Tax Challenges Arising from the Digitalisation of the Economy*, 2021. https://www.oecd.org/tax/beps/statement-on-a-two-pillar-solution-to-address-the-tax-challenges-arising-from-the-digitalisation-of-the-economy-october-2021.pdf (accessed April 19, 2022)

OECD and Africa Initiative. https://www.oecd.org/tax/transparency/what-we-do/technical-assistance/africa-initiative.htm (accessed April 19, 2022)

OECD and Global Forum. *Exchange of Information on Request: Handbook for Peer Reviews 2016–2020*, 2016 Terms of Reference. https://www.oecd.org/tax/transparency/documents/terms-of-reference.pdf (accessed April 19, 2022)

OECD and Global Forum on Transparency and Exchange of Information for Tax Purposes. *Tax Transparency in Africa 2021: Africa Initiative Progress Report*. https://www.oecd.org/tax/transparency/documents/tax-transparency-in-africa-2021.htm (accessed April 19, 2022)

OECD and Global Forum on Transparency and Exchange of Information for Tax Purposes. *Tax Transparency in Africa 2022: Africa Initiative Progress Report*. https://

www.oecd.org/tax/transparency/documents/tax-transparency-in-africa-2022.pdf (accessed April 25, 2023)

Signé Landry, Sow Mariama, and Madden Payce. "Illicit Financial Flows in Africa-Drivers, Destinations, and Policy Options," *Africa Policy Initiative Policy Brief*, 2020. https://www.brookings.edu/wp-content/uploads/2020/02/Illicit-financial-flows-in-Africa.pdf (accessed April 18, 2022)

UN. https://www.un.org/press/en/2021/sga2051.doc.htm (accessed April 20, 2022)

UN Committee of Experts on International Cooperation in Tax Matters. *Report on the Twenty-Third Session*, 2021. https://www.un.org/development/desa/financing/sites/www.un.org.development.desa.financing/files/2022-02/N2140002E.pdf (accessed April 22, 2022)

UNCTAD. *Economic Development in Africa Report: Tackling Illicit Financial Flows for Sustainable Development in Africa*, 2020. https://unctad.org/system/files/official-document/aldcafrica2020_en.pdf (accessed April 15, 2022)

UNESCO and World Bank. *Education Finance Watch*, 2022. https://thedocs.worldbank.org/en/doc/e52f55322528903b27f1b7e61238e416-0200022022/related/EFW-2022-Jul1.pdf (accessed April 26, 2023)

UN Office of the High Commissioner for Human Rights. *The Right to Development and Taxation*. https://www.ohchr.org/sites/default/files/Documents/Issues/RtD/InfoNote_Taxation.pdf (accessed April 21, 2022)

UN Sustainable Development Goals. *SDG Indicators, Metadata Repository*. https://unstats.un.org/sdgs/metadata/?Text=&Goal=&Target=16.4 (accessed April 21, 2022)

World Bank. *The World Bank Group's Response to Illicit Financial Flows: A Stocktaking*, 2016. https://documents1.worldbank.org/curated/en/502341468179035132/pdf/104568-BR-SecM2016-0112-IDASecM2016-0071-IFC-SecM2016-00423-MIGA-SecM2016-0044-Box394878B-PUBLIC-disclosed-4-5-16.pdf (accessed April 24, 2022)

World Bank and the OECD. *Few and Far, The Hard Facts on Stolen Asset Recovery: Stolen Asset Recovery Series*, 2014. Publishing and Knowledge Division, World Bank

World Health Organization. *Global Spending on Health: Rising to the Pandemics Challenges*, Global Report 2021. https://apps.who.int/iris/bitstream/handle/10665/350560/9789240041219-eng.pdf?sequence=1&isAllowed=y (accessed April 27, 2023)

World Health Organization. *Global Spending on Health: Rising to the Pandemics Challenges*, Global Report 2022. https://apps.who.int/iris/bitstream/handle/10665/365133/9789240064911-eng.pdf (accessed April 27, 2023)

Zucman Gabriel. "Taxing across Borders: Tracking Personal Wealth and Corporate Profits," *Journal of Economic Perspectives* 28, 2014. https://gabriel-zucman.eu/files/Zucman2014JEP.pdf (accessed April 20, 2022)

Chapter 5

State Complicity in Impairing Its Development Rights

Salient Lessons from the Nigerian Halliburton Bribery Scandal

Marie-Louise F. Aren

INTRODUCTION

The latter half of the twentieth century marked a turning point in the crusade against colonialism in many African states.[1] Coinciding with the de-colonisation movement was a stronger global recognition and (enforcement) of human rights values such as fundamental freedoms, liberalisation, and development, among others. Together, these contributed to laying the groundwork for the subsequent economic liberalisation policies that became the forerunner of globalisation.[2] As global prosperity grew, development-related challenges like poverty and inequality began to emerge.[3] This is because globalisation, 'the integration of poor countries into a world economy of open competition', created and still creates a situation where states at different stages of advancement interact using the same rulebook that is more favourable to advanced states, thereby amplifying global injustices.[4] The continuous exploitation of Africa's wealth at the expense of African development for the benefit of others in the guise of globalisation ignited discourse on Africa's right to its development.[5]

As a recent human rights concept, the nature and significance of the Right to Development remain strongly contested by the global north and global south, creating political polarisation and difficulty in reaching a comprehensive governmental consensus on its meaning and practical import.[6] Regardless of the global debate on the nature of the Right to Development, certain core elements of the Right to Development can be gleaned from the various international human rights instruments, like the International Covenant on

Economic, Social and Cultural Rights and the 17-point United Nations Sustainable Development Goals (SDGs).[7]

Development from these instruments starts with human beings and the Right to Development essentially revolves around human development. To this end, an effective development process incorporates human right principle and values to be impactful, promotes social and economic fairness, and ensures the participation of development subjects. Another element of the Right to Development is its shared responsibility element where the actualisation of the development is concurrently shared among development actors, however, states have the primary responsibility for realising the Right to Development.[8] The responsibility of states as the primary duty bearers is discussed in the subsequent sections.

DEVELOPMENT: A HUMAN RIGHTS APPROACH

The United Nations Declaration of the Right to Development culminates from the recognition of the interrelationship between human rights and development.[9] The Right to Development as a human right became firmly established through global trends, especially in the fall of communist European governments in the 1980s.[10] Consequently, the view that respect for human rights, the rule of law, and responsible political institutions are critical components of all development and fair distribution of resources, led to the birth of the human rights approach to the Right to Development.[11] The Right to Development was first documented as a collective and individual human right in the African Charter on Human and Peoples' Rights as a definitive individual and collective right.[12] It became fully documented as a universal human right by the 1986 UN Declaration on the Right to Development (UNRTD) as a collective right of people and a distinct individual right.[13] Article 1 of the UNRTD defines it as:

> *The right to development is an inalienable human right under which every human person and all peoples are entitled to participate in, contribute to, and enjoy economic, social, cultural and political development, in which all human rights and fundamental freedoms can be fully realized.* (emphasis in original)

The UN's adoption of the Right to Development stems from the premise of development as a comprehensive economic, social, cultural, and political process, dependent on the active and meaningful participation of persons in the development process and the fair distribution of benefits.[14] Other international human and other agreements have emerged from the recognition of the Right to Development such as the 1993 Vienna Declaration and Programme of Action, and the Declaration on the Rights of Indigenous Peoples, among others. The Right to Development as a human right appears to gradually shed the concept of development rooted in Western notions of aid and paternalistic welfare colonialism. Though welfare aid has been used in providing some development infrastructure like roads and schools, the inequality gap between rich and poor continues to widen. Hence, development from a human right perspective is useful, as it places stronger responsibility on the state for creating the enabling environment for development to occur. It also places collective and individual responsibility on citizens as beneficiaries of development to work towards achieving development goals. The reality in many African states tells a different story.[15]

The implementation of development from a human rights perspective began with the Millennium Development Goals (MDGs), a set of SMART goals and targets for combating development challenges of inequality and rising poverty.[16] The obligatory implementation of the Right to Development is conditioned into the UN's human rights observing system as part of its mission. The effectiveness of a human rights-based approach to development requires that laws, policies, and institutions at the global and national levels facilitate the responsibilities present in the international human rights conventions.[17] According to Hamm, the human rights approach to development also stems from the recognition of the legal responsibility of the international community of nations as members of human rights treaties to facilitate cooperation in development efforts.[18] Development is approached as obligatory rather than complementary—as a goodwill gesture from states. The calibration of development from a human rights perspective also provides a principle-based framework for implementing the Right to Development at different levels.

Development as a human right on the one hand has produced significant contributions ranging from global acknowledgement to delivering civil and political liberties. It has translated development from an ideological and intellectual concept into a 'reality of making development' happen. On the other hand, it has not fully addressed the issue of rising inequality and social justice present in the world. Modern global inequality level is almost at their twentieth-century level at the height of Western colonialism.[19] Within Africa, the average income inequality of the top 10 per cent is almost thirty times higher than the income of the bottom 50 per cent, which is above the values of other severe inequality regions like the Middle East.[20]

Several reasons may account for the massive inequality present in Africa, but from a legal perspective, it may be attributable to placing the responsibility for implementing development squarely on states, without similar responsibilities placed on other development-influencing actors.[21] Understandably, the decision to place responsibility on states for implementing the Right to Development flows from the social contract as a conferral of public trust and legitimacy, however, globalisation has changed that established dynamics due to the emergence of new and influential players.[22] There is no similar responsibility placed on global influencers and non-state actors such as third-party states, multinational corporations (MNCs), and mega-financial institutions specifically. The explosion and influence of non-state actors in national and international affairs have led some scholars like Robert Keohane and Joseph Nye and Martin Carnoy to argue the declining relevance of states relative to the influence wielded by non-state actors.[23]

The UN Guiding Principles while providing soft law rights-based guidance for states and MNCs in their business activities under the Protect, Respect and Remedy Framework, the fact remains that it is not a binding legal framework.[24] It cannot be enforced against most dominant non-state actors for their role in undermining the Right to Development through sustaining extreme inequality, poverty, and illicit financial flows. Another dimension to enforcing development from a human rights angle is the challenge of navigating the delicate balance between the state's responsibility for central planning and administering the economy while providing access to the private sector or markets. If development rights are both people and individual-centred, which determines how state resources and the economy will serve the public good, then it may create a conflict for the private sector as stakeholders in the development process through their innovation and financial access.

The components and path of the development from a human rights perspective remain unclear.[25] It appears as a blend of all human rights, which affects its independence and justiciability. There also appears to be an absence of agreed and clear key performance indicators to measure and evaluate the performance of enforcing development as a human right. Tsikata, however, argues that accountability, participation, and people-centredness should be the normative guidance for the development and measuring the Right to Development should be based on its transformation value to development practice.[26] The global north mostly doubts its value of strengthening development from a human rights approach.

Despite these looming issues, the fact remains that development as a human right is critical for delivering SDGs and states have a huge responsibility to play in fostering development given their institutional legitimacy and roles as a custodian of human rights. States are also primarily responsible for ensuring good governance and accountability as indispensable pieces to the realisation of human rights in general and in the successful provision of public goods. The placement of development policy with human rights values remains one of the most effective mechanisms for actualising development at a national and regional level.

STATES AS PRIMARY DUTY BEARERS OF THE RIGHT TO DEVELOPMENT

The United Nations and regional bodies like the African Union Commission play an important role in facilitating global discourse on the Right to Development. Like other rights, many international law instruments and institutions recognise that the first duty bearer of the Right to Development is the state. The role of the State in implementing the RTD was seen in the *Centre for Minority Rights Development (Kenya) and Minority Rights Group International on behalf of Endorois Welfare Council v Kenya (Endorois case)*, where the African Union Commission decided that the unlawful eviction of the Endorois people from the Lake Bogoria area in central Kenya interfered with their right to participate in their development by the Kenyan Government.[27] The Vienna Declaration and Programme of Action reaffirm the Right to Development while enjoining states to corporate with each other for the actualisation of the Right to Development.[28]

Article 3(1) of the DTRD provides that states have the primary responsibility for the creation of national and international conditions favourable to the realisation of the Right to Development. Article 3(3) confers to all states the duty to cooperate in ensuring development and eliminating obstacles to development. Article 4(1) makes it the duty of states to take steps individually and collectively to formulate international development policies to facilitate the full realisation of the Right to Development. Article 6(1) of the Declaration instructs states to cooperate in promoting, encouraging, and strengthening universal respect for human rights and fundamental freedoms for all. Article 10 provides that states acting nationally and internationally are enjoined to take steps to ensure the full exercise and progressive enhancement of the right through the formulation, adoption, and implementation of policy, legislative, and other measures.

The placement of the primary responsibility on states is a step in the right direction. It promotes a shift from the paternalism of imperialist systems to the responsible participation of governments in their development. Likewise, consistency with other international human rights conventions, where states are primary duty bearers, is maintained. There are, however, inherent challenges in making states alone primary duty bearers of the Right to Development. Owing to the soft law nature of the DRTD, there is a lack of compelling sanctions for non-compliance by states in failing to enforce the Right to Development for its people's benefit, which could create accountability challenges.[29]

As a result, a few African states have taken concrete steps to incorporate the rights and obligations of development into their Constitution and domestic legislations as enforceable rights by citizens and other citizen representative organisations.[30] For example, in Nigeria, the Constitution recognises development as a fundamental objective and directive principle of State policy, not an autonomous human right like the fundamental rights in Chapter III of the same Constitution.[31] Consequently, it is unenforceable as a human or people's right. The failure to incorporate the Right to Development as an enforceable right in national laws affects the enforceability of these rights when infringed, particularly in dualist states. The Right to Development when translated into legal rights at the national level invokes a sense of obligation on the state to implement. It also ensures the right-holders can legally demand that the state be accountable for carrying out their development responsibilities. Incorporating the Right to Development into the legislative system ensures that the national law and policies work as tools to monitor, adjudicate their performance, and proscribe remedies for breaches.[32]

The State's primary responsibility for implementing the Right to Development is undermined by the absence of an implementation blueprint and process in the DRTD and the UN systems. Instead, states decide on how best to implement these rights, meaning different states will have different development concepts and goals. The Declaration is silent on guidelines or steps in utilising state resources in the fulfilment of development rights. In fairness to the UN, this could be out of respect for states' sovereignty. Also, the Right to Development would depend on having strong governance and institutional structures in place to implement the right, which is absent in many African countries. Appropriate mechanisms are vital for accountability in enforcing development rights. In Africa, the African Court might play that role for states and people in addressing development rights violations, since the African Charter protects the Right to Development. However, the success and effectiveness of the accountability system of the African Court would be dependent on the willingness of states to fully trust and submit to the jurisdiction of the court.

The DRTD only holds the international community of states as a complementary duty bearer to the RTD through the duty to cooperate. Even though the international community might not make direct pro-development policies in respective states, they do have the economic and political leverage to foster or mar the development trajectory of states, especially the MNCs and their home states. Therefore, the identification and articulation of the obligations of external development actors in concrete terms would prove relevant in assisting states implement their development rights obligation with little *development-sabotaging* activities from external actors. For example, instances where the protection of foreign investments impinge on states' pro-development policy-making space. Stronger obligations placed on dominant members of the international community of states would guarantee a recognised responsibility on the international community of states in 'contributing to the immediate realisation of the minimum essential level of socio-economic rights globally'.[33] Salomon gives three compelling reasons why stronger cooperative responsibilities should be placed on the international community of states.[34]

First, the activities of powerful actors external to the developing state may sometimes encourage underdevelopment. Second, the pervasive influence of international economic organisations like the World Trade Organisation who push neoliberal capitalist agenda disguised as development. Third, erosion of the State's domestic autonomy limits the ability of states—particularly poor and less influential states—to independently decide their own economic and social policies, which impacts its ability to implement the Right to Development.[35] So far, the provisions in RTD for other states to cooperate with a State in actualising its goal for development are insufficient and overlook the influence of external states and actors on the Right to Development. Regardless, African states work within the regulatory and implementation space available in implementing development. The next section examines the vitiating impact of IFFs on states' enforcement responsibilities and/or obligation.

AFRICAN IFFS AND IMPACT ON STATE RESPONSIBILITY TO ENFORCE THE RIGHT TO DEVELOPMENT

According to the GFI, Africa has documented losses of about US$1.4 trillion from the period of 1970–2015.[36] The GFI figures based on comprehensive data available for trade-related IFFs show a total value of US$1.6 trillion of the value gaps identified in trade between 134 developing countries and their trading partners in 2018.[37] Two African countries of the Gambia and Malawi have the largest value gaps identified in US Dollars in the bilateral trade at 45 per cent and 37 per cent respectively.[38] Likewise, estimates from the United Nations Economic Commission for Africa (UNECA) illustrate that during the period 2000–2015, net IFFs from Africa to the rest of the world averaged USD$73 billion (at 2016 prices) per year from trade misinvoicing alone.[39] In other words, there was more financial flow out of Africa than financial flow into Africa. IFFs out of Africa represent an opportunity cost of forgone socio-economic investment income which could foster economic growth and tackle prolonged poverty in the continent.

Although IFFs occur through different methods like criminal financing, commercial-type IFFs are the most used channel of IFFs, followed by organised crime and public sector corrupt activities.[40]

The cumulative IFFs magnitude based on countries in Africa is led by Nigeria, followed by Egypt and South Africa.[41] The extractive industry, specifically the petroleum and minerals industry takes the lion's share of IFFs through tax abuses, regulatory abuses, and corrupt practices.[42] The size of these figures reveals IFFs as one of the main factors responsible for the reduced capacity of African states to enforce the Right to Development, especially across social and economic lines.

In acknowledgement of the impact of IFFs on Africa's development out of the continent, some regional and national initiatives have emerged over the years. In 2015, a High-Level Working Group on Illicit Financial Flows from Africa was established to raise awareness among African governments and propose policies to combat IFFs.[43] The good reception of the findings of the high-level panel eventually precipitated the launching of The African Union's initiative on winning the Fight against Corruption: A Sustainable Path for Africa's Transformation 2018.[44] A multi-door partnership/project was created in 2020 to tackle IFF in Africa.[45] The multi-door project was surrounded by broader international initiatives, culminating in the resolution on the Impact of IFFs on Development Finance and the African Union (AU) Special Declaration on IFFs.[46] The AU has also entered into strategic partnerships for effective collaboration in addressing the difficulties and breaches in the battle against illicit outflows. Some strategic partnerships include the African Tax Administration Forum (ATAF) partnership, the Global Forum partnership, and others.

At the sub-regional level within the Regional Economic Communities (REC), some institutions combat money laundering aspects of IFFs. In Economic Community for West African States (ECOWAS), the Intergovernmental Action Group against Money Laundering in West Africa exists, the East and Southern Africa regions have the joint Eastern and Southern Africa Anti-Money Laundering Group, the North Africa Region has the Financial Action Task Force; and Central Africa region has the Central African Action Group against Money Laundering.[47] At the national level, several African countries have taken steps to establish anti-corruption legislation, reform present laws, and create anti-IFFs mechanisms. Several African countries have associate membership or observer status in international groups like the Inter-Governmental Action Group against money laundering in the Financial Action Task Force, the Financial Crimes Enforcement Network, and the Egmont Group of Financial Intelligence Units.[48] While these institutional and regulatory strides are vital to combating IFFs, there are still dissatisfactory results in curbing illicit outflows out of Africa, which is traceable to policy and institutional incoherence from being on diverse IFFs forums.

As African IFFs continue, inadequate enforcement capacity in the face of IFFs mechanism sophistication, and lack of accountability from the public, among others impede enforcement. Funding and resource shortages force regional and national enforcement agencies to be at the mercy of stringent foreign assistance conditions. Despite these drawbacks, the role of political will in addressing corruption as an important component in the fight against IFF is critical.[49]

FACTUAL OVERVIEW OF THE HALLIBURTON SCANDAL AND NIGERIAN GOVERNMENT'S COMPLICITY IN UNDERMINING ITS RTD

Developing states sometimes undermine their development rights through corruption, IFFs, and a failure to design and implement concrete long-ranging development plans.[50] The Halliburton case dates back to 1994–2004 when a network of secretive banks (HSBC in London) and offshore tax havens (Switzerland) were used to funnel US$182 million in bribes to Nigerian officials.[51] This was done in exchange for awarding a US$6 billion engineering and construction contract for the Bonny Island Natural Liquefied Gas Projects to an international consortium of companies (the KBR, a former subsidiary of Halliburton, an American multinational oil field service corporation, Japanese firm JGC Corporation, Paris-based Technip, as well as Italy's ENI S.p.A/Snamprogetti). The scandal implicated high-level personalities including the Nigerian Head of State and political elites such as General Abdul Salami Abubakar and Dick Cheney former US vice president, who was the chairman and CEO of Halliburton at the time. His representatives denied his involvement and diplomatic deals were made to hush more public scrutiny.

The Halliburton Bribery Scandal showcases the role of states in their truncating their right through development through corruption, bribery, and IFFs, in conjunction with external enablers such as lawyers and anti-development foreign laws. For example, the British Lawyer facilitated the movement and concealment of the bribe money, aided by porous laws like England and Switzerland's famous bank secrecy and beneficial ownership laws that encourage the use of these countries as a base for laundering and moving bribe money from a KBR former subsidiary of Halliburton to Nigerian officials, presidents, and vice presidents. Also, we see the role of multinational banks' failure to alert the authorities to suspicious financial flows, under the guise of respecting bank secrecy laws.

Eventually, investigations were carried out, leading to the indictment and conviction of some of the foreign companies in the consortium and their top executives. Punishments included paid penalties totalling more than US$1.5 billion for their role in the bribery and some imprisonments. These actions showed some cooperation from the international community in discouraging bribery and corruption. The Nigerian government, however, did not and still has not taken serious action in convicting and confiscating the bribe money received by its officials. Some of the officials entered plea bargains that allowed them to retain a substantial portion of the bribe. Also, a tiny settlement was reached with the Nigerian government, where Halliburton agreed to pay only US$32.5 million penalties and US$2.5 million in legal expenses for a US$6 billion contract bribery.

The Halliburton scandal shows at first glance the connivance of many African governments through its officials in undermining its development trajectory through illicit financial flows, facilitating IFFs, lack of transparency, absence of political will in anti-corruption efforts, and a general lack of impunity. In the Halliburton scandal, while the CEO of some of the consortium companies were punished with jail time and the imposition of hefty fines, Nigerian officials involved went scot-free to enjoy with impunity to enjoy the corrupt proceeds of the bribes received. Nigerian government by implication undercut its Right to Development under the DRTD to put systems in place to enforce its development rights. One of these systems is appropriate sanctions enforcement for development saboteurs like corrupt public officials. Nigeria breached its primary development duty by accepting bribes to facilitate the exploitation of its mineral resources, overlooking its development interests and development-friendly due process.[52] Taken a step further, under the African Charter Provisions, Nigeria set back its development rights by failing to undertake concrete steps to 'eliminate all forms of foreign exploitation particularly that practised by international monopolies to enable their peoples to fully benefit from the advantages derived from their national resources'.[53]

The foreign companies and their officials failed in their cooperative duties to Nigeria's Right to Development by bribing Nigerian officials and politicians, resulting in the illicit flow of development funds. However, their role in the scandal is secondary to Nigeria's role. The DRTD and the African Charter enjoins the state to create an enabling environment, conducive to actualising their Right to Development. The Nigerian government went contrary to this mandate. Instead, the Nigerian government created (and still creates) a conducive environment for bribery, corruption, and illicit financial outflows to thrive, under-developing Nigeria in the process. Nigeria undermined (and continues to undermine) by failing to prosecute the erring politicians and officials behind the Halliburton Bribery Scandal, even though the foreign officials responsible for the scandal were prosecuted in their countries. The implication of failure to prosecute its corrupt public officials involved in the scandal sends a message of unseriousness to other states willing to cooperate with Nigeria in assisting Nigeria's development. It showcases a pitiful national irresponsibility that is anti-thematic to development.

The scandal reveals Nigeria's culpability in failing to implement its development rights and fairly administer resources for the common good.

Arguably, no entity can promote the interest of development better than the states themselves because states have more to lose in abdicating their development rights than external development actors as currently seen in Sri Lanka.[54] The lack of determination by the Nigerian state in its discharging development obligation under international and regional instruments inadvertently signals other stakeholders to join in the development sabotage. The collective lack of urgency in prioritising development rights in Nigeria at all leadership levels in public institutions will continue to concentrate political and economic power in corrupt hands who unfortunately control the State.[55] By failing to put stronger legal frameworks and enforceable mechanisms in place to minimise breaches and crimes by its officials and institutions, Nigeria failed in its primary responsibility to enforce its Right to Development.

The Halliburton scandal also shows the glaring unwillingness despite the payment of lip service to fighting IFFs made by African Leadership. The government appears to lack the political will to fight corruption and IFFs, especially when political cronies of a running administration are indicted. Nigerian officials and politicians who received kickbacks of over US$182 million to overlook due process in awarding contracts of US$6 billion to MNCs have not been successfully prosecuted.[56] The foreign culprits of the scandal have been sentenced in the USA and France using the American Foreign Corrupt Practices Act (FCPA) and the Convention on Combating Bribery of Foreign Public Officials in International Business Transactions 1997.[57] In all, Nigeria's involvement in the scandal makes it an active willing participant in the re-colonisation scramble for its and Africa's valuable resources and wealth.

LESSONS FROM THE HALLIBURTON BRIBERY SCANDAL

Link between Corruption, Underdevelopment, and the Gradual Erosion of Sovereignty

Sovereignty or the right to make decisions with little external interference is the hallmark of statehood.[58] However, since the end of colonisation and its replacement with neoliberal globalisation, the entrance of new domestic and international development actors into the activities of the state's domestic economy has added an intrusive dimension to the state's governance of its domestic affairs. Globalisation disguised as development has caused states to open up their territory and legislative space to trade, and investment, resulting in external political and economic influences on state decision-making. This has led to the rise of powerful MNCs that have more economic and political muscle than states who have no choice but to toe the line of the MNCs, diminishing their sovereignty in the process. The role and interference of MNCs in the domestic affairs of states in furtherance of their profit-motivated interests have not gone unnoticed and have a strong impact on sovereignty.[59]

The globalisation of property rights and ensuing disputes have eroded the territorial and legislative autonomy of states and property rights. States' resources over time have steadily shifted from national to transnational arenas.[60] As Grinin rightly observes from tracing the European state's evolution from the interwar years that 'the range of the state's internal affairs where nobody intervenes and which are regulated only by national law and traditions, are contracting and international law or law of a definite community (of collective participation)'.[61]

Without a doubt, globalisation significantly changes the scope of national sovereignty and weakens the position of a state as a primary provider of development through reduced state autonomy. Sovereignty is further eroded when the internal governance structures in society get gradually influenced by laws, policies, and practices of other states as officials attempt to justify certain conduct in such comparative terms. This interference often exhibits through diplomatic lobbying and at worse bribery and corruption as the Halliburton Bribery Scandal shows. Corruption affects development and national sovereignty by taking pro-development policies in ways that jeopardise human development, affect the right of states' citizens to fully enjoy its resources and undermine fundamental rights and freedoms.[62]

The Halliburton Bribery Scandal shows first-hand how corruption especially in developing countries reveals itself in the collapse of governance institutions and law enforcement processes. This in turn creates an unsustainable atmosphere of impunity that affects the proper functioning of democracy. It also signals to the external parties the signs of a failing state where unethical conduct from external parties would be tolerated. These parties, in other words, are given the licence to prey on the state's resources in a way that truncates its development. Accordingly, states adjust to the gradual erosion of their people's civil, political, and socio-economic rights.

The rule of law is only protected when states fulfil their primary development obligations by creating and maintaining a predictable legal system that addresses developmental and governance challenges in a transparent, fair, and reasonable manner. States' legal, institutional, judicial, and constitutional efforts against corruption should be oriented towards empowering the citizenry against corruption, rather than just combating corruption.[63] The Nigerian state failed in setting up these necessary institutional measures in place in a way that empowers its people (and officials) against corruption.

Increases Financing Gap in Achieving the Sustainable Development Goals

First, illicit capital flight significantly reduces the US$200 billion financing gap African countries face in achieving their SDG targets. This manifests as a high balance of payment deficit in the current account of countries, resulting in all kinds of the domestic market and policy effects. A deficit in BOP forces countries to depend on international sources or foreign exchange reserves to balance their current account balance, leading to drastic market and policy changes.[64] These changes are manifested as higher and fluctuating interest rates, weaker exchange rates, reduced market-related activities, budget austerity for public services, and so on. Furthermore, IFFs puts undue pressure on the fiscal system of states due to falling tax revenues arising from tax evasion. This encourages states to increase consumption taxes like VAT to make up for the shortfall in budgeted revenue, leading to less economic spending and money circulating in the economy. IFFs intensifies economic problems through draining foreign exchange, trade imbalances, and macroeconomic instability which is one of the reasons why countries with abundant resources are underachieving economically.

The connection and significance between the rising sovereign debt level and its impact on human rights and development are not new.[65] As Kampel reflects, the connection between the development rights infringement and debt emerged from financial globalisation in the post-war era and its linkage to authoritarian regimes in Latin America.[66] In Africa, rising debt levels, exacerbated by IFFs may not bode well for human rights observance and achieving SDGs.

Based on the latest data, ACTSA calculates that external government debt payments from Southern Africa amounted to at least US$21.1 billion in 2018 alone.[67] Of the US$21.1 billion total, US$1.9 billion was paid to multilateral institutions (international financial institutions), US$11.2 billion was paid to bilateral institutions (other governments) and US$8 billion was paid to the private sector. ACTSA estimates that about two-thirds of IFF in Southern Africa take the form of principal payments with the remainder as interest payments.[68] In 2020, the South African active scenario medium-term budget balances debt servicing cost was at ZAR 236.4 billion for 2019/2020, with an estimated increase in debt servicing cost to ZAR263.1 billion in 2021/2022 and ZAR 301.1 billion in 2022/2023, respectively. This impacts public spending revenue from the opportunity cost forgone for infrastructure investment, channelled into debt servicing.

Threaten National and Regional Peace and Security through Widening Inequality

Unchecked Illicit flows deepen systemic inequalities because it excessively affects the poorest and most vulnerable groups in the lower end of the economic class. In other words, the poor are made poorer by the fiscal system, primarily due to increased consumption taxes. It also impacts the legitimacy of democratic governance structures which may lead to damage to damage and low levels of trust in formal governance and the rule of law. This might fuel conflicts and threaten peace and security in Africa from the weakening of state institutions and growing corruption – through offshore financial centres with a high level of financial secrecy, thereby fostering a lack of transparency and accountability.

Goal 16 of the SDGs calls for the promotion of peaceful and inclusive societies for sustainable development, provision of access to justice for all and building effective, accountable and inclusive institutions at all levels.[69] The elimination of IFFs falls within the ambit of this SDG, via the strengthening of institutions responsible for the reduction of IFFs and substantial reduction of illicit financial and arms flows, strengthening the recovery and return of stolen assets and combating all forms of organised crime. The significant reduction of corruption and bribery in all forms encourages the development of transparent institutions at all levels. Given their development responsibility to states, it is in the best interest of African states to develop the political resolve to combat IFFs owing to sabotaging effects on states' developmental course and governance structures.

RECOMMENDATIONS AND CONCLUSION

Redefine African Development in Concrete and Implementable Measures

While global partnership and collaboration are important, the first response should begin at the national level as the DRTD, and African Charter proscribe. This is because international cooperation may not be very effective if the national system and structures enforcing the Right to Development are non-existent. A shift contextualising development in concrete, implementable measures and an ideological reorientation that requires understanding the political-economic game of resource control and the global dominance involved are paramount. African government/leadership must collectively desire at a personal, institutional, and national level to stop playing second fiddle and being at the bottom of the global development food chain. African states should utilise their legislative autonomy to consistently review legislation and establish rules/guidelines that strengthen existing institutions with more capacity to implement the RTD, tampered with accountability in due process regulation. African governments are encouraged to include the Right to Development as a human and communal right at the national level. This will foster accountability. Enhanced institutional coordination at the national level, the state level and the local government level should be given priority attention. These steps will help in translating the Right to Development from a political campaign statement to measurable development practice.

Implement Global Financial Anti-Corruption Measures into National Laws

More African states especially resource-rich states should adopt and incorporate some of the FATF recommendations on Anti-Money Laundering and Beneficial Ownership disclosure and definition into their domestic laws. The original mission of the task force was to prevent the utilisation of the banking system and financial institutions for money laundering and to consider additional preventive efforts in this field, including the adaptation of the legal and regulatory systems to enhance multilateral judicial assistance. Ghana and Botswana have implemented some of the FATF recommendations and other African countries can do the same. African governments should enact beneficial ownership disclosure laws domestically and incorporate beneficial ownership disclosure clauses in new and reviewed investment agreements perhaps as an addendum. Existing loan agreements should be reviewed, like Mozambique did saving the government US$200 million in debt and more in debt servicing payments. Countries should also revisit existing tax agreements with unfavourable rules/terms and unite along RECs to reformulate favourable rules as seen in the Caribbean Community Multi-Lateral Tax Treaty of 2004 that gives more capital importing countries which a lot of African countries greater taxing rights over corporate income.

Active Involvement of African Civil Society Organisations in Implementing Development

Governments should encourage the routine involvement of civil society organisations (CSO) at the national level to track illicit capital outflows. CSOs are helpers in the fight against IFFs. CSOs may be useful in engaging the political willingness component in the fight against IFF by contributing to policy-oriented research, building capacity for officials responsible for fighting illicit flows and drawing awareness of citizens to the menace of IFFs. CSOs may also be valuable in bringing together all stakeholders involved in IFF-development partners, the private sector, parliamentarians, policymakers, and the public under a common platform to find sustainable solutions in curbing massive illicit outflows. In 2021, the inaugural African Conference on Debt and Development (AfCoDD) by the African Forum and Network on Debt and Development (AFRODAD) started a new African Debt campaign aimed at fostering new outlooks on issues of African domestic resource mobilisation and international development finance mechanisms. The campaign and conference culminated in The Harare Declaration 2021. African governments can collaborate with CSOs in providing independent advice, and up-to-date statistical research data on IFF, useful in designing policies that bring solutions to IFF in Africa.

Increase Public Access and Input on Public Finances and Development Projects

Increased accountability and transparency in public financial affairs are recommended. Government procurement agencies should be required to inform the public of high-level projects, especially mining contracts as a matter of public policy for scrutiny and input. Some of these bogus development projects are disguised channels for IFFs, yet the development burden of their failure falls on the public through regressive taxes, VAT increments, the rising cost of living, and reduced public spending. It is recommended that members of the public fulfilment of their collective and individual Right to Development under the DRTD development projects/loans and have a direct say on matters that affects them This is because the national parliament is gradually losing sight of its duty in informing citizens who elected them to protect their development interests, especially in curbing IFF and a fair redistribution of resources.

The Right to Development is a primary human right which supports the fulfilment of other human rights. States have the primary duty to ensure that national policies incorporate the Right to Development, while the international community of states have a cooperation duty. Developing states, especially in Africa sabotage their development rights and goals through IFFs, leaving undesirable consequences for development and rights. Sustainable development largely depends on the soundness of socio-economic policies and measures taken to implement these measures. The Halliburton Bribery Scandal showcases the passivity of developing states in the execution of their development rights, misuse of state resources for corrupt private interests, and the unwillingness to prosecute development saboteurs. States' failure to accept and address their complicity in undermining development will potentially affect economic growth, divert resources for infrastructure development and unpopularise governance which might lead to state system collapse. African states should formulate and vigorously implement simultaneous development and anti-corruption measures, engage responsible non-state actors and reform existing institutions for effective enforcement of development rights.

NOTES

1. Yusuf Bangura, *Britain and Commonwealth Africa: The Politics of Economic Relations 1951–75* (Manchester: Manchester University Press, 1983), 4–44.

2. UN General Assembly, Universal Declaration of Human Rights, 10 December 1948, 217 A (III).

3. Paul Krugman and Anthony J. Venables, "Globalization and the Inequality of Nations," *The Quarterly Journal of Economics* 110, no. 4 (1995): 857–80.

4. Luke Martell, *The Sociology of Globalization, 2016-Introduction* (Polity, 2017), 138.

5. Edwini Kessie and Yvonne Apea, "The Participation of African Countries in the Multilateral Trading System," *African Yearbook of International Law Online/ Annuaire Africain de droit international Online* 12, no. 1 (2004): 9–66.

6. Khurshid Iqbal, "The Declaration on the Right to Development and Implementation," *Political Perspectives CIP* 1, no. 10 (2007): 1–15.

7. The International Covenant on Economic, Social and Cultural Rights 16 December 1966 (993 U.N.T.S 3), entered into force on 3 January 1976. *See* also United Nations Transforming Our World: The 2030 Agenda for Sustainable Development A/RES/70/1 https://sustainabledevelopment.un.org/content/documents/21252030%20Agenda%20for%20Sustainable%20Development%20web.pdf.

8. *Id.*

9. UN General Assembly, Declaration on the Right to Development: resolution / adopted by the General Assembly, 4 December 1986, A/RES/41/128, available at: https://www.refworld.org/docid/3b00f22544.htm.

10. Icelandic Human Rights Centre, "Human Rights and Development," https://www.humanrights.is/en/human-rights-education-project/human-rights-concepts-ideas-and-fora/human-rights-in-relation-to-other-topics/human-rights-and-development.

11. *Id.*

12. Organization of African Unity (OAU), African Charter on Human and Peoples' Rights ("Banjul Charter"), 27 June 1981, CAB/LEG/67/3 rev. 5, 21 I.L.M. 58 (1982), available at: https://www.refworld.org/docid/3ae6b3630.html. Article 22(122) provides that 'All peoples shall have the right to their economic, social and cultural development with due regard to their freedom and identity and in the equal enjoyment of the common heritage of mankind.'

13. Supra note.

14. *Id.*

15. S. Vyas-Doorgapersad, "Lack of Citizen Participation and Inefficient Service Delivery at the Local Level in South Africa," *International Journal of Environmental, Cultural, Economic and Social Sustainability* 5, no. 1 2009: 87–97.

16. At the UN Millennium Summit in 2000.

17. UN General Assembly, International Covenant on Civil and Political Rights, 16 December 1966, United Nations, Treaty Series, vol. 999, p. 171, available at: https://www.refworld.org/docid/3ae6b3aa0.html and UN General Assembly, *International Covenant on Economic, Social and Cultural Rights*, 16 December 1966, United

Nations, Treaty Series, vol. 993, p. 3, available at: https://www.refworld.org/docid/3ae6b36c0.html.

18. Brigitte I. Hamm, "A Human Rights Approach to Development," *Human Rights Quarterly* 23, no. 4 (2001): 1005–31. JSTOR, http://www.jstor.org/stable/4489369, accessed 24 April 2023.

19. L. Chancel and T. Piketty, "Global Income Inequality, 1820–2020: The Persistence and Mutation of Extreme Inequality," *Journal of the European Economic Association* 19, no. 6 (2021): 3025–62.

20. L. Chancel, D. Cogneau, A. Gethin, and A. Myczkowski, How Large Are African Inequalities? Towards Distributional National Accounts in Africa, 1990–2017 (2019).

21. Chris Jochnick, "The Human Rights Challenge to Global Poverty," (1999).

22. Arjun Sengupta's, "The Right to Development as a Human Right," (2000).

23. R. O. Keohane and J. S. Nye, *Power and Interdependence: World Politics in Transition* (New York: Harper Collins Publishers, Second Edition, 1989); M. Carnoy, "Multinationals in a Changing World Economy: Whither the Nation-State," in M. Carnoy et al. (Eds.), *The New Global Economy in the Information Age* (University Park, PA: Pennsylvania State University Press, 1993), 45–96.

24. Guiding Principles on Business and Human Rights: Implementing the United Nations "Protect, Respect and Remedy" Framework (1 January 2012).

25. James C.N. Paul, "The Human Right to Development: It is Meaning and Importance," *Third World Legal Studies* 11 (1992), Article 2.

26. Dzodzi Tsikata, "The Rights-based Approach to Development: Potential for Change or More of the Same?" (2004).

27. Communication 276 / 2003. The Commission Recommended the Return of the Endorois' Lands by the Kenyan Government.

28. Art 10. UN General Assembly, Vienna Declaration and Programme of Action, 12 July 1993, A/CONF.157/23.

29. *Id.*

30. Ghai and Pao, *supra* note xxxi. Ghai and Pao maintain that some developing states have no intention of implementing the right at the national level, and are only concerned with its usefulness to make claims at the international level.

31. Chapter II Constitution of the Federal Republic of Nigeria Cap C23 LFN 2004.

32. Laure-Hélène Piron, *Rights and Humanity An Emerging Consensus on the Right to Development: Some Current Initiatives Relevant to the Implementation of the RTD* (Right to Development Report, 2000), 1–48, https://www.scribd.com/document/94283797/Right-to-Develp.

33. Margot E. Salomon, "Legal Cosmopolitanism and the Normative Contribution of the Right to Development," *LSE Legal Studies Working Paper No. 16/2008* (2008): 1–15.

34. Margot E. Salomon, "International Economic Governance and Human Rights Accountability," in Margot E. Salomon, Arne Tostensen, and Wouter Vandenhole (Eds.), *Casting the Net Wider: Human Rights, Development and New Duty Bearers* (Intersentia, 2007), 153.

35. *Id. See* also A.E Oji and M. V. C. Ozioko, "Effect of Globalization on Sovereignty of States," *Nnamdi Azikiwe University Journal of International Law and Jurisprudence* 2 (2011): 257–270. Christopher Chase-Dunn, "Globalization: A World-systems Perspective," *Journal of World-Systems Research* 5, no. 2 (1999): 188.188–215.

36. B Iorio, "Out of Africa: Capital Flight" Global Financial Integrity (2019), https://gfintegrity.org/out-of-africa-capital-flight/.

37. GFI Report, Trade-Related Illicit Financial Flows in 134 Developing Countries 2009–2018 (2018), https://gfintegrity.org/report/trade-related-illicit-financial-flows-in-134-developing-countries-2009-2018/.

38. *Id.*

39. UNECA A Study on the Global Governance Architecture for Combating Illicit Financial Flows (2018), https://archive.uneca.org/sites/default/files/PublicationFiles/global-governance_eng_rev.pdf.

40. AU/ECA, Illicit Financial Flow Report of the High-Level Panel on Illicit Financial Flows from Africa (2015), https://www.unodc.org/documents/NGO/AU_ECA_Illicit_Financial_Flows_report_EN.pdf.

41. *Id.*

42. *Id.*

43. At the request of the joint AU/ECA Conference of Ministers of Finance, Monetary Affairs, Economic Planning and Integration of the African Union and the Conference of African Ministers of Finance.

44. https://au.int/sites/default/files/newsevents/conceptnotes/38416-cn-final_english-_hld_concept_note_design.pdf.

45. African Union Press Releases, African Union Commission is set to launch a Multi-Donor Action against Illicit Financial Flows in Africa 1st December 2020. https://au.int/en/pressreleases/20201201/african-union-commission-set-launch-multi-donor-action-against-illicit, accessed 5 December 2021. The multi-door initiative/project on IFF is co-financed by the European Union (EU), the German Federal Ministry of Economic Development and Cooperation (BMZ) and implemented by the Deutsche Gesellschaft für Internationale Zusammenarbeit (GIZ) through the Good Financial Governance in Africa Programme. The project achieves its IFF mandate through the implementation of country pilot measures using established and active African networks African Tax Administration Forum (ATAF); the Collaborative Africa Budget Reform Initiative (CABRI); the African Organisation of Public Accounts Committees (AFROPAC); and the African Organisation of Supreme Audit Institutions (AFROSAI).

46. AU, ASSEMBLY SPECIAL DECLARATION ON ILLICIT FINANCIAL FLOWS Doc. Assembly/AU/17(XXIV) https://au.int/sites/default/files/documents/29831-doc-assembly_declaration_on_illicit_financial_flow_-_english.pdf.

47. FATF Members and Observers https://www.fatf-gafi.org/about/membersandobservers/.

48. *Id.*

49. S. S. Ankamah and S. M. Manzoor e Khoda, "Political Will and Government Anti-corruption Efforts: What Does the Evidence Say?" *Public Administration and Development* 38, no. 1 (2018): 3–14.

50. Olusola Joshua Olujobi, "Nigeria's Upstream Petroleum Industry Anti-corruption Legal Framework: The Necessity for Overhauling and Enrichment," *Journal of Money Laundering Control* ahead-of-print (2021): 2–3.

51. Will Fitzgibbon and Musikilu Mojeed, Files Open New Window on $182-Million Halliburton Bribery Scandal in Nigeria International Consortium of Investigative Journalist Investigations. *ICIJ* February 10, 2021, https://www.icij.org/investigations/swiss-leaks/files-open-new-window-182-million-halliburton-bribery-scandal-nigeria/.

52. *See* Articles 2 and 4 DRTD 1986.

53. Art 21 (5) African Charter.

54. Benjamin Parkin and Mahendra Ratnaweera, "Sri Lanka Appeals for Food Aid as Debt Crisis Worsens," *Financial Times*, June 1, 2022, https://www.ft.com/content/c89a972c-df31-449c-a824-ba3ccd54a4da.

55. Victor E. Dike, "'Why Nations Fail' to Develop: The Case of Nigeria," *SAGE Open* 5, no. 4 (2015): 1–12: 2158244015611714.

56. Okechukwu I Eme and Okoh Chukwuma Inya, "The Role of Efcc in Combating Political Corruption," *Arabian Journal of Business and Management Review* 1, no. 3 (2011): 46–68.

57. Kathleen A. Lacey, "Investigation of Halliburton Co./TSKJ's Nigerian Business Practices: Model for Analysis of the Current Anti-Corruption Environment on Foreign Corrupt Practices Act Enforcement," *Journal of Criminal Law and Criminology* 96, no. 2 (2006): 2–5.

58. James R. Crawford, *Brownlie's Principles of Public International Law* (Oxford: OUP, 2012), 128, 447–49.

59. MNC interference in state affairs. *See* John M. Kline, "MNCs and Surrogate Sovereignty," *The Brown Journal of World Affairs* 13, no. 1 (2006): 123–33.

60. Christopher Saporita, "Reconciling Human Rights and Sovereignty: A Framework for Global Property Law," *Indiana Journal of Global Legal Studies* 10 (2003): 255–60.

61. Leonid E. Grinin, "State Sovereignty in the Age of Globalization: Will it Survive?" *Globalistics and Globalization Studies* (2012): 211–37. *See* also Leonid E. Grinin, "Globalization and Problems of National Sovereignty," *Materials of 'The round table', devoted to the Day of Philosophy UNESCO* (2004): 39–47. *See* also Richard Falk's "Sovereignty and Human Rights: The Search for Reconciliation," *Issues of Democracy* 5, no. 1 (2000): 29–35. *See* also Michael P. Donnelly, "Democracy and Sovereignty vs International Human Rights: Reconciling the Irreconcilable?" *The International Journal of Human Rights* 24, no. 10 (2020): 1429–50 on the reconcilability between human rights, sovereignty and democracy democratic-majority-rule system of governance decide the rules of law by which they live.

62. UNDHR *supra note ii.*

63. Raj C. Kumar, "Corruption and Human Rights: Promoting Transparency in Governance and the Fundamental Right to Corruption-free Service in India," *Columbia Journal of Asian Law* 17 (2003): 31.

64. Alex Erskine and Fredrik Eriksson, "Improving Coherence in the Illicit Financial Flows Agenda." U4 Illicit financial flows: https://www.u4.no/publications/improving-coherence-in-the-illicit-financial-flows agenda.pdf (2018): 30–33.

65. Ilias Bantekas and Cephas Lumina, *Sovereign Debt and Human Rights* (Oxford: OUP, 2013), 289–301.

66. Daniel Kampel, "Sovereign Debt Restructuring and the Right to Development: Challenges from an Incomplete Framework," *Global Campus Human Rights Journal* 1 (2017): 1–16.

67. IMF (2019) https://www.imf.org/en/Countries; World Bank (2019) https://databank.worldbank.org/data/source/world-development-indicators.

68. Action for Southern Africa The Money Drain How Trade Mis-invoicing and Unjust Debt Undermine Economic and Social Rights in Southern Africa Briefing Paper 2019, 7–9. https://actsa.org/wp-content/uploads/dlm_uploads/2019/08/ACTSA-The-Money-Drain-FINAL.pdf.

69. United Nations #Envision2030 Goal 16: Peace, Justice and Strong Institutions https://www.un.org/development/desa/disabilities/envision2030-goal16.html, accessed 20 December 2021.

BIBLIOGRAPHY

155/96: Social and Economic Rights Action Center (SERAC) and Center for Economic and Social Rights (CESR) / Nigeria.

Abi-Saab, Georges. "The Legal Formulation of a Right to Development." In *Le droit au développement au plan international, Académie de droit international de La Haye*, edited by René-Jean Dupuy, 139. Hague: Sijthoff & Noordhoff, 1981.

Action for Southern Africa the Money Drain How Trade Mis-Invoicing and Unjust Debt Undermine Economic and Social Rights in Southern Africa Briefing Paper 2019 7–9. https://actsa.org/wp-content/uploads/dlm_uploads/2019/08/ACTSA-The-Money-Drain-FINAL.pdf.

African Commission on Human and Peoples Rights v Kenya (006/2012) [2017] AFCHPR 28; (26 May 2017).

African Union Commission. "'Agenda 2063: The Africa We Want' Aspirations 1 and 7." 2015. Accessed 23 June 2022. http://www.un.org/en/africa/osaa/pdf/au/agenda2063-first10yearimplementation.pdf.

Alston, Philip. "Ships Passing in the Night: The Current State of the Human Rights and Development Debate Seen Through the Lens of the Millennium Development Goals." *Human Rights Quarterly* 27, no. 3 (2005): 755–829.

Arts, Karin, and Atabongawung Tamo. "The Right to Development in International Law: New Momentum Thirty Years Down the Line?" *Netherlands International Law Review* 63, no. 3 (2016): 221–49.

Bangura, Yusuf. *Britain and Commonwealth Africa: The Politics of Economic Relations, 1951–75*. Manchester University Press, 1983.

Bantekas, Ilias and Cephas Lumina. *Sovereign Debt and Human Rights*, 289–301. Oxford: OUP, 2013.

Barsh, Russel Lawrence. "The Right to Development as a Human Right: Results of the Global Consultation." *Human Rights Quarterly* 13, no. 3 (1991): 322–38.

Bedjaoui, Mohammed. "The Right to Development." In *International Law: Achievements and Prospects*, edited Bedjaoui Mohammed, 1177. Dordrecht: Martinus Nijhoff Publishers, 1991.

Bunn, Isabella D. "The Right to Development: Implications for International Economic Law." *American University International Law Review* 15 (1999): 1425.

Chase-Dunn, Christopher. "Globalization: A World-Systems Perspective." *Journal of World-Systems Research* 5, no. 2 (1999): 188.

Communication 276 / 2003. "The Commission Recommended the Return of the Endorois' Lands by the Kenyan Government."

Constitution of the Federal Republic of Nigeria Cap C23 LFN 2004.

Crawford, James R. *Brownlie's Principles of Public International Law* (8th edn), 128, 447–49. Oxford: OUP, 2012.

Davidson, Basil. *The Black Man's Burden: Africa and the Curse of the Nation-State*. Times Press, 1993.

Dike, Victor E. "'Why Nations Fail' to Develop: The Case of Nigeria." *SAGE Open* 5, no. 4 (2015): 1–12.

Donnelly, Michael P. "Democracy and Sovereignty vs International Human Rights: Reconciling the Irreconcilable?" *The International Journal of Human Rights* 24, no. 10 (2020): 1429–50.

Eme Okechukwu, I., and Okoh Chukwuma Inya. "The Role of EFCC in Combatting Political Corruption." *Arabian Journal of Business and Management Review* 1, no. 3 (2011): 46–68.

Erskine, Alex, and Fredrik Eriksson. "Improving Coherence in the Illicit Financial Flows Agenda." *U4 Illicit Financial Flows* (2018): 30–33. https://www.u4. no/publications/improving-coherence-in-the-illicit-financial-flowsagenda.pdf.

Espiell, Hector Gros. "The Right of Development as a Human Right." *Texas International Law Journal* 16 (1981): 189.

Falk, Richard. "Sovereignty and Human Rights: The Search for Reconciliation." *Issues of Democracy* 5, no. 1 (2000): 29–35.

Financial Action Task Force Recommendations. https://www.ft.com/content/c89a972c-df31-449c-a824-ba3ccd54a4da.

Fitzgibbon, Will and Musikilu Mojeed. "Files Open New Window on $182-Million Halliburton Bribery Scandal in Nigeria." *International Consortium of Investigative Journalist Investigations ICIJ* (February 10, 2021). https://www.icij.org/investigations/swiss-leaks/files-open-new-window-182-million-halliburton-bribery-scandal-nigeria/.

Ghai, Yash P., and Y. K. Pao. *Whose Human Right to Development?* Commonwealth Secretariat, 1989.

Global Financial Integrity. 2019. https://www.gfintegrity.org/issues/data-by-country/.

Grinin, Leonid E. "Globalization and Problems of National Sovereignty." *Materials of 'the Round Table', Devoted to the Day of Philosophy UNESCO* (2004): 39–47.

Grinin, Leonid E. "State Sovereignty in the Age of Globalization: Will It Survive?" In *Globalistics and Globalization Studies*, edited by Grinin E. Leonid et al., 211–37. Volgograd: Uchitel Publishing, 2012.

Ibhawoh, Bonny. "The Right to Development: The Politics and Polemics of Power and Resistance." *Human Rights Quarterly* 33 (2011): 76.

IMF. 2019. https://www.imf.org/en/Countries; World Bank. 2019. https://databank.worldbank.org/data/source/world-development-indicators.

Iqbal, Khurshid. "The Declaration on the Right to Development and Implementation." *Political Perspectives CIP* 1, no. 10 (2007): 1–39.

Islam, Faisal, and Claudia Mitchell. "Neoliberal Globalization, Multilateral Development Agencies and HIV and AIDs Education in South Africa: Looking Back to Look Ahead." In *Critical Perspectives on Neoliberal Globalization, Development and Education in Africa and Asia*, edited by Dip Kapoor, 121–34. Leiden: Brill, 2011.

Kamga, Serges Djoyou, and Tendai Shephard Mbanje. "International Law, the United Nations Security Council, Coloniality of Power and the Realization of the Right to Development in Africa: Some Reflections." In *The Right to Development in Africa: Issues, Constraints and Prospects*, edited by Serges Djoyou Kamga, 57–69. Pan-African University Press, 2020.

Kampel, Daniel. "Sovereign Debt Restructuring and the Right to Development: Challenges from an Incomplete Framework." *Global Campus Human Rights Journal* 1 (2017): 1–16.

Kessie, Edwini, and Yvonne Apea. "The Participation of African Countries in the Multilateral Trading System." *African Yearbook of International Law Online/ Annuaire Africain de droit international Online* 12, no. 1 (2004): 9–66.

Kline, John M. "MNCs and Surrogate Sovereignty." *The Brown Journal of World Affairs* 13, no. 1 (2006): 123–33.

Krugman, Paul, and Anthony J. Venables. "Globalization and the Inequality of Nations." *The Quarterly Journal of Economics* 110, no. 4 (1995): 857–80.

Kumar, C. Raj. "Corruption and Human Rights: Promoting Transparency in Governance and the Fundamental Right to Corruption-Free Service in India." *Columbia Journal of Asian Law* 17 (2003): 31.

Lacey, Kathleen A. "Investigation of Halliburton Co./TSKJ's Nigerian Business Practices: Model for Analysis of the Current Anti-Corruption Environment on Foreign Corrupt Practices Act Enforcement." *Journal of Criminal Law and Criminology* 96, no. 2 (2006): 2–5.

Martell, Luke. *The Sociology of Globalization, 2016-Introduction*. Polity, 2017. https://www.perlego.com/book/1536101/the-sociology-of-globalization-pdf?utm_source=google&utm_medium=cpc&campaignid=15853719261&adgroupid=133053562278&gclid=CjwKCAjwqJSaBhBUEiwAg5W9p6ZFGr3GT56XK12OY9EqOg2HEM8JBScZ6MzXufII3FVKS7qyD-ErxxoCbw0QAvD_BwE.

Mohan, Giles, and Jeremy Holland. "Human Rights & Development in Africa: Moral Intrusion or Empowering Opportunity?" *Review of African Political Economy* 28, no. 88 (2001): 177–96.

Nielson, Lynge. "Classification of Countries Based on their Level of Development." *WP/11/31 IMF Working Papers* (2011).

Ngang, Carol C. "The Right to Development in Africa and the Implications of its Non-Realisation to Prospects for Development on the Continent." In *The Right to Development in Africa: Issues, Constraints and Prospects*, edited by Serges Djoyou Kamga, 151–69. Pan-African University Press, 2020.

Oji, A. E., and M. V. C. Ozioko. "Effect of Globalization on Sovereignty of States." *Nnamdi Azikiwe University Journal of International Law and Jurisprudence* 2 (2011): 257–70.

Olujobi, Olusola Joshua. "Nigeria's Upstream Petroleum Industry Anti-Corruption Legal Framework: The Necessity for Overhauling and Enrichment." *Journal of Money Laundering Control* 26, no. 7, (2023): 2–3.

Organization of African Unity (OAU), African Charter on Human and Peoples' Rights ("Banjul Charter"), 27 June 1981, CAB/LEG/67/3 rev. 5, 21 I.L.M. 58 (1982), entered into force 21 October 1986.

Parkin, Benjamin and Mahendra Ratnaweera. "Sri Lanka Appeals for Food Aid as Debt Crisis Worsens." *Financial Times*, June 1, 2022. https://www.ft.com/content/c89a972c-df31-449c-a824-ba3ccd54a4da.

Pempel, Thomas J. "The Developmental Regime in a Changing World Economy." In *The Developmental State*, edited by Meredith Woo-Cummings, 137–81. Ithaca: Cornell University Press, 1999

Piron, Laure-Hélène. *Rights and Humanity "An Emerging Consensus on the Right to Development: Some Current Initiatives Relevant to the Implementation of the RTD.* Right to Development Report, 2000. https://www.scribd.com/document/94283797/Right-to-Develp.

Salomon, Margot E. "International Economic Governance and Human Rights Accountability." In *Casting the Net Wider: Human Rights, Development and New Duty Bearers,* edited by Margot E. Salomon, Arne Tostensen, and Wouter Vandenhole, 153. Intersentia, 2007.

Salomon, Margot E. "Legal Cosmopolitanism and the Normative Contribution of the Right to Development." *LSE Legal Studies Working Paper No. 16/2008* (2008): 1–15.

Sano, Hans-Otto. "Development and Human Rights: The Necessary, but Partial Integration of Human Rights and Development." *Human Rights Quarterly* 22 (2000): 734.

Santhi, S., and A. Saravanakumar. "The Economic Development of Singapore: A Historical Perspective." *Aut Research Journal* 11 (2020): 441–59.

Saporita, Christopher. "Reconciling Human Rights and Sovereignty: A Framework for Global Property Law." *Indiana Journal of Global Legal Studies* 10 (2003): 255–60.

The 1993 Vienna Declaration and Programme of Action.

The 2002 Monterrey Consensus.

The 2005 World Summit Outcome Document.

The 2007 Declaration on the Rights of Indigenous Peoples.

The International Covenant on Economic, Social and Cultural Rights 16 December 1966 (993 U.N.T.S 3), entered into force on 3 January 1976.

Udombana, Nsongurua J. "The Third World and the Right to Development: Agenda for the Next Millennium." *Human Rights Quarterly* 22, no. 3 (2000): 753–87.

United Nations, Charter of the United Nations, 24 October 1945, 1 UNTS XVI entered into force 24 September 1973.

United Nations Conference on Environment and Development Rio de Janeiro, Brazil. *Agenda 21: Programme of Action for Sustainable Development; Rio Declaration on Environment and Development; Statement of Forest Principles: The Final Text of Agreements Negotiated by Governments at the United Nations Conference on Environment and Development (UNCED), 3–14 June 1992, Rio De Janeiro, Brazil.* United Nations Dept. of Public Information, 1993.nt.

United Nations General Assembly, Declaration on the Right to Development: resolution / adopted by the General Assembly, 4 December 1986, A/RES/41/128.

United Nations General Assembly, Universal Declaration of Human Rights, 10 December 1948, 217 A (III).

United Nations General Assembly, Vienna Declaration and Programme of Action, 12 July 1993, A/CONF.157/23.

United Nations Millennium Declaration 2000.

United Nations Transforming Our World: The 2030 Agenda for Sustainable Development A/RES/70/1. Accessed 20 June 2022. https://sustainabledevelopment.un.org/content/documents/21252030%20Agenda%20for%20Sustainable%20Development%20web.pdf.

United Nations #Envision2030 Goal 16: Peace, Justice and Strong Institutions. Accessed 20 December 2021. https://www.un.org/development/desa/disabilities/envision2030-goal16.html.

World Bank. "How Does the World Bank Classify Countries?" *World Bank Data.* https://datahelpdesk.worldbank.org/knowledgebase/articles/378834-how-does-the-world-bank-classify-countries.

Yew, Lee Kuan. *From the Third World to First: The Singapore Story, 1965–2000.* Marshall Cavendish International Asia Pte Ltd, 2012.

Chapter 6

Advocating for a Human Rights-Based Approach to Combatting Illicit Financial Flows

Annelie de Man

INTRODUCTION

The African continent continues to experience high levels of poverty and inequality, with limited access to education, adequate housing, healthcare, water, and sanitation.[1] Although rich in natural resources, very few of the resources of African countries are reaching the most vulnerable. This has a significant impact on the fulfilment of economic and social rights on the continent, as poverty is multidimensional and inextricably linked to human rights, in particular the Right to Development. Illicit financial flows (IFFs) compound on these issues as essential resources are diverted from development programmes. Goal 16.4 of the 2030 Agenda for Sustainable Development[2] and the Addis Ababa Action Agenda[3] call for a significant reduction in IFFs as they impose an immense obstacle to realising the Right to Development.[4] This is especially true regarding peoples' right to self-determination, including the right to full sovereignty over all their natural wealth and resources. Linked to these rights is the duty of states to create an enabling environment conducive to development.

In 2020, Africa was estimated to lose around $86.2 billion annually due to IFFs.[5] This is almost equal to the amount of Official Development Assistance received during this time.[6] In light of Africa's development challenges, a loss of resources of this magnitude will have grave consequences for economic and social development. The High Level Panel on Illicit Financial Flows from Africa estimates that IFFs amounted to a loss of $1 trillion over the past fifty years.[7] Even though these financial losses are difficult to measure precisely due to the secrecy and illegality surrounding IFFs, Herkenrath argues that consensus has been reached that IFFs flowing out of developing countries far exceed development aid flowing into these countries.[8] This makes IFFs a significant challenge to development programming on the continent.[9] In a 2015 study conducted by Global Financial Integrity, it was estimated that in thirty-five developing countries, IFFs were more than the annual expenditure related to education for the same period (2008–2012).[10]

Arguments in support of curbing IFFs are usually based on one of two grounds: economics or ethics. From an economic perspective, it is argued that IFFs dispossess developing countries of resources essential for development. On the other hand, ethical proponents argue that governments' inaction in dismantling the structures that allow IFFs to occur is 'morally unjustifiable'.[11] Traditional approaches employed in curbing IFFs have focused primarily on prosecution and recovering stolen assets. However, in light of the statistics provided above, it can be argued that this is not enough to sufficiently curb the existence of this phenomenon.

This chapter argues for a human rights-based approach to be employed in the fight against IFFs. Specifically, this chapter focuses on corruption by government officials as one of the ways through which IFFs can occur. It will be argued that attention should shift to preventive measures provided under a human rights-based approach.[12] A human rights-based approach recognises that states have specific legally binding duties founded in international, regional, and domestic human rights law, including practising due diligence in managing domestic resources. Following this approach in combatting corruption can hold numerous advantages, the main of which is the value added by framing the impact of corruption in human rights language and identifying and relying on the legal obligations that rest on states. It is argued that a human rights-based approach should be employed in conjunction with the standard approaches already implemented in curbing corruption specifically and IFFs in general. This chapter will focus on the domestic human rights obligations of states, as created under international and regional human rights law, and not on their duties in terms of international co-operation in combatting IFFs, as this is a lengthy discussion in its own right.

The chapter will commence with an overview of what IFFs are, followed by a discussion on the impact of IFFs in general and corruption, as a form of IFFs, on human rights, particularly the Right to Development. From there, the content and principles of the human rights-based approach will be analysed, including the duties imposed on state actors. Even though these respective duties are highly interrelated, and each carries importance in a holistic approach to combatting IFFs, this chapter will only consider obligations pertinent to the principle of accountability as it forms part of the human rights-based approach to development and as it relates to corruption committed by government officials. The United Nations Convention against Corruption[13] underscores the importance of this principle by calling for accountability and transparency in government structures to ensure development. The 2003 United Nations Convention against Corruption was adopted to 'promote and strengthen measures to prevent and combat corruption more efficiently and effectively'.[14] To this end, the Convention contains a comprehensive set of accountability measures that member states can apply to strengthen their legal and regulatory regimes to fight corruption. The chapter will conclude with an outline of the advantages gained if a human rights-based approach is employed in curbing corruption as a subset of IFFs.

OVERVIEW OF DEFINITION AND FORMS OF IFFS

The various definitions of IFFs have already been outlined in the introduction to this collection. However, it is worth pointing out that IFFs can occur through various mediums (although these can be interlinked with one enabling the other and vice versa), namely (a) commercial activities (this can occur through 'tariff, duty and revenue offences, tax evasion, competition offences and market manipulation')[15]; (b) criminal activities (this includes 'any type of trafficking in goods, such as drugs and firearms, or services, such as smuggling of migrants. IFFs emerge from transnational trade in illicit goods and services and cross-border flows from managing the illicit income from such activities'.[16] Terrorism financing and exploitative activities, such as kidnapping or extortion, can also constitute an IFF when a related flow of value occurs across borders)[17]; and (c) corruption (acts such as 'bribery, embezzlement, abuse of functions, trading in influence, illicit enrichment and other acts of corruption' will constitute IFFs when they result in a cross-border flow of value).[18]

Generally, IFFs have been found to have four specific features. First, it is '[i]llicit in origin, transfer or use'.[19] A 'flow of value' will be considered illicit if 'it is illicitly generated (e.g. originates from criminal activities or tax evasion), illicitly transferred (e.g. violating currency controls) or illicitly used (e.g. for financing terrorism)'.[20] Second, is an 'exchange of value'. This means more than financial transfers and includes the exchange of goods and services and financial and non-financial assets.[21] Third, 'IFFs measure a flow of value over a given time'.[22] Lastly, IFFs require a flow of value across a border.[23]

The rest of this chapter will focus on IFFs that result from grand-scale corruption. Although no single definition of corruption exists, the most common definition is that of the World Bank, that is, 'the abuse of public office for private gain'.[24] However, it has been argued that the World Bank's definition does not recognise the victim element of corruption and its impact on human well-being.[25] Olaniyan has formulated the following definition, which is more fitting for the purpose of this article:

> [T]he deliberate, intentional mass stealing of public wealth and resources by senior state officials entrusted with its fair and honest management for the common good and achievement of human rights, whether carried out individually or collectively, but with the support, encouragement, or acquiescence of the state, combined with a refusal to genuinely, thoroughly and transparently investigate and/or prosecute the mass stealing and recover stolen assets, which violates the human rights of the economically and socially vulnerable.[26]

In line with the thesis of this chapter, the definition provided by Olaniyan will be relied on going forth as it demonstrates the social harm caused by corrupt acts and omissions, as well as the duties of states as it relates to preventing and combatting corruption.

IMPACT OF IFFS AND CORRUPTION ON THE RIGHT TO DEVELOPMENT

The Independent Expert on the Effects of Foreign Debt, Cephas Lumina, makes it clear that '[i]n essence, the failure to counter IFFs and recover stolen assets is a denial of access to basic healthcare, education, safe water and sanitation, adequate housing and infrastructure, all of which are basic conditions for the enjoyment of human rights'.[27] Corruption, on the other hand, 'diverts funds intended for investment in public services, . . . distorts justice systems, interferes with political processes, and affects the delivery of public services. In other words, corruption bears human rights costs'.[28] This is also evident from Olaniyan's definition provided earlier.

The most direct and evident impact of corruption is the loss of revenue that could have been employed in state budgets providing for crucial service delivery to meet the basic needs of its people and fulfil socio-economic rights.[29] These include 'security and justice to basic social services such as health and education'.[30] This disproportionately affects the poor and most vulnerable by limiting their access to quality and affordable social services, such as housing, education, and healthcare.[31] In turn, poverty and underdevelopment is exasperated which violates the principle of equality and non-discrimination as contained in core international human rights instruments.[32]

Article 2 of the International Covenant on Economic, Social and Cultural Rights (CESCR) obliges states to fulfil the rights contained in the Covenant to 'the maximum of its available resources'.[33] Due to the loss of financial resources, corruption impede states' ability to employ their maximum available resources to realise economic and social rights.[34] This duty will be expanded upon later.

In particular, where states fail to fulfil this duty, it can be argued that the Right to Development is violated. This is based on the argument that any consideration of the Right to Development includes a review of the full spectrum of civil, political, economic, social, and cultural rights due to the interrelated nature of all human rights.[35] Development and human rights have an intertwined relationship. Improvement in one area will inevitably result in progress in the other. In accordance with Article 1 of the Declaration on the Right to Development, the Right to Development underscores this relationship as it 'calls for an enabling environment for development and human rights, and the mobilisation of resources for development'.[36] Therefore, IFFs, and in this case corruption, can be seen as violating the Right to Development.[37]

The Vienna Declaration and Programme of Action,[38] the outcome document of the 1993 World Conference on Human Rights, recognises that the Right to Development is a fundamental human right. This right finds further legal recognition in Article 22 of the African Charter on Human and Peoples' Rights.[39] It is also argued that it has transcended to the level of customary international law.[40]

Moreover, the Declaration acknowledges the right of peoples to self-determination, including the right to full sovereignty over all their natural wealth and resources (Article 1(2)). The right to self-determination is also realised in common Article 1 of the International Covenant on Civil and Political Rights and CESCR. This right has 'clear implications for activities that undermine the ability of other States to raise revenue and fund their own development'.[41] It can be argued that corruption is one of the 'activities' referred to due to their potential to significantly reduce domestic resources available for development programming. As highlighted by Muchhala to the United Nations Human Rights Council, '[r]ealizing this right requires the generation of sufficient financial resources, for which the recovery of illicit financial flows is imperative'.[42]

Moreover, adequate domestic resources enable states to formulate and implement national development policies that cater to their needs rather than relying on external resources that reflect the preferences and conditionalities of foreign donors. This provides states with more policy space to create an environment conducive to development and eventually realising economic and social rights.[43] Kamga argues that corruption violates the right of people to have full sovereignty over their resources.[44] Muchhale also points out:

> IFFs undermine articles of the [Declaration on the Right to Development] which establish the link between the human right to development and the right of peoples to self-determination, and the duties of states and the international

community to ensure an enabling environment for development at both national and global levels, mainly through international cooperation.[45]

The Declaration places the primary obligation on states to create 'national and international conditions favourable for realising the right to development'.[46] As already mentioned, corruption related IFFs result in significant resources leaving a country. This creates restrictive resource conditions which limit the development objectives that can be pursued. States' obligations under the Right to Development include the duty to respect international law (Article 3), eliminate any obstacles to development (Article 3), and take steps to 'ensure the full exercise and progressive enhancement of the Right to Development, including the formulation, adoption and implementation of policy, legislative and other measures at the national and international levels' (Article 10). Therefore, states must implement adequate measures, in line with international law, to prevent corruption as it creates an obstacle to development programming.

Looking at corruption through this lens, the prevention thereof becomes a human rights imperative.[47] At this point, a human rights-based approach to combatting corruption comes to the fore. In the following sections, it will be argued that this approach relies on certain fundamental human rights principles that can strengthen existing measures to combat corruption.

A HUMAN RIGHTS-BASED APPROACH: DEFINITION AND PRINCIPLES

The human rights-based approach to development emerged during the 1990s from the discourse on the relationship between human rights and development as two separate but highly interlinked fields. It has been recognised that these two areas share the same ultimate goal, the promotion of 'well-being and freedom, based on the dignity and equality of all people', by securing fundamental liberties (e.g. to be free from hunger) and providing enabling opportunities (for instance equal access to education).[48] Since then, numerous national and international development agencies (including governments) have adopted this approach.

A human rights-based approach 'puts human rights at the heart of human development'.[49] This approach finds its value in drawing attention 'to legitimate institutions and substantive parameters regulating the distribution of power and resources and the peaceful settlement of grievances'.[50] A human rights-based approach is also in line with Article 1 of the Declaration on the Right to Development, which holds that every person is entitled to an approach that takes account of their rights in development programming that affects them.[51] Although no single or exclusive definition of a human rights-based approach exists, some useful definitions can be drawn from the literature.[52]

The United Nations Office of the High Commissioner for Human Rights has defined this approach as 'a conceptual framework for the process of human development that is normatively based on international human rights standards and operationally directed to promoting and protecting human rights'.[53] De Beco relies on the definition of Hansen and Sano, which defines a human rights-based approach as a 'means of integrating human rights principles and aspirations into measures of planned and institutional change'.[54] Langford et al. argue that '[t]his conception draws from the multiple sources and understandings of human rights and tries to anchor them in an operational public policy context that is relevant for tackling development and poverty issues'.[55]

Under this approach, development claims are linked to the 'legal power of internationally recognised human rights'.[56] Therefore, this approach is based on the idea that states have legally binding obligations, which they voluntarily agreed to, under international, regional and national human rights law. Rights and entitlements are regarded as legitimate claims against the duty-bearer. The latter is then under a legal obligation to ensure that the right-holder is secure in their rights.[57] The objectives of a human rights-based approach are to identify rights-holders, their rights, corresponding duty-bearers, and their obligations and to enlarge the capacity of rights-holders to claim their rights from duty-bearers.[58] Many international and regional treaties, declarations and authoritative interpretations of rights have provided a clear and coherent framework from which to determine the legal content of rights, as well as corresponding obligations.[59]

According to Asjbørn Eide's tripartite framework of rights, states have the following duties under human rights law: (a) the obligation to respect, meaning to refrain from interfering in the enjoyment of human rights; (b) the obligation to protect, which requires states to ensure that the actions of others do not threaten rights and to bring violators of human rights to account; and (c) the obligation to fulfil which is divided into two separate duties. First is the obligation to facilitate access to rights fulfilment by establishing an enabling environment under which a right can be progressively realised. Second, the obligation to provide 'a specific right when an individual or group is unable, for reasons beyond their control, to realise the right themselves by means at their disposal'.[60]

Furthermore, in the case of socioeconomic rights, three obligations can be identified that are of immediate effect: (a) the obligation not to discriminate between groups of people in the realisation of rights; (b) the obligation to take deliberate steps towards the full realisation of all rights; and (c) the obligation to monitor the progress of steps taken and to have accessible accountability measures available to rights-holders in the case of violations of rights.[61] The entire set of obligations applicable to a country can be derived from national, regional, and international standards.[62]

Moreover, the approach calls for the realisation of economic, social, and cultural rights as the objective of development, and that human rights principles and standards are upheld throughout all phases of the development process. Human rights principles must also 'guide the formulation of policies, laws, strategies, and other appropriate measures in the administrative, budgetary, judicial, educational, political, social, and other fields' that impact development programming.[63]

The principles of a human rights-based approach are legally binding upon states to the extent that they are underscored by human rights contained in international and regional treaties to which a specific state is a party, as well as domestic law. These principles, which create an 'explicit normative framework',[64] are (a) equality and non-discrimination, (b) equal and meaningful participation, (c) empowerment, and (d) accountability and transparency. The Right to Development also underscores these principles.[65] Former United Nations High Commissioner for Human Rights, Navi Pillay, has stated that 'corruption violates these core principles' and conversely 'when upheld and implemented, are the most effective means to fight corruption'.[66] Due to the interrelated nature of the principles, each will be briefly discussed later. However, special attention will be paid to the principle of accountability as the most relevant principle to the problem at hand.

Equality and Non-discrimination

According to the Universal Declaration of Human Rights, all human beings are entitled to human rights, without discrimination on any ground, based merely on the fact that they are human.[67] Therefore, human rights must be guaranteed to all persons and fulfilled in an equal manner.[68] This principle ensures that the rights of the most marginalised and vulnerable are not overlooked and that inequalities are rectified. Adherence to this principle requires addressing unjust power relations and unfair distribution of resources as required under Article 8 of the Declaration on the Right to Development.[69] Corruption violate this principle as resources accrue to a few, which hampers the full realisation of the rights of all on a fair and equal basis. If the standards of the Declaration on the Right to Development are upheld, equal access to rights fulfilment and benefits from development opportunities will be ensured. The Right to Development requires states to ensure the fair and equal distribution of development opportunities and basic resources. When domestic resources unfairly and illegitimately accrue to few, states are under an obligation to adequately prevent and investigate such occurrences.

Participation

Article 2(3) of the Declaration on the Right to Development recognises the right of people to participate, in a free, active and meaningful manner, in development programming that affects them. Everyone should be able to participate on an equal basis without discrimination. Participation enables duty-bearers to become aware of the unique challenges faced by different parts of society and understand how to address them effectively. Moreover, popular participation is required at the formulation, implementation, and monitoring stages of national policies.[70]

To ensure meaningful participation, there is an obligation on the duty-bearer to build the capacities of rights-holders. This should include empowering people to address unequal structures and practices, such as IFFs.[71] The rights to freedom of expression and assembly are vital components of the principle of participation.[72] States must rely on interpretations of these rights in international and regional instruments to ensure it is adequately respected and protected.

By having their voice heard, disadvantaged communities can highlight the impact of corruption and advocate for their prevention as a priority for sustainable development and rights fulfilment. Civil society and watchdog organisations have a unique role to play in preventing and curbing corruption by providing a platform for the reporting of corruption and compiling reports that highlight areas of concern, the specific impact thereof, and recommendations for future prevention and investigation. State actors must provide freedom to these organisations to operate and include them in the formulation, implementation, and monitoring of national strategies to curb corruption.

Empowerment

Under a human rights-based approach, individuals are empowered to move from being beneficiaries with needs to be met to rights-holders with legitimate claims that can be enforced through accountability measures. This is based on the notion that poverty is not merely a lack of access to resources and social services, but is exasperated by issues of disempowerment and powerlessness.[73] Under this principle, people can become agents of change and influence public policy.[74] This principle is fundamental in the fight against corruption. It enables the disadvantaged to claim the fulfilment of the various obligations by duty-bearers outlined in this chapter and adhere to the duty of accountability and due diligence in managing domestic resources (which will be elaborated on below).

Accountability

Human rights instruments provide clearly defined and agreed-upon rights and rights-holders, as well as corresponding duties and duty-bearers. When development is linked to human rights, development challenges can be addressed through the entirety of the international, regional, and national human rights frameworks.[75] Domestic law (and therefore the extent to which international and regional human rights law has been translated into national human rights law) provides rights-holders with the most accessible accountability measures.

Langford et al. argue that under a human rights-based approach the non-fulfilment of rights is understood as 'the *failure* of the duty-bearer'. As rights-holders, individuals are empowered to call on duty-bearers to '*change* its behaviour' or to take steps to develop 'the necessary *capacity* to realise its duties'.[76] States' obligations to respect, promote, protect, and fulfil human rights include the duty to address hindrances to development that can be linked to violations of their human rights obligations. When challenges to development problems, such as the lack of resources due to corruption, are reformulated as violations of human rights, it becomes a legal obligation of the state to rectify them.

Under a human rights-based approach, empowered rights-holders can use local political, administrative, judicial, or quasi-judicial mechanisms to hold states accountable to their human rights and development obligations.[77] These mechanisms include legal enforcement via courts, international reporting obligations, parliamentary oversight, and pressure from independent media and non-governmental organisations.[78] National and international human rights monitoring bodies can also be approached to hold states accountable.[79] A human rights-based approach requires that all available accountability and redress measures be equally available to all. Where necessary, the state must build the capacity of rights-holders to make use of these measures.[80]

The precise content of human rights and their corresponding obligations can be found in treaties, interpretations by domestic courts, authoritative interpretations of rights, recommendations by treaty monitoring bodies, working groups, special rapporteurs, and so on.[81] The following section will explore some of the more relevant treaties that outline the obligations of states as it relates to addressing corruption which can be relied upon in line with the principle of accountability as outlined.

International Covenant on Economic, Social, and Cultural Rights

As mentioned, Article 2 of CESCR places the obligation on states:

> to *take steps*, individually and through international assistance and co-operation, especially economic and technical, to the *maximum of its available resources*, with a view to *achieving progressively the full realisation* of the rights

> recognised in the present Covenant *by all appropriate means*, including particularly the adoption of legislative measures. (my emphasis)

This requires states to be diligent in employing all their accessible resources towards achieving the rights contained in the Covenant. As a general duty, states must adopt legislation, policies, and practices that actively work towards preventing corruption by their agents and or third parties, especially when it comes to the provision of social services.[82] Suppose a state fails in its due diligence over the use of available resources, and resources are illegally diverted. In that case, it can be viewed as a violation of the state's duty to protect the enjoyment of rights, which includes the right to sovereignty over resources as part of the Right to Development.[83] This is also in accordance with the Maastricht Guidelines on Violations of Economic, Social, and Cultural Rights.[84] This obligation places the duty on states to do everything within their capabilities to prevent resource losses via corruption. This duty can be outlined as follows:

> (a) Governments must mobilise domestic resources to their utmost ability; (b) government expenditures must be efficient and effective; (c) *failure to tackle corruption constitutes a failure to comply with the obligation*; (d) funds earmarked in the budget for economic, social and cultural rights must not be diverted to non-economic, social and cultural rights areas; (e) funds earmarked for economic, social and cultural rights must be fully expended for that purpose.[85] (my emphasis)

Furthermore, under the duty to progressively realise rights, states must address all harmful practices that constitute an unjustified decrease in public expenditure (which can happen as a result of IFFs and/or corruption) aimed at the fulfilment of economic and social rights that form part of the Right to Development.[86] Lastly, the duty of employing all appropriate means to realise rights includes adopting measures and legislation to combat the theft and or mismanagement of state resources.[87] The Special Rapporteur on the Right to Food, Jean Ziegler, argues that the obligation to protect includes a duty to fight corruption. This duty rests on all states party to CESCR.[88] Another element of the responsibility to protect is the duty of states to adequately investigate and prosecute claims of corruption which can also form part of the duty to employ all appropriate means.[89]

Any violation of the responsibilities outlined above and thus the rights contained in CESCR can be brought before domestic courts, national human rights organisations and Committee on ESCR to oblige states to fulfil their legally binding human rights obligations.

United Nations Convention against Corruption

The Convention states that 'a comprehensive and multidisciplinary approach is required to prevent and combat corruption effectively'.[90] It places the obligation on all states to prevent and eradicate corruption.[91]

One of the aims of the Convention is to promote accountability and proper management of public resources.[92] Transparency is crucial to ensure the effectiveness of accountability measures and is emphasised in articles 5, 10, and 13 of the United Nations Convention against Corruption. Article 5(1) obliges state parties to

> develop and implement or maintain effective, coordinated anti-corruption policies that promote the participation of society and reflect the principles of the rule of law, proper management of public affairs and public property, integrity, transparency and accountability.

The Convention places several obligations on states to be employed to prevent corruption. For instance, Article 6(1) requires state parties to establish bodies that work towards eradicating corruption. Article 8 requires the adoption and implementation of codes of conduct for public officials, while Article 35 of the Convention requires states to provide effective and equally accessible remedies to victims of corruption. States' adherence to the obligations contained in the Convention is assessed via a peer review mechanism and periodic reporting to the Conference of State Parties.[93]

The measures outlined in the Convention can create legally binding obligations to the extent that they are translated into domestic law. As already outlined, the prevention of corruption and the subsequent loss of resources is essential in realising the Right to Development. Moreover, adherence to the Convention's provisions carries political value that can strengthen advocacy for more robust accountability measures. This will be elaborated later.

Other Relevant Human Rights Instruments

The African Union Convention on Preventing and Combatting Corruption[94] provides several provisions similar to the United Nations Convention against Corruption. With respect to space limitations, these will not be repeated. The African Union Convention's objective is to '[p]romote and strengthen the development in Africa by each State Party, of mechanisms required to prevent, detect, punish, and eradicate corruption and related offences in the public and private sectors'.[95] Adherence to the provisions of the Convention by state parties is monitored through the Advisory Board on Corruption.

Similar provisions related to accountability measures can also be found in the Addis Ababa Action Agenda, the Third International Conference on Financing for Development outcome document. It is stated that this Agenda is 'devoted to the financing for development, with the fight against IFFs at the heart of its strategy'.[96] Under the Agenda, curbing IFFs is recognised as 'an explicit priority'.[97] It is argued that the same priority can be read from the 2030 Agenda for Sustainable Development and the Declaration on the Right to Development.[98] The latter also provides for many other obligations that rest on states regarding the Right to Development, some of which have already been discussed earlier.

All the instruments highlighted above can play a crucial role in realising the Right to Development. It is argued that under the principle of accountability, citizens are in the position to hold their states accountable when they fail to fulfil their obligations outlined in these instruments. Therefore, if it can be demonstrated that an individual state does not have adequate measures to prevent corruption, then citizens can hold states accountable for the non-realisation of rights, particularly the Right to Development.

VALUE ADDED BY A HUMAN RIGHTS-BASED APPROACH

The United Nations Human Rights Council has acknowledged the need for a human rights-based approach to eliminate corruption.[99] Following a human rights-based approach can hold many advantages.[100] However, only those advantages most pertinent to this discussion will be briefly outlined below.

Creation of Legally Binding Obligations

According to the High Level Panel on Illicit Financial Flows from Africa, curbing corruption requires the political will of governments.[101] However, under a human rights-based approach, it becomes the legal responsibility of the state to address corruption that can hamper the fulfilment of human rights obligations. When development objectives are framed in terms of human rights, any failure to achieve these objectives can constitute a violation of human rights.

Moreover, as the Right to Development has legal recognition under the African Charter on Human and Peoples' Rights (article 22), cases can be brought before the African Court and African Commission on Human and Peoples' Rights to mandate states to keep to their human rights commitments as it relates to this right (which includes the duty of due diligence towards domestic resources). This is also true for the full spectrum of human rights that underscores the Right to Development.

A human rights-based approach provides accountability measures and remedies at the international, regional, and domestic levels that meet international standards based on human rights commitments, which states have voluntarily agreed to. This ensures transparency and can expose alternative priorities that undermine development.[102] Corruption reproduces itself when the powerful do not face any consequences for their actions, and the disadvantaged cannot demand the protection of their rights.[103] Moreover, when accountability measures are continuously implemented and accessible, they can deter corruption and IFFs.[104]

Accountability measures that can be employed include those provided for under CESCR, the United Nations Convention Against Corruption and the African Union Convention on Preventing and Combatting Corruption. The African Court and Commission on Human and Peoples' Rights and domestic courts can also be approached to order states to fulfil their human rights obligations that are contravened due to corruption and to redress violations of human rights.

The human rights-based approach provides an explicit framework of the content of rights and duties. This further strengthens advocacy and accountability measures, especially where the content of these rights and duties have been fleshed out in authoritative interpretations of rights. This includes positive measures duty-bearers can and should employ to ensure the fulfilment of rights.[105] These measures can also be employed to monitor whether states have put in place effective measures to prevent corruption.

Political Value and Strengthened Advocacy Measures

As already mentioned, one of the strengths of a human rights-based approach lies in its advocacy value. By framing corruption in terms of human rights violations, it can add value in placing the prevention of corruption prominently on the agendas of international and regional forums.[106] Moreover, political pressure can be strengthened by bringing a 'human face' to the impacts of corruption.[107] Advocacy for curbing corruption can also rely on recommendations from international human rights mechanisms that identify areas of concern in fulfilling rights.[108] Country- and /or rights-specific reports from United Nations treaty bodies and Special Rapporteurs that enjoy a significant degree of social and political legitimacy can assist in identifying human rights challenges and violations that can impede development and pressure states to implement preventive measures.[109] This includes reports on the harmful impact of corruption. Even though recommendations resulting from these processes are non-binding, it is widely acknowledged that they carry significant moral and political value.[110]

Looking at corruption through a Right to Development lens creates a vital advocacy tool to push states towards creating an enabling environment for development as required under the Declaration, which requires doing everything within its power to prevent corruption.[111] Reports from United Nations bodies and international and national non-governmental organisations can be employed as a basis to show that a respective country does not have adequate measures in place to curb corruption and that this results in challenges in the realisation of the Right to Development within the country. These reports can be used to garner international support for a call for more effective preventive measures or as a basis for litigation against a state. Furthermore, a human rights-based approach places particular focus on eliminating inequalities in the distribution of wealth and resources.[112] This allows for the identification of disadvantaged groups or rights that have not been fully realised due to resource constraints.[113] Empowering individuals to demand the realisation of their rights limits the ability of the powerful to get away with corrupt practices. The human rights framework also provides a shared language for practitioners from different areas (human rights, development, economics, political studies, etc) to come together to eliminate corruption.[114]

Other Advantages

Despite their legal and political value, human rights also imply a moral duty. Based on the idea of respect for human dignity, the human rights framework provides a set of moral values.[115] These normative standards can form the basis 'for implementing long-term, durable, sustainable, and broad legal and institutional reforms' necessary to combat corruption.[116]

Moreover, under the human rights framework, development related to the fulfilment of rights is a global responsibility.[117] Therefore, accountability for corruption resulting in IFFs is extended to other states and transnational actors such as international donors, inter-governmental organisations and international non-governmental organisations.[118] The Maastricht Principles on Extraterritorial Obligations can be employed to determine the obligations of respective states in preventing or redressing IFFs.[119] The responsibility of international co-operation in combatting IFFs has repeatedly been recognised.[120] This is a significant responsibility in its own right, but unfortunately, it falls outside this article's scope. It suffices to say that this responsibility is also strengthened under a human rights-based approach. Lastly, a human rights-based approach towards repatriating and reallocating stolen assets can also ensure that these funds are not again mismanaged or misappropriated.[121]

CONCLUSION

Corruption have caused significant damage to African countries, and the numbers related to lost revenue are astounding. The most evident impact of corruption is the loss of resources that could have been employed for social services and development. Moreover, corruption impedes the ability of states to utilise their maximum available resources in realising economic and social rights. Under the current landscape, it has been highlighted that it is essential for Africa to generate the resources necessary for development on the continent. Corruption creates a gap between the state's resources and those required for domestic development and rights fulfilment. This has a particular impact on the Right to Development, as it encompasses most other human rights, particularly the rights to self-determination and sovereignty over one's own natural resources.

This article argued for a human rights-based approach to be employed in curbing corruption. A human rights-based approach relies on the principles and legal obligations of states as contained in international, regional, and national human rights instruments. The objectives of a human rights-based approach are to identify rights-holders, their rights, corresponding duty-bearers, and their obligations and to enlarge the capacity of rights-holders to claim their rights from duty-bearers.

Various human rights instruments obligate states to be accountable and transparent in using domestic resources. The principle of accountability underscores this as part of the human rights-based approach. Under this principle, states' obligations to respect, promote, protect, and fulfil human rights include the duty to address hindrances to development that can be linked to violations of their human rights obligations. Impediments to development, such as the impact of corruption, are reformulated as human rights violations, which states are legally obliged to rectify. Moreover, empowered rights-holders are provided with a platform to claim redress and demand the fulfilment of their rights. This article provided an overview of some human rights instruments that provide avenues to hold states accountable to do everything within their capacity to prevent corruption.

Following a human rights-based approach in the fight against corruption holds several advantages, the most important of which is the creation of legally binding obligations on states. This empowers the most vulnerable and provides them with an avenue to hold states accountable for the failure to create an enabling environment for realising the Right to Development. Another strength of this approach lies in its advocacy value. By framing IFFs in terms of human rights violations, political pressure can be put on states to adopt effective accountability and due diligence measures.

Therefore, it is submitted that to ensure sustainable development for all on the African continent, employing a human rights-based approach to curbing corruption is crucial. The tools for the use of this approach are already in place. What is needed is for local, regional, and international organisations in the field of human rights and development (including government departments, non-governmental organisations, and individual human rights activists) to spread awareness and assist the most vulnerable in demanding the fulfilment of their legally recognised rights.

NOTES

1. High Level Panel on Illicit Financial Flows from Africa, *Track it! Stop it! Get it! Illicit financial flows* (Commissioned by the African Union Commission/ United Nations Economic Commission for Africa Conference of African Ministers on Finance, Planning and Economic Development, 2015), 13.
2. 2030 Agenda for Sustainable Development: Transforming our World (2015).
3. Addis Ababa Action Agenda of the Third International Conference on Financing for Development (2015), para 23.
4. 'Goals', Sustainable Development, United Nations Department of Economic and Social Affairs, accessed 25 November 2022, https://sustainabledevelopment.un.org/sdg16; Serges D. Kamga, 'Illicit financial flows, asset recovery, the power game and the right to development in Africa,' *Comparative and International Law Journal of Southern Africa* 51, no. 2 (2019): 194.
5. 'Economic development in Africa: tackling illicit financial flows for sustainable development in Africa', United Nations Conference on Trade and Development, 2020, para 19, https://unctad.org/system/files/official-document/aldcafrica2020_en.pdf.
6. High Level Panel on Illicit Financial Flows from Africa, *Track it! Stop it! Get it! Illicit financial flows*, 13.
7. High Level Panel on Illicit Financial Flows from Africa, *Track it! Stop it! Get it! Illicit financial flows*, 13.
8. Marc Herkenrath, 'Illicit financial flows and their developmental impacts: an overview', *International Development Policy* (2014): para 2 https://doi.org/10.4000/poldev.1863. See also OECD, '*Illicit financial flows from developing countries: measuring OECD responses*' (2014), 15, https://www.oecd.org/corruption/illicit_financial_flows_from_developing_countries.pdf.
9. Herkenrath, 'Illicit financial flows and their developmental impacts: an overview,' 2.

10. Joseph Spanjers and Håkon F. Foss, *Illicit financial flows and development indices: 2008–2012* (Global Financial Integrity, 2015), 30–33, http://www.gfintegrity.org/wp-content/uploads/2015/05/Illicit-Financial-Flows-and-Development-Indices-2008-2012.pdf.

11. 'Illicit financial flows, human rights, and the post-2015 development agenda', Global Financial Integrity & ERI Institute, October 2014, 1, https://www.gfintegrity.org/wp-content/uploads/2016/12/IFFs-HR-Post-2015DevAgenda.pdf.

12. Global Financial Integrity & ERI Institute, 'Illicit financial flows,' 9.

13. United Nations Convention against Corruption (2003).

14. Art 1(a).

15. 'SDG Indicator Metadata,' UNSTATS, last updated March 31, 2023, https://unstats.un.org/sdgs/metadata/files/Metadata-16-04-01.pdf.

16. UNSTATS, 'SDG Indicator Metadata.'

17. UNSTATS, 'SDG Indicator Metadata.'

18. UNSTATS, 'SDG Indicator Metadata;' High Level Panel on Illicit Financial Flows from Africa, *Track it! Stop it! Get it! Illicit financial flows*, 24; OECD, '*Illicit financial flows from developing countries: measuring OECD responses*,' 16.

19. UNSTATS, 'SDG Indicator Metadata.'

20. UNSTATS, 'SDG Indicator Metadata.'

21. UNSTATS, 'SDG Indicator Metadata.'

22. UNSTATS, 'SDG Indicator Metadata.'

23. UNSTATS, 'SDG Indicator Metadata.'

24. World Bank, *Helping countries combat corruption: The role of the World Bank* (World Bank, 1997), 8. See also Sarah Bracking, 'Political development and corruption: why "right here, right now!"?,' in *Corruption and development*, ed. Sarah Bracking (Hampshire: Palgrave Macmillan, 2007), 3–4.

25. Kolawole Olaniyan, *Corruption and human rights law in Africa* (Oxford: Hart Publishing, 2014), 25, 51.

26. Olaniyan, *Corruption and human rights law in Africa*, 20.

27. Cephas Lumina, *The negative impact of the non-repatriation of funds of illicit origin on the enjoyment of human rights. Final report of the Independent Expert on the effects of foreign debt and other related international financial obligations of States on the full enjoyment of all human rights, particularly economic, social and cultural rights, Cephas Lumina* (United Nations Human Rights Council, 2014), 15.

28. Raoul Wallenberg Institute, *The nexus between anti-corruption and human rights: a review by the Raoul Wallenberg Institute of Human Rights and Humanitarian Law* (Raoul Wallenberg Institute, 2018), executive summary. See also Olaniyan, *Corruption and human rights law in Africa*, 115.

29. Kamga, 'Illicit financial flows,' 195; Global Financial Integrity, 'Illicit Financial Flows;' OECD, *Measuring OECD responses to illicit financial flows*, 15.

30. OECD, *Measuring OECD responses to illicit financial flows*, 15.

31. 'Combatting corruption,' World Bank, March 15, 2023, https://www.worldbank.org/en/topic/governance/brief/combating-corruption#:~:text=The%20World%20Bank%20Group's%20approach,risks%20that%20have%20been%20identified.

See also Evangelos A. Mantzaris, 'Corruption as a violation of basic human rights in South Africa and Russia,' *African Journal of Public Affairs* 9, no. 8 (2017): 18–19.

32. Leslie Holmes, *Corruption: a very short introduction* (Oxford: Oxford University Press, 2015), 25; Cecily Rose, 'The application of human rights law to private sector complicity in governmental corruption,' *Leiden Journal of International Law* 24, no. 3 (2011): 715; Bhumika Muchhala, *The right to development and illicit financial flows: realizing the Sustainable Development Goals and financing for development* (United Nations Human Rights Council, 2018), para 23. These include the Universal Declaration of Human Rights (1948), art 1; International Covenant on Civil and Political Rights (1966), art 2; International Covenant on Economic, Social and Cultural Rights (CESCR) (1966), art 2.

33. See Muchhala, *The right to development and illicit financial flows*, para 33.

34. Lumina, *The negative impact of the non-repatriation of funds*, para 24.

35. Muchhala, *The right to development and illicit financial flows*, para 5.

36. Muchhala, *The right to development and illicit financial flows*, para 35.

37. Gerard E. Kamdem Kamga, 'Linkages between illicit financial flows and the non-realisation of the right to development in Africa,' *Comparative and International Law Journal of Southern Africa* 51, no. 2 (2019): 171.

38. Vienna Declaration and Programme of Action (1993).

39. African Charter on Human and Peoples' Rights (1981).

40. Kamga, 'Illicit financial flows,' 209.

41. Magdalena Sepùlveda Carmona, *Report of the Special Rapporteur on extreme poverty and human rights, Magdalena Sepùlveda Carmona* (United Nations Human Rights Council, 2014), para 19. See also Muchhala, *The right to development and illicit financial flows*, para 47.

42. Muchhala, *The right to development and illicit financial flows*, para 54. See also Kamga, 'Illicit financial flows,' 211.

43. Muchhala, *The right to development and illicit financial flows*, paras 50–51.

44. Kamga, 'Illicit financial flows,' 196.

45. Muchhala, *The right to development and illicit financial flows*, para 46.

46. Art. 3.

47. Muchhala, *The right to development and illicit financial flows*, summary.

48. United Nations Office of the High Commissioner for Human Rights (OHCHR), *Frequently asked questions on a human rights-based approach to development cooperation* (Geneva: United Nations Publications, 2006), 7.

49. Emilie Filmer-Wilson, 'The human rights-based approach to development: the right to water,' *Netherlands Quarterly of Human Rights* 23, no. 2 (2005): 213.

50. Mac Darrow and Amparo Tomas, 'Power, capture, and conflict: a call for human rights accountability in development cooperation,' *Human Rights Quarterly* 27, no. 2 (2005): 490.

51. Richard F Oppong, 'Trade and human rights: a perspective for agents of trade policy using a rights-based approach to development,' *African Human Rights Law Journal* 6, no. 1 (2006): 126.

52. Allessandra Lundström Sarelin, 'Human rights-based approaches to development cooperation, HIV/AIDS, and food security,' *Human Rights Quarterly* 29, nr.

2 (2007): 475; Varun Gauri and Siri Gloppen, 'Human rights-based approaches to development: concepts, evidence and policy,' *Polity* 44, no. 4 (2012): 486.

53. OHCHR, *Frequently asked questions on a human rights-based approach to development cooperation*, 15. See also Malcolm Langford, Andy Sumner, and Alicia Ely Yamin, 'Introduction: situating the debate,' in *The Millennium Development Goals and human rights: past, present and future*, ed. Malcolm Langford, Andy Sumner, and Alicia Ely Yamin (New York: Cambridge University Press, 2013), 25.

54. Gauthier De Beco, 'The interplay between human rights and development the other way around: the emerging use of quantitative tools for measuring the progressive realisation of economic, social and cultural rights,' *Human Rights and International Legal Discourse* 4, no. 2 (2010): 268.

55. Langford et al., 'Introduction: situating the debate,' 24. See also Victor Abramovich, 'The rights-based approach in development: policies and strategies,' *CEPAL Review* 88 (April 2006): 33.

56. Paul Nelson, 'Human rights, the Millennium Development Goals, and the future of development cooperation,' *World Development* 35, no. 12 (2007): 2042. See also Filmer-Wilson, 'The human rights-based approach to development,' 230–32.

57. Caroline Moser et al., *To claim our rights: livelihood security, human rights and sustainable development* (London: Overseas Development Institute, 2001), 10. See Siobhan McInerney-Lankford, 'International development actors and human rights,' in *The Millennium Development Goals and human rights: past, present and future*, ed. Malcolm Langford, Andy Sumner, and Alicia Ely Yamin (New York: Cambridge University Press, 2013), 179.

58. 'The human rights-based approach to development cooperation: towards a common understanding among UN agencies,' United Nations Development Group, accessed October 13, 2003, https://unsdg.un.org/resources/human-rights-based-approach-development-cooperation-towards-common-understanding-among-un.

59. Filmer-Wilson, 'The human rights-based approach to development,' 216, 230–32; Philip Alston, *A human rights perspective on the Millennium Development Goals* (Millennium Project Task Force on Poverty and Economic Development, 2004), para 106.

60. Darrow and Tomas, 'Power, capture and conflict,' 529–30; OHCHR, *Frequently asked questions on a human rights-based approach to development cooperation*, 2.

61. OHCHR, *Frequently asked questions on a human rights-based approach to development cooperation*, 3.

62. Alston, *A human rights perspective*, para 103.

63. Darrow and Tomas, 'Power, capture and conflict,' 498.

64. OHCHR, *Principles and guidelines for a human rights approach to poverty reduction strategies* (OHCHR, 2006), para 16.

65. Muchhala, *The right to development and illicit financial flows*, para 36. See also Lumina, *The negative impact of the non-repatriation of funds*, paras 29–34.

66. 'The human rights case against corruption,' OHCHR, last updated March 27, 2013, https://www.ohchr.org/EN/NewsEvents/Pages/HRCaseAgainstCorruption.aspx. See also Olaniyan, *Corruption and human rights law in Africa*, 65–66.

67. Preamble, art 1.

68. Moser et al., *To claim our rights*, 19;

69. OHCHR, *Frequently asked questions on a human rights-based approach to development cooperation*, 8.

70. 'Limburg principles on the implementation of the International Covenant on Economic, Social and Cultural Rights,' ESCR-Net, accessed November 25, 2021, para 11, https://www.escr-net.org/resources/limburg-principles-implementation-international-covenant-economic-social-&-cultural.

71. OHCHR, *Draft guidelines: a human rights approach to poverty reduction strategies* (OHCHR, 2002), para 86.

72. United Nations Development Programme (UNDP), *Human rights and the Millennium Development Goals: making the link* (UNDP, 2006), 21.

73. OHCHR, *Draft guidelines*, para 5; Abramovich, 'The rights-based approach in development,' 38.

74. Alexandre A. Frediani, 'Sen's capability approach as a framework to the practice of development,' *Development in Practice* 20, no. 2 (2010): 182.

75. Filmer-Wilson, 'The human rights-based approach to development,' 216.

76. M. Langford et al., 'Introduction: situating the debate,' 24.

77. Darrow and Tomas, 'Power, capture and conflict,' 512. See also Abramovich, 'The rights-based approach in development,' 45.

78. Siobhan McInerney-Lankford, 'International development actors and human rights,' in *The Millennium Development Goals and human rights: past, present and future*, ed. Malcolm Langford, Andy Sumner, and Alicia Ely Yamin (New York: Cambridge University Press, 2013), 164.

79. UNDP, *Human rights and the Millennium Development Goals*, 24; Philip Alston, 'Ships passing in the night: the current state of the human rights and development debate seen through the lens of the Millennium Development Goals,' *Human Rights Quarterly* 27, no. 3 (2005): 813.

80. OHCHR, *Frequently asked questions on a human rights-based approach to development cooperation*, 24; UNDP, *Human rights and the Millennium Development Goals*, 24.

81. OHCHR, *Frequently asked questions on a human rights-based approach to development cooperation*, 3.

82. Maastricht Guidelines on Violations of Economic, Social, and Cultural Rights (1997), para 14(g); United Nations Committee on Economic, Social and Cultural Rights (Committee on ESCR), *General comment 14: The right to the highest attainable standard of health (art 12)* (OHCHR, 2000), para 52.

83. International Council on Human Rights Policy (ICHRP) and Transparency International, *Corruption and human rights: making the connection* (Geneva: International Council on Human Rights Policy, 2009), 25.

84. See para 14(g) and para 15(e).

85. Lumina, *The negative impact of the non-repatriation of funds*, para 19.

86. Committee on ESCR, *General Comment 3: the nature of states parties' obligations (Art 2, Para 1, of the Covenant)* (OHCHR, 1990); Rose, 'The application of human rights law,' 718–19; Boersma, *Corruption*, 232–33.

87. United Nations Human Rights Committee, *CCPR General Comment 27: article 12 (freedom of movement)* (OHCHR, 1999), secs 12, 19; Martine Boersma, *Corruption: A violation of human rights and a crime under international law?* (Cambridge: Intersentia Limited, 2012), 228, 230, 233.

88. See Jean Ziegler, *Report of the Special Rapporteur on the right to food* (United Nations Human Rights Council, 2001), para 28. See also Boersma, *Corruption*, 157, 160–61.

89. ICHRP & Transparency International, *Corruption and Human Rights*, 42. See also *Glenister v President of the Republic of South Africa & Others* 2011 (3) SA 347 (CC) paras 175–76, 198.

90. Preamble.

91. Preamble.

92. Art 1(c).

93. See art 63.

94. African Union Convention on Preventing and Combatting Corruption (2003).

95. Art 2(1).

96. Kamdem Kamga, 'Linkages between illicit financial flows,' 179.

97. Muchhala, *The right to development and illicit financial flows*, para 85.

98. Muchhala, *The right to development and illicit financial flows*, para 91.

99. Muchhala, *The right to development and illicit financial flows*, para 34.

100. See for instance Samuel Hickey and Diana Mitlin, eds., *Rights-based approaches to development: exploring the potential and pitfalls* (Sterling: Kumarian Press, 2009); Paul Gready, 'Rights-based approaches to development: What is the value-added?' *Development in Practice* 18, no. 6 (2008): 735–47.

101. High Level Panel on Illicit Financial Flows from Africa, *Track it! Stop it! Get it! Illicit financial flows*, 3.

102. Alicia Ely Yamin, 'Will we take suffering seriously? Reflections on what applying a human rights framework to health means and why we should care,' *Health and Human Rights* 10, no. 1 (2008): 48. See also OHCHR, *Frequently asked questions on a human rights-based approach to development cooperation*, 17.

103. ICHRP & Transparency International, *Corruption and Human Rights*, 5.

104. ICHRP & Transparency International, *Corruption and Human Rights*, 6.

105. Alston, 'Ships passing in the night,' 823.

106. ICHRP & Transparency International, *Corruption and Human Rights*, 6.

107. Olaniyan, *Corruption and human rights law in Africa*, 14, 114.

108. Simone Cecchini and Francesco Notti, 'Millennium Development Goals and human rights: faraway, so close?,' *Journal of Human Development and Capabilities: A Multi-Disciplinary Journal for People-Centred Development* 12, no. 1 (2011): 123.

109. Abramovich, 'The rights-based approach in development,' 36. For examples of the contributions that these processes can make see Boersma, *Corruption*, 135–74.

110. Boersma, *Corruption*, 146.

111. Muchhala, *The right to development and illicit financial flows*, para 39.

112. Guido Schmidt-Traub, 'The Millennium Development Goals and human rights-based approaches: moving towards a shared approach,' *The International Journal of Human Rights* 13, no. 1 (2009): 79.

113. Oppong, 'Trade and human rights,' 131–32; Cecchini and Notti, 'Millennium Development Goals and human rights,' 123.

114. Paul Gready, 'Reasons to be cautious about evidence and evaluation: rights-based approaches to development and the emerging culture of evaluation,' *Journal of Human Rights Practice* 1, no. 3 (2009): 387. See also OHCHR, *Frequently asked questions on a human rights-based approach to development cooperation*, 19–20.

115. Olaniyan, *Corruption and human rights law in Africa*, 348.

116. Olaniyan, *Corruption and human rights law in Africa*, 13.

117. OHCHR, *Draft guidelines*, para 13.

118. Andrea Cornwall and Celestine Nyamu-Musembi, 'Putting the "rights-based approach" to development into perspective,' *Third World Quarterly* 25, no. 8 (2004): 1417.

119. Olaniyan, *Corruption and human rights law in Africa*, 174. See FIAN International, *Maastricht Principles on Extraterritorial Obligations of States in the Area* (FIAN, 2013).

120. See for example Kamga, 'Illicit financial flows;' Muchhala, *The right to development and illicit financial flows*, para 75.

121. Lumina, *The negative impact of the non-repatriation of funds*, para 30.

BIBLIOGRAPHY

2030 Agenda for Sustainable Development: Transforming our World. 2015.

Abramovich, Victor. "The rights-based approach in development: policies and strategies." *CEPAL Review* 88 (April 2006): 33–48.

Addis Ababa Action Agenda of the Third International Conference on Financing for Development. 2015.

African Charter on Human and Peoples' Rights. 1981.

African Union Convention on Preventing and Combatting Corruption. 2003.

Alston, Phillip. *A human rights perspective on the Millennium Development Goals.* Millennium Project Task Force on Poverty and Economic Development, 2004.

Alston, Phillip. "Ships passing in the night: the current state of the human rights and development debate seen through the lens of the Millennium Development Goals." *Human Rights Quarterly* 27, no. 3 (2005): 755–829.

Boersma, Martine. *Corruption: a violation of human rights and a crime under international law?* Cambridge: Intersentia Limited, 2012.

Bracking, Sarah. "Political development and corruption: Why 'right here, right now!'?" In *Corruption and development*, edited by Sarah Bracking, 3–27. Hampshire: Palgrave Macmillan, 2007.

Cecchini, Simone and Notti, Francesco. "Millennium Development Goals and human rights: faraway, so close?" *Journal of Human Development and Capabilities: A Multi-Disciplinary Journal for People-Centred Development* 12, no. 1 (2011): 121–33.

Cornwall, Andrea and Nyamu-Musembi, Celestine. "Putting the 'rights-based approach' to development into perspective." *Third World Quarterly* 25, no. 8 (2004): 1415–37.

Darrow, Mac and Tomas, Amparo. "Power, capture, and conflict: a call for human rights accountability in development co-operation." *Human Rights Quarterly* 27, no. 2 (2005): 471–538.

De Beco, Gauthier. "The interplay between human rights and development the other way around: the emerging use of quantitative tools for measuring the progressive realisation of economic, social and cultural rights." *Human Rights and International Legal Discourse* 4, no. 2 (2010): 265–87.

Declaration on the Right to Development. 1986.

Ely Yamin, Alicia. "Will we take suffering seriously? Reflections on what applying a human rights framework to health means and why we should care." *Health and Human Rights* 10, no. 1 (2008): 45–63.

ESCR-Net. "Limburg principles on the implementation of the International Covenant on Economic, Social and Cultural Rights." Accessed November 25, 2021. https://www.escr-net.org/resources/limburg-principles-implementation-international-covenant-economic-social-&-cultural.

FIAN International. *Maastricht principles on extraterritorial obligations of states in the area.* FIAN, 2013.

Filmer-Wilson, Emilie. "The human rights-based approach to development: the right to water." *Netherlands Quarterly of Human Rights* 32, no. 1 (2005): 213–41.

Frediani, Alexandre A. "Sen's capability approach as a framework to the practice of development." *Development in Practice* 20, no. 2 (2010): 173–87.

Gauri, Varun and Gloppen, Siri. "Human rights-based approaches to development: concepts, evidence and policy." *Polity* 44, no. 4 (2012): 485–503.

Glenister v President of the Republic of South Africa & Others 2011 (3) SA 347 (CC).

Global Financial Integrity. "Illicit financial flows." Accessed November 25, 2021. https://gfintegrity.org/issue/illicit-financial-flows/.

Global Financial Integrity & ERI Institute. "Illicit financial flows, human rights, and the post-2015 development agenda." October 2014. https://www.gfintegrity.org/wp-content/uploads/2016/12/IFFs-HR-Post-2015DevAgenda.pdf.

Gready, Paul. "Rights-based approaches to development: what is the value-added?" *Development in Practice* 18, no. 6 (2008): 735–47.

Gready, Paul. "Reasons to be cautious about evidence and evaluation: rights-based approaches to development and the emerging culture of evaluation." *Journal of Human Rights Practice* 1, no. 3 (2009): 380–401.

Herkenrath, Marc. "Illicit financial flows and their developmental impacts: an overview." *International Development Policy* (2014). https://doi.org/10.4000/poldev.1863.

Hickey, Samuel and Mitlin, Diana, eds. *Rights-based approaches to development: exploring the potential and pitfalls.* Sterling: Kumarian Press, 2009.

High Level Panel on Illicit Financial Flows from Africa. *Track it! Stop it! Get it! Illicit financial flows.* Commissioned by the African Union Commission/United Nations Economic Commission for Africa Conference of African Ministers on Finance, Planning and Economic Development, 2015.

Holmes, Leslie. *Corruption: a very short introduction.* Oxford: Oxford University Press, 2015.

International Council on Human Rights Policy and Transparency International. *Corruption and human rights: making the connection.* Geneva: International Council on Human Rights Policy, 2009.

International Covenant on Civil and Political Rights. 1966.

International Covenant on Economic, Social and Cultural Rights. 1966.

Kamdem Kamga, Gerard E. "Linkages between illicit financial flows and the non-realisation of the right to development in Africa." *Comparative and International Law Journal of Southern Africa* 51, no. 2 (2019): 169–92.

Kamga, Serges D. "Illicit financial flows, asset recovery, the power game and the right to development in Africa." *Comparative and International Law Journal of Southern Africa* 51, no. 2 (2019): 193–214.

Langford, Malcolm, Sumner, Andy, and Ely Yamin, Alicia. "Introduction: situating the debate." In *The Millennium Development Goals and human rights: past, present and future,* edited by Malcolm Langford, Andy Sumner, and Alicia Ely Yamin, 1–36. New York: Cambridge University Press, 2013.

Lumina, Cephas. *The negative impact of the non-repatriation of funds of illicit origin on the enjoyment of human rights. Final report of the Independent Expert on the effects of foreign debt and other related international financial obligations of States on the full enjoyment of all human rights, particularly economic, social and cultural rights, Cephas Lumina.* United Nations Human Rights Council, 2014.

Lundström Sarelin, Alessandra. "Human rights-based approaches to development co-operation, HIV/AIDS, and food security." *Human Rights Quarterly* 29, no. 2 (2007): 460–88.

Maastricht Guidelines on Violations of Economic, Social, and Cultural Rights. 1997.

Mantzaris, Evangelos A. "Corruption as a violation of basic human rights in South Africa and Russia." *African Journal of Public Affairs* 9, no. 8 (2017): 15–30.

McInerney-Lankford, Siobhan. "International development actors and human rights." In *The Millennium Development Goals and human rights: past, present and future,* edited by Malcolm Langford, Andy Sumner, and Alicia Ely Yamin, 160–208. New York: Cambridge University Press, 2013.

Moser, Caroline et al. *To claim our rights: livelihood security, human rights and sustainable development.* London: Overseas Development Institute, 2001.

Muchhala, Bhumika. *The right to development and illicit financial flows: realising the Sustainable Development Goals and financing for development.* United Nations Human Rights Council, 2018.

Nelson, Paul. "Human rights, the Millennium Development Goals, and the future of development cooperation." *World Development* 35, no. 12 (2007): 2041–55.

Olaniyan, Kolawole. *Corruption and human rights law in Africa.* Oxford: Hart Publishing, 2014.

Oppong, Richard F. "Trade and human rights: a perspective for agents of trade policy using a rights-based approach to development." *African Human Rights Law Journal* 6, nr. 1 (2006): 123–45.

Organisation for Economic Co-operation and Development. *Measuring OECD responses to illicit financial flows.* Paris: OECD, 2013.

Organisation for Economic Co-operation and Development. *Illicit financial flows from developing countries: measuring OECD responses.* 2014. https://www.oecd.org/corruption/Illicit_Financial_Flows_from_Developing_Countries.pdf.

Raoul Wallenberg Institute. *The nexus between anti-corruption and human rights: a review by the Raoul Wallenberg Institute of Human Rights and Humanitarian Law.* Raoul Wallenberg Institute, 2018.

Rose, Cecily. "The application of human rights law to private sector complicity in governmental corruption." *Leiden Journal of International Law* 24, no. 3 (2011): 715–40.

Schmidt-Traub, Guido. "The Millennium Development Goals and human rights-based approaches: moving towards a shared approach." *The International Journal of Human Rights* 13, no. 1 (2009): 72–85.

Sepùlveda Carmona, Magdalena. *Report of the Special Rapporteur on extreme poverty and human rights, Magdalena Sepùlveda Carmona.* United Nations Human Rights Council, 2014.

Spanjers, Jospeh and Foss, Håkon F. *Illicit financial flows and development indices: 2008–2012.* Global Financial Integrity, 2015.

United Nations Committee on Economic, Social and Cultural Rights. *General Comment 3: the nature of states parties' obligations (Art 2, Para 1, of the Covenant).* OHCHR, 1990.

United Nations Committee on Economic, Social and Cultural Rights. *General Comment 14: the right to the highest attainable standard of health (art 12).* OHCHR, 2000.

United Nations Conference on Trade and Development. "Economic development in Africa: tackling illicit financial flows for sustainable development in Africa." 2020. https://unctad.org/system/files/official-document/aldcafrica2020_en.pdf.

United Nations Convention against Corruption. 2003.

United Nations Department of Economic and Social Affairs. "Goals." Sustainable Development. Accessed November 25, 2022. https://sustainabledevelopment.un.org/sdg16.

United Nations Development Group. "The human rights-based approach to development co-operation: towards a common understanding among UN agencies." Accessed October 13, 2022. https://unsdg.un.org/resources/human-rights-based-approach-development-cooperation-towards-common-understanding-among-un.

United Nations Development Programme. *Human rights and the Millennium Development Goals: making the link.* UNDP, 2006.

United Nations Human Rights Committee. *CCPR General Comment 27: article 12 (freedom of movement)*. OHCHR, 1999.

United Nations Office of the High Commissioner for Human Rights. *Draft guidelines: a human rights approach to poverty reduction strategies*. OHCHR, 2002.

United Nations Office of the High Commissioner for Human Rights. *Frequently asked questions on a human rights-based approach to development co-operation*. Geneva: United Nations Publications, 2006.

United Nations Office of the High Commissioner for Human Rights. *Principles and guidelines for a human rights approach to poverty reduction strategies*. OHCHR, 2006.

United Nations Office of the High Commissioner for Human Rights. "The human rights case against corruption." Last updated March 27, 2013. https://www.ohchr.org/EN/NewsEvents/Pages/HRCaseAgainstCorruption.aspx.

Universal Declaration of Human Rights. 1948.

UNSTATS. "SDG Indicator Metadata." Last updated March 31, 2023. https://unstats.un.org/sdgs/metadata/files/Metadata-16-04-01.pdf.

Vienna Declaration and Programme of Action. 1993.

World Bank. *Helping countries combat corruption: the role of the World Bank*. World Bank, 1997.

World Bank. "Combatting corruption." Last updated September 22, 2020. https://www.worldbank.org/en/topic/governance/brief/anti-corruption.

Ziegler, Jean. *Report of the Special Rapporteur on the right to food*. United Nations Human Rights Council, 2001.

Chapter 7

South African Banks, State Capture, Illicit Financial Flows, and Violation of the Right to Development

Marianne Séverin

INTRODUCTION

Recognised in 1986 by the United Nations Declaration of the Right to Development (UNDRTD),[1] the Right to Development (RTD) consists of a plurality of civil, political, and socioeconomic rights. The RTD is understood as a 'solidarity right' which is 'necessarily linked to the duties or responsibilities that exist mutually between individuals and their families, communities and societies'.[2] Under Article 1 of the UNDRTD, the RTD is defined as:

> An inalienable human right by virtue of which every human person and all peoples are entitled to participate in, contribute to, and enjoy economic, social, cultural and political development, in which all human rights and fundamental freedoms can be fully realized.[3]

This declaration has been reinforced, since 1993, by the Vienna Declaration and Programme of Action (adopted by 171 countries) which affirms:

> That all human rights derive from the dignity and worth inherent in the human person, and the human person is the central subject of human rights and fundamental freedoms, and consequently should be the principal beneficiary and should participate actively in the realization of these rights and freedoms.[4]

Seen as a universal right, it is emphasised in Article 22 of the African Charter on Human and Peoples' Rights (ACHPR)[5] that the RTD has particular and strong aspects in an African context. According to Serges D. Kamga, the RTD and its implementation 'entails addressing numerous [African] issues, including the sanctity of the rule of law, African cultures, development assistance, corruption, the gender question, and the migration crisis'.[6] Consequently, the RTD through the African prism must be read as follows—the RTD holders being the African peoples and the duty bearers the African states:

1. All peoples shall have the right to their economic, social and cultural development with due regard to their freedom and identity and in the equal enjoyment of the common heritage of mankind.
2. States shall have the duty, individually or collectively to ensure the exercise of the Right to Development (Art. 22).[7]

As Obiora Chinedu Okafor explains, while 'all peoples' shall enjoy the provision of ACHPR's Article 22, African states under Article 1[8] must:

> Assume the obligation to adopt legislative or other measures to give effect to the rights protected under that treaty. States are . . . required to enact laws that support the recreation of an environment in which people can develop their full potential and lead productive, creative lives in accordance with their needs and interests.[9]

Most African countries signed and ratified the African Charter,[10] and so the RTD through its Article 22. Nevertheless, in reality, African states are far removed from realising the RTD. The issue with the RTD is the combination of weak states and institutions, poor governance, lack of democracy, corruption/illicit financial flows (IFFs), and weak socioeconomic contexts.[11] South Africa must be included in this description (except for the lack of democracy as South Africa could be seen as a stable democracy). Although the RTD is not mentioned in the 1996 South African Constitution, it is translated through its Chapter 2—Bill of Rights.[12] This is also echoed by the preamble to the Constitution which calls for social justice in building and egalitarian society which also underpins the RTD. It emphasises the need to 'heal the divisions of the past and establish a society based on democratic values, social justice and fundamental human rights',[13] because

> the apartheid system had a severe impact on human well-being and livelihood security, the emphasis on human rights is not only crucial for reshaping South African society but, importantly, also for determining how these entitlements should be formulated to define development priorities in a transformative manner.[14]

The originality of the South African case is that the RTD concept must be seen as having taken root, with the writing and adoption of a historical document namely, the Freedom Charter in 1955[15] during apartheid. This document which informs the governing party policies articulated the aspirations of a 'liberated South Africa where all citizens enjoy the rights of equity in access to opportunities and redistributive justice in the allocation of resources'.[16] More than twenty years before the African Charter, the South African Freedom Charter articulated what became Article 22 of the African Charter, regarding the right of 'all peoples' to their economic, social and cultural development with due regard to their freedom and identity and in equal enjoyment of the common heritage of mankind (Art. 22(1)).[17]

The end of apartheid and the new political context created the opportunity to write a new South African Constitution, making the Freedom Charter its keystone through the Bill of Rights which:

1- Is a cornerstone of democracy in South Africa. It enshrines the rights of all people in our country and affirms the democratic values of human dignity, equality, and freedom.
2- The state must respect, protect, promote, and fulfil the rights in the Bill of Rights (Art. 7(1&2).[18]

Despite the democratic dispensation enshrined in the Constitution in a bid to address past injustices, since 1994 the new democratically elected regime led by the African National Congress (ANC) has failed to realise and promote the RTD in South Africa. The proliferation of IFFs and corruption that divert resources that could have contributed to poverty alleviation illustrate this. The chapter argues that the state, which is the primary duty bearer of the RTD, and the private sector 'the other organ of the state' violate the RTD by becoming accomplice of IFFs. To this end, the chapter identifies and tries to unpack the mechanisms at the heart of the South African state capture and its correlation with IFFs, in which South African banks played an instrumental role. In so doing the chapter will review the situation across the Free State province, a province involved in a serious corruption scandal. It epitomises IFFs from this province and their impact on people's lives in the Free State. The chapter further portray the extent to which a bank can be involved in a money laundering system and thereby infringing the RTD in this province.

In this chapter, a general definition of state capture and IFFs depict their mechanisms at the provincial level through a criminal/political and financial network responsible for money laundering/IFFs from Free State to Dubai. In addition, the chapter refers to two specific Enablers of IFFs: First National Bank (FNB) and Standard Bank, both being the oldest banks in the country, and on the African continent in general. FNB was established in 1838 while Standard Bank was set up twenty-four years later in 1862 under the name Standard Bank of South Africa. Part of the so called 'Big Five Banks' of the country, FNB is part of the First Rand Group, the larger financial services conglomerate and side to the Johannesburg Stock Exchange.[19] In addition,

FNB 'provides personal, private, business, commercial and corporate banking services to millions of customers across South Africa'.[20] In assessing their role in IFFs environment and the infringement of the RTD, the chapter provides an overview of the banking system and human rights/RTD as well as the major anti-money laundering tools to prevent human rights/RTD violation in South Africa. In terms of structure, the chapter is divided into five sections including this introduction. The second section explores the duty bearers of the RTD while the third one examines the case study of the Free State province in a context of state capture/IFFs. The penultimate section focuses on the bank enablers of IFFs and how their action violates the RTD whereas the final section provides recommendations.

THE DUTY BEARERS OF THE RIGHT TO DEVELOPMENT

The state and the private sectors are the duty bearers of the Right to Development.

The State

The Declaration of UNDRTD is explicit in its article 2(3) regarding the state as a duty bearer having the obligation to implement the RTD:

> States have the right and the duty to formulate appropriate national development policies that aim at the constant improvement of the well-being of the entire population and of all individuals, on the basis of their active, free and meaningful participation in development and in the fair distribution of the benefits resulting therefrom.[21]

and its article 6(3) which states that

> States should take steps to eliminate obstacles to development resulting from failure to observe civil and political rights, as well as economic social and cultural rights.[22]

While the UNDHR leaves a broad margin in what constitutes the duty bearers, the UNDRTD exclusively mentions the states as duty bearers. According to Chapter 2 of the South African Constitution, the State 'must respect, protect, promote and fulfil the rights in the Bill of Rights'.[23] In so doing, the South African state can be referred to as the first RTD duty bearer. The government of South Africa, represented by the ANC is yet to give effect to the RTD, due to the involvement of its members (at the national and provincial levels) up to the highest levels of the State in the state capture scandal.[24]

The Private Sector

Based on the preamble to the Universal Declaration of Human Rights—UDHR—(1948), the definition of the duty bearers has some latitude. The UDHR states

> Every individual and every organ of society . . . shall strive by teaching and educating to promote respect for these rights and freedoms and by progressive measures, national and international, to secure their universal and effective recognition and observance, both among the peoples of Members States . . . .[25]

Serges D. Kamga states that, 'this provision calls upon every entity in the society or 'organ of society' to ensure that human rights are observed'.[26] While the Bill of Rights creates binding obligations on the state to provide for its citizens the private sector, not explicitly named in this Chapter 2 of the SA Constitution, has also binding duties towards the South African people, and *de facto*, is the other RTD holder. As a matter of fact:

> A company, an organisation or private individual can be held to account for violations of Rights . . . Not only the government, but also, in appropriate circumstances, private individuals, companies or other bodies [must] respect the Rights.[27]

The private sector is indeed the duty bearer of the RTD even though originally the doctrine was of the view 'that this sector of the society did not need to take responsibility in human rights issues on the ground that governments are the violators of human rights and not private companies'.[28]

With the launch of the United Nations Global Compact (26 July 2000),[29] the idea of private companies being outside the human rights corpus became against the grain. All private sectors were invited to meet human rights values.[30] In a context of global processes where companies have 'the opportunity to expand their web of networks as well as exchange experiences and good practices',[31] a UN draft document 'Norms on the responsibilities of Transnational Corporations and Other Business Enterprises with regard to Human Rights (2003 Norms)' was submitted on 30 May 2003,[32] adopted in 2008 and endorsed by the United Nations Human Rights of the High Commissioner in 2011 as the Guiding Principles on Business and Human Rights (Guiding Principles).[33]

With South Africa being bound to the UNDHR, the UNDRTD, and the ACHPR, and then the Guiding principles, the state and private companies in South Africa are arguably the duty bearers of the RTD. Thereby, FNB and Standard Bank shall respect, implement, and protect South African holders' human rights/RTD. It is this observation that underpins this analysis of the South African banks' contribution to the violation of the Bill of Rights, in a context of state capture. One must raise the following questions: Why has the South African banking system been involved in an extensive system of illicit financial transactions from South Africa to a tax haven? Why were South African 'larger banks (collectively, materially important)' co-conspirators in the violation of the RTD, when they 'show a developed understanding of their money laundry risks and seem better at implementing mitigating measures commensurate with their risks'?[34]

STATE CAPTURE, IFFS FROM SOUTH AFRICA: THE CASE STUDY OF THE FREE STATE PROVINCE

Understanding the State Capture and the IFFs from South Africa

The 'State capture' shall be seen as a sophisticated system of 'Grand corruption' involving two groups of powerful individuals who cooperate to 'carry out fraudulent or deceptive activities'.[35] In short, because of being in a position of power, they use public funds for private gains while ignoring remorselessly the consequences of their own acts on the community, notably the most vulnerable people.[36]

With the South African case study, the 'Grand corruption'—known as State capture—is one of the biggest scandals in the post-apartheid area. Not only was this country the victim of 'actors' who were only concerned by their selfish interests in a context of fraudulent collusion and recurrent chains of corrupt acts[37]—state capture actors—but it was also 'betrayed' by private agencies[38] which, as we will see, helped, and/or allowed IFFs from South Africa to tax havens—'IFFs enablers'.

The State Capture, a Sophisticated System of Grand Corruption[39]

State capture is a particular context where companies and institutions of powerful individuals use corruption such as the buying of laws, amendments, decrees, or sentences, as well as illegal contributions to political parties and candidates, to influence and shape a country's policy and legal environment, and economy in their own interests.[40] State capture also refers to an environment where 'institutions—as legislative, executive, judiciary, regulatory agencies, public works ministries as well as private companies, political leaders, high ranking officials, or interest groups are captured'.[41] This is mainly possible because a minority of actors—'oligarchs' (also called 'captors')—are given the opportunity to manipulate policy formation, and even shape the emerging rules of the game, to their own substantial advantage,[42] while social interests of all citizens are denied.

When it comes to the African context[43] neopatrimonialism is the main reason why the state capture system can take root is another complex system, conceptualised by S.N Eisenstadt[44] and further advanced by Jean-François Médard. As defined by Max Weber, neopatrimonialism consists of categories of authorities which might be traditional (authority being held by an individual whose power has been designed by tradition and by custom),[45] charismatic (an extraordinary quality of power outside everyday life and not accessible by the 'common man' which is a personal charisma, or referring to charisma of function which is impersonal and based on a recognition of a holder's exceptional quality given by an institution),[46] or a rational-legal authority (an authority given by 'an impersonal bureaucratic logic governed by law and reason').[47] Within the African context, while states sound like a bureaucratic one, they are made by 'power holders' who use a sophisticated system for their survival and selfish financial interests (corruption):

> Patrimonialism and neopatrimonialism . . . denote systems in which political relationships are mediated through, and maintained by personal connections between leaders and subjects, or patrons and clients. . . . While patrimonialism is said to cement social bonds in small-scale situations through a reliance on trust, reciprocity, and material exchanges, it is believed to distort power, corrupt authority, and fuel personal aggrandizement when it permeates large political institutions such as bureaucracies and state.[48]

South Africa is not an exception to that definition. On the one hand, the ruling party – ANC – has become a neopatrimonialism system where loyalty, patronage, and factionalism are the 'rules', and on the other hand, a group of powerful people has met within an informal entity which retains secretly the decision-making power of the state beyond the legal; the 'deep state' or 'state within a state'.[49] Thereby, in 2012, the political analyst Aubrey Matshiqi described already the 'deep state' as a system which is 'materialized when senior officials, sections of business, members of criminal syndicates and intelligence operatives in the State and the private sector act in pursuit of mutually beneficial interests . . . When the coffins of members of the criminal and business underworld are draped in the colors of the dominant party, senior police officials seem to be engaging in nefarious activities with the criminal and business underworld.'[50] Four years later, Matshiqi was much more specific by pointing to powerful actors who manipulated public authorities to their own ends – the Gupta and Zuma families:

> They are the tip of the iceberg when it comes to . . . politics of patronage and corruption, and the possibility that parts of the state are being criminalized. . . . South African politics and . . . economy operate, in part, on the basis of deep-state projects and other nefarious political and economic activities that mimic the deep state.[51]

The South African neo-patrimonial case study is identified especially during the 'Jacob Zuma era' where the State Capture/IFFs and consequently the RTD/Bill of Rights violation have their roots. It was Professor Tom Lodge who best described this system in 2014, while he was referring the ANC in the following terms:

> Increasingly within the ANC, leadership behavior appears to be characterized by neo-patrimonial predispositions and, while formal distinctions between private and public concerns are widely recognized, officials nevertheless use their public powers for private purposes. Other symptoms of neo-patrimonial political behavior [having] also appeared, [as] factionalism that is the emergence of internal rival groups constituted by personal loyalty rather than shared ideological beliefs.[52]

It is very important to acknowledge that when we talk about state capture in South Africa, we also refer to actors deeply involved in this system.[53] If at first the purpose of this case study is not personalising our analysis, with the neopatrimonialism definition and one of the state capture aspects, it is unrealistic to not name the protagonists of this Grand corruption system, while the majority of South African newspapers, the three volumes of the Judicial Commission of Enquiry into State Capture, or the non-governmental organisation (NGO) Open Secrets as well as South African Civil Society Organisations (e.g. OUTA[54] or Forensics for Justice[55]) exposed all of them, in a strategy of naming and shaming all 'state capture actors'.[56]

These sources show that South Africa had seen the growth of two networks of actors, who protected their own interests, particularly their financial interests. They built up 'political capital' that they transformed into a vast and powerful network which undermined a range of state institutions and woven into illicit financial transactions from South Africa.[57] These actors organised themselves into 'political-family and friendship networks' which are represented by the former Head of State Jacob Zuma, his close relatives and his 'ANC comrades', and the Gupta family, settled in SA since 1990s and its own friendship networks.[58] When 'Zuma won the Presidency the alliance between the President and the Gupta brothers would make both the Gupta family and

Zuma's family fabulously wealthy'[59] and they protected their own interests in terms of financial interests.

While broadening this 'political and financial capital', a 'shadow state' (deep state or state within the state as we defined before) was set up by them, throughout the time, their networks of relationships crossed and bound them together as they need to act for 'whatever reason in secretive ways so that they can either effectively hide, actively deny or consciously "not know" that which contradicts their formal roles in the "constitutional state"'.[60]

The networks we describe are usually seen at the national level, but as we will demonstrate subsequently, it extends beyond. The state capture also applies to the provincial level. The duplication of the state capture from the national level to the provincial was only possible because provincial high-ranking officials – political allies to the former president Jacob Zuma – had also benefited from the proximity of the Guptas while helping them in their criminal activity (IFFs from the Free State to Dubai) with the 'blessing' of two important South African banks.[61]

IFFs from South Africa

From a South African perspective, the country is regarded as one of the most affected by IFFs on the Continent. Regardless of legal and judicial arrangements to counteract the illicit transactions, a 'corrupt upper-class' get richer while the socioeconomic landscape has been weakening.[62] To illustrate our point, a succession of data can be given as an example. In 2013 with the loss of $29.13 billion, South Africa was ranked number ninth in terms of IFFs. Far from improving, Global Financial Integrity (GFI) report showed 'South Africa moving into the top 10, jumping from the 13th to the 10th'.[63] It is within this context that the president of GFI coined in 2013 that South Africa had beaten all the records[64] as the country lost more than $100.7 billion only for the period 2002–2011. Similarly, 2015 and 2016, the country lost a large amount of money, up to R60 billion.[65] The Reserve Bank of South Africa then 'referred to a dead loss of billions if not tens of billions'.[66] It is important to note that the increase in money lost due to IFFs amounted to the recapture of Zuma-Guptas' political and financial network in South Africa,[67] thereby putting the country's economy at risk as it is bound, according to the Revenue Services, to

> South African world-class financial systems, along with the large extractive industry of mining and resources, the presence of large multinational corporations, and South African open economy and tradable currency.[68]

More importantly, the Financial Intelligence Centre mentioned in March 2017 that about R 9 million could have been dubious transactions, while at the same time, R 6.8 billion were linked to another seventy-two dubious transactions due to the illegal actions of the Gupta family.[69]

What we have just described in relation to this 'political and financial network' responsible for illegal financial transactions at the upper level of power, echoes what has been happening to the South African provincial government. The Free State province is the best case study to illustrate how the ANC neopatrimonialism system emphasised the rules of loyalty, patronage, and factionalism and as a result a scheme of IFFs at a provincial/local level. This case study of the Free State province shows a specific violation of the RTD by a decentralised government, at first, and by a private sector which was also supposed to realise the RTD in a provincial/local landscape, in a context of 'provincial state capture'.

UNDERSTANDING THE 'PROVINCIAL STATE CAPTURE': FROM THE CONCRETISATION OF THE RTD TO IFFS FROM THE FREE STATE

To understand what the 'Free State province capture' is about, it is necessary to provide the context through the description of an integrated diary project namely Estina project in the rural town, Vrede. In fact, this initiative was leaked according to Pieter-Louis Myburgh in his book on the former Premier of the Free State province, Ace Magashule,[70] to a very new and unknown company called Estina (which may be regarding as a company screen for the Guptas[71]). This company which signed a contract with the Department for Agriculture and Rural Development was 'appointed as the implementing agent for a diary project'.[72] It was supposed to provide a 'capital investment of R 228 million' while 'the provincial department would invest R 342 million over a period of three years'.[73] The idea of such a project was to identify and mainstreamed eighty 'emerging dairy farmers in an Agri-BEE company'. They would have got '51% stake in this Agri-BEE company while the Estina would keep the remaining shares'. In fact, the all idea was supposed to be transformative in a poor area and advance the realization of the RTD.[74] On paper and according to the Free State government announcement (February 2013), this project was 'to create business run by black people and redress the historical wrongs of apartheid',[75] and 'to empower the local community, eventually being ceded to local dairy farmers trained to use the sophisticated facilities'.[76] The reality is quite different. The project turned out to be a serious financial fraud organised by criminal/political networks, that violated the RTD of the people in the Free State province, especially the most vulnerable.[77]

In fact, under the control of the ANC, since the first provincial elections in 1994, the Free State has always been the breeding ground for factionalism, as demonstrated in the excellent article of Chitja Twana,[78] and thus responsible for corruption as the work of Pieter-Louis Myburg documents very well.[79] The latter shows the degree of corruption led by the protagonists of the Free State capture, Ace Magashule (former Premier at this time) and his 'comrades in crime' and the Guptas which was discussed at length earlier what we shall return to in this section. According to him:

> The Free State became one of the foremost sites of capture. For years, Magashule's own patronage networks had operated mostly independently from role-players outside Free State . . . around 2012, the Guptas and other business linked to Zuma began to infiltrate the province in earnest. Magashule evidently had no qualms about his boss's friends feasting on Free State contracts along with his own associates . . . synergy and aligned interests were the order of the day. The nexus between Zuma, Magashule and the Guptas is a case point.[80]

Based on these two publications as well as South African media, reports of the commission of inquiry and NGOs papers, we are dealing here with a specific case of major corruption and money laundering and that deeply involved Free State ANC officials and corrupted businessmen (the Guptas). They are the ones who led to the infringement of the RTD in this province, through the Estina/Vrede integrated diary project, which was to be the concretisation of the RTD.

ESTINA DIARY PROJECT: A CONCRETISATION OF THE RTD IN THE FREE STATE PROVINCE

As a public-private partnership the Estina diary project was presented at first in 2012 during the Budget vote of the Department of Agriculture and Rural Development.[81] The speech shall be analysed through the concretisation of the RTD in the province. It also highlights the fundamental role of the duty bearers to the implementation of the RTD. Prior to further elucidation, it is important to emphasise the historical rhetoric the ANC provincial government, through its Department of Agriculture, used to 'show' its commitment to the RTD. For that, the speech referred of two ANC heroes, both born in the Free State (former Orange Free State province) and sons of farmers—who fought for equal rights among all South Africa and so all South African farmers in the province:

> the country celebrates the life and times of the third President of the African National Congress (ANC), ZR Mahabane under the theme 'All shall have equal rights.'
>
> this sitting takes place in the birthplace of Ntate Thabo Mofutsanyane, one of our heroes and stalwarts. He is the son of a farmer who during that time went

> through the hardship of dishonesty and undermined by his fellow white commercial farmers which prompted him to join the struggle. We stand here today as this generation both black and white to correct those imbalances which Thabo Mofutsanyana fought for.[82]

As we will soon portray, the memory and commitments of these former political leaders were betrayed in the name of financial and selfish interests of a minority at the expense of the most vulnerable in the Free State. Nevertheless, we shall acknowledge that this Budget vote speech in putting agriculture in the centre of rural development, through a partnership between the private sector and the provincial state entities (as the Department of Agriculture) should have ensured the implementation of the RTD. This Estina diary project should have been part of

> the Provincial Growth and Development Strategy for the agriculture and rural development sector [through] a multi-year mega Public and Private Partnership business concept that deals with income generation through farming in the rural area of the province, the creation of on- and off-farm agri-business, value chain enterprises and Black Economic Empowerment. This overarching strategic intent is underscored by a dedication to make the long term more urgent . . . [With such a strategy, the province [shall be able to] enable faster economic growth, job creation and food security for all.[83]

So, to implement this strategy the Department of Agriculture and Rural Development announced an allocation of 'R 131,8 million for the financial year 2012/13 to projects'.[84] While the contours of this project seemed coherent with the concretisation and implementation of the RTD, inconsistencies, irregularities, and financial fraud soon appeared.

FINANCIAL FRAUD AND CRIMINAL NETWORKS

According to Myburgh, the Estina project turned out to be a considerable financial fraud, implying what we once called before a 'politico-criminal networks' that spread across the Free State province.[85] South African investigative press,[86] or investigative journalists' book,[87] as well as civil society organisation reports[88] or academic papers,[89] and before that the report of the South African Public Protector[90] and finally more recently the Zondo Commission[91] have meticulously described how irregularities, poor governance and especially a money laundering system have tainted the realisation and implementation of the RTD that should have benefited a vulnerable segment of the province's population formerly discriminated against. All these sources show the reality of the Estina Project. While being supposed to foster the enjoyment of socio-economic rights in this province, the project was created to siphoning around R280.2 million fund, in eight instalments from the Department of Agriculture between June 2012 and May 2016:

> It is now incontrovertible that the Estina/Vrede Dairy Project was, from start to finish . . . to loot Free State government funds. Indeed, an analysis of banking records and other documentation by Shadow World Investigations has revealed that the vast majority of the R280.2 million paid to Estina by the Free State government was transferred into accounts owned or controlled by the Gupta enterprise.[92]

In 2017, the #GuptaLeaks revealed 'how millions milked from Free State government'.[93] Just for the year 2013, the Free State government transferred R114 million for the diary project to Estina, but between 11 August and 24 September 2013[94] R84 million were sent to one of the Guptas' businesses, Gateway in Dubai. In fact, all evidence referring to various transfers of money from the Free State province outside South African borders have highlighted how 'public funds were laundered from the province',[95] first because of political and private sector connections and collusion. To summarise, on the one hand, the Guptas, along with their close relatives, and on the other hand, the three provincial high-ranking officials, who have in common not only their connexion with the Guptas but also with the former president Jacob Zuma and his relatives. As Pieter-Louis Myburg put it,

> the Free State became one of the foremost sites of capture, as for years Magashule's own patronage networks had operated mostly independently from role-players outside Free State. . . . Around 2012, the Guptas and other business-people linked to Zuma began to infiltrate the province in earnest . . . Magashule became increasingly prominent within the Guptas' social circles after he became Premier . . . By 2015, at the pinnacle of their capture of the State, the Gupta view Magashule as one of their most important allies in the government.[96]

The Open Secrets report also shows the connections between Peter Thabethe, Monzebanzi Zwane, and the Guptas:

> Thabethe's connections to the Gupta enterprise were multiple. First, it must be recalled that in 2012, Thabethe conducted research into international dairy companies that might undertake the project and landed on Paras Dairy. Between 29 February and 4 March 2012, Thabethe travelled to India to meet with Paras. He was accompanied on the trip by Ashok Narayan. Narayan was a key lieutenant in the Gupta enterprise.[97]
>
> Mosebenzi Zwane has long-running connections to the Gupta enterprise . . . , in relation to Estina . . . in October 2012, the Gupta enterprise began arranging

> for Zwane's choir to take an all-expenses-paid trip to India. The Gupta enterprise was responsible for arranging visas for . . . Mosebenzi Zwane himself. It also paid for the flights and hotels, and arranged a touring itinerary, including tickets for the Taj Mahal.[98]

Furthermore, the other and most important reason why this financial fraud—money laundering—could continue with impunity is because the South African banking system was used to 'facilitate multiple suspicious transactions that should have been flagged and reported'.[99] But as we will see in the following section, where anti-money laundering legislation in South Africa can be seen as biting, it is strange to note the involvement of two major South African banks in the violation of the RTD.

THE ENABLERS OF IFFS: THE CASE OF FNB AND STANDARD BANK

Before looking at the case of the two major South African banks involved in illicit transactions, it is useful to link the issue of the banking system to its obligation to be an actor of the RTD. It is also important to identify banking tools to prevent from RTD violation.

Banking System and Human Rights/RTD

Part of the business sector, the banking system shall be bound to 'Guiding Principles on Business and Human Rights',[100] and so, to the principles of RTD in general and to the Bill of Rights in South African case. According to Bank Track, 'banks must contribute to adverse human rights impacts, through their provision of finance', meaning that 'banks are not only directly linked to the impact through their finance, but contribute to it'.[101] As the 'Guiding Principles' put it, the corporate—banks—must stick to its foundational principles which state:

1. Business enterprises should avoid infringing on the human rights of others and should address adverse human impacts with they are involved, meaning taking adequate measures for their prevention, mitigate and, where appropriate, remediation.
2. Business enterprises should not undermine State's abilities to meet their own human rights obligations.
3. The responsibility to respect human rights requires that business:
   a) Avoid causing or contributing to adverse human rights impacts through their own activities, address such impacts when they occur.

b) Seek to prevent of mitigate adverse human rights that are directly linked to their operations, products, or services by their business relationships, even if they have not contributed to those impacts.[102]

The core of their activity being linked to the provision of finance, all-bank systems shall prevent any negative impacts on human rights; banks finance, in all cases, involving either contributions to or direct linkage with human rights impacts.[103] So, the bank system is invited to introduce human rights notions and practices in its own processes to prevent from causing any harm, as well as to stop its own clients or entities from using it to violate such rights. The banks are required to know their own clients (and activities) so as to prevent any human rights violation. It is in this context that the Guiding Principles on Business and Human Rights emphatically encourage a 'Human Rights due diligence' which is:

> The process [that] should include assessing actual and potential human rights impacts, integrating, and acting upon the findings, tracking responses, and communicating how impacts address human rights due diligence.[104]

While the guiding principles is clear on the urgent need for banks to respect human rights, the reality is different. Indeed, regarding the discourse on IFFs from Africa and the violation of the RTD, the 2015 Report of the High-Level Panel on Illicit Financial Flows from Africa is self-explanatory about the role of the banks in illicit transactions:

> IFFs will at some point pass through banks and the financial system. The international banks sometimes facilitate IFFs even when they know that the money is tainted, as became evident in several asset recovery cases. Even where banks have an obligation to file suspicious transactions reports, this requirement is often overlooked in some countries in transactions emanating from small, rural branches. Indeed, banks sometimes knowingly establish infrastructure to facilitate IFFs moving to financial secrecy jurisdictions.[105]

The case of South Africa or more specifically of the 'Free State capture' illustrates this assertion as the banking system of the country was one of the 'Enablers' of IFFs from the Free State province to tax haven. Despite the country's robust anti-money laundering legal architecture such as the prevention of Organisation Crime Act[106] and the Financial Intelligence Centre Act,[107] two major South African banks found themselves at the heart of IFFs from the Free State province to Dubai and vice versa. This is inconsistent with the fact that South African banks are major role players in the Financial Action Task Force (FATF)[108] and the legal anti-money laundry, aimed at shielding the RTD against plagues such as IFFs that divert resources from development financing initiatives. The significance of South Africa's subscription to these mechanisms cannot be overemphasised.

FATF has the responsibility 'to set standards and promotes effective legal, regulatory, and operational measures for combating money laundering, the financing of terrorism and other threats to the international systems'.[109] Within this framework, South Africa is committed to implement the international standards in its own anti-money laundering legal architecture with the Prevention of Organised Crime Act 121 of 1998 (POCA)[110] and the Financial Intelligence Centre Act 38 of 2001 (FICA) (amended twice in 2003 and 2017)[111] which are the 'fundamental pillars' of South Africa's anti-money laundering legal architecture).[112] In other words, the FATF's requirement and recommendations place important obligations on South African national banks as 'accountable institutions'. As a result, the banking sector must comply and set up anti-money laundering systems, as due diligence and keep records of all transactions. In addition, they must know their customers and report all suspicious transactions to the Financial Intelligence Unit, according to Section 29 of FICA. With the anti-money laundering legal architecture and obligations imposed on South African bank systems one can reasonably raise the question as to know what went wrong with FNB and Standard Bank.

FNB AND STANDARD BANK'S FAILURE TO PROTECT THE RTD IN THE FREE STATE PROVINCE

While the Estina diary integrated project was to meet the objectives of the RTD at the provincial level, it appeared to be a way to capture the Department of Agriculture funds, but more importantly to put in place a sophisticated money laundering system: 'when the Asset Forfeiture Unit attempted to seize funds related to the Estina project, they failed to understand fully the sophisticated banking methods used by the Gupta enterprise'.[113] In fact, the strategy was to use several laundering methods to achieve the three main steps of laundering – placement, layering and integration, such as the 'round-tripping' and 'loan-backs' schemes.

> As the name suggests, 'round-tripping' involves transferring funds into a number of placeholder accounts, from where they are paid onto a further set of intermediary accounts, before being repaid and reintegrated into the original transmitting account. 'Loan-back' systems involve taking out personal or business loans secured against the proceeds of crime. The proceeds of crime are laundered by 'loaning' them 'back', hence the name. Both of these techniques become difficult to investigate and trace if, at any stage in the process, the funds travel to offshore secrecy jurisdictions.[114]

It was these methods and means that between June 2012 and May 2016 R280.2 million was stolen from the Free State government and transferred to Dubai, from Standard Bank and FNB to Standard Bank offshore in Dubai.[115]

The sophistication of this money laundering system does not explain the failure of these two banks to prevent the illicit transaction from the Free State province to Dubai. Indeed, they did not take into account the 'red flags'. According to Open Secrets and Shadow World Investigations, Standard Bank failed to monitor the project which was under the control of a right-hand man who did not have any experience in agriculture.[116] More importantly, this bank did not report immediately the transfer of funds to offshore compagnies in Dubai. The FNB did also hold an Estima account where two significant transfers from the Free State Agriculture department (R60 million—8 Mays 2015; R48 million—5 May 2016)[117] occurred. This account was in fact a stopping-off point before the immediate transfer of funds. Given that Standard Bank failed to conduct its due diligence regarding the project and the Guptas, this has not only resulted in the transfer of the entire public fund offshore which unfortunately may never be recovered. The reputation of these two banks has been tarnished, given their failure to comply with the anti-money laundering mechanisms put in place by the South African legislator. Moreover, their failure to prevent IFFs amounts to a violation of the RTD as demonstrated by the staggering amount siphoned from the Estina Diary farm.[118]

CONCLUSION

This chapter has focused on the South African banks involved in the violation of the RTD, in a context of state capture/IFFs from the Free State province. In its third part, after searching to understand the outbreak of the state capture/IFFs in South Africa, this chapter analysed the 'provincial state capture'. Through the case study of a public-private partnership, Estina diary project, the chapter showed how the concretisation of the RTD was betrayed, through the implementation of a huge money laundry money system. This was made possible because of a politico-criminal networks in the Free State government, on one side, and a South African banking system, on the other. Ultimately, the chapter found that for the RTD to be realised, the state at national and provincial level should plays its role of duty bearer. It also found that 'every' organ with specific attention to the private sector, namely FNB and Standard Bank, should also take their responsibility in avoiding IFFs to ensure that RTD fund reach their beneficiaries.

NOTES

1. Declaration on Right to Development, 4 December 1986, https://www.ohchr.org/en/instruments-mechanisms/instruments/declaration-right-development.

2. Shadrack Gutto, 'The Right to Development: An Implied Right in South Africa's Constitutional Order,' in *Reflections on Democracy and Human Rights: A Decade of the South African Constitution (Act 108 of 1996)*, ed. South African Human Rights Commission (Johannesburg: South African Human Rights Commission, 2006), 111, chap. 13, https://www.sahrc.org.za/home/21/files/Reports/Reflection%20of%20democracy%20and%20human%20rights_10%20year%20review_%20200.pdf.

3. Declaration on Right to Development.

4. Vienna Declaration and Programme of Action, 25 June 1993, https://www.ohchr.org/en/instruments-mechanisms/instruments/vienna-declaration-and-programme-action.

5. African Charter on Human and Peoples' Rights, 27 June 1981, https://au.int/en/treaties/african-charter-human-and-peoples-rights.

6. Serges D. Kamga, *The Right to Development in Africa: Issues, Constraints and Prospects* (Austin, Texas: African University Press, 2020), 6.

7. African Charter on Human and Peoples' Rights, 27 June 1981, https://au.int/en/treaties/african-charter-human-and-peoples-rights.

8. African Charter on Human and Peoples' Rights.

9. Obiora Chinedu Okafor, 'A Regional Perspective: Article 22 of the African Charter on Human and Peoples' Rights,' in *Realizing the Right to Development*, ed. United Nations Human Rights of the High Commissioner (New York and Geneva: United Nations, 2013), 381, chap. 27, https://www.ohchr.org/sites/default/files/Documents/Publications/RightDevelopmentInteractive_EN.pdf.

10. African Charter on Human and Peoples' Rights.

11. Anzanilifuno Munyai and Avitus A Agbor, 'The Impact of Corruption on the Right to Development in Africa,' in *Perspectives on the Right to Development*, ed. Carol C. Ngang, Serges D. Kamga, and Vusi Gumde (Pretoria: Pretoria University Law Press, 2018), 72–73.

12. Constitution of South Africa, 1996 – Bill of Rights, https://www.gov.za/documents/constitution/chapter-2-bill-rights.

13. Constitution of South Africa, 1996 – Preamble, https://www.gov.za/documents/constitution-republic-south-africa-1996-preamble.

14. Carol C Ngang, 'Radical Transformation and a Reading of the Right to Development in the South African Constitutional Order,' *South African Journal on Human Rights* 35, no. 1 (January 2019): 36.

15. History of the Freedom Charter, https://www.dffe.gov.za/sites/default/files/docs/publications/history_freedomcharter.pdf.

16. Ngang, 'Radical Transformation and a Reading of the Right to Development in the South African Constitutional Order,' 33.

17. African Charter on Human and Peoples' Rights.

18. Constitution of South Africa, 1996—Bill of Rights.

19. First National Bank, https://www.fnb.co.za/about-fnb/about-us.html; Banks around the world, https://www.relbanks.com/africa/south-africa/first-national-bank.

20. SandonCity, First National Bank, https://www.sandtoncity.com/shops/first-national-bank/.

21. Declaration on Right to Development.

22. Declaration on Right to Development.

23. Constitution of South Africa, 1996 – Bill of Rights.

24. Marianne Séverin, 'Civil Society and the Fight against Illicit Financial Flows in Africa. The Case Study of OUTA and the "State Capture in South Africa",' in *Illicit Financial Flows from South Africa. Decolonial Perspectives on Political Economy and Corruption*, ed. Serges D Kamga (London and New York: Routledge, 2022), 123.

25. Universal Declaration of Human Rights, 10 December 2018, https://www.un.org/en/udhrbook/pdf/udhr_booklet_en_web.pdf.

26. Serges D Kamga, *The Right to Development in the African Human Rights System* ((London and New York: Routledge 2018), chap. 3, Kobo eBooks.

27. Role of the Bill of Rights, https://ourconstitution.constitutionhill.org.za/south-african-constitution/our-constitution-explained/role-the-bill-of-rights/.

28. Kamga, *The Right to Development in the African Human Rights System*, chap. 3.

29. United Nations Global Compact, 26 July 2000, https://www.unglobalcompact.org/what-is-gc/mission/principles.

30. United Nations Global Compact.

31. Kamga, *The Right to Development in the African Human Rights System*, chap. 3.

32. United Nations Economic and Social Council, 'Norms on the responsibilities of Transnational Corporations and Other Business Enterprises with regard to Human Rights,' E/CN.4/Sub.2/2003/12 (30 May 2003), https://digitallibrary.un.org/record/498842.

33. United Nations Human Rights Office of the High Commissioner, 'Guiding Principles on Business and Human Rights,' https://www.ohchr.org/sites/default/files/documents/publications/guidingprinciplesbusinesshr_en.pdf.

34. Financial Action Task Force (FATF), *South Africa's Measures to Combat Money Laundering and Terrorist Financing* (October 2021), 10, https://www.fatf-gafi.org/media/fatf/documents/reports/mer4/Mutual-Evaluation-Report-South-Africa.pdf.

35. Evaristus Okechukwu Ekwueme, 'What am I doing When I am Being Corrupt? An Epistemology of Corruption,' in *Corruption in Africa. A Threat to Justice and Sustainable Peace*, ed. Elizabeth Nduku and John Tenamwenye (Geneva: Globethics.net Focus 14, 2014), 61, https://www.globethics.net/documents/4289936/13403252/GE_Focus_14_web.pdf.

36. Kamga, *The Right to Development in the African Human Rights System*, chap. 3

37. Séverin, 'Civil Society and the Fight against Illicit Financial Flows in Africa. The Case Study of OUTA and the "State Capture in South Africa",' 123.

38. Open Secrets and Shadow World Investigations, *The Enablers, The Bankers, Accountants and Lawyers that Cashed in on State Capture* (Southern Africa Office, 2020), https://www.opensecrets.org.za/wp-content/uploads/TheEnablers_web.pdf.

39. Séverin, 'Civil society and the Fight Against Illicit Financial Flows in Africa. The Case Study of OUTA and the "State Capture in South Africa"'; Marianne Séverin, 'Civil Society, Corruption and the Realisation of the Right to Development in African: The Case of Forensics for Justice and 'State Capture' in South Africa,' in *The Right to Development in Africa: Issues, Constraints and Prospects*, ed. S D Kamga (Austin, Texas: Pan-African University Press, 2020).

40. Maira Martini, 'Anti-corruption Helpdesk. State Capture: An Overview,' *Transparency International* (March 2014), 2, https://knowledgehub.transparency.org/helpdesk/state-capture-an-overview.

41. Judith February, 'South Africa Pays the Price of State Capture,' *Institute for Security Studies* (ISS) (April 2017), https://issafrica.org/isstoday/south-africa-pays-the-price-of-state-capture.

42. Joel Hellman & Daniel Kauffmann, 'Confronting the Challenge, of State Capture in Transition Economies,' *International Monetary Fund* 38, no. 3 (September 2001), https://www.imf.org/external/pubs/ft/fandd/2001/09/hellman.htm.

43. Jean-François Médard, « L'État néo-patrimonial » in *États d'Afrique: formation, mécanismes et crise*, ed. Jean-François Médard (Paris: Karthala, 1992), 323–55.

44. Anne Pitcher, Mary H. Moran and Michael Johnson, 'Rethinking Patrimonialism and Neopatrimonialism in Africa,' *African Studies Review* 52, no. 1 (April, 2009): 125–26.

45. Hubert Treiber, « La sociologie de la domination de Max Weber à la lumière de publications récentes, » *Revue française de sociologie* 45, no. 4 (2005): 871–82; Elizabeth Kauffmann, « Les trois types purs de la domination légitime de Max Weber: Les paradoxes de la domination et de la liberté » *Sociologie* 5, no. 3 (2014): 307–17.

46. Treiber, « La sociologie de la domination de Max Weber à la lumière de publications récentes »; Hellman & Kauffmann, « Les trois types purs de la domination légitime de Max Weber: Les paradoxes de la domination et de la liberté ».

47. Pitcher, Moran and Johnson, 'Rethinking Patrimonialism and Neopatrimonialism in Africa,' 130.

48. Pitcher, Moran and Johnson, 'Rethinking Patrimonialism and Neopatrimonialism in Africa,' 129–30.

49. Thuli Gqubule, *No Longer Whispering to Power. The Story of Thuli Madonsela* (Johannesburg & Cape Town: Jonathan Ball Publishers SA, 2017), 151.

50. Aubrey Matshiqi, 'Rise of Deep State has Me Ducking for the Duvet,' *Business Day*, 16 April 2012, https://www.pressreader.com/south-africa/business-day/20120416/281887295295817.

51. Aubrey Matshiqi, 'The Guptas? They're just the Tip of the Iceberg,' *Rand Daily Mail*, 9 February 2016, https://www.businesslive.co.za/rdm/politics/2016-02-09-the-guptas-theyre-just-the-tip-of-the-iceberg/.

52. Tom Lodge, 'Neo-patrimonial Politics in the ANC,' *African Affairs* 113, no. 450 (January 2014): 1.

53. Séverin, 'Civil Society and the Fight against Illicit Financial Flows in Africa. The Case Study of OUTA and the "State Capture in South Africa".'

54. Séverin, 'Civil Society and the Fight against Illicit Financial Flows in Africa. The Case Study of OUTA and the "State Capture in South Africa".'

55. Séverin, 'Civil Society and the Fight against Illicit Financial Flows in Africa. The Case Study of OUTA and the "State Capture in South Africa".'

56. Séverin, 'Civil Society and the Fight against Illicit Financial Flows in Africa. The Case Study of OUTA and the "State Capture in South Africa",' 123.

57. Séverin, 'Civil Society and the Fight against Illicit Financial Flows in Africa. The Case Study of OUTA and the "State Capture in South Africa",' 123.

58. To understand the relationship between the Zuma and Gupta families, see Adriaan Basson, *Zuma Exposed* (Johannesburg & Cape Town: Jonathan Ball Publishers SA, 2012); Richard Calland, *The Zuma Years. South Africa's Changing Face of Power* (Cape Town: Zebra Press, 2013); Pieter-Louis Myburgh, *The Republic of Gupta. A Story of State Capture* (Cape Town: Penguin Books, 2017); Jacques Pauw, *The President's Keepers. Those Keeping Zuma in Power and Out Prison* (Cape Town: Tafelberg Publishers Ltd, 2017).

59. Vashna Jagarnath, 'Ajay Come to Jo'burg: From Selling Shoes to Assailing the State,' *Daily Maverick*, 28 October 2016, https://www.dailymaverick.co.za/opinionista/2016-10-28-ajay-comes-to-joburg-from-selling-shoes-to-assailing-the-state/#.Wvw_pYiFPIU.

60. Haroon Bhorat, et al. *Betrayal of the Promise: How South Africa is being Stolen* (May 2017), 6, https://pari.org.za/betrayal-promise-report/.

61. 'How the Guptas of Saharanpur Came to be known as the Zuptas of the South Africa,' *The Economic Times*, 20 August 2017, https://economictimes.indiatimes.com/news/company/corporate-trends/how-the-guptas-of-saharanpur-came-to-be-known-as-the-zuptas-of-south-africa/articleshow/60101573.cms.

62. Séverin, 'Civil Society and the Fight against Illicit Financial Flows in Africa. The Case Study of OUTA and the "State Capture in South Africa",' 123.

63. Global Financial Integrity (GFI), *New Study: Crime, Corruption, Tax Evasion Drained a Record U$$991.2 Billion in Illicit Financial Flows from Developing Economies in 2012.*

64. Sarah Evans, 'R147bn Lost through Money Illegally Leaving SA,' *Mail and Guardian*, 16 December 2014, https://mg.co.za/article/2014-12-16-billions-lost-through-illegal-outflows.

65. Llewellyn Prince, 'Almost R60 billion Flows Out of SA Illicitly,' *City Press*, 16 March 2017, https://city-press.news24.com/News/almost-r60-billion-flows-out-of-sa-illicitly-20170316.

66. Prince, 'Almost R60 billion Flows Out of SA Illicitly'.

67. Makhura B. Rapanyane and Chuene C. Ngoepe, 'The Impact of Illicit Financial Flows on South African Political Economy under Jacob Zuma, 2009–2018,' *Journal of Public Affairs* 20, no. 1 (September 2019): 4.

68. African Monitor, *State of Illicit Financial Flows in South Africa. A Scoping Exercise* (April 2017), 2, http://www.africanmonitor.org/wp-content/uploads/2017/04/IFF-Report-1.pdf.

69. 'How the Guptas of Saharanpur Came to be known as the Zuptas of the South Africa,' *The Economic Times*, 20 August 2017, https://economictimes.indiatimes.com/news/company/corporate-trends/how-the-guptas-of-saharanpur-came-to-be-known-as-the-zuptas-of-south-africa/articleshow/60101573.cms.

70. Pieter-Louis Myburgh, *Gangster State. Unravelling Ace Magashule's Web of Capture* (Cape Town: Penguin Books, 2019), chap. 14, Kindle.

71. See Public Protector South Africa, *Allegation of Maladministration against the Free State Department of Agriculture Vrede Integrated Dairy Project, Report n°:31 of 2017/18*, https://www.gov.za/sites/default/files/gcis_document/201802/vrede-report1.pdf; Judicial Commission of Inquiry into state capture report, Part VI, Vol. 1, *Vrede Diary Project/Estina and Closure of Gupta Bank Accounts* (2022), https://www.gov.za/sites/default/files/gcis_document/202206/electronic-state-capture-commission-report-part-vi-vol-i_0.pdf.

72. Myburgh, *Gangster State. Unravelling Ace Magashule's Web of Capture*, chap. 14.

73. Myburgh, *Gangster State. Unravelling Ace Magashule's Web of Capture*, chap. 14.

74. David Pilling and Joseph Cotterill, 'Jacob Zuma, the Guptas and the Selling of South Africa,' *Financial Times Magazine*, 30 November 2017, https://www.ft.com/content/707c5560-d49a-11e7-8c9a-d9c0a5c8d5c9.

75. Pilling and Cotterill, 'Jacob Zuma, the Guptas and the selling of South Africa.'

76. Open Secrets and Shadow World Investigations, *The Enablers, The Bankers, Accountants and Lawyers that Cashed in on State Capture*, 87.

77. David Pilling and Joseph Cotterill, 'Jacob Zuma, the Guptas and the Selling of South Africa,' *Financial Times Magazine*, 30 November 2017, accessed April 15, 2022, https://www.ft.com/content/707c5560-d49a-11e7-8c9a-d9c0a5c8d5c9.

78. Chitja Twana, 'The Demon of Factionalism in an African National Congress (ANC)—Led Free State Province (1994–2004). A Reality?' *Southern Journal for Contemporary* 30, no. 3 (December 2005).

79. Myburgh, *Gangster State. Unravelling Ace Magashule's Web of Capture*, chap. 14.

80. Myburgh, *Gangster State. Unravelling Ace Magashule's Web of Capture*, chap. 14.

81. Budget Vote Speech of the Free State Department of Agriculture and Rural Development Tabled by the Honourable MJ Zwane, MEC for Agriculture and Rural Development, 22 March 2012, https://www.gov.za/budget-vote-speech-free-state-department-agriculture-and-rural-development-tabled-honourable-mj.

82. Budget Vote Speech of the Free State Department of Agriculture and Rural Development Tabled by the Honourable MJ Zwane, MEC for Agriculture and Rural Development.

83. Budget Vote Speech of the Free State Department of Agriculture and Rural Development Tabled by the Honourable MJ Zwane, MEC for Agriculture and Rural Development.

84. Budget Vote Speech of the Free State Department of Agriculture and Rural Development Tabled by the Honourable MJ Zwane, MEC for Agriculture and Rural Development.

85. Myburgh, *Gangster State. Unravelling Ace Magashule's Web of Capture*, chap. 14.

86. For example, Tabelo Timse and Stefaans Brummer, 'Gupta's Farm Cash Cows in Free State,' *Mail and Guardian*, 31 May 2013, https://mg.co.za/article/2013-05-31-00-guptas-farm-cash-cows-in-free-state/. amaBhungane and Scorpio, '#GuptaLeaks: The Dubai Laundromat—How millions Milked from Free State Government Paid for Sun City Wedding,' *amaBhungane*, 30 June 2017, https://amabhungane.org/stories/guptaleaks-the-dubai-laundromat-how-millions-milked-from-free-state-government-paid-for-sun-city-wedding/.

87. Myburgh, *Gangster State. Unravelling Ace Magashule's Web of Capture*, chap. 14.

88. Open Secrets and Shadow World Investigations, *The Enablers, The Bankers, Accountants and Lawyers that Cashed in on State Capture*; Shadow World Investigations (SWI), *Estina/Vrede Integrated Dairy Project* (2019), https://shadowworldinvestigations.org/wp-content/uploads/2019/12/SWI-Submission-to-the-Zondo-Commission-Estina-and-the-Gupta-Enterprise.pdf.

89. Léonce Ndikumana, Karmen Naido, and Adam Aboobaker, 'Capital Flight From South Africa: A Case Study,' *Peri Working Paper Series: Capital Flight from Africa*, WP 516 (June 2020).

90. Public Protector South Africa, *Allegation of Maladministration against the Free State Department of Agriculture 'Vrede Integrated Dairy Project'*.

91. Judicial Commission of Inquiry into state capture report, Part VI, Vol. 1 *Vrede Diary Project/Estina and Closure of Gupta Bank Accounts*.

92. Open Secrets and Shadow World Investigations, *The Enablers, The Bankers, Accountants and Lawyers that Cashed in on State Capture*, 88.

93. amaBhungane and Scorpio, '#GuptaLeaks: The Dubai Laundromat—How millions Milked from Free State Government Paid for Sun City Wedding.'

94. amaBhungane and Scorpio, '#GuptaLeaks: The Dubai Laundromat—How millions Milked from Free State Government Paid for Sun City Wedding.'

95. amaBhungane and Scorpio, '#GuptaLeaks: The Dubai Laundromat—How millions Milked from Free State Government Paid for Sun City Wedding.'

96. Myburgh, *Gangster State. Unravelling Ace Magashule's Web of Capture*, chap. 13.

Ace Magashule who was the Premier of the Free State province (2009–2018).

97. Open Secrets and Shadow World Investigations, *The Enablers, The Bankers, Accountants and Lawyers that Cashed in on State Capture*, 95.

Peter Thabethe, was the Head of the Free State Agriculture Department at this time and Monzebanzi Zwane served Member of the Executive Councxil (MEC) in the Portfolio of Agriculture and Rural development.

98. Open Secrets and Shadow World Investigations, *The Enablers, The Bankers, Accountants and Lawyers that Cashed in on State Capture*, 96.

99. Open Secrets and Shadow World Investigations, *The Enablers, The Bankers, Accountants and Lawyers that Cashed in on State Capture*, 17.

100. United Nations Human Rights Office of the High Commissioner, 'Guiding Principles on Business and Human Rights'.

101. Bank Track, *Human Rights Briefing Paper: How Banks Contribute to Human Rights Violations* (December 2017), 1, https://www.banktrack.org/download/how_banks_contribute_to_human_rights_abuses/180416_how_banks_contribute_human_rights_1.pdf.

102. United Nations Human Rights Office of the High Commissioner, 'Guiding Principles on Business and Human Rights,' 13.

103. Bank Track, *Human Rights Briefing Paper: How Banks Contribute to Human Rights Violations*, 1.

104. United Nations Human Rights Office of the High Commissioner, 'Guiding Principles on Business and Human Rights,' 17.

105. United Nations Economic Commission for Africa (UNECA), *Report of the High-Level Panel on Illicit Financial Flows from Africa*, 37.

106. Prevention of Organised Crime Act 121 of 1998, https://www.gov.za/documents/prevention-organised-crime-act.

107. Financial Intelligence Centre Act 38 of 2001, https://www.fic.gov.za/Resources/Pages/Legislation.aspx.

108. The Financial Action Task Force (FATF) is an in an intergovernmental organisation which South Africa is one of the thirty-six member countries, that provides recommendations to fight against IFFs. Established in 1989 by a group of seven (G-7) at the Paris Summit and intergovernmental institution, the Financial Action Task Force (FATF).

109. Financial Action Task Force (FATF), https://www.anti-moneylaundering.org/fatf.aspx.

110. Prevention of Organised Crime Act 121 of 1998.

111. Financial Intelligence Centre Act 38 of 2001.

112. Open Secrets and Shadow World Investigations, *The Enablers, The Bankers, Accountants and Lawyers that Cashed in on State Capture*, 21.

113. Open Secrets and Shadow World Investigations, *The Enablers, The Bankers, Accountants and Lawyers that Cashed in on State Capture*, 97.

114. Open Secrets and Shadow World Investigations, *The Enablers, The Bankers, Accountants and Lawyers that Cashed in on State Capture*, 97.

115. Open Secrets and Shadow World Investigations, *The Enablers, The Bankers, Accountants and Lawyers that Cashed in on State Capture*, 102–4.

116. Open Secrets and Shadow World Investigations, *The Enablers, The Bankers, Accountants and Lawyers that Cashed in on State Capture*, 102–4.

117. Open Secrets and Shadow World Investigations, *The Enablers, The Bankers, Accountants and Lawyers that Cashed in on State Capture*, 102–4.

118. Appel and Erin on Estina Laundromat: Complicity of banks. Available at https://www.biznews.com/global-citizen/2022/05/19/estina-laundromat-banks-complicity.

BIBLIOGRAPHY

African Charter on Human and Peoples' Rights. June 27, 1981. Accessed April 15, 2022. https://au.int/en/treaties/african-charter-human-and-peoples-rights.

African Monitor. *State of Illicit Financial Flows in South Africa: A Scoping Exercise*, April 2017. Accessed April 15, 2022. http://www.africanmonitor.org/wp-content/uploads/2017/04/IFF-Report-1.pdf.

amaBhungane and Scorpio. '#GuptaLeaks: The Dubai Laundromat – How Millions Milked from Free State Government Paid for Sun City Wedding.' *amaBhungane*, June 30, 2017. Accessed April 15, 2022. https://amabhungane.org/stories/guptaleaks-the-dubai-laundromat-how-millions-milked-from-free-state-government-paid-for-sun-city-wedding/.

Banks Around the World. Accessed April 15, 2022. https://www.relbanks.com/africa/south-africa/first-national-bank.

Bhorat, Haroon et al. *Betrayal of the Promise: How South Africa Is Being Stolen*, May 2017. Accessed April 15, 2022. https://pari.org.za/betrayal-promise-report/.

Budget Vote Speech of the Free State Department of Agriculture and Rural Development Tabled by the Honourable MJ Zwane, MEC for Agriculture and Rural Development, March 22, 2012. Accessed April 15, 2022. https://www.gov.za/budget-vote-speech-free-state-department-agriculture-and-rural-development-tabled-honourable-mj.

Constitution of South Africa, 1996—Bill of Rights. Accessed April 15, 2022. https://www.gov.za/documents/constitution/chapter-2-bill-rights.

Constitution of South Africa, 1996—Preamble. Accessed April 15, 2022. https://www.gov.za/documents/constitution-republic-south-africa-1996-preamble.

Declaration on Right to Development. December 4, 1986. Accessed April 15, 2022. https://www.ohchr.org/en/instruments-mechanisms/instruments/declaration-right-development.

Ekwueme, Evaristus Okechukwu. 'What am I Doing When I am Being Corrupt? An Epistemology of Corruption.' In *Corruption in Africa: A Threat to Justice and Sustainable Peace*, edited by Elizabeth Nduku and John Tenamwenye, 49–68. Geneva: Globethics.net Focus 14, 2014.

February, Judith. 'South Africa Pays the Price of State Capture.' *Institute for Security Studies* (ISS), April 2017. Accessed April 15, 2022. https://issafrica.org/isstoday/south-africa-pays-the-price-of-state-capture.

Financial Action Task Force (FATF). Accessed April 15, 2022. https://www.anti-moneylaundering.org/fatf.aspx.

Financial Action Task Force (FATF). *South Africa's Measures to Combat Money Laundering and Terrorist Financing*, October 2021. Accessed April 15, 2022. https://www.fatf-gafi.org/media/fatf/documents/reports/mer4/Mutual-Evaluation-Report-South-Africa.pdf.

Financial Intelligence Centre Act 38 of 2001. Accessed April 15, 2022. https://www.fic.gov.za/Resources/Pages/Legislation.aspx.

First National Bank. Accessed April 15, 2022. https://www.fnb.co.za/about-fnb/about-us.html.

Global Financial Integrity (GFI). *New Study: Crime, Corruption, Tax Evasion Drained a Record U$$991.2 Billion in Illicit Financial Flows from Developing Economies in 2012*, December 2014. Accessed April 15, 2022. https://www.gfintegrity.org/wp-content/uploads/2014/12/EMBARGOED-Press-Release-Illicit-Financial-Flows-from-Developing-Countries-2003-2012.pdf.

Gqubule, Thuli. *No Longer Whispering to Power: The Story of Thuli Madonsela.* Johannesburg & Cape Town: Jonathan Ball Publishers SA, 2017.

Gutto, Shadrack. 'The Right to Development: An Implied Right in South Africa's Constitutional Order.' In *South African Human Rights Commission Reflections on Democracy and Human Rights: A Decade of the South African Constitution (Act 108 of 1996)*, edited by South African Human Rights Commission, 109–18. Johannesburg: South African Human Rights Commission, 2006.

Hellman, Joel and Daniel Kauffmann. 'Confronting the Challenge, of State Capture in Transition Economies.' *International Monetary Fund* 38, no. 3 (September 2001). Accessed April 15, 2022. https://www.imf.org/external/pubs/ft/fandd/2001/09/hellman.htm.

History of the Freedom Charter. Accessed April 15, 2022. https://www.dffe.gov.za/sites/default/files/docs/publications/history_freedomcharter.pdf.

Jagarnath, Vashna. 'Ajay Come to Jo'burg: From Selling Shoes to Assailing the State.' *Daily Maverick*, October 28, 2016. Accessed April 15, 2022. https://www.dailymaverick.co.za/opinionista/2016-10-28-ajay-comes-to-joburg-from-selling-shoes-to-assailing-the-state/#.Wvw_pYiFPIU.

Judicial Commission of Inquiry into State Capture Report, Part VI, Vol. 1. *Vrede Diary Project/Estina and closure of Gupta Bank Accounts (2022).* Accessed June 10, 2022. https://www.gov.za/sites/default/files/gcis_document/202206/electronic-state-capture-commission-report-part-vi-vol-i_0.pdf.

Kamga, Serges D. *The Right to Development in Africa: Issues, Constraints and Prospects.* Austin: Pan-African University Press, 2020.

Lodge, Tom. 'Neo-Patrimonial Politics in the ANC.' *African Affairs* 113, no. 450 (January 2014): 1–23.

Martini, Maira. 'Anti-Corruption Helpdesk: State Capture: An Overview.' *Transparency International*, March 2014. Accessed April 15, 2022. https://knowledgehub.transparency.org/helpdesk/state-capture-an-overview.

Matshiqi, Aubrey. 'Rise of Deep State Has Me Ducking for the Duvet.' *Business Day*, April 16, 2012. Accessed April 15, 2022. https://www.pressreader.com/south-africa/business-day/20120416/281887295295817.

Matshiqi, Aubrey. 'The Guptas? They're Just the Tip of the Iceberg.' *Rand Daily Mail*, February 9, 2016. Accessed April 15, 2022. https://www.businesslive.co.za/rdm/politics/2016-02-09-the-guptas-theyre-just-the-tip-of-the-iceberg/.

Mbuga, David K. 'Corruption and Human Rights Moral Theorical Perspectives.' In *Corruption in Africa: A Threat to Justice and Sustainable Peace*, edited by Elizabeth Nduku and John Tenamwenye, 217–44. Geneva: Globethics.net Focus 14, 2014.

Médard, Jean-François. « L'État néo-patrimonial. » In *États d'Afrique : formation, mécanismes et crise*, edited by Jean-François Médard, 323–55. Paris: Karthala, 1992.

Munyai, Anzanilifuno and Avitus A. Agbor. 'The Impact of Corruption on the Right to Development in Africa.' In *Perspectives on the Right to Development*, edited by Carol C. Ngang, Serges D. Kamga, and Vusi Gumede, 70–96. Pretoria: Pretoria University Law Press (PULP), 2018.

Myburgh, Pieter-Louis. *Gangster state. Unravelling Ace Magashule's web of capture*. Cape Town: Penguin Books, 2019, Kindle.

Ndikumana, Léonce et al. 'Capital Flight from South Africa: A Case Study.' *Peri Working Paper Series: Capital Flight from Africa*, WP 516 (June 2020). Accessed April 15, 2022. https://peri.umass.edu/publication/item/1323-capital-flight-from-south-africa-a-case-study.

Ngang, Carol C. 'Radical Transformation and a Reading of the Right to Development in the South African Constitutional Order.' *South African Journal on Human Rights* 35, no. 1 (January 2019): 25–49.

Okafor, Obiora Chinedu. 'A Regional Perspective: Article 22 of the African Charter on Human and Peoples' Rights.' In *Realizing the Right to Development*, edited by United Nations Human Rights of the High Commissioner, 373–84. New York and Geneva: United Nations, 2013.

Open Secrets and Shadow World Investigations. *The Enablers, The Bankers, Accountants and Lawyers that Cashed in on State Capture.* Southern Africa Office, Last modified, April 2020. Accessed April 15, 2022. https://www.opensecrets.org.za/what_we_do/investigations/the-enablers/.

Pilling, David and Joseph Cotterill. 'Jacob Zuma, the Guptas and the Selling of South Africa.' *Financial Times Magazine*, November 30, 2017. Accessed April 15, 2022. https://www.ft.com/content/707c5560-d49a-11e7-8c9a-d9c0a5c8d5c9.

Pitcher, Anne et al. 'Rethinking Patrimonialism and Neopatrimonialism in Africa.' *African Studies Review* 52, no. 1 (April 2009): 125–56.

Prevention of Organised Crime Act 121 of 1998. Accessed April 15, 2022. https://www.gov.za/documents/prevention-organised-crime-act.

Public Protector South Africa. 'Allegation of Maladministration Against the Free State Department of Agriculture "Vrede Integrated Dairy Project".' *Report n°:31 of 2017/18*. Accessed April 15, 2022. https://www.gov.za/sites/default/files/gcis_document/201802/vrede-report1.pdf.

Rapanyane, Makhura B. and Chuene C. Ngoepe. 'The Impact of Illicit Financial Flows on South African Political Economy Under Jacob Zuma, 2009–2018.' *Journal of Public Affairs* 20, no. 1 (September 2019): 1–7. https://doi.org/10.1002/pa.2020.

Role of the Bill of Rights. Accessed April 15, 2022. https://ourconstitution.constitutionhill.org.za/south-african-constitution/our-constitution-explained/role-the-bill-of-rights/.

SandonCity, First National Bank. Accessed April 15, 2022. https://www.sandtoncity.com/shops/first-national-bank/.

Séverin, Marianne. 'Civil Society and the Fight Against Illicit Financial Flows in Africa: The Case Study of OUTA and the "State Capture in South Africa".' In *Illicit Financial Flows from South Africa*, edited by Serges D. Kamga, 119–34. London and New York: Routledge, 2022.

Séverin, Marianne. 'Civil Society, Corruption, and the Realisation of the Right to Development in African: The Case of Forensics for Justice and "State Capture" in South Africa.' In *The Right to Development in Africa: Issues, Constraints and Prospects*, edited by Serges D. Kamga, 265–83. Austin: Pan-African University Press, 2020.

South African Human Rights Commission. *Reflections on Democracy and Human Rights: A Decade of the South African Constitution (Act 108 of 1996).* Johannesburg: SAHRC, 2006.

Timse, Tabelo and Stefaans Brummer. 'Gupta's Farm Cash Cows in Free State.' *Mail and Guardian*, May 31, 2013. Accessed April 15, 2022. https://mg.co.za/article/2013-05-31-00-guptas-farm-cash-cows-in-free-state/.

Twana, Chitja 'The Demon of Factionalism in an African National Congress (ANC)—Led Free State Province (1994–2004): A Reality?' *Southern Journal for Contemporary* 30, no. 3 (December 2005): 109–31.

Universal Declaration of Human Rights, December 10, 2018. Accessed April 15, 2022. https://www.un.org/en/udhrbook/pdf/udhr_booklet_en_web.pdf.

United Nations Economic Commission for Africa (UNECA). *Report of the High-Level Panel on Illicit Financial Flows from Africa*, 2015. Accessed April 15, 2022. https://repository.uneca.org/handle/10855/22695?locale-attribute=en&.

United Nations Economic and Social Council. 'Norms on the Responsibilities of Transnational Corporations and Other Business Enterprises with Regard to Human Rights.' E/CN.4/Sub.2/2003/12, May 30, 2003. Accessed April 15, 2022. https://digitallibrary.un.org/record/498842.

United Nations Global Compact. July 26, 2000. Accessed April 15, 2022. https://www.unglobalcompact.org/what-is-gc/mission/principles.

United Nations Human Rights Office of the High Commissioner. 'Guiding Principles on Business and Human Rights.' Accessed April 15, 2022. https://www.ohchr.org/sites/default/files/documents/publications/guidingprinciplesbusinesshr_en.pdf.

Vienna Declaration and Programme of Action. June 25, 1993. Accessed April 15, 2022. https://www.ohchr.org/en/instruments-mechanisms/instruments/vienna-declaration-and-programme-action.

Chapter 8

Neoliberal Legality, Illicit Financial Flows, and the Complicity of the South African Banking Sector

Isaac Shai and Felix Dube

INTRODUCTION

The law is a product of political ideologies prevailing at defining historical moments, such as constitution-making, and is shaped and engineered to achieve particular political, social, and economic outcomes. This is particularly evident when one looks at the adoption of the Constitution of the Republic of South Africa, 1996, and subsequent legislation adopted to move South Africa from the apartheid system to a constitutional democracy. Economically, the law entrenches specific institutional models that make it possible for specific economic, financial, and developmental ideas to thrive. In post-apartheid South Africa, as well as the rest of colonial Africa, the central role of the law in embracing Western ideas of economic development, often seen under the umbrella of capitalism and its connotations of market supremacy,[1] is particularly amplified. This economic approach, enhanced and reinforced by the law through regulation and deregulation, has come to be known as neoliberalism.[2] The law, and what at face value appears to be state regulation – when, in fact, it constitutes negative regulation – is essential to the neoliberal project. An argument could be made, albeit in parenthesis, that neoliberalism requires a strong state, guided by a strong constitution and judiciary, to ensure that its interests, as opposed to the interests of states, are safeguarded.

Whereas the role of neoliberalism in shaping post-colonial Africa and most of the Global South is acknowledged in critical scholarship,[3] efforts to tame its influence have been minimal, if any. In our understanding, none have succeeded so far. This is demonstrated by the prevalence of illicit financial flows, which cost Africa at least $88 billion per year.[4] In an economically challenged continent, this is a massive figure. For its part, South Africa loses at least $5 billion each year to illicit financial flows, totalling about R80 billion per annum.[5] This is not sustainable in a country whose economy is struggling and which faces severe socioeconomic challenges.[6] Illicit financial flows do not only rob the *fiscus* of much-needed revenue but also perpetuate corruption and the financing of terrorism.[7] There is a multitude of reasons for the perpetuation of illicit financial flows in South Africa.[8] These range from tax evasion, corruption, and other subtle and outright criminal acts. Whereas these reasons are important, our focus in this chapter is on the contribution of neoliberal legality to illicit financial flows from South Africa.

As we will describe it in this chapter, neoliberal legality refers to the role of the law in advancing neoliberalism. We argue that since illicit financial flows require a legitimate banking system to move money around and given that illicit financial flows would be impossible without an enabling banking environment, neoliberal legality enables banks to deliberately 'look away', thus making them complicit in illicit financial flows. Their participation in illicit financial flows is made possible by neoliberal legality that has entrenched itself in laws regulating the banking sector in South Africa. We suggest that despite the limitations of law as an instrument to combat the deleterious effects of neoliberalism, there is an opportunity to reorient the laws regulating banking with the purpose of addressing rampant illicit financial flows.

We dedicate the first section of this chapter to an analytic exposition of neoliberalism and neoliberal legality. In the second section, we analyse the policy framework that informs the laws dealing with banking in South Africa. In the third section, we discuss the legal framework for the regulation of the banking sector and how the laws manifest neoliberal legality to the extent of aiding illicit financial flows. It is in this section that we illustrate how illicit financial flows find fertile ground in neoliberal legality as expressed in the laws regulating banks. We conclude in the fourth section and make recommendations on how South Africa can address the deleterious effects of neoliberal legality.

CONNECTING NEOLIBERALISM WITH NEOLIBERAL LEGALITY

It is said that ontologically, neoliberalism was about changing 'man himself'.[9] But how was this to be achieved? In this section, we provide a general overview of neoliberalism to answer this question and link it with neoliberal legality. We begin by observing that the term neoliberalism 'carries a bewildering set of meaning'[10] because it is generally approached as an ideology and a set of economic policies informed by this ideology.[11] It 'is the often ill-defined shorthand that has come to represent the dominant ideology, political economy, and policy approach internationally from the 1980s onward'.[12] Its roots date to the 1930s when ordoliberals in Europe and the Chicago School in the United States proposed a new way to learn from history and dodge the mistakes of 'classical *laissez-faire* liberalism, socialism, totalitarianism, and the welfare state'.[13] The central idea of this philosophical approach was to express a utopia in which neoliberals could realise their freedom and enhance their quality of life by harnessing the benefits of pursuing self-interests in a market defined by autonomous transactions, that is, capitalism.[14] In this context, one can view neoliberalism as harnessing freedom and democratic opportunities for the benefit of markets. Thus, neoliberalism is not just about the workings of financial markets and their regulation, but it also influences political and economic conditions that define legal relationships on which individual freedom to harness the markets is exercised.[15] This makes neoliberalism 'a set of discourses, practices and apparatus that determine a new model of government of human beings in accordance with the universal principle of competition'.[16]

What we see so far is that neoliberalism provides the foundation on which capitalism thrives. This explains why some say that neoliberalism is incapable of 'grasping the novelty of capitalism'.[17] Understood this way, neoliberalism is also characterised as 'fundamentally a rationality'[18] of 'contemporary capitalism' which not only disciplines the actions of the rulers but also of the ruled.[19] Dardot and Laval argue that 'the principal characteristic of neo-liberal rationality is the generalisation of competition as a behavioural norm and of the enterprise as a model of subjectivism'.[20] The shift instantiated by neoliberalism, and which qualitatively distinguishes it from liberal capitalism, is that neoliberalism imposes a new set of rules that not only affect the trajectory of capital accumulation but have the effect of fundamentally changing society and subjectivities in particular.[21] It is in this sense that neoliberalism is at once an ontological and epistemological redefinition of liberalism. It constitutes the redefinition of the theoretical bases of liberalism.[22]

As Brabazon notes, 'neoliberalism strives to *manage* difference and inequality, rather than to *address* them'.[23] In South Africa, this has profound implications for efforts to overcome inequalities caused by excesses of the apartheid order. Institutions which should ideally be at the forefront of overcoming these inequalities, such as banks, are actually doing the opposite and remain beholden to the erstwhile way of doing things. An example can be easily found in the role of banks in stamping out what they term as corruption and illicit financial flows when it comes to certain categories of persons while at the same time ignoring similar acts by others. The closure of the bank accounts of some individuals by leading financial institutions on the grounds of corruption while at the same time not extending similar treatment to entities that have pleaded guilty to these crimes is confounding. The judgement of the Equality Court (also sitting at the High Court of South Africa, Western Cape Division, Cape Town) in *Surve v Nedbank* is an illustration of these inequalities.[24] This judgement is yet to be reported in the official law reports, despite obvious interest to the public.

Through the state, neoliberalism creates a legal framework that corresponds with and advances the interests of neoliberalism. It requires laws to be enacted and interpreted to achieve its ends, regardless of the needs of the nation at the time. Neoliberalism also requires the state to enforce and protect certain rights, such as property rights and contractual rights.[25] To achieve this, neoliberal legality gives corporations legal status and confers to them all constitutional rights except those that may only be exercised by human beings. This is achieved within the understanding that commercial law and labour law are prerequisites for advancing the logic of neoliberalism.[26] Neoliberalism creates a new legal framework and order 'wherein private initiative subject to competition could unfold in complete freedom'. We understand this to mean that neoliberal legality does not impose but prohibits separation of the economy from the legal and institutional framework within which it operates, thereby creating a competitive market order that is firmly grasped by the tentacles of neoliberalism. Neoliberal legality ensures no part of society remains in a state in which it cannot advance the interests of neoliberalism.

It is accepted that capitalism and its philosophical underpinnings, such as neoliberalism, is a result of legal rules. Laval says that in this regard, capitalism and its crisis is a result of the laws of capital accumulation (Laval loc 257). Therefore, overcoming the crisis of capitalist accumulation requires juridico-institutional changes (Dardot and Laval, loc 263). It has been noted that the law plays an active role in mediating political, social, and economic life in a manner that advances the ends of neoliberalism. Brabazon terms this 'juridification'.[27] Hors says that 'the significance of the increased reach of law extends beyond the content of the laws in question to the form of law itself, which this volume contends has been essential to the development and spread of the neoliberal social and economic order'.[28] This puts the rule of law firmly within the grip of neoliberalism since the rule of law 'embodies key characteristics of the legal, most notably the notion of formal equality – that all are equal before the law'.[29] Viewed in this light, the law enhances the neoliberal agenda by creating an illusion that instead of focusing on advancing equality, redistributing resources and striving for justice, the state must instead create conditions that are optimal for facilitating the transactions of corporations. This is often justified in the public interest, that is, the public interest and democratic commands require the creation of conditions for individuals driven by self-interest to thrive.[30] In other words, for capitalism to respond to the crisis of accumulation, the forces of neoliberalism require legal intervention to enhance and protect its needs. This makes capitalism an 'economico-juridico' complex, which we now discuss with reference to the influence of neoliberalism on the policy approach to the regulation of the banking sector in South Africa.

SOUTH AFRICA'S NEOLIBERAL POLICY APPROACH TO THE REGULATION OF THE BANKING SECTOR

The legal dimensions of neoliberalism and their influence on domestic and international laws and the institutions which enforce these laws need to be studied.[31] This is because the bulk of the literature on neoliberalism focuses on ideas and policies which define neoliberalism and pays little to no attention to how neoliberalism embeds itself in the law and the institutions which create, interpret and enforce those laws.[32] Neoliberalism embeds itself in the law and its institutions through neoliberal legality, which is the focus of this section. In this section, we proceed from the premise that in South Africa, illicit financial flows can be traced to the phenomenon of financialisation, which arises as a result of neoliberal restructuring. Financialisation is a direct result of neoliberal legality and neoliberal restructuring. We argue that the ineffectiveness of banking laws is inherent in that these laws do not constitute state intervention but constitute negative regulation, that is, regulation to ensure the absence of regulation. As such, they create conditions and possibilities for illicit financial flows. We elaborate on this line of the argument below.

We begin by noting that neoliberal legality enhances illicit financial flows by requiring the state to restructure its economics through policy and statutory adjustments that create ideal conditions for illicit financial flows. In Africa, these economic structural adjustments have been adopted under the tutelage of Western financial institutions such as the International Monetary Fund and the World Bank. Like many of its counterparts, South Africa has experienced the debilitating effects of neoliberal restructuring but perhaps not as badly as its counterparts. South Africa's move to economic adjustment might have started with the adoption of the Reconstruction and Development Programme (RDP), which acknowledged the need to 'modify regulations and support innovative financial institutions and instruments which mobilise private domestic savings'.[33] While on face value this observation seems to be a noble one, it, in effect, created fertile ground for the weakening of the state's oversight over financial institutions, thereby allowing them to work with the private sector in ways which would later be revealed to be facilitating and enabling illicit financial flows. Whereas on its own the RDP did not have immediate implications on the financial sector, its successor did, with far-reaching consequences on illicit financial flows.

The Growth, Employment, and Distribution macroeconomic plan, popularly known as GEAR, was adopted after the RDP. It focused on the privatisation of some state enterprises and the removal of exchange controls.[34] In what it termed 'exchange control liberalisation', GEAR called for the loosening of foreign access to domestic credit, doubling the limits for asset swaps, increasing foreign currency transfers and offsetting the costs of procuring imports against exports.[35] This obviously had one main outcome: the creation of an enabling environment for the private sector to move large amounts of funds under relaxed exchange controls. This relaxation of exchange controls resulted in illicit financial flows due to the abuse of a relaxed regulatory framework for crime, corruption, tax evasion, and other economic crimes disguised as legitimate transactions under the liberalised exchange control framework created by GEAR. The obvious implication of these is that these illicit financial flows pass through the banking network.

To understand how regulations enacted in the implementation of both the RDP and GEAR facilitate illicit financial flows, it is imperative to note the following defining components of illicit financial flows in South Africa.

> The main domestic proceeds-generating crimes in South Africa have been identified as tax crimes, corruption and bribery, fraud, those linked to credit card abuse, and environmental and resource type crimes. Tax crimes encompass evasion of a broad range of taxes and fees, including corporate and personal income and customs and excise taxes as well as tax fraud (e.g. VAT fraud). Fraud includes Ponzi schemes, other investment, cyber-fraud, and digital banking frauds as well as those involving virtual assets. Criminal proceeds from these activities, income disguised as donations or gifts, or legal income earned are often illicitly channelled outside the country and into IFCs thereby contravening exchange control regulations. Given the criminality associated with the manner in which they are generated, such activities are unlikely to be tax compliant. They may also involve foreign investment allowances, crypto assets, financial emigration or funds that are transferred through Common Monetary Area (CMA) countries.[36]

In identifying the nature of these illicit financial flows, we hope to ascertain regulatory issues that create an enabling environment for these illicit activities. We address each of these below. Tax crimes include all crimes relating to the evasion of taxes such as income tax, corporate tax, customs and excise taxes, and fraud concerning value-added tax.[37] These crimes occur notwithstanding that South Africa has a comprehensive legal framework for taxation.[38] Despite the fact that legislation gives the South African Revenue Service, working with other law enforcement agencies, powers to enforce tax compliance, tax crimes are on the rise in South Africa. This is because there are gaps in the enforcement of tax legislation.[39] There are also rising cases of undeclared wealth, contrary to section 5 of the Income Tax

Act, which imposes an obligation on South African tax residents to pay tax on their worldwide income. The gaps in the enforcement of legislation that make it possible for tax evasion and hiding of foreign sources of wealth to flourish can only lead to one thing—illicit financial flows. The question may then be asked: for whose benefit is the government not fully enforcing its tax system?

Some of the major drivers of illicit financial flows are corruption and bribery, which manifest in illegal *quid pro quo* activities in which those in charge of administration and regulatory enforcement receive, solicit, or otherwise obtain gratification for turning a blind to illegalities or doing something to enhance such illegalities. Corruption and bribery have profound implications on a nation's ability to curb illicit financial flows. This has been acknowledged at the United Nations levels as follows:

> Corruption and related financial flows do not only undermine States' ability to mobilise resources for financing sustainable development and for realising human rights. They also weaken state institutions and undermine the rule of law and the functioning of the criminal justice systems.[40]

In South Africa, corruption is endemic despite the enactment of robust anti-corruption legislation.[41] The problem with corruption is that not only does it create conditions and incentives for facilitating illicit financial flows—it also makes it harder to recover the proceeds of corruption.[42] Hence, corruption is a double-edged sword—it incentivises illicit financial flows while also making it notoriously difficult to recover such illicit flows.

In addition to illicit financial flows flowing from tax crimes, corruption, and bribery, South Africa is fast becoming a fraud hub, as seen by the increasing number of Ponzi schemes, banking fraud (including credit card fraud), and crimes committed through virtual assets such as cryptocurrencies.[43] These crimes require sophisticated planning and delivery, all of which involve a measure of illicit financial flows along the chain. For these crimes to succeed, a form of laundering and concealment must be employed. In total, the proceeds of tax crimes, corruption, and fraud which are laundered and disguised in one way or another may be usable and moved across jurisdictions. The proliferation of all sorts of non-governmental organisations and gifting of prominent persons and their families are some of the manifestations of this.[44] The laundering of the proceeds of crimes involves the banking sector as funds have to be moved to and from banks. Whether banks are directly complicit in such crimes or not remains a subject of debate, although we argue that they know, or ought to know, that such activities are occurring through their systems.

NEOLIBERAL REGULATION OF THE BANKING SECTOR IN SOUTH AFRICA

We began our discussion with the hypothesis that illicit financial flows require a legitimate banking system to move money around and that without an enabling banking environment, illicit financial flows would be impossible. In this section, we take the discussion further and present case studies that show that the deliberate 'looking away' by banks not only makes banks complicit in illicit financial flows but further makes banks participants in illicit financial flows. We hope to illustrate that the ability of banks to 'look away' is made possible by neoliberal legality that has entrenched itself in laws regulating banking in South Africa.

However, it is imperative for us to note that while neoliberal regulation has its hands all over the banking system in South Africa, resulting in *regulation for deregulation*, South Africa generally has a well-grounded legal regime whose weakness is not so much in the framing of legislation but in its enforcement.[45] Hence, it is not surprising that South Africa has a plethora of statutes that govern the banking sector and which, when enforced properly, could significantly reduce illicit financial flows. These include the *Banks Act*,[46] the *Financial Intelligence Centre Act*,[47] and anti-laundering and anti-corruption legislation, such as the *Protection of Constitutional Democracy Against Terrorist and Related Activities Act*.[48] These statutes created regulatory and oversight institutions which, in addition to the Reserve Bank of South Africa, include the Financial Intelligence Centre, the Prudential Authority, the Johannesburg Securities Exchange, the Financial Services Board, and the Asset Forfeiture Unit, to mention but a few. These institutions were established to supervise the financial sector—including banks—and to ensure that these statutes are implemented by, *inter alia*, the reporting of suspicious transactions, tracing and recovery of illicit funds, and acting as a buffer against illicit financial flows. These institutions supplement ordinary criminal investigation and prosecution institutions such as the South African Police Service and the National Prosecuting Authority.

Given so many statutes, and in the light of so many regulatory institutions in the banking and financial sectors, the question arises as to why South Africa continues to see an increase in illicit financial flows. We have identified this reason before—lack of enforcement of regulation and the structuring of legislation in such a way that potentially incentivises lack of compliance in specific circumstances. On the issue of lack of enforcement of laws and regulations, it has become evident that South Africa has lost a crucial part of its enforcement mechanisms. This might be traced to a decade or back when the country disbanded the Scorpions (official known as the Directorate of Special Operations), a serious crimes investigations unit that cracked some of the most notorious criminals involved in illicit financial flows and related crimes.[49] The conviction of the former National Commissioner, Jack Selebi, was largely due to the Scorpions. However, the Scorpions were disbanded and replaced by the Directorate for Priority Crime Investigation (the Hawks),[50] under whose watch South Africa has seen continuous growth of serious financial crimes, including illicit financial flows.

There is a reason for rising illicit financial flows: there is too much legislative and institutional focus on anti-money laundering and a corresponding neglect of other illicit financial flows.[51] The South African Reserve Bank, which has constitutional oversight over the banking system in South Africa, has occasionally been fining banks for their laxity of controls in matters involving money laundering.[52] While the Reserve Bank has been quick to say that its fines were not indicative of the complicity of banks in financing these illicit financial flows, the fact is that without the banking environment, these illicit transactions would not have occurred. It also remains clear that these illicit financial flows occurred in the banking system under a supposedly tight regulatory environment, meaning that there are gaps in the regulatory system that can be exploited for illicit financial flows. What makes it possible is that notwithstanding that it does not have an urgent and real threat of terrorism, South Africa is focusing too much on anti-money laundering and the financing of terrorism.[53]

> The reason for increasing institutional focus in these areas is the influence of Western powers, particularly the United States and the European Union, who provide technical and other training support to local regulators.[54] While this may be good as a pre-emptive strike against terrorism and its financing, it illustrates a much deeper problem—too much neoliberal influence on the South African economy, government and regulators. As such, it is safe to assume that with so much neoliberal influence on the country's centres of power and law-making bodies, the result can only be neoliberal legality, as these Western powers are not providing this technical 'help' out of benevolence but as part of looking after their own interests, which include access to resources for their companies and easy-to-access funds. This is illustrated by the fact that 'illicit financial outflows from developing countries ultimately end up in banks in developed countries like the United States and the United Kingdom, as well as in tax havens like Switzerland, British Virgin Islands, or Singapore'.[55]
>
> It has been reported that more than 60 per cent of illicit financial flows out of Africa are for the benefit of 'multinational companies through transfer pricing, trade mispricing and other corporate malpractices'.[56] As custodians of their own systems, and given their vast experience, the banks in the destination countries know, or perhaps, to put it mildly, ought to know, when suspicious transactions occur in their networks. The same can be said of South African banks. The lack of capacity to combat these illicit financial flows and to enforce regulatory

> compliance by South African institutions has been flagged as one of the reasons for rising illicit financial outflows.[57] This inadequacy is exacerbated by exemptions granted under the Financial Intelligence Centre Act to certain categories of entities, resulting in a 'back hole' through which exempted institutions might work as conduits for illicit financial flows. The exemptions include certain members of exchanges and investment managers.[58] Ironically, these are persons at whose disposal lie vast amounts of money which can be moved illicitly without proper regulatory scrutiny and oversight. Granting them exemptions essentially means *carte blanche* licence to do as they please.

While the regulatory environment is governed by strict legislation (notwithstanding the back holes created by exemptions), another area of weakness is that the banking sector is left to decide on who to deal with. This raises the issue of the duplicity of the banking sector when it comes to illicit financial flows and the management of 'reputational risk'. To maximise the full potential of their 'good reputations', these banks retain full power and sole discretion to close bank accounts of clients they suspect of corruption and, by extension, illicit financial flows (often after sensational headlines in the papers)[59] but not extending the same courtesy to persons and institutions that have actually committed corrupt activities or conducted themselves in ways detrimental to South Africa's interests. The most glaring issue about this is that the closure of some of the bank accounts has been done on a racially motivated basis, as alleged in the *Surve* case.[60] Often, where there is discrimination, there is excessive scrutiny of those discriminated, while those who benefit from the discrimination get a free pass. As a result, opportunities for illicit financial flows are created as those deemed to be 'less risky' are given a free pass from scrutiny.

CONCLUSION

In this chapter, we have argued that neoliberal legality and its influence on the regulation of the financial sector and the enforcement (and lack thereof) of laws on the banking sector creates conditions for illicit financial flows by enhancing possibilities for corruption, tax evasion, operation of illegal markets, exploitative activities and the financing of terrorism. At the time of writing, there is no question about the endemic nature of corruption in South Africa and the risks of the financing of terrorism caused by a laxity of regulations in the banking sector. Without the financial sector, these illicit financial flows would not occur. Notwithstanding the risks of harm to human life due to the financing of terrorism, illicit financial flows also rob South Africa of fiscal revenue to grow its economy, build infrastructure and provide social and economic services to its population. Issues such as corruption and the financing of terrorism do not board well with legitimate investors and might, as a result, push them away from investing in the country. It undermines public confidence in the commitment and ability of the state to enforce its laws. We conclude that the deleterious effects of neoliberalism on South Africa's economy, particularly its role in facilitating illicit financial flows, can only be addressed if they are recognised and addressed. This requires the state to advance its role in fostering democracy, encouraging collective action and addressing inequalities.

NOTES

1. Honor Brabazon, 'Introduction: Understanding Neoliberal Legality' in Honor Brabazon (ed), *Neoliberal Legality: Understanding the Role of Law in the Neoliberal Project* (Routledge, 2017), 1.

2. Jamie Peck, Neil Brenner and Nik Theodore, 'Actually Existing Neoliberalism' in Damien Cahill and others (eds), *The Sage Handbook of Neoliberalism*, Vol. 1 (2018) 3.

3. See, for instance, Graham Harrison, 'Economic Faith, Social Project and a Misreading of African Society: The Travails of Neoliberalism in Africa' (2005) 26 Third World Quarterly 1303; Sagie Narsiah, 'Neoliberalism and Privatisation in South Africa' (2002) 57 GeoJournal 3; Graham Harrison, 'Authoritarian Neoliberalism and Capitalist Transformation in Africa: All Pain, No Gain' (2019) 16 Globalizations 274; Lee Wengraf, *Extracting Profit: Imperialism, Neoliberalism and the New Scramble for Africa* (Haymarket Books 2018).

4. Francois Charlier, 'Tackling Illicit Financial Flows to Secure Africa's Future, Curb Conflict' (*United Nations*, 2021) <https://0-www-un-org.ujlink.uj.ac.za/africarenewal/magazine/february-2021/tackling-illicit-financial-flows-secure-africas-future-curb-conflict> accessed 17 June 2022.

5. See OECD, *Assessing Tax Compliance and Illicit Financial Flows in South Africa* (OECD Publishing, 2022) for a full assessment.

6. See Goal 16 of the Sustainable Development Goals, which requires states to 'significantly reduce illicit financial flows and arms flows, strengthen the recovery and return of stolen assets and combat all forms of organised crime' – United Nations, 'Transforming Our World: The 2030 Agenda for Sustainable Development' <https://sustainabledevelopment.un.org/content/documents/21252030%20Agenda%20for%20Sustainable%20Development%20web.pdf>

7. OECD, *Assessing Tax Compliance and Illicit Financial Flows in South Africa* 31 illustrates that the defining features of illicit financial flows have been analysed to include illicit tax and other commercial activities that result in tax evasion, the use of illegal markets, corrupt activities, and the exploitative activities, including the financing of terrorism and related crimes. There is already evidence that South Africa's laxity in tackling illicit financial flows is leading to the financing of terrorism – see Financial Intelligence Centre, 'South Africa's Inherent Riska Nd Vulnerabilities to Terror Financing Risks Identified' (*Financial Intelligence Centre,* 2022) <https://

www.fic.gov.za/Documents/Media%20release%20-%20TF%20national%20risk%20assessment%2012%20April%202022.pdf> accessed 10 June 2022; Financial Intelligence Centre, 'South African National Terrorism Financing Risk Assessment' (*Financial Intelligence Centre,* 2022) <https://www.fic.gov.za/Documents/TF%20NRA%2031%20March%202022.pdf> accessed 10 June 2022.

8. In chapter, illicit financial flows should be understood as monies that are earned, transferred, or used. Hence, illicit financial flows can be distinguished from legitimate movements of funds such as capital flight and other movements of huge funds abroad by residents and non-residents in search of better returns because they include all 'revenue or proceeds derived from corruption, commercial activities or crime'—OECD, *Assessing Tax Compliance and Illicit Financial Flows in South Africa* 30.

9. Pierre Dardot and Christian Laval, *The New Way of the World: On Neoliberal Society* (Verso Books, 2014), 65.

10. Costas Douzinas, *Critical Jurisprudence: The Political Philosophy of Justice* (Hart, 2005), 284.

11. Dardot and Laval, *The New Way of the World: On Neoliberal Society,* 1.

12. Brabazon, 'Introduction: Understanding Neoliberal Legality' 3.

13. Ibid., 3.

14. Ibid.

15. Andrés Palacios Lleras, 'Neoliberal Law and Regulation' in Honor Brabazon (ed), *Neoliberal Legality: Understanding the Role of Law in the Neoliberal Project* (Routledge, 2017), 62.

16. Dardot and Laval, *The New Way of the World: On Neoliberal Society*, 114.

17. Ibid., 12.

18. Ibid., 9.

19. Ibid.

20. Ibid.

21. Ibid., 242.

22. Laval, 56.

23. Brabazon, 'Introduction: Understanding Neoliberal Legality' 6.

24. *Surve and Others V Nedbank Limited and Another* [2022] ZAWCHC 19.

25. Under the South African Constitution, this is illustrated in section 25 (the property clause), and its strong protection of property rights. It is also evident from the Bill of Rights, which bestows corporations with rights, except only those rights that can only be exercised by humans, such as the right to vote.

26. Laval, 58.

27. Brabazon, 'Introduction: Understanding Neoliberal Legality' 6.

28. Ibid.

29. Ibid., 7.

30. Ibid.

31. Lleras, 'Neoliberal Law and Regulation' 61.

32. Ibid.

33. South African Government, *White Paper on Reconstruction and Development Programme* (GN 1954 in *GG* 16085 of 23 November 1994).

34. See National Treasury, 'Growth, Employment, and Redistribution' <http://www.treasury.gov.za/publications/other/gear/chapters.pdf> accessed 20 June 2022 for a full account of GEAR.

35. Ibid., 12.

36. OECD, *Assessing Tax Compliance and Illicit Financial Flows in South Africa*, 34.

37. Ibid.

38. The major taxation statutes include the Income Tax Act 58 of 1962; Value-Added Tax Act 89 of 1991; Tax Administration Act 28 of 2011.

39. OECD, *Assessing Tax Compliance and Illicit Financial Flows in South Africa* 95.

40. Michele Bachelet, 'Combatting Corruption and Illicit Financial Flows' (*United Nations Human Rights Commissioner,* 2022) <https://www.ohchr.org/en/statements/2022/02/combatting-corruption-and-illicit-financial-flows#:~:text=Corruption%20and%20related%20financial%20flows,of%20the%20criminal%20justice%20systems.> accessed 20 June 2022.

41. The major anti-corruption statutes are the Prevention and Combatting of Corrupt Activities Act 12 of 2004; Executive Members Ethics Act 82 of 1998; and the Prevention of Organised Crime Act 121 of 1998.

42. Andrew Dornbierer, 'Introduction' in Andrew Dornbierer (ed), *Illicit Enrichment* (A Guide to Laws Targeting Unexplained Wealth, Basel Institute on Governance 2021) 11.

43. OECD, *Assessing Tax Compliance and Illicit Financial Flows in South Africa* 34.

44. Ibid.

45. African Monitor, 'Regulatory Framework for Illicit Financial Flows in South Africa' <http://www.africanmonitor.org/wp-content/uploads/2017/04/IFF-Report-2.pdf> accessed 7 July 2022.

46. Banks Act 94 of 1990.

47. Financial Intelligence Centre Act 38 of 2001.

48. Protection of Constitutional Democracy against Terrorist and Related Activities 33 of 2004.

49. See, for example, *Selebi V S* [2012] 1 All SA 332 (SCA).

50. The Scorpions were disbanded through the South African Police Service Amendment Act 57 of 2008. This statute was unsuccessfully challenged in *Glenister V President of the Republic of South Africa* 2011 (3) SA 347 (CC).

51. African Monitor, 'Regulatory Framework for Illicit Financial Flows in South Africa' 8.

52. See, for instance, Anti-corruption Authorities, 'South Africa's Reserve Bank Fines Top Four Banks over Anti-Money Laundering Controls' 2022 <https://www.acauthorities.org/news/south-africas-reserve-bank-fines-top-four-banks-over-anti-money-laundering-controls> accessed 11 June 2022.

53. African Monitor, 'Regulatory Framework for Illicit Financial Flows in South Africa' 8.

54. Ibid.

55. Global Financial Integrity, 'Illicit Financial Flows' (*GFI,* 2021) <https://gfintegrity.org/issue/illicit-financial-flows/> accessed 22 June 2022.

56. Dev Kar and Joseph Spanjers, 'Illicit Financial Flows from Developing Countries: 2004–2013' <https://secureservercdn.net/50.62.198.97/34n.8bd.myftpupload.com/wp-content/uploads/2015/12/IFF-Update_2015-Final-1.pdf> 11.

57. African Monitor, 'Regulatory Framework for Illicit Financial Flows in South Africa' 9.

58. See, for instance, South African Government, *Finanncial Intelligence Centre Act (38/2001): Exemptions in Terms of the Act* (GN 749 in *GG* 26487 of 21 June 2004).

59. See *Surve and Others V Nedbank Limited and Another* para 5.

60. Ibid para 16.

BIBLIOGRAPHY

African Monitor, 'Regulatory Framework for Illicit Financial Flows in South Africa' <http://www.africanmonitor.org/wp-content/uploads/2017/04/IFF-Report-2.pdf> accessed 7 July 2022

Anti-Corruption Authorities, 'South Africa's Reserve Bank Fines Top Four Banks over Anti-Money Laundering Controls' (2022) <https://www.acauthorities.org/news/south-africas-reserve-bank-fines-top-four-banks-over-anti-money-laundering-controls> accessed 11 June 2022

Bachelet M, 'Combatting Corruption and Illicit Financial Flows' (United Nations Human Rights Commissioner, 2022) <https://www.ohchr.org/en/statements/2022/02/combatting-corruption-and-illicit-financial-flows#:~:text=Corruption%20and%20related%20financial%20flows,of%20the%20criminal%20justice%20systems.> accessed 20 June 2022

Brabazon H, 'Introduction: Understanding Neoliberal Legality' in Brabazon H (ed), *Neoliberal Legality: Understanding the Role of Law in the Neoliberal Project* (Routledge, 2017)

Charlier F, 'Tackling Illicit Financial Flows to Secure Africa's Future, Curb Conflict' (United Nations, 2021) <https://0-www-un-org.ujlink.uj.ac.za/africarenewal/magazine/february-2021/tackling-illicit-financial-flows-secure-africas-future-curb-conflict> accessed 17 June 2022

Dardot P and Laval C, *The New Way of the World: On Neoliberal Society* (Verso Books, 2014)

Dornbierer A, 'Introduction' in Dornbierer A (ed), *Illicit Enrichment* (A Guide to Laws Targeting Unexplained Wealth, Basel Institute on Governance, 2021)

Douzinas C, *Critical Jurisprudence: The Political Philosophy of Justice* (Hart, 2005)

Financial Intelligence Centre, 'South Africa's Inherent Riska Nd Vulnerabilities to Terror Financing Risks Identified' (Financial Intelligence Centre, 2022) <https://www.fic.gov.za/Documents/Media%20release%20-%20TF%20national%20risk%20assessment%2012%20April%202022.pdf> accessed 10 June 2022

Financial Intelligence Centre, 'South African National Terrorism Financing Risk Assessment' (Financial Intelligence Centre, 2022) <https://www.fic.gov.za/Documents/TF%20NRA%2031%20March%202022.pdf> accessed 10 June 2022

Global Financial Integrity, 'Illicit Financial Flows' (GFI, 2021) <https://gfintegrity.org/issue/illicit-financial-flows/> accessed 22 June 2022

Harrison G, 'Authoritarian Neoliberalism and Capitalist Transformation in Africa: All Pain, No Gain' (2019) 16 Globalizations 274

Harrison G, 'Economic Faith, Social Project and a Misreading of African Society: The Travails of Neoliberalism in Africa' (2005) 26 Third World Quarterly 1303

Kar D and Spanjers J, 'Illicit Financial Flows from Developing Countries: 2004–2013' <https://secureservercdn.net/50.62.198.97/34n.8bd.myftpupload.com/wp-content/uploads/2015/12/IFF-Update_2015-Final-1.pdf>

Lleras AP, 'Neoliberal Law and Regulation' in Brabazon H (ed), *Neoliberal Legality: Understanding the Role of Law in the Neoliberal Project* (Routledge, 2017)

Narsiah S, 'Neoliberalism and Privatisation in South Africa' (2002) 57 GeoJournal 3

National Treasury, 'Growth, Employment, and Redistribution' <http://www.treasury.gov.za/publications/other/gear/chapters.pdf> accessed 20 June 2022

OECD, *Assessing Tax Compliance and Illicit Financial Flows in South Africa* (OECD Publishing, 2022)

Peck J, Brenner N and Theodore N, 'Actually Existing Neoliberalism' in Cahill D and others (eds), *The Sage Handbook of Neoliberalism*, Vol. 1 (2018).

United Nations, 'Transforming Our World: The 2030 Agenda for Sustainable Development' <https://sustainabledevelopment.un.org/content/documents/21252030%20Agenda%20for%20Sustainable%20Development%20web.pdf>

Wengraf L, *Extracting Profit: Imperialism, Neoliberalism and the New Scramble for Africa* (Haymarket Books, 2018)

Chapter 9

The Gendered Impact of Illicit Financial Flows

Women's Participation and Contribution in Curbing Illicit Financial Flows from Africa with Focus on Nigeria and South Africa

Olayinka Oluwakemi Adeniyi and John Oluwadamilare Olawuyi

INTRODUCTION

Illicit financial flows can be defined as money illegally earned, transferred, or utilised and thus constituting a threat to sustainable development and one of the greatest contemporary challenges to global development.[1] This illicit act affects economic growth and legitimate trade, depriving governments of the financial resources they might otherwise invest in public ventures, such as health, education, and infrastructure. Illicit financial flows do not exist in isolation only within the context of money laundering/embezzlement, among other things, but also involve illicit-arms trade, drug trafficking, and the commodities used in supporting and aiding conflicts.[2]

An estimated $88.6 billion, which is equivalent to 3.7 per cent of Africa's gross domestic product (GDP), leaves the African continent as illicit financial flows.[3] Illicit financial flows include activities such as corruption, theft, tax evasion, money laundering, and all other illegal financial businesses.[4] Illicit financial flows also originate from sources like revenues from illegal activities, abusive profit-shifting, trade misinvoicing, corruption, and many others.[5] It is an act perpetrated by the government, public officers, companies, business organisations, and individuals. The analysis from the perpetrators' viewpoint may break illicit financial flows into three components of commercial activities, criminal activities, and corruption which is a good description of how it plays out in Africa.[6] The effect of illicit financial flows is far-reaching; apart from the loss of money which affects individuals and the development of the larger society,[7] it particularly affects the issue of gender equality.[8] It also touches on the area of the socio-economic right to health,[9] resulting in issues of concern like the high rate of maternal mortality and morbidity in Africa.[10] These touch on the issue of development,[11] exacerbate inequalities in the society,[12] and are connected to the Right to Development as it inhibits women's participation and contribution to development.[13] It is trite that the attainment of good health and well-being is a Sustainable Development Goal (SDG).[14]

In a nutshell, illicit financial flow is an issue that affects development and could adversely affect or thwart the Right to Development.[15] The Right to Development is the human right by which every human is entitled to participate, contribute, and enjoy economic, social, cultural, and political development.[16] This right is to be enjoyed irrespective of gender, sex, age, or status.[17]

Women are not left out of engaging in the activities of illicit financial flows and imperatively since the effect of illicit financial flows affects women more adversely or in a different way from men, women should also have a role to play in combating and curbing it.[18] However, studies on women's inclusion or participation and impact in the reduction of illicit financial flows are scarce.[19] How women participate in, and what women can do to contribute to the reduction of illicit financial flows is necessarily a gendered aspect of the discourse and is worthy of research. This study engages with this.

This chapter is divided into six sections. The first section is the introduction. The second section contains the discourse on illicit financial flows and their status in Nigeria and South Africa. The third section discusses illicit financial flows and its connection to the Right to Development in Africa. The fourth section discusses women's engagement with illicit financial flows in Africa and the effect of illicit financial flows on women's rights with a focus on women's socio-economic rights in the two countries. The fifth section discusses the Innovative strategies to stall or limit illicit financial flows from Africa through women-inclusive measures for development. The sixth section concludes the chapter.

ILLICIT FINANCIAL FLOWS AND THEIR STATUS IN NIGERIA AND SOUTH AFRICA

Illicit financial flows is a global phenomenon with developing regions being more vulnerable to it.[20] This is why it is said that illicit financial flows have adverse effects on the development of developing countries.[21] Illicit financial flows encompass the international transfer of amounts of money generated by bribery, tax evasion, and illegal markets.[22] It also includes criminal activities, drug trade, human trafficking, illegal arms dealing, smuggling of contraband, acts of corruption, bribery, and theft.[23] It is said that illicit financial flows out of sub-Saharan Africa surpass the foreign aid inflows into the continent.[24] The statistics and status of illicit financial flows in Africa can be shocking.[25] From 1980 to 2018 Africa exported an aggregate of $1.3 trillion of illicit financial flows.[26] As of 2019, the losses were estimated to be around USD 50 and 80 billion annually.[27] Resource-rich countries in oil and the size of economic activities are pointers to illicit financial flows,[28] these countries also tend to have higher rates of corruption.[29] Southern and West African regions of the continent are said to have the highest illicit financial flows.[30] South Africa and Nigeria are leading countries in the continent, and among the top four emitters of illicit flow (including the Democratic Republic of Congo [DRC] and Ethiopia).[31] In terms of the volume of illicit financial flows, Nigeria, Egypt, and South Africa led the regional outflows.[32] The high share of illicit outflows by South Africa and Nigeria may be partly related to the size of the net inflow of Foreign Direct Investment FDI into the two countries.[33] This section looks briefly at the status of illicit financial flows in the two countries.

South Africa

Of all the countries in the Southern African region, South Africa is arguably the most affected by illicit financial flows.[34] The majority of the illicit financial flows from the country arise from the transfer pricing from the mining sector.[35] In 2019, mining contributed R360.9 billion or 8.1 per cent to the GDP.[36] Illicit financial flows are the reason for the low human development in southern African countries.[37] The illicit financial flows experienced in South Africa is not of any benefit to both the public and private sectors.[38] South Africa is one of the largest emitters and receivers of illicit flows in sub-Saharan Africa.[39] Illicit financial flows are the reason why social and labour plans are not implemented.[40] Illicit financial flows in South Africa was US$ 9,978,535 in 2005 and by 2012 it was US$ 39,179,944, as a proportion of GDP, the inflow was 5.58 per cent.[41] In quantum terms, the illicit financial flows for South Africa as of 2015 was US$196,335,868 in total.[42] Research reports that in South Africa alone, about one-third of the country's GDP is lost to corruption and organised crime.[43] The update as of 2018 is daunting, and as such, the fact of its affecting the economy and development in the country cannot be overlooked. This is why special attention needs to be paid to the issue in the country.[44]

Nigeria

Nigeria is rated the highest in illicit financial flows in West Africa.[45] The country alone accounts for 10 per cent of the illicit financial flows from

Africa annually.[46] A significant percentage of Nigeria's foreign exchange is earned from oil exports, but it is obvious that illegal money is easy to move out of the country.[47] As of 2017, Nigeria was reported to be the largest importer of the US dollar.[48] Effects of criminal activities connected to illicit financial flows evident in Nigeria include its use for firearms, the cases of kidnapping, bombing, and the general high insecurity state of the country.[49] The aggregate illicit financial flow for Nigeria was US$87,739,590 and the inflow was US$114,410,096 representing an average of about 9.77 per cent as a proportion of the GDP in absolute terms for the period 2005 to 2015.[50] Between 1980 to 2018 Nigeria's illicit financial flows in total in million dollars was 67,058 totalling 3.4 per cent of total trade.[51] It is argued that the current scale of illicit financial flows originating in developing countries like Nigeria cannot be measured, but the estimated volume is staggering and still increasing.[52]

EFFECT OF ILLICIT TRANSFER AND ITS CONNECTION TO THE RIGHT TO DEVELOPMENT

The first impact of illicit financial flows is a reduction in domestic expenditure and investment – both public and private.[53] The varied face or presentations of illicit financial flow is damaging to the economy, with public money from public use being diverted to private consumption for goods like luxury cars, and investments in expensive real estate, art, or precious metals.[54] Over and over, the major effect of illicit financial flows is on the development of the country in question.[55] Apart from the loss of money or income, it is about the concerns of what the lost financial resources could have been used for. Illicit financial flows affect the development of countries, especially in the areas of education, health, and other basic needs.[56] In South Africa, the money lost to illicit financial flows through drugs and organised crimes is alarming, the money that should be used to provide basic infrastructure, water, sanitisation, accommodation, and schools.[57]

The spillover of illicit financial flows and criminal activities can be seen in increased instability, violence, and terrorism in Nigeria.[58] Illicit financial flows stemming from illegal activities such as crime and corruption erode the functioning of criminal justice systems, reduce state revenues, erode the tax base, and weaken state institutions.[59]

Illicit financial flows are linked to the Right to Development in different ways, robbing citizens of contribution and participation, as these are core principles of the Right to Development.[60]

The Right to Development aims to create an enabling environment for peace, development, and human rights, including women's rights, and the mobilisation of resources for inclusive development.[61] In sub-Saharan Africa, southern Africa of which South Africa takes the lead was identified as the region with the highest rate of income inequality.[62] Compared to Netherlands and some other developed countries, maternal mortality is still high in South Africa,[63] situations like these are a display of inadequate funds for such programmes. This not unconnected to the impact of illicit financial flows.

Although the Right to Development calls for full and equal inclusion of women in policy and governance,[64] illicit financial flows have restricted the fulfilment of this mandate because of its impact on the socio-economic development of Nigeria and South Africa.[65]

The Right to Development is a two-way act, one which places the greater part of the responsibility on the state to look after the people it governs by providing means and avenues which improve their standards and conditions of living.[66] The second is due to the availability of these options by the state, the individual can play their role or part in seizing the opportunity to exercise, experience, and enjoy this Right to Development.[67]

The Right to Development is about responsibility; it requires the participation or contribution of persons individually and collectively to development.[68] A situation where women are not allowed to contribute to development in their societies whether in their capacities as business entrepreneurs or politically in any way is against this provision.[69]The government must provide the enabling platform or conducive environment whether through policies, regulations, or other necessities for individuals to facilitate the fulfilment of this right.[70]

The Right to Development requires resources that are being limited and restricted by illicit financial flows.[71] The inhibiting features of illicit financial flows have the tendency of affecting a large number of citizens in the long run rather than just few individuals. Because of this effect on the Right to Development, as a human right, it is the responsibility of the government to focus on curbing it so that development is not obstructed.[72]

The Right to Development specifically requires the government to put effective measures in place to ensure that women have active roles in the development process.[73] The government also must ensure the existence of policies to provide for the full realisation of the Right to Development.[74]

Looking at the provision and the situation or level at which the two countries of Nigeria and South Africa are at present with regard to the enjoyment or realisation of the Right to Development and with particular emphasis on the contribution and involvement of women, it can be argued that the status quo is the fault of the government of the states.[75] The considerable gender gap in terms of policies and interventions on the issue of equality attests to this. A look at this issue from the lens of government's non-response to help women entrepreneurs to prevent tax evasion or involvement in informal cross-border businesses is one example.[76]

WOMEN'S ENGAGEMENT WITH ILLICIT FINANCIAL FLOWS IN AFRICA AND THE EFFECT OF ILLICIT FINANCIAL FLOWS ON WOMEN'S RIGHTS WITH A FOCUS ON SOCIO-ECONOMIC RIGHTS IN THE TWO COUNTRIES

This section seeks to analyse women's involvement or engagement with illicit financial flows. It then goes further to look at the effect of illicit financial flows on women with a focus on their socio-economic rights.

Women's Engagement with Illicit Financial Flows

First looking at the three categories of illicit financial flows that emanate from (i) corruption through embezzlement and bribery by officials in government; (ii) from money laundering from different forms of illegal activities; and (iii) that emanate from tax evasion and attempts by firms to move money between borders.[77] Only a few women are in full-time formal employment compared to 33 per cent of men across seventeen countries in sub-Saharan Africa.[78] In 2019, statistics for female unemployment stood at 30 per cent in South Africa.[79] Although increasing in recent times, the number of women in the working force in Nigeria is still low compared to men.[80]

In South Africa, female informal employment constitutes 92 per cent of total female employment.[81] The informal sector forms part of the private sector of large companies, and small and medium-scale enterprises.[82] Within the informal sector, women are even more in trade, especially in informal cross-border trade.[83] Within this informal cross-border trade, they can engage in tax evasion and maybe to an extent what might amount to illegal trading or export of restricted materials.[84] Cross-border illicit financial flows is an acknowledged phenomenon in Nigeria.[85] The participation of women in Nigeria in cross-border trade is also evident in research.[86] In the cross-border trade of South Arica and its neighbours, men prefer not to cross borders but women are in the business and even employ men.[87] The reality of informal cross-border trade may be firms or individuals evading trade-related regulations and duties wholly or partially, for example, avoiding official border crossing posts or resorting to illegal practices like under-invoicing.[88] Maybe, it is to this extent that women can be said to engage with illicit financial flows, that is through tax evasion within informal cross-border trade.

Meanwhile, the loss of funds from SMEs and individuals in cross-border trade is low compared to what is lost by the corruption of multinational companies and government public officers.[89]

There are few women in the formal sector of government employment as opposed to the informal sector. Hence it can be argued that their involvement in corruption in public service space is slim. This is relevant concerning how women engage with the issue of corruption that plays out in the sector. Research provides that women compared to men are less likely to engage in corrupt acts.[90] Irrespective of their low number within the public sector, it is established that there are women who engage in these illicit acts.[91] There are records of women in public or political offices who have been corrupt and embezzled money transferring them into private accounts outside the country.[92] However, the existence of women in public offices has been associated more with the reduction of corruption than participation.[93] It is said that women are important in the fight against corruption.[94] Research finds that women have higher standards of ethical behaviour compared to men, and thus are less likely to involve in obnoxious acts.[95] Women are also less likely to sacrifice the public good to achieve personal benefit. It goes without saying that the involvement of women in parliament/leadership or public service will likely reduce corruption than increase it. The resonance of the argument is that there are few women in public offices but more in trade and especially cross-border trade. As a result of the scenario, women can be argued to participate less in corruption from the angle of public office. Again, even in public offices, women are known to be strict and more preventive of corruption than men. However, because of lack of government aid in the area of cross-border trade it is likely that women contribute to illicit financial flows in this aspect.

Meanwhile because women are vulnerable, they are more or differently affected than men by the effects of illicit financial flows. How this plays out in Nigeria and South Africa is discussed presently.

Effect of Illicit Financial Flows on Women's Socio-economic Rights

The practices of illicit financial flows are damaging to the social and economic life of Nigeria.[96] Notwithstanding women's participation or not in illicit financial flows, it is glaring that the acts affect women differently and even more than men.[97] In a 2017 UN report on the state of inequality in sub-Saharan Africa, Southern Africa was identified as the region with the highest rate of income inequality.[98] Research confirmed that illicit financial flows are negatively impacting socio-economic development in South Africa.[99] Illicit financial flows affect the provisions of social amenities, which in turn affects issues like maternal care, immunization, family planning, all of which impact women more than men.[100]

Government investment in the services of health, education, housing, social protection, electricity and water provision, or transport infrastructure, alleviate the burden that women shoulder, without the tax money for these, women would be particularly affected in the care for themselves, the children, the aged in their families and care which would also affect the fulfilment of their responsibility to participate and contribute to the development of their society.[101] This responsibility is a provision of the Right to Development.[102]

Women are more dependent on social services. Women are mostly among the lowest income earners in every country, VAT takes the largest share from those with the lowest income.[103] South Africa depends on tax revenue for its social amenities, like many African countries.[104] When export and import are tampered with through illicit financial flows or corruption, the tax base is eroded. In this situation, social amenities that are provided with tax money cannot be performed.[105] And women including their children will be mostly affected.

Human trafficking generates illicit financial flows, this crime is known to target more women than men.[106] In the case of human trafficking, women are more victims than participants.[107] The exploitation and control over the victims deprive them of their dignity as humans and excludes them from the provisions of the Right to Development.[108]

Illicit financial flows hamper development and the guarantee of basic human rights.[109] These glaring rights are mostly related to socio-economic rights.[110] Illicit financial flows affect employment and education, especially that of women and children.[111] The state of university education in Nigeria and the state of its medical relapse is an example.[112] Lack of infrastructure and non-payment of teachers are all the result of corruption in public office, misappropriation of public funds, or tax problems.[113]

The impact of illicit flows falls more on issues of poverty[114] and in this aspect, women are more affected.[115] Public revenue is essential for the realisation of socio-economic rights, women's rights and development.[116] The fact is that where economic development is affected, unemployment is high, maternal mortality is high, equality is difficult to attain and women's development is hampered.[117]

The analysis within this section is that women's engagement with illicit financial flows can be positive and negative. The negative aspect is their participation in the existence or promotion of illicit financial flows. The positive aspect is with regards to their contribution to reducing or curbing illicit financial flows. Considering that the impact of illicit financial flows lies more heavily on women than men, their efforts to curb the acts will bring more gains to them and the societies too. For example, women can play an important role to counter corruption, which is an important element in reducing illicit financial flows.[118] The aspect of their inclusion in contributing to and participating in the curbing of illicit financial flows to enjoy the benefits can be explained within the provisions of the Right to Development,[119] and the possibilities can be explored.

INNOVATIVE STRATEGIES TO STALL OR LIMIT ILLICIT FUND TRANSFER FROM AFRICA THROUGH WOMEN-INCLUSIVE MEASURES FOR DEVELOPMENT

Research reveals that women bring strength to leadership roles,[120] but they are few in leadership positions in public offices. This low number of women is not unconnected to the perception of women and gender bias or discrimination that restricts women from gaining and accessing work in public offices and attaining leadership positions.[121] Also, the loss of funds by individuals and Small Medium Enterprises SMEs is low compared to what is lost by the corruption of multinational companies and government public officers.[122] Thus the involvement of women in cross-border trade as individuals or SMEs is low compared to the loss brought about by other sectors where men are more involved like the corruption in public offices or by male public officers.[123] This corruption level in the public sector can be described as the perpetration of illicit finances.

Political will and visionary leadership are key factors that will be needed to make a change in the discourse.[124] Public consultation, policy consultation, and policy promulgation will be necessary.[125]

Issues of Tax as they relate to illicit financial flows are important aspects of the discussion, especially concerning development.[126] Many women are in the informal cross-border trade and can engage in tax evasion practices because the laws for operating legally are too rigid and restrictive of women's engagement.[127] Again criminal activities like trafficking are mostly done by men while women are more of the victims.[128]

To correct the issues discussed, the solution seems clear, more women should be included in leadership positions in public offices where they can be included in processes of policy-making prevention of corruption, and such actions. Research provides that women are less likely to tolerate corruption, and involving them in leadership positions or law enforcement roles can help curb illicit financial flows.[129] Despite the low impact of SMEs in the discourse of illicit financial flows and women, it is still an area that deserves engagement. Addressing customs and police corruption can help the border trade issues.[130] Already, suggested strategies to curb illicit financial flows include the enactment of effective trade laws, trade regulations, automatic exchange of information on tax issues, guidelines on anti-money laundering, and such related issues.[131] The AfCFTA should be investigated for its women-inclusive provisions.[132] Gender-specific financial inclusion policies will be necessary. Women are generally acknowledged cleaners to curb illegalities in society and thus have a role in curbing illicit financial flows.[133] To do this, women need to hold positions in leadership, parliament, and policy-making to make a difference in the corruption activities that affect illicit financial flows.[134]

Including women in leadership positions is pertinent in the discourse of change for development in Africa.[135] Through the active participation of women in policy amendments or personal involvement in business, this can be achieved.[136] The coming together of women's associations or groups to tackle the issue of illicit financial flows can also be assessed.[137]

Opening up higher education for women, including business management skills and training, will be necessary.[138] Customs and laws, religious practices, financial constraints, political impediments, women's perceptions of politics, and family responsibilities which are the fundamental challenges to women's inclusion and participation in leadership positions should be dealt with.[139] However, the first step to putting the strategies in place is a change of perception about women.[140]

The government of South Africa and Nigeria should increase their efforts on financial inclusion for women.[141] It is evident that there still exists a considerable gender gap in terms of policies and interventions that would help women entrepreneurs which should be closed.[142] Other factors to improve women's inclusion in leadership include movements and activism, gender quotas, electoral and political leadership systems, and women empowerment.[143] Banking institutions should put efforts into aiding women entrepreneurs, especially with funds or loans for business.[144]

CONCLUSION

Illicit financial flow is a human rights issue and impacts socio-economic rights and the Right to Development. The issue affects women differently from men. Women's engagement in the acts/crime/process mostly is in default. Women are few in the formal job sector and out of these few, only a few hold leadership positions. In this situation, they only work out orders of the superior if they engage in corruption. In the informal trade sector, women engage in tax evasion because of the strict rules that make it difficult for them to trade, and in the criminal acts of illicit financial flow especially in human trafficking, women are mostly victims rather than perpetrators. Women however have a role to play in curbing illicit financial flows. With the illicit financial flows currently happening within the African society, especially in Nigeria and South Africa, trusting a woman to be at the helm of control in the government should be considered.

At the family level, it is a proven fact that it is in a woman's nature to ensure organisation, satisfaction, and protection for her own; hence, the opportunity to give a woman the role of leading may bring more togetherness, growth, and accountability in the state offices. Legal and socio-legal systems and structures to make this feasible in South Africa and Nigeria should be established, strengthened, and implemented. However, the starting point will be an understanding of the role and importance of women in contributing to and curbing illicit financial flows. This is necessary to change the perceptions or narratives. Then, government must put systems and institutions that are women-inclusive in place. This must not be only in rhetoric as most African countries are known to have the practice of legislating without enforcement but must aid the effective implementation.

In essence, the discourse of affirmative action should move beyond rhetoric to reality. Women should be motivated and encouraged to come together to support each other in leadership and integrity. Women's self-development and moral discipline are needed. Policies should include moral teachings, integrity, and social responsibilities in school curricula. Empirical research especially participatory action research should be explored to bring out the need for this teaching in schools. The research would result in policy recommendations that will reach the authorities and government. Advocacy to move the government to include this in curricula is necessary. Activities, of engagement and collaborative work of stakeholders, civil societies' involvement, or extracurricular activities will be useful. The government must provide this right, it should put all law, policies, education, enforcement, and so on in place to deal with poverty and greed to deal with corruption.

NOTES

1. OECD, *Illicit Financial Flows: The Economy of Illicit Trade in West Africa*, OECD Publishing (2018), Paris, https://doi.org/10.1787/9789264268418-en.
2. OECD, *Illicit Financial Flows* (2018), https://doi.org/10.1787/9789264268418-en.
3. UNCTAD (2020) *Tackling Illicit Financial Flows for Sustainable Development in Africa Economic Development in Africa Report* 2020.
4. UNODC (2014) *Illicit Financial Flows Report of the High-Level Panel on Illicit Financial Flows from Africa* 2014.
5. Defining, estimating, and disseminating statistics on illicit financial flows in Africa UNCTAD, https://unctad.org/project/defining-estimating-and-disseminating-statistics-illicit-financial-flows-africa, accessed 18 June 2022.
6. OECD, *Domestic Resource Mobilization: Fighting against Corruption and Illicit Financial Flows*, African Union Commission (2019), Tax-Transparency-in-Africa-2020.pdf (oecd.org).
7. Emma Farge, 'Illegal Money Flows from Africa Near $90 billion,' *Reuters* September 28, 2020, https://www.reuters.com/article/us-un-africa-idUSKBN26J2UV.
8. UNHR, 'Illicit Financial Flows Threaten Progress on Gender Equality,' *United Nations Human Rights Office of the High Commissioner*, IFFGender07July (ohchr.org).

9. OT Osigbesan, '"Medical Brain Drain" and its Effect on the Nigerian Healthcare Sector' (Ph.D. diss., Walden University, 2021).

10. J. Imafidon, 'One Way Traffic: Nigeria's Medical Brain Drain A Challenge for Maternal Health and Public Health System' (Ph.D. thesis, University of California, Los Angeles, 2018).

11. GE Kamdem Kamga, 'Linkages between Illicit Financial Flows and the Non-realisation of the Right to Development in Africa,' *The Comparative and International Law Journal of South Africa* 52, no. 2 (2019).

12. Chloe Maurel, *Illicit Financial Flows Hinder Development in Africa—the UN Must Rise to the Challenge of Ending this Equal Times*, https://www.equaltimes.org/illicit-financial-flows-hinder?lang=en#.YXGeQp5Bw2w.

13. De Schutter Olivier, 'Taxing for the Realization of Economic, Social and Cultural Rights,' *Tax, Inequality and Human Rights* (New York: Oxford Academic, 2019), 59–79, https://doi.org/10.1093/oso/9780190882228.003.0003.

14. M Yara and C Williams, 'The Role of Digital Health in Making Progress toward Sustainable Development Goal (SDG) 3 in Conflict-affected Populations,' *International Journal of Medical Informatics* 14 (2018): 114–20, https://doi.org/10.1016/j.ijmedinf.2017.11.003.

15. AA Agbor, 'A Delineation of the Impact of Illicit Financial Flows on the Right to Development: Details from Cameroon's Special Criminal Court,' *Journal of Financial Crime*, (2022), A delineation of the impact of illicit financial flows on the right to development: details from Cameroon's special criminal court | Emerald Insight.

16. Art 1 Declaration on the Right to Development.

17. Art 1 Declaration on the Right to Development. Development is a human right UN https://www.un.org/en/events/righttodevelopment/, accessed 24 June 2022.

18. O Merkle and M Kirya, 'The Gendered Dimensions of Illicit Financial Flows,' *Transparency International* (2019): 9, https://www.jstor.org/stable/pdf/resrep20495.pdf.

19. Merkle and Kirya, 'The Gendered Dimensions of Illicit Financial Flows' 9.

20. OECD, *Domestic Resource Mobilization: Fighting against Corruption and Illicit Financial Flows*, African Union Commission (2019), Tax-Transparency-in-Africa-2020.pdf (oecd.org).

21. GE Kamdem Kamga, 'Linkages between Illicit Financial Flows and the Non-Realisation of the Right to Development in Africa,' *The Comparative and International Law Journal of South Africa* 52, no. 2 (2019); Chloe Maurel, *Illicit Financial Flows Hinder Development in Africa' – the UN Must Rise to the Challenge of Ending this Equal Times* https://www.equaltimes.org/illicit-financial-flows-hinder?lang=en#.YXGeQp5Bw2w.

22. Peter Reuter, 'Illicit Financial Flows and Governance: The Importance of Disaggregation, World Development Report Background Paper' (Washington, DC: World Bank, 2017) Illicit Financial Flows and Governance: The Importance of Disaggregation (worldbank.org).

23. OECD, *Domestic Resource Mobilization: Fighting against Corruption and Illicit Financial Flows*, African Union Commission (2019), Tax-Transparency-in-Africa-2020.pdf (oecd.org).

24. Vusi Gumede and David Fadiran, 'Illicit Financial Flows in Southern Africa: Exploring Implications for Socio-economic Development,' *Africa Development* XLIII, no. 4 (2018): 127–53.

25. Luckystar Miyandazi, 'The Complexities of Tackling Illicit Financial Flows in Practice the Example of Tanzania,' Discussion Paper, *ECDPM* no.255 (2019) The complexities of tackling illicit financial flows in practice: The example of Tanzania—ECDPM.

26. Landry Signé, Mariama Sow, and Payce Madden, 'Illicit Financial Flows in Africa Drivers, Destinations, and Policy Options,' *Africa Growth Initiative* (2020) Illicit-financial-flows-in-Africa.pdf (brookings.edu).

27. OECD, *Domestic Resource Mobilization: Fighting against Corruption and Illicit Financial Flows* African Union Commission (2019), Tax-Transparency-in-Africa-2020.pdf (oecd.org).

28. OECD, *Domestic Resource Mobilization* (2019), Tax-Transparency-in-Africa-2020.pdf (oecd.org).

29. Landry Signé, Mariama Sow, and Payce Madden, 'Illicit Financial Flows in Africa Drivers, Destinations, and Policy Options,' *Africa Growth Initiative* (2020) Illicit-financial-flows-in-Africa.pdf (brookings.edu).

30. OECD, *Domestic Resource Mobilization: Fighting against Corruption and Illicit Financial Flows*, African Union Commission (2019), Tax-Transparency-in-Africa-2020.pdf (oecd.org).

31. Landry Signé, Mariama Sow, and Payce Madden, 'Illicit Financial Flows in Africa Drivers, Destinations, and Policy Options,' *Africa Growth Initiative* (2020) Illicit-financial-flows-in-Africa.pdf (brookings.edu).

32. *Illicit Financial Flows and the Problem of Net Resource Transfers from Africa: 1980–2009 Joint Report by African Development Bank and Global Financial Integrity May 2013.*

33. Onanuga Abayomi, 'Comparing the Illicit Financial Flows in Some African Countries: Implications for Policy' *African Journal of Economic Review* VI, Issue II (July 2018).

34. OECD, *Domestic Resource Mobilization: Fighting against Corruption and Illicit Financial Flows*, African Union Commission (2019), Tax-Transparency-in-Africa-2020.pdf (oecd.org).

35. Landry Signé, Mariama Sow, and Payce Madden, 'Illicit Financial Flows in Africa Drivers, Destinations, and Policy Options,' *Africa Growth Initiative* (2020) Illicit-financial-flows-in-Africa.pdf (brookings.edu).

36. Thando Ngozo, 'Illicit Financial Flows in the Mining Industry in South Africa' (South Africa *OXFAM* 2020), oxfam_illicit-financial-flows-report_fin_web.pdf.

37. Vusi Gumede and David Fadiran, 'Illicit Financial Flows in Southern Africa: Exploring Implications for Socio-economic Development,' *Africa Development* XLIII, no. 4 (2018): 127–53.

38. Onanuga Abayomi, 'Comparing the Illicit Financial Flows in Some African Countries: Implications for Policy,' *African Journal of Economic Review* VI, Issue II (July 2018).

39. Landry Signé, Mariama Sow, and Payce Madden, 'Illicit Financial Flows in Africa Drivers, Destinations, and Policy Options,' *Africa Growth Initiative* (2020) Illicit-financial-flows-in-Africa.pdf (brookings.edu).

40. Vusi Gumede and David Fadiran, 'Illicit Financial Flows in Southern Africa: Exploring Implications for Socio-economic Development,' *Africa Development* XLIII, no. 4 (2018): 127–53.

41. Onanuga Abayomi, 'Comparing the Illicit Financial Flows in Some African Countries: Implications for Policy,' *African Journal of Economic Review* VI, Issue II (July 2018).

42. Onanuga, 'Comparing the Illicit Financial Flows' 2018.

43. UNODC Counters Illicit Financial Flows in Africa, United Nations Office on Drugs and Crime UNODC at https://www.unodc.org/unodc/frontpage/2020/November/unodc-counters-illicit-financial-flows-in-africa.html, accessed 11 May 2023.

44. M. B. Rapanyane and C. C. Ngoepe, 'The Impact of Illicit Financial Flows on the South African Political Economy under Jacob Zuma, 2009–2018,' *Journal of Public Affairs*, 20, no. 2 (2020): e2020.

45. OECD, *Domestic Resource Mobilization: Fighting against Corruption and Illicit Financial Flows*, African Union Commission (2019), Tax-Transparency-in-Africa-2020.pdf (oecd.org).

46. B Umar and Z Mohammed, 'The Effects of Illicit Financial Flows on Oil and Gas Revenue Generation in Nigeria,' *Journal of Money Laundering Control* 24, no. 1 (2021): 177–86, https://doi.org/10.1108/JMLC-07-2020-0081.

47. Pallavi Roy, Simeon Obidairo, and Ifejesu Ogunleye, 'How Exchange Rate (mis)Management Leads to Illicit Financial Flows: A Political Economy Analysis of Feasible Reform in Nigeria Anti Corruption Evidence' Working Paper 043, 2022, How exchange rate (mis)management leads to illicit financial flows: a political economy analysis of feasible reform in Nigeria—ace (soas.ac.UK).

48. Peter Reuter, 'Illicit Financial Flows and Governance: The Importance of Disaggregation, World Development Report Background Paper' (Washington, DC: World Bank, 2017) Illicit Financial Flows and Governance: The Importance of Disaggregation (worldbank.org).

49. GI Ayodeji, 'Illicit Financial Flows, Insecurity and Challenges of Governance in Nigeria,' *Studies in Politics and Society, Journal of Political Economy* 6 (2018): 271 Challenges of Curbing Illicit Financial Flows and Insecurity in Governance: Insights from Nigeria | Semantic Scholar.

50. Onanuga Abayomi, 'Comparing the Illicit Financial Flows in Some African Countries: Implications for Policy,' *African Journal of Economic Review* VI, Issue II (July 2018).

51. Pallavi Roy, Simeon Obidairo, and Ifejesu Ogunleye, 'How Exchange Rate (mis)Management Leads to Illicit Financial Flows: A Political Economy Analysis of Feasible Reform in Nigeria Anti Corruption Evidence' Working Paper 043, 2022, How exchange rate (mis)management leads to illicit financial flows: a political economy analysis of feasible reform in Nigeria—ace (soas.ac.UK).

52. M. A. Eneji, A. E. Bitrus, H. Haruna, D. O. Yilkes, and J. Sani, 'Impact of Governance on Fiscal Discipline and Illicit Financial Flows in Nigeria,' *Net Journal of Social Sciences* 10, no. 2 (2020): 19–31.

53. OECD, 'Illicit Financial Flows from Developing Countries: Measuring OECD Responses,' OECD Publishing (2014), Paris, https://doi.org/10.1787/9789264203501-en.

54. OECD, 'Illicit Financial Flows from Developing Countries.'

55. OECD, 'Domestic Resource Mobilization: Fighting against Corruption and Illicit Financial Flows,' African Union Commission (2019), Tax-Transparency-in-Africa-2020.pdf (oecd.org).

56. Onanuga Abayomi, 'Comparing the Illicit Financial Flows in Some African Countries: Implications for Policy,' *African Journal of Economic Review* VI, Issue II (July 2018).

57. UNODC Counters Illicit Financial Flows in Africa, United Nations Office on Drugs and Crime UNODC at https://www.unodc.org/unodc/frontpage/2020/November/unodc-counters-illicit-financial-flows-in-africa.html, accessed 11 May 2023.

58. OECD, 'Illicit Financial Flows: The Economy of Illicit Trade in West Africa,' *OECD Publishing* (2018), Paris, https://doi.org/10.1787/9789264268418-en.

59. UNODC and UNACTD, 'Conceptual Framework for the Statistical Measurement of Illicit Financial Flows' 2020, Microsoft Word—IFF Conceptual Framework_for publication_FINAL.docx (unctad.org).

60. De Schutter Olivier, 'Taxing for the Realization of Economic, Social and Cultural Rights,' *Tax, Inequality and Human Rights* (New York: Oxford Academic, 2019), 59–79, https://doi.org/10.1093/oso/9780190882228.003.0003.

61. UNHR, 'Illicit Financial Flows Threaten Progress on Gender Equality,' *United Nations Human Rights Office of the High Commissioner*, IFFGender07July (ohchr.org).

62. F. Adeleke, 'Illicit Financial Flows and Inequality in Africa: How to Reverse the Tide in Zimbabwe,' *South African Journal of International Affairs* 26, no. 3 (2019): 367–393, Illicit financial flows and inequality in Africa: How to reverse the tide in Zimbabwe | Request PDF (researchgate.net).

63. Maternal Health UNFPA East and Southern Africa 2023 at https://esaro.unfpa.org/en/topics/maternal-health, accessed 12 May 2023.

64. Art 8 Declaration on the Right to Development.

65. M. A. Eneji, A. E. Bitrus, H. Haruna, D. O. Yilkes, and J. Sani, 'Impact of Governance on Fiscal Discipline and Illicit Financial Flows in Nigeria,' *Net Journal of Social Sciences* 10, no. 2 (2022): 19–31.

66. Art 10 Declaration on the Right to Development.

67. Art 2(2) Declaration on the Right to Development.

68. Art 2(2) Declaration on the Right to Development.

69. Art 2(3) Declaration on the Right to Development.

70. Art 3(1) Declaration on the Right to Development.

71. A. A. Agbor, 'A Delineation of the Impact of Illicit Financial Flows on the Right to Development: Details from Cameroon's Special Criminal Court,' *Journal of Financial Crime* (2022), A delineation of the impact of illicit financial flows on

the right to development: details from Cameroon's special criminal court | Emerald Insight.

72. Art 6(3) Declaration on the Right to Development.

73. Art 8(1) Declaration on the Right to Development.

74. Art 10 Declaration on the Right to Development.

75. Art 10 Declaration on the Right to Development.

76. T. A. Ojo, 'A Study of Financial Inclusion and Women's Empowerment in South Africa: The Case of Female Entrepreneurs in Gauteng' (Ph.D. Thesis University of Pretoria, 2020).

77. Vusi Gumede and David Fadiran, 'Illicit Financial Flows in Southern Africa: Exploring Implications for Socio-economic Development,' *Africa Development* XLIII, no. 4 (2018): 127–53.

78. 4IRSA, 'The Future of Artificial Intelligence in Africa' https://www.4irsa.org/news/the-future-of-artificial-intelligence-in-africa/, accessed 13 September 2021.

79. N. Rizk, 'AI and Gender in Africa' https://knowledgemaze.wordpress.com/2020/08/17/ai-and-gender-in-africa/, accessed 13 September 2021.

80. Okeoma John-Paul Okeke, 'Nigerian Culture: A Barrier to the Career Progress of Women in Nigeria,' *Global Journal of Human Resource Management* 5, no. 5 (2017): 1–11.

81. F. Bonnet *et al.*, 'Women and Men in the Informal Economy: A Statistical Brief,' *WIEGO* (Manchester, UK, 2019) [PDF] Women and men in the informal economy: a statistical brief | Semantic Scholar.

82. Jeffrey Kurebwa, 'Implications of Illicit Financial Flows on Africa's Democratic Governance,' *International Journal of Politics and Good Governance* IX, no. 9.1 (2018).

83. Vivian Malta, Ms. Lisa L Kolovich, Angelica Martinez, and Ms. Marina Mendes Tavares, 'Informality and Gender Gaps Going Hand in Hand,' issue 112, 2019, https://doi.org/10.5089/9781498314718.001.

84. J. P. Bohoslavsky, 'Tax-Related Illicit Financial Flows and Human Rights,' *Journal of Financial Crime* 25, no. 3 (2018): 750–69, https://doi.org/10.1108/JFC-04-2017-0029.

85. C. P. Chinwe, 'Illicit Financial Flow a Cog in the Wheel of Political and Economic Development of Nigeria,' *Journal of Public Administration and Social Welfare Research* 3, no. 2 (2018).

86. T. O. George, M. I. Ozoya, and E. O. Amoo, 'Women in Informal Cross-border Trading along Nigeria and Benin Republic Border: Challenges and Coping Strategies,' *International Journal of Applied Business and Economic Research* (2017).

87. A. Chikanda and I. Raimundo, 'Informal Entrepreneurship and Cross-Border Trade between Mozambique and South Africa,' *African Human Mobility Review* 3, no. 2 (2017).

88. Jean-Guy K. Afrika and Gerald Ajumbo, 'Informal Cross Border Trade in Africa: Implications and Policy Recommendations,' *Africa Economic Brief* 3, no. 10 (2012), OPEV Newsletter (afdb.org).

89. Lovell Fernandez, 'A Survey of Corruption and Anti-Corruption Initiatives in Africa,' *Journal of Anti-corruption Law* 2, no. 1 (2018): 31–57.

90. A. Guerra and T. Zhuravleva, 'Do Women always Behave as Corruption Cleaners?'. *Public Choice* 191 (2022): 173–92, https://doi.org/10.1007/s11127-022-00959-5.

91. Ortrun Merkle, Transparency International, 2019, Transparency International Knowledge Hub | Knowledge Hub.

92. Bakare Majeed, 'Why We Have Not Auctionized N14 billion Jewellery, Assets Seized from Diezani,' *Premium Times,* May 28, 2021, https://www.premiumtimesng.com/news/headlines/464339-why-weve-not-auctioned-n14-billion-jewellery-assets-seized-from-diezani-efcc.html.

93. Monika Bauhr, Nicholas Charron, and Lena Wängnerud, 'Exclusion or Interests? Why Females in Elected Office Reduce Petty and Grand Corruption,' *European Journal of Political Research* 58 (2018): 1043–65, https://doi.org/10.1111/1475-6765.12300.

94. Clara Kasser-Tee, 'The Role of Women in the Fight against Corruption in Ghana,' *Development in Practice* 31, no. 4 (2020): 477–83, https://doi.org/10.1080/09614524.2020.1856789.

95. Mahmoud Salari and Hamid Noghanibehambari, 'Natural Resources, Women and Corruption,' *Resource Policy* 74 (2021), https://doi.org/10.1016/j.resourpol.2021.102412.

96. C. P. Chinwe, 'Illicit Financial Flow a Cog in the Wheel of Political and Economic Development of Nigeria,' *Journal of Public Administration and Social Welfare Research* 3, no. 2 (2018), (iiardjournals.org).

97. Jason Hickel, 'The "Girl Effect": Liberalism, Empowerment and the Contradictions of Development,' *Third World Quarterly* 35, no. 8 (2014): 1355–73.

98. Adeleke Fola, 'Illicit Financial Flows and Inequality in Africa: How to Reverse the Tide in Zimbabwe,' *South African Journal of International Affairs* 26, no. 3 (2019): 367–93.

99. Vusi Gumede and David Fadiran, 'Illicit Financial Flows in Southern Africa: Exploring Implications for Socio-economic Development,' *Africa Development* XLIII, no. 4 (2018): 127–53.

100. Bienvenido Ortega, Jesus Sanjuan, and Antonio Casquero, 'Illicit Financial Flows and the Provision of Child and Maternal Health Services in Low- and Middle-Income Countries,' *Open Access* 20, no. 15 (2020), https://doi.org/10.1186/s12914-020-00236-w.

101. De Schutter Olivier, 'Taxing for the Realization of Economic, Social and Cultural Rights,' *Tax, Inequality and Human Rights* (New York: Oxford Academic, 2019), 59–79, https://doi.org/10.1093/oso/9780190882228.003.0003.

102. Art 2 Declaration on the Right to Development.

103. UNHR, 'Illicit Financial Flows Threaten Progress on Gender Equality,' *United Nations Human Rights Office of the High Commissioner*, IFFGender07July (ohchr.org).

104. Michelle Rufaro MaziwisaI and Patricia Lenaghan, 'Rethinking the Right to Water in Rural Limpopo,' *African Human Rights Law Journal* 20, no. 1 (2020).

105. Michelle and Patricia, 'Rethinking the Right to Water in Rural Limpopo' (2020).

106. R. O. Iroanya, G. Nguluwe, and S. Ndapulamo, 'Human Trafficking and Illicit Financial Flows in Africa,' *Journal of Namibian Studies* 25 (2019): 47–70, https://namibian-studies.com/index.php/JNS/article/view/8327.

107. Iroanya, Nguluwe, and Ndapulamo, 'Human Trafficking and Illicit Financial Flows in Africa,' 47–70.

108. Iroanya, Nguluwe, and Ndapulamo, 'Human Trafficking and Illicit Financial Flows in Africa,' 47–70.

109. Ortrun Merkle, Transparency International, 2019, Transparency International Knowledge Hub | Knowledge Hub.

110. Moorosi Leshoele and Vusi Gumede, *Social and Economic Effects of Illicit Financial Flows in South Africa*, ed. Serges Dyjou Kamga (South Africa: Vusi Gumede Publications, 2021), 1–18, Academic Paper 2.pdf (vusigumede.com).

111. D. Serges, 'Illicit Financial Flows, Assets Recovery, the Power Game and the Right to Development in Africa,' *Comparative and International Law Journal of Southern Africa* 52, no. 2 (2019): 193–214.

112. O. N. Jacob, H. F. Josiah, and A. T. Josiah, 'Effects of Corruption on Public Universities Administration in Nigeria,' *Emergent: Journal of Educational Discoveries and Lifelong Learning* 2, no. 7 (2021): 5–18.

113. Igiebor and Godstime O, 'Political Corruption in Nigeria: Implications for Economic Development in the Fourth Republic,' *Journal of Developing Societies* 35, no. 4 (2019): 493–513, (sagepub.com).

114. De Schutter Olivier, 'Taxing for the Realization of Economic, Social and Cultural Rights,' *Tax, Inequality and Human Rights* (New York: Oxford Academic, 2019), 59–79, https://doi.org/10.1093/oso/9780190882228.003.0003.

115. Jason Hickel, 'The "Girl Effect": Liberalism, Empowerment and the Contradictions of Development,' *Third World Quarterly* 35, no. 8 (2014): 1355–73.

116. Declaration, Berne, and Tax Justice Network. 'State Responsibility for the Impacts of Cross-border Tax Abuse on Women's Rights & Gender Equality,' *Centre for Economic and Social Right*s (2016).

117. Ortrun Merkle, Transparency International, 2019, Transparency International Knowledge Hub | Knowledge Hub.

118. O Merkle and M Kirya, 'The Gendered Dimensions of Illicit Financial Flows,' *Transparency International* (2019), https://www.jstor.org/stable/pdf/resrep20495.pdf.

119. M. Bauhr and N. Charron, 'Will Women Executives Reduce Corruption? Marginalization and Network Inclusion,' *Comparative Political Studies* 54, no. 7 (2021): 1292–1322 (sagepub.com).

120. D. L. Rhode, 'Women and Leadership' (Oxford University Press, 2017) (getsmarter.com).

121. Rhode, 'Women and Leadership.'

122. Lovell Fernandez, 'A Survey of Corruption and Anti-Corruption Initiatives in Africa,' *Journal of Anti-Corruption Law* 2, no. 1 (2018): 31–57.

123. Lovell, 'A Survey of Corruption and Anti-Corruption Initiatives in Africa,' 31–57.

124. OECD, 'Domestic Resource Mobilization: Fighting against Corruption and Illicit Financial Flows,' *African Union Commission* (2019), Tax-Transparency-in-Africa-2020.pdf (oecd.org).

125. Lovell Fernandez, 'A Survey of Corruption and Anti-Corruption Initiatives in Africa,' *Journal of Anti-Corruption Law* 2, no. 1 (2018): 31–57.

126. J. P. Bohoslavsky, 'Tax-related Illicit Financial Flows and Human Rights,' *Journal of Financial Crime* 25, no. 3 (2018): 750–69, https://doi.org/10.1108/JFC-04-2017-0029.

127. I. Sheneyeh, C. Abonge, and L. Fonjong, 'Rethinking the Nature, Implications, and Challenges of Informal Cross Border Trade by Women from Cameroon across the Cameroon-Nigeria Southwestern Borders,' *Open Journal of Social Sciences* 9 (2021): 248–66, 10.4236/jss.2021.910018.

128. E. O. Sotande, 'Transnational Organised Crime and Illicit Financial Flows: Nigeria, West Africa and the Global North' (Ph.D. Thesis, University of Leeds, 2016).

129. Makmur and Kartini Laras, 'Women and Dirty Money: How Women are Affected by, Involved, and Counter Money Laundering,' *Jurnal Hukum Prasada* 9, no. 1 (2022): 35–44. Academia.edu.

130. I. Sheneyeh, C. Abonge and L. Fonjong, 'Rethinking the Nature, Implications, and Challenges of Informal Cross Border Trade by Women from Cameroon across the Cameroon-Nigeria Southwestern Borders,' *Open Journal of Social Sciences* 9 (2021): 248–66, 10.4236/jss.2021.910018.

131. Bello Umar, MA Abu, and Zayyanu Mohammed, 'Strategies for Preventing Illicit Financial Flows in Developing Countries,' *Journal of Money Laundering Control* 23, no. 3 (2020): 601–608, https://doi.org/10.1108/JMLC-02-2020-0017.

132. Bukola Oyaleke, 'Regulating Trade-based Illicit Financial Activities in Nigeria' (LLM, University of Pretoria, 2019).

133. Brenna Armstrong et al., 'Corruption, Accountability, and Women's Access to Power' *The Journal of Politics* 84, no. 2 (2022).

134. Chandan Kumar Jha and Sudipta Sarangi, 'Women and Corruption: What Positions Must They Hold to Make a Difference?' *Journal of Economic Behavior and Organization* 151 (2018): 219–33.

135. Monde Ephraim Faku et al., 'Bridging the Gender Gap and Promoting Representation of Women in the National Parliament' a comparative analysis study of South Africa and Lesotho 2019 Gender Questions.

136. T. A. Ojo, 'A Study of Financial Inclusion and Women's Empowerment in South Africa: The Case of Female Entrepreneurs in Gauteng' (Ph.D. Thesis University of Pretoria, 2020).

137. Lovell Fernandez, 'A Survey of Corruption and Anti-Corruption Initiatives in Africa,' *JACL* 2 (2018): 31.

138. Nannerl O. Keohane, 'Women, Power & Leadership,' *Daedalus* 149, no. 1 (2020): 236–50, https://doi.org/10.1162/daed_a_01785.

139. I. Mbukanma and K. Strydom, 'Theoretical Exploration on Improving Women Inclusiveness and Participation: A Study of South African Foreign Policy Decision-Making,' *Gender and Behaviour* 9, no. 1 (2021).

140. Mbukanma and Strydon, 'Theoretical Exploration.'

141. T. A. Ojo, 'A Study of Financial Inclusion and Women's Empowerment in South Africa: The Case of Female Entrepreneurs in Gauteng' (PhD Thesis University of Pretoria, 2020).

142. T. A. Ojo, 'A Study of Financial Inclusion and Women's Empowerment in South Africa: The Case of Female Entrepreneurs in Gauteng' (Ph.D. Thesis University of Pretoria, 2020).

143. I. Mbukanma and K. Strydom, 'Theoretical Exploration on Improving Women Inclusiveness and Participation: A Study of South African Foreign Policy Decision-Making,' *Gender and Behaviour* 9, no. 1 (2021).

144. OECD, 'Domestic Resource Mobilization: Fighting against Corruption and Illicit Financial Flows,' African Union Commission (2019), Tax-Transparency-in-Africa-2020.pdf (oecd.org).

BIBLIOGRAPHY

4IRSA, "The Future of Artificial Intelligence in Africa." Accessed September 13, 2021. https://www.4irsa.org/news/the-future-of-artificial-intelligence-in-africa/.

A. Chikanda, and I. Raimundo, "Informal Entrepreneurship and Cross-Border Trade between Mozambique and South Africa." *African Human Mobility Review* 3(2), (2017): 943–74.

A. Guerra and T. Zhuravleva, "Do Women Always Behave as Corruption Cleaners?" *Public Choice* 191(1–2), (2022): 173–92. https://doi.org/10.1007/s11127-022-00959-5.

A. A. Agbor, "A Delineation of the Impact of Illicit Financial Flows on the Right to Development: Details from Cameroon's Special Criminal Court." *Journal of Financial Crime* 30(4), (2022): 877–90. Emerald Insight.

Adeleke Fola, "Illicit Financial Flows and Inequality in Africa: How to Reverse the Tide in Zimbabwe." *South African Journal of International Affairs* 26(3), (2019): 367–93.

B. Umar and Z. Mohammed, "The Effects of Illicit Financial Flows on Oil and Gas Revenue Generation in Nigeria." *Journal of Money Laundering Control* 24(1), (2021): 177–86. https://doi.org/10.1108/JMLC-07-2020-0081.

Bakare Majeed, "Why We Have Not Auctionized N14 Billion Jewellery, Assets Seized from Diezani." *Premium Times* (May 28, 2021). https://www.premiumtimesng.com/news/headlines/464339-why-weve-not-auctioned-n14-billion-jewellery-assets-seized-from-diezani-efcc.html.

Bienvenido Ortega, Jesus Sanjuan, and Antonio Casquero, "Illicit Financial Flows and the Provision of Child and Maternal Health Services in Low- and Middle-Income Countries." *Open Access* 20(15), (2020). https://doi.org/10.1186/s12914-020-00236-w.

Brenna Armstrong, T. D. Barnes, D. Z. O'Brien, M. M. Taylor-Robinson, "Corruption, Accountability, and Women's Access to Power." *The Journal of Politics* 84(2), (2022): 1–7.

Bukola Oyaleke, "Regulating Trade-Based Illicit Financial Activities in Nigeria." LLM, University of Pretoria, 2019.

C. P. Chinwe, "Illicit Financial Flow a Cog in the Wheel of Political and Economic Development of Nigeria." *Journal of Public Administration and Social Welfare Research* 3(2), (2018). iiardjournals.org.

Chandan Kumar Jha and Sudipta Sarangi, "Women and Corruption: What Positions Must They Hold to Make a Difference?" *Journal of Economic Behavior and Organization* 151, (2018): 219–233.

Chloe Maurel, *Illicit Financial Flows Hinder Development in Africa—The UN Must Rise to the Challenge of Ending This Equal Times*. https://www.equaltimes.org/illicit-financial-flows-hinder?lang=en#.YXGeQp5Bw2w.

Clara Kasser-Tee, "The Role of Women in the Fight Against Corruption in Ghana." *Development in Practice* 31(4), (2020): 477–83, https://doi.org/10.1080/09614524.2020.1856789.

D. Serges, "Illicit Financial Flows, Assets Recovery, the Power Game and the Right to Development in Africa." *Comparative and International Law Journal of Southern Africa* 52(2), (2019): 193–214.

D. L. Rhode, Women and Leadership, Oxford University Press, 2017. getsmarter.com.

De Schutter Olivier, "Taxing for the Realization of Economic, Social and Cultural Rights." In *Tax, Inequality and Human Rights*, Oxford Academic, New York, 2019, 59–79. https://doi.org/10.1093/oso/9780190882228.003.0003.

Declaration, Berne, and Tax Justice Network. "State Responsibility for the Impacts of Cross-Border Tax Abuse on Women's Rights & Gender Equality." Centre for Economic and Social Rights, 2016.

E. O. Sotande, "Transnational Organised Crime and Illicit Financial Flows: Nigeria, West Africa and the Global North." PhD thesis, University of Leeds.

Emma Farge, "Illegal Money Flows from Africa Near $90 Billion," U.N study says *Reuters* September 29 2020 at Reuters.com/article/ozatp-uk-un-africa-idAFKBN26K131=OZATP accessed 14/11/2023.

F. Adeleke, "Illicit Financial Flows and Inequality in Africa: How to Reverse the Tide in Zimbabwe." *South African Journal of International Affairs* 26(3), (2019): 367–393, Illicit financial flows and inequality in Africa: How to reverse the tide in Zimbabwe | Request PDF (researchgate.net).

F. Bonnet et al., "Women and Men in the Informal Economy: A Statistical Brief." *WIEGO,* Manchester, 2019. [PDF] Women and men in the informal economy: a statistical brief | Semantic Scholar.

G. E. Kamdem Kamga, "Linkages between Illicit Financial Flows and the Non-Realisation of the Right to Development in Africa." *The Comparative and International Law Journal of Southern Africa* 52(2), (2019): 169–92.

G. I. Ayodeji, "Illicit Financial Flows, Insecurity and Challenges of Governance in Nigeria." *Studies in Politics and Society Journal of Political Economy* 6, (2018): 271 Challenges of Curbing Illicit Financial Flows and Insecurity in Governance: Insights from Nigeria | Semantic Scholar.

Godstime Osariyekemwen Igiebor, "Political Corruption in Nigeria: Implications for Economic Development in the Fourth Republic." *Journal of Developing Societies* 35(4), (2019): 493–513. sagepub.com.

I. Mbukanma and K. Strydom, "Theoretical Exploration on Improving Women Inclusiveness and Participation: A Study of South African Foreign Policy Decision-Making." Gender and Behaviour 19(1), (2021): 17696–712.

I. Sheneyeh, C. Abonge, and L. Fonjong, "Rethinking the Nature, Implications, and Challenges of Informal Cross Border Trade by Women from Cameroon across the Cameroon-Nigeria Southwestern Borders." *Open Journal of Social Sciences* 9(10), (2021): 248–266, https://doi.org/10.4236/jss.2021.910018.

J. Imafidon, One Way Traffic: Nigeria's Medical Brain Drain A Challenge for Maternal Health and Public Health System. Ph.D. thesis, University of California, Los Angeles, 2018.

J. P. Bohoslavsky, "Tax-Related Illicit Financial Flows and Human Rights." *Journal of Financial Crime* 25(3), (2018): 750–769. https://doi.org/10.1108/JFC-04-2017-0029.

Jason Hickel, "The 'Girl Effect': Liberalism, Empowerment and the Contradictions of Development." *Third World Quarterly* 35(8), (2014): 1355–73.

Jean-Guy K. Afrika and Gerald Ajumbo, "Informal Cross Border Trade in Africa: Implications and Policy." *Africa Economic Brief* 3(10), (2012): 1–13.

Jeffrey Kurebwa, "Implications of Illicit Financial Flows on Africa's Democratic Governance." *International Journal of Politics and Good Governance* IX(9), (2018): 1.

Kartini Laras Makmur, "Women and Dirty Money: How Women Are Affected by, Involved, and Counter Money Laundering." *Jurnal Hukum Prasada* 9(1), (2022): 35–44. Academia.edu.

Landry Signé, Mariama Sow, and Payce Madden, "Illicit Financial Flows in Africa Drivers, Destinations, and Policy Options." *Africa Growth Initiative,* 2020. Illicit-financial-flows-in-Africa.pdf (brookings.edu).

Lovell Fernandez, "A Survey of Corruption and Anti-Corruption Initiatives in Africa." *JACL* 2, (2018): 31.

Lovell Fernandez, "A Survey of Corruption and Anti-corruption Initiatives in Africa." *Journal of Anti-corruption Law* 2(1), (2018): 31–57.

Luckystar Miyandazi, "The complexities of tackling illicit financial flows in practice the example of Tanzania", Discussion Paper, ECDPM No.255, 2019. The Complexities of Tackling Illicit Financial Flows in Practice: The Example of Tanzania—ECDPM.

M. Bauhr and N. Charron, "Will Women Executives Reduce Corruption? Marginalization and Network Inclusion." *Comparative Political Studies* 54(7), (2021): 1292–1322. (sagepub.com).

M. Yara and C. Williams, "The Role of Digital Health in Making Progress Toward Sustainable Development Goal (SDG) 3 in Conflict-Affected Populations." *International Journal of Medical Informatics* 14, (2018): 114–20, https://doi.org/10.1016/j.ijmedinf.2017.11.003.

M. A. Abu Bello Umar, and Zayyanu Mohammed, "Strategies for Preventing Illicit Financial Flows in Developing Countries." *Journal of Money Laundering Control* 23(3), (2020): 601–8. https://doi.org/10.1108/JMLC-02-2020-0017.

M. A. Eneji, A. E. Bitrus, H. Haruna, D. O. Yilkes, and J. Sani, "Impact of Governance on Fiscal Discipline and Illicit Financial Flows in Nigeria." Net Journal of Social Sciences 10(2), (2022): 19–31.

M. B. Rapanyane and C. C. Ngoepe, "The Impact of Illicit Financial Flows on the South African Political Economy under Jacob Zuma, 2009–2018." *Journal of Public Affairs* 20(2), (2020): e2020.

Mahmoud Salari and Hamid Noghanibehambari, "Natural Resources, Women and Corruption." *Resources Policy* 74, (2021). https://doi.org/10.1016/j.resourpol.2021.102412.

Maternal Health UNFPA East and Southern Africa 2023. https://esaro.unfpa.org/en/topics/maternal-health accessed 12 May 2023.

Michelle Rufaro Maziwisa, and Patricia Lenaghan, "Rethinking the Right to Water in Rural Limpopo." *African Human Rights Law Journal* 20(1), (2020): 233–260.

Monde Ephraim Faku et al., "Bridging the Gender Gap and Promoting Representation of Women in the National Parliament." A Comparative Analysis Study of South Africa and Lesotho 2019 Gender Questions7(1): 1–15.

Monika Bauhr, Nicholas Charron, and Lena Wängnerud, "Exclusion or Interests? Why Females in Elected Office Reduce Petty and Grand Corruption." *European Journal of Political Research* 58(4), (2018): 1043–65. https://doi.org/10.1111/1475-6765.12300.

Moorosi Leshoele and Vusi Gumede, "Social and Economic Effects of Illicit Financial Flows in South Africa," ed. Serges Djoyou Kamga. South Africa: Vusi Gumede Publications, 2021, 1–18, Academic Paper 2.pdf (vusigumede.com).

N. Rizk, "AI and Gender in Africa." Accessed September 13, 2021. https://knowledgemaze.wordpress.com/2020/08/17/ai-and-gender-in-africa/.

Nannerl O. Keohane, "Women, Power & Leadership." *Dædalus* 149(1), (2020): 236–50. https://doi.org/10.1162/daed_a_01785.

O. Merkle, and M. Kirya, "The Gendered Dimensions of Illicit Financial Flows." *Transparency International* (2019): 9. https://www.jstor.org/stable/pdf/resrep20495.pdf.

O. N. Jacob, H. F. Josiah, and A. T. Solomon, "Effects of Corruption on Public Universities Administration in Nigeria." *Emergent: Journal of Educational Discoveries and Lifelong Learning* 2(7), (2021): 5–18.

O. T. Osigbesan, "Medical Brain Drain and its Effect on the Nigerian Healthcare Sector." Ph.D. diss., Walden University, 2021.

OECD, *Domestic Resource Mobilization: Fighting against Corruption and Illicit Financial Flows African Union Commission, Tax-Transparency-in-Africa 2020.pdf (oecd.org)*, 2019.

OECD, *Illicit Financial Flows from Developing Countries: Measuring OECD Responses*, OECD Publishing, Paris, 2014. https://doi.org/10.1787/9789264203501-en.

OECD, *Illicit Financial Flows: The Economy of Illicit Trade in West Africa*, OECD Publishing, Paris, 2018. https://doi.org/10.1787/9789264268418-en.

Okeoma John-Paul Okeke, "Nigerian Culture: A Barrier to the Career Progress of Women." *Global Journal of Human Resource Management* 5(5), (2017): 1–11.

Onanuga Abayomi, "Comparing the Illicit Financial Flows in Some African Countries: Implications for Policy." *African Journal of Economic Review* VI(II July), (2018): 172–95.

Ortrun Merkle and Transparency International. Transparency International Knowledge Hub | Knowledge Hub, 2019.

Pallavi Roy, Simeon Obidairo, and Ifejesu Ogunleye, "How Exchange Rate (Mis) Management Leads to Illicit Financial Flows: A Political Economy Analysis of Feasible Reform in Nigeria Anti Corruption Evidence." Working Paper 043, (2022) How Exchange Rate (MIS) Management Leads to Illicit Financial Flows: A Political Economy Analysis of Feasible Reform in Nigeria—ace (soas.ac.UK).

Peter Reuter, “Illicit Financial Flows and Governance the Importance of Disaggregation.” World Development Report Background Paper, World Bank, Washington, DC, 2017, Illicit Financial Flows and Governance: The Importance of Disaggregation (worldbank.org).

R. O. Iroanya, G. Nguluwe, and S. Ndapulamo, “Human Trafficking and Illicit Financial Flows in Africa.” *Journal of Namibian Studies* 25, (2019): 47–70. https://namibian-studies.com/index.php/JNS/article/view/8327.

Recommendations.“Informal Cross Border Trade in Africa: Implications and Policy” *Africa Economic Brief* 3(10), (2012), 1–13 chrome-extension://efaidnbmnnnibpcajpcglclefindmkaj/https://www.afdb.org/fileadmin/uploads/afdb/Documents/Publications/Economic%20Brief%20-%20Informal%20Cross%20Border%20Trade%20in%20Africa%20Implications%20and%20Policy%20Recommendations%20-%20Volume%203.pdf accessed 14/11/2023.

T. A. Ojo, “A Study of Financial Inclusion and Women’s Empowerment in South Africa: The Case of Female Entrepreneurs in Gauteng.” Ph.D. thesis, 2020 University of Pretoria.

T. O. George, M. I. Ozoya, and E. O. Amoo, “Women in Informal Cross-Border Trading along Nigeria and Benin Republic Border: Challenges and Coping Strategies.” *International Journal of Applied Business and Economic Research* 15(26) (2017): 155–63.

Thando Ngozo, (2020), Illicit Financial Flows in the Mining Industry in South Africa, South Africa *OXFAM* 2020, oxfam_illicit-financial-flows-report_fin_web.pdf.

UNCTAD, “Defining, Estimating, and Disseminating Statistics on Illicit Financial Flows in Africa.” Accessed June 18, 2022. https://unctad.org/project/defining-estimating-and-disseminating-statistics-illicit-financial-flows-africa.

UNCTAD, *Tackling Illicit Financial Flows for Sustainable Development in Africa Economic Development in Africa Report 2020*, 2020.

UNHR, “Illicit Financial Flows Threaten Progress on Gender Equality.” *United Nations Human Rights Office of the High Commissioner*, IFFGender07July (ohchr.org).

United Nations Declaration on the Declaration on the Right to Development, 1986 chrome-extension://efaidnbmnnnibpcajpcglclefindmkaj/https://www.ohchr.org/sites/default/files/Documents/Issues/Development/RTD_booklet_en.pdf accessed 14/11/2023.

UNODC, *Illicit Financial Flows Report of the High-Level Panel on Illicit Financial Flows from Africa 2014*, 2014.

UNODC and UNACTD, “Conceptual Framework for the Statistical Measurement of Illicit Financial Flows.” 2020. Microsoft Word—IFF Conceptual Framework_for publication_FINAL.docx (unctad.org).

UNODC Counters Illicit Financial Flows in Africa, United Nations Office on Drugs and Crime UNODC. https://www.unodc.org/unodc/frontpage/2020/November/unodc-counters-illicit-financial-flows-in-africa.html accessed 11 May 2023.

Vivian Malta, Ms. Lisa L. Kolovich, Angelica Martinez, and Ms. Marina Mendes Tavares, “Informality and Gender Gaps Going Hand in Hand.” *IMF Working Papers* 2019(112), (2019). https://doi.org/10.5089/9781498314718.001.

Vusi Gumede and David Fadiran, “Illicit Financial Flows in Southern Africa: Exploring Implications for Socio-economic Development.” *Africa Development* XLIII(4), (2018): 127–53.

Part 2

ILLICIT FINANCIAL FLOWS, MULTINATIONAL CORPORATIONS, AND NATURAL RESOURCE EXPLOITATION IN AFRICA

Chapter 10

Digging for Development

The Impact of Illicit Financial Flows on the Realisation of the Right to Development in Africa's Mineral and Petroleum Exploration Industries

Rita Ozoemena and Chané Henney

INTRODUCTION

Illicit financial flows (IFFs) generally refer to financial capital illegally transferred across the border that contravenes national and/or international laws.[1] This can be connected to any illegal activity and should be broadly interpreted to accommodate various approaches such as corruption, illegal markets, the funding of terrorism, theft, tax evasion, and other illegal commercial practices, and these forms of IFFs are not mutually exclusive.[2] Consequently, IFFs have a detrimental impact on the people and the economy of developing African countries such as South Africa, Zimbabwe, and Nigeria. Wasted expenditures are capital that are necessary to realise the socioeconomic rights of citizens which, have seen enormous decline yet in Nigeria, the petroleum exploration industry contributes significantly to the government's revenue and exportation earnings.[3] South Africa ranks sixth as the world's largest producer of diamonds by volume but the socio-economic benefits of this natural resource remain unrealisable for the majority of the people.[4] Zimbabwe boasts the second largest platinum deposit and chromium ores globally and is rich in almost forty minerals, and thus, the mineral exploration industry contributes significantly to this country's GDP.[5] Clearly, mineral and oil exploration industries are important for Africa's growth and development. Unfortunately, too often, natural resources create an ideal environment for corruption and IFFs. There is a correlation between the protection of Africa's natural resources for her own development benefit and the Right to Development as provided in articles 21 and 22 of the African Charter on Human and Peoples' Rights (African Charter). Consequently, it is a right to sovereignty of the people over their natural resources.[6] In other words, this affirms the people as 'sovereigns' and the ensuing right over their natural resources that must be respected, promoted, and fulfilled.

The Right to Development (RTD) consists of several basic human rights, which ultimately aims to give people the right to enjoy, contribute, and participate in the constant development of their well-being, and can be seen as a vector of rights which includes the right to food, housing, health, education, and other social, cultural, and economic rights.[7] Thus, failing to eliminate illegal financial and trading activities driven by corruption undermines development. Moseneke J and Cameron J stated:

> There can be no gainsaying that corruption threatens to fell at the knees virtually everything we hold dear and precious in our hard-won constitutional democracy. It blatantly undermines the democratic ethos, the institutions of democracy, rule of law and the foundational values of our nascent constitutional project. It fuels maladministration and public fraudulence and imperils the capacity of the state to fulfil its obligations to respect, protect, promote and fulfil all the rights in the Bill of Rights. When corruption and organized crime flourish, sustainable development and economic growth are stunted. And in turn, the stability and security of society is put at risk.[8]

The ripple effect of IFFs as noted from the corrupt commercial activities presented by the mining and petroleum exploration in these countries significantly affects the realisation of the Right to Development. The Right to Development presents a critical lens in examining the adverse impact of IFFs on the realisation of the socioeconomic development of the people of these countries and the continent. In the first place, this chapter discusses the RTD from an African context in which the concept gives the world a view of development as a right, and protection of its natural resources. Second, the chapter examines the challenge of IFFs on these countries and the various forms in which the problem undermines Africa's development agenda. In the third place, the chapter examines the potential for recovery of stolen assets and funds with a view to exploring ways of accountability and transparency in the mining industry for optimum development of the people.

THE RIGHT TO DEVELOPMENT: AN AFRICAN CONTEXT

The RTD, as enshrined in the African Charter on Human and People's Rights (African Charter) promotes a new view of economic order that aims to put people and their well-being first. However, the realisation of the RTD in Africa has proved difficult for a number of reasons. Firstly, the exploitation of African natural resources by European colonialists left the continent greatly underdeveloped on social, economic, political, and cultural spheres.[9] As such, even after African countries gained independence, the dire effects of colonialism were and are still apparent. Secondly, the continued exploitation of natural resources stunts Africa's growth whereas these natural resources are sufficient to drive Africa's development. The Right to Development was first recognised in a binding instrument in 1981 in the African Charter.[10] Accordingly, article 22 provides:

1. All peoples shall have the right to their economic, social, and cultural development with due regard to their freedom and identity and in the equal enjoyment of the common heritage of mankind.
2. States shall have the duty, individually or collectively, to ensure the exercise of the Right to Development.

Pursuant to article 22 of the African Charter, all people have the right to economic, cultural, and social development that promotes their well-being. In other words, the process of development or the development in itself must not be at the detriment of the people. In the *Social and Economic Rights Action Center and the Center for Economic and Social Rights v Nigeria,* the African Commission held that a state party to the African Charter has the responsibility to regulate the actions of a non-state actor violating human rights in a community, and therefore their RTD.[11] Thus, any illegal acts, such as illicit financial flows, that violate people's RTD should be addressed by the state. It is instructive we argue, that article 21 of the African Charter be read in conjunction with Right to Development in article 22. Thus, article 21 specifically states that state parties

> shall undertake to eliminate all forms of foreign exploitation particularly that practised by international monopolies so as to enable their peoples to fully benefit from the advantages derived from their national resources.[12]

It is, therefore, the duty of the state to ensure that its people benefit from the wealth of natural resources. Since it applies to every human being and all peoples, the RTD is both an individual and collective right.[13] Furthermore, the African Charter places a duty on all member States to ensure that this right is exercised by all people.[14] In *the Centre for Minority Rights Development (Kenya) and Minority Rights Group International on behalf of Endorois Welfare Council v Kenya*, the African Commission emphasised the importance of the state as the primary duty bearer for the Right to Development, as well as the importance of participation, accountability and choice needed in all areas of development.[15] In most African countries including those under review in this chapter, majority of people hardly participate or have a choice in the development process that concerns them.

On 4 December 1986 the United Nations General Assembly through the adoption of *Resolution 41/128*, the UN Declaration on the Right to Development (UN Declaration on the RTD) affirms the nature and content to the Right to Development. In terms of this Declaration, the centrality of the human person as the beneficiary of development is clear requiring effort of every individual and group through participation advance this entitlement to development.[16] In terms of article 3 of the UN Declaration on the RTD, states have the duty to develop policies on a national and international level that aim to realise the RTD.[17] Consequently, the UN Declaration on the RTD calls on the cooperation of states in ensuring a favourable environment where the RTD can be realised, as well as eradicate obstacles to the realisation of the RTD.[18] This declaration also aims to affirm each person's fundamental human right as enshrined in the Universal Declaration of Human Rights. The Universal Declaration of Human Rights in its entirety affirms fundamental human rights such as equality and the right to an effective remedy for acts violating fundamental human rights.[19] Additionally, numerous treaties support the idea of the RTD, such as the International Covenant on Economic, Social and Cultural Rights; the International Covenant on Civil and Political Rights and the UN Draft Convention on the Right to Development.

The RTD must be interpreted broadly. It consists of several fundamental human rights, which ultimately aims to give people the right to enjoy, contribute and participate in the constant development of their well-being. In the UN Declaration on the RTD, the RTD is defined as

> an inalienable human right by virtue of which every human person and all peoples are entitled to participate in, contribute to, and enjoy economic, social, cultural and political development, in which all human rights and fundamental freedoms can be fully realized.[20]

Due to the fact that the RTD is an inalienable right, its violation or any act that infringes on this right must be greatly discouraged with appropriate remedial actions. Despite the status of RTD on the continental treaty framework, African countries are still plagued by illegal commercial activities such as IFFs and corruption which directly pose a threat to the development of its people. IFFs in the oil and mining industries, therefore, pose a problem to the realisation of the inalienable RTD due to its weakening of the state's capacity to provide basic services that promote the well-being of the people.

Accountability, equity, choice, and non-discrimination that are core contents of RTD[21] are undermined by IFFs Nigeria, South Africa, and Zimbabwe.

The United Nations Conference of Trade and Development (UNCTAD) estimated in 2020 that Africa loses about $88.6 billion annually to illicit capital flight.[22] Not only does this have a detrimental impact on the economies of African countries, such as Nigeria, South Africa and Zimbabwe, but it also a major obstacle in realising the inalienable Right to Development. Much-needed resources and funds are being diverted from developing countries, without hospitals that are functional with medicines and trained doctors, the schools without libraries or science labs or the women and men that die daily from treatable diseases who are in desperate need of it, to only a handful of beneficiaries. IFFs is a scourge that continues to destabilise African development agenda if it remains unchecked and dealt with decisively.

CHALLENGE OF ILLICIT FINANCIAL FLOWS ON THE REALISATION OF THE RIGHT TO DEVELOPMENT

Nigeria, South Africa, and Zimbabwe are rich with natural resources, but IFFs in the oil and mining industry have hindered the people's right to fully enjoy the benefits of this wealth. The aim of target 16.4 of the United Nations' Sustainable Development Goals is to 'significantly reduce illicit financial and arms flows, strengthen the recovery and return of stolen assets and combat all forms of organized crime' by the year 2030. However, thus far reaching this goal seems near impossible for Nigeria, South Africa, and Zimbabwe due to the prevalence of IFFs in the oil and mining industry.

Illicit Financial Flow in Context

The combined earnings to the GDP for oil exploration and mining in the three countries in this study account for about 29 per cent of GDP earnings.[23] In fact, the oil industry brought in 600 billion USD over the past sixty years for Nigeria.[24] This country is Africa's top oil producer and contributes approximately 80 per cent to the government's revenue. Additionally, the oil industry contributes approximately 9 per cent to the Nigeria's (GDP) annually and according to the data from the Central Bank of Nigeria, the country made a sum of 195 billion USD from the export of crude oil between 2017 and 2021 at the average of 39 billion USD per annum.[25] The exploration of oil in Nigeria since 1958 was expected to set the country on a positive socioeconomic trajectory yet according to World Bank, Nigeria ranks 150 out of 157 in 2020 Human Capital Index.[26] The economic outlook seems bleak due to the risk of throwing more than 5 million people under the poverty line in 2021/2022.[27] The World Bank projects that in 2022, 95.1 million will be living in poverty.[28] In 2018, about 83 million people were living below the poverty line and additional 53 million people were vulnerable.[29] Clearly, due to illicit financial flows, Nigeria may not meet the obligations to the people as well as the targets on Sustainable Development Goals.

Similar to Nigeria, South Africa is extremely rich in natural resources ranking as the second largest producer of gold,[30] and the fourth largest producer of diamonds on the African continent.[31] The Chamber of Mines estimated that the mining industry contributed around R286 billion to South Africa's economy in 2015.[32] According to Statistics South Africa, the mining industry generated R527.5 billion in total sales in 2019, of which 61 per cent thereof were sourced from outside of the country,[33] and are vulnerable to IFFs. The people are caught in this cycle of digging for development, they see and hear how much the mining executives earn as income and yet, many of the people working underground to mine these minerals live in poverty and squalor. This was the core reason for the strikes that took place in Marikana, South Africa when miners demanded an increase in salary. What was a peaceful protest for wage increase turned violent and thirty-four miners were killed in one day by policemen.[34]

Zimbabwe also has a diverse mining sector and boasts occurrences of almost forty different minerals. Among these minerals are gold, nickel, copper, platinum, chrome, coal, and diamonds.[35] Zimbabwe is the third largest producer of platinum in the world, and its mining sector contributes 12 per cent to the country's GDP.[36] Due to the mining industry's significant contribution to the country's GDP, it clearly plays a major role in the country's development. Unfortunately, widespread corruption has made it difficult for citizens to reap the benefits these lucrative industries have to offer in terms of growth and development for these countries and the continent as a whole. Complete enjoyment of the profits generated by the mining industry is hindered by corruption and tax evasion.

IFFs in Nigeria, South Africa and Zimbabwe's oil and mining industries are largely characterised by trade misinvoicing, both underinvoicing and overinvoicing. The aim of trade misinvoicing, which forms a large component of IFFs, is to conceal or accumulate money in different jurisdictions through the misrepresentation of the cost or number of imports or exports.[37] Misinvoicing may occur through either underinvoicing of exports (which aims to reduce income tax liability and move money across borders), or overinvoicing of imports (meaning more than the normal prices are paid for imports).[38]These methods are commonly used for purposes of tax evasion, money laundering or avoidance of custom duties. Due to the fact that IFFs are hidden, data on trade misinvoicing proves challenging.

As a result of IFFs, the oil and mining industry has failed to make significant contribution to the development of the people, with the poor suffering the most. In Zimbabwe, 97.88 per cent of IFFs can be linked to the mining sector and the remaining linked to timber, fisheries, and wildlife.[39] According to Tendai Biti, the two minerals that are closely linked to IFFs are platinum and chrome.[40] It is estimated that from 2009 to 2012 alone, Zimbabwe lost 239 million USD due to export underinvoicing.[41] There are also cases of export overinvoicing. During 2009 to 2012, export overinvoicing accumulated to approximately 2.79 billion USD. About 97 per cent of this can be linked to South Africa which is the biggest trading partner to Zimbabwe.[42] According to Kwaramba *et al*, there is about 49 per cent unrecorded capital inflows from South Africa into Zimbabwe.[43] Results also indicate that unrecorded capital outflows occurred through trade with other countries including, Italy, Belgium, South Africa, and Australia.[44]

On the part of Nigeria, for example, most people who benefit from Nigeria's oil wealth are a limited number of elite beneficiaries, such as government officials, instead of the Nigerian people as a collective. Consequently, the country accounts for about 25 per cent of the top emitters of IFFs in Africa, of which most are linked to natural resources in this instance, oil and gas.[45] It is estimated that from 1996 to 2014, Nigeria's oil export misinvoicing amounted to 44 billion USD, while import misinvoicing amounted to 45 billion USD.[46] Usually, the funds are hidden in offshore accounts and assets hidden in other countries. For instance, former governor of one of the states of the oil-producing Niger Delta was found with about 1 million British pound cash on him and another 1.8 million British Pounds in cash and accounts in the United Kingdom.[47] Several Nigerian elites with private oil blocks are also implicated in these forms of illicit transactions, for instance, Famfa Oil in 1993 sold 40 per cent to Star Deepwater, a Texaco Company, which sold 8 per cent of its stake to Brazil's Petrobas defeating the purpose of the Indigenisation policy that allows for more local participation in the oil sector.[48] Thus, Illicit offshore financial centres are used to harbour illicit money under the guise of fake foundations, anonymous trusts and Nigeria's trade misinvoicing is also characterised by import underinvoicing as well as export underinvoicing.[49]

The Netherlands is one of Nigeria's most prominent trading partners, but there are discrepancies when comparing these two countries' reports on the exports and imports of crude oil. In numerous cases, both imports from and exports to the Netherlands were not recorded by Nigeria and vice versa.[50] According to UNCTAD, misinvoicing during the period of 1996 to 2014 between the Netherlands and Nigeria amounted to 44.6 billion USD. There is also substantial underinvoicing of crude oil to the United States, which from the period of 1996 to 2014 amounted to 69.7 billion USD, followed by

Germany which amounted to 23.9 billion USD.[51] Although these provided statistics demonstrate only a few instances of IFFs that occurred between Nigeria and their major trading partners, it remains a huge loss with a detrimental impact on development. It is common knowledge that health is one of the indicators for development. In Nigeria for more than a decade now, the health budget has never met the sector commitment. It always falls short by 10.66 per cent since 2001, and unfortunately, the allocation to the health sector in 2022 is about 4.34 per cent.[52] It is not surprising or ethically inappropriate to find that Nigerian politicians and their families seek medical care abroad in countries like the United Kingdom because they have not developed the healthcare system in Nigeria to any standard.

Like Nigeria, IFFs in South Africa is rampant. From 2010 to 2014 the South African government lost a total of 37 billion USD in revenue from the mining industry. This translates to around 7.4 billion USD annually.[53] The UN estimates that gold exports from South Africa worth 78 billion USD were not declared for the period of 2000 to 2014.[54] Additionally, from 2011 to 2014, South Africa recorded 1.3 billion USD export overinvoicing.[55] The Netherlands, Japan, and China accounted for the bulk of export misinvoicing during this period. In 2000–2014, silver and platinum export underinvoicing in South Africa amounted to 19 billion USD.[56] Of these total exports, 65.7 per cent were to Japan, China, and the United States.[57] It is also estimated that 62 per cent of iron ore was exported to China. South Africa also indicates large exports of iron ore to the Netherlands.[58] However, these reports do not appear in the Netherlands' records.[59] There are also discrepancies between the value of gold South Africa declared and the value reported by South Africa's major gold trading partners such as India, China, and Japan.[60] The extent and depth of IFFs indicate failure not only in these countries but also with the international trading system according to Barbara Curson.[61] This is a huge indictment of the international trading system in contributing to the non-realisation of the international economic order that protects the people in Africa as envisaged in the Right to Development.

According to the UN's Office of Drugs and Crime, the profit generated by illicit oil and mineral mining and trafficking in precious minerals has outgrown the profits associated with other serious crimes, including drug trafficking.[62] Theoretically, due to these countries' wealth, people's livelihoods should be improving at a reasonable rate. Instead, poverty reigns supreme. In fact, 40 per cent of Nigerian citizens live below the country's poverty line.[63] Even though Nigeria has committed itself to promote and ensure the RTD, poor governance and lack of efficient implementation of laws create obstacles in realising this right, especially those dealing with IFFs that create the perfect environment for corruption to thrive.[64] On 16 August 2021, President Muhammadu Buhari passed the Petroleum Industry Act,[65] with the aim of reforming the oil industry and addressing the grievances of citizens impacted by the sector.[66] It remains to be seen whether this legislation will effectively address IFFs in the oil industry and be implemented in such a way that it will hold culprits accountable, as well as prevent future corruption. The introduction of the 2021–2025 National Action Plan and the new Petroleum Industry Act seems promising and highlights a certain level of commitment to improve the realisation of the peoples' RTD in Nigeria and promote sustainable growth.

Seen as an opportunity to promote growth in Nigeria, Heirs Holdings purchased a substantial percentage of Shell Nigeria's Oil ML 17 field in 2021.[67] Shell announced its completion of Oil ML 17 in Nigeria in early 2021. Heirs Holdings, in partnership with Transcorp,[68] purchased 45 per cent of Shell's Oil ML 17 for approximately 530 million USD. This agreement is by far the largest oil financing in Africa in more than ten years. The goal of this deal is to 'create Africa's first integrated energy multinational, a global quality business, uniquely focused on Africa and Africa's energy needs'.[69] It is worth noting that although this deal might lead to much-needed profit, Shell Nigeria has been criticised in the past for oil spills in the delta, oil theft, and asset sabotage. This brings another set of problems that negatively impacts the people's RTD, especially since Nigeria is well-known for corruption among their government officials. In April 2016, private documents (referred to as the 'Panama Papers') that contained information pertaining to a system of crime that enabled corruption, including financial secrecy, illegal offshore accounts and other financial crimes were leaked. In the Panama Papers,[70] politically exposed people in Nigeria were linked to money laundering, which enabled the purchase of luxury mansions, vehicles, private jets, yachts, and other goods. Most of these luxury goods, property, and money were hidden in offshore accounts in London and Dubai.[71] Recovering these assets has proved difficult over the years. The loss of revenue through IFFs has a detrimental impact on service delivery, which infringes on Nigerian citizens' basic human rights with the basic needs of citizens not being met. Access to healthcare, food, education, water, and shelter is impeded due to stolen funds that could have been utilised for the improvement of livelihoods and well-being of people in Nigeria. It seems that in Nigeria, oil is almost inextricably linked to corruption, to the detriment of immediate and long-term development. In the *African Union Report on Illicit Financial Flows*, it is asserted that countries that export oil form the largest share of IFFs from the African Continent. From 1970 to 2009, Nigeria lost approximately 217.7 billion USD to IFFs. At that time, Nigeria represented approximately 31 per cent of IFFs out of Africa.[72]

According to Sala-I-Martin and Subramanian, from 1965 to 2000, Nigeria's oil revenues accumulated to 350 billion USD.[73] Despite this, the standard of living is not improving as much as needed. Poor governance and lack of political will have created an environment for IFFs to thrive, to the detriment of citizens, especially vulnerable and minority groups. Instead of Nigeria's oil wealth being utilised to ensure development of all people, the poverty situation remains dire. Despite its oil wealth, Nigeria still experiences significant underdevelopment due to IFFs and mismanagement of funds.

Like Nigeria, South Africa suffers from unemployment and poverty. South Africa's unemployment rate is currently 34.4 per cent,[74] indicating a lack of employment opportunities, which is one of the primary causes of poverty. Worse off than South Africa is Zimbabwe. According to the Borgen Project, half of Zimbabwe's population live below the food poverty line and around 74 per cent of Zimbabweans live on only 5.50 USD per day. Zimbabweans struggle with access to safe drinking water, education, sanitary products, and food.[75] The change to US dollars as Zimbabwe's currency due to its local currency being rendered worthless more than a decade ago did not address these concerns.[76] It attests to the fact that poor governance and corruption have led to the country experiencing severe economic crises, with the poor being affected the most.

In Zimbabwe, the mining industry is under tight political control creating an environment for IFFs to thrive, because those who commit corruption are among the elite.[77] The arrest of Henrietta Rushwaya, politician and president of the Zimbabwe Miners Federation, for gold smuggling attests to this.[78] According to Zimbabwe's minister of home affairs, Kazembe Kazembe, IFFs cost Zimbabwe 100 million USD per month for lost revenue due to gold smuggling.[79] Money and resources lost due to IFFs severely impacts the people's RTD. The economy is currently underdeveloped and Zimbabweans are not able to improve their quality of life. There are also fewer investments in countries where corruption is rampant. The huge portions of money generated from the mining industry that have been illicitly transferred abroad, could have greatly contributed to the development of the people as envisaged in art 22 of the African Charter. It can thus be argued that IFFs in the mining industry can be closely linked to lack of development among marginalised and vulnerable communities.

As long as these corrupt activities continue to thrive, the realisation of the RTD will remain an inconceivable dream. These funds, if it were utilised properly, could have made a significant contribution to improving the livelihoods of people and communities, by improving the state of public hospitals, addressing the lack of quality medication and treatment for those without medical aid, ensuring adequate housing, and addressing food insecurity. According to the UNCTAD, there is an annual financing gap of about 2.5 trillion USD for developing countries to achieve their key sustainable development objectives[80] hence, the urgent need to plug the leak and recover funds for development agenda.

RECOVERY OF STOLEN ASSETS

Seizing and recovering the proceeds of corruption—asset recovery—can be a powerful tool in combating IFFs and holding perpetrators accountable. It has the potential to have a powerful developmental impact when the returns are used for development purposes.[81] Nigeria's Economic and Financial Crimes Commission Act gives the Commission (EFCC) the authority to trace and attach assets acquired as a result of economic and financial crime.[82] In the past, Nigeria has had success in recovering hundreds of millions of US dollars in stolen assets.[83] However, attempts to recover some of the stolen or looted funds have been far from satisfactory. In response to some of the stolen funds that were identified, Itse Sagay states that

> One third of the stolen funds could have provided 635.18 kilometres of roads, 36 ultra-modern hospitals per state, 183 schools, and educated 3,974 children from primary to tertiary level at 25.24 million per child and built 20,042 units of 2-bedroom houses.[84]

The above statement by Sagay depicts the enormity of the challenges and the importance of recovery for development. However, the amount of capital lost far exceeds the assets recovered, making it difficult for Nigeria to benefit from it. This is further exemplified by the many warnings against the federal government of Nigeria's plan to redistribute about 322 million USD recovered 'Abacha Loot'. This plan comes amidst the re-election bid of President Buhari who has failed to deliver on any of his election promises in 2015. His government seeks to redistribute funds without any social assistance model in the country's governance system.[85] This is antithetical to development.

In South Africa, the Prevention of Organised Crime Act provides that property obtained through unlawful means can be forfeited to the state. South Africa also has several anti-corruption units such as the Special Investigation Unit, the Financial Intelligence Centre, the Asset Forfeiture Unit, Anti-Corruption Task Team and the Investigating Directorate that are central to the process and efforts of recovering assets.

Zimbabwe's Anti-Corruption Commission Act established the Anti-Corruption Commission to combat fraud and corruption.[86] This Commission is central in the process of recovering assets and financial investigations. In 2020, the Commission recovered 100 million USD worth of assets.[87] Zimbabwe has also adopted a number of policies to curb IFFs such as 'Look East Policy (2003), Community Share Ownership (2011) established for the purposes of wealth redistribution and the Indigenization and Economic Empowerment Act (2007) that required 51 per cent local ownership of mining companies'.[88]

In these countries, there is no short of legislation, policies, or institutional armour to address IFFs. The issue is rather that these tools are not being used sufficiently. The high cost of asset recovery and the necessary expertise required are some of the primary barriers that agencies face.[89] While stolen assets are being recovered, it is not enough to alleviate the socioeconomic problems people are facing in these developing countries.

RECOMMENDATIONS

IFFs pose a significant risk to social, economic, political, and cultural rights. It is an obstacle in Africa's path to realise every individual's Right to Development. It is imperative that these risks be identified on a national and international level in order to curb IFFs. To tackle corruption, a human rights-based approach is needed.

The five core human rights principles that underpin a human rights-based approach to tackle corruption are participation, accountability and transparency, non-discrimination and equality, empowerment of rights-holders and legality.[90] This approach empowers people to have knowledge of their rights, as well as claim it. It also increases accountability of individuals and institutions who are responsible for respecting, protecting, and fulfilling human rights. It is about ensuring that the standards and the principles of human rights are integrated into policymaking, as well the day to day running of organisations.

It is clear that radical change is needed to address the issue of IFFs. Firstly, the implementation of clear and comprehensive tax and trade legislation is imperative. Along with legislation, cooperation between countries to investigate, prevent, and recover illicit capital should curb IFFs. Anonymous shell companies need to be eliminated, tax evasion deterred, and transparency of corporations improved. Technology has also come a long way in regulating financial flows. Regulatory technology and artificial intelligence may improve the identification and disruption of illicit financial trails. It can track disguised ownership, identify misinvoicing and compare it to tax data in real time. Thus, investing in technology, while expensive, seems to have the potential to truly track illicit flows. For example, TRACE (a project launched by the EU) will be able to improve the identification and disruption of illicit financial trails. Its aim is to provide a 'flexible open-source platform to detect and analyse cross-border money trails used by criminals'. Naturally, implementation will be challenging and it will not be able to defeat IFF's on its own, but it may assist in recovering and preventing substantial amounts of money that could be utilised for development within these countries. Proper legislation aimed at enforcing transparency from state and non-state actors must be implemented. For example, the goal of the Extractives Industries Transparency Initiative (EITI) is strengthening governance through the improvement of transparency and accountability.

As previously mentioned, asset recovery is one of the methods that can be utilised to address IFFs. The Stolen Assets Recovery (StAR) Initiative was created by the World Bank and UNODC and between the years of 2006 and 2012, 2.6 billion USD was frozen. Unfortunately, only 423.5 million USD was returned to the countries of origin.[91] Asset recovery also depends on the level of cooperation between international bodies, as well as agencies. StAR relies on voluntary reporting, which makes it difficult to see the entire process through.

Additionally, corporations should review policies on an annual basis. This also allows corporations to update policies and regulations related to financial crime risk management, in accordance with international and national laws. It is important to foster a culture of integrity and encourage people to speak up when having concerns. Collaboration between corporations should also be encouraged. It is imperative to capitalise on experts that can identify and eradicate corruption in public procurement, and global supply chain such as accountants, financial and legal advisors, bankers as well as sustainability experts.[92]

Due to IFFs being a global phenomenon, international and regional cooperation is needed to strengthen information exchanges. Institutions that were created to deal with complex financial crimes should be effectively managed and given autonomy to investigate and prosecute crimes without political influence. Enough resources are needed to effectively combat IFFs, as well as expert personnel competent enough to prevent, investigate and prosecute crimes related to IFFs.

CONCLUSION

In this chapter, it was argued that IFFs in the oil and mining industry has a detrimental impact on the Right to Development in Nigeria, South Africa, and Zimbabwe. Nigeria's oil industry is the mainstay of the economy for more than five decades and contributes immensely to the country's GDP. However, IFFs and corruption have been decimated the institutional ability of the state to advance the people's RTD. South Africa and Zimbabwe's mining sectors make significant contribution to each country's revenue. It was argued that IFFs is inextricably linked to natural resources and as such hinders the inalienable Right to Development in Nigeria, South Africa, and Zimbabwe. These three countries are legally obligated, under the African Charter, to promote the RTD. While the RTD is not explicitly referred to in legislation in these countries, social, economic, political, and cultural rights as enshrined in their Constitutions form part of the RTD.

Nigeria, South Africa, and Zimbabwe have committed to numerous international obligations to realise the right of development and tackling illicit financial flows. These three countries have also ratified numerous international instruments including the

- International Covenant on Economic, Social and Cultural Rights
- International Covenant on Civil and Political Rights
- African Charter on Human and People's Rights
- United Nations Declaration on Human Rights
- United Nations Sustainable Development Goals

Thus, all three countries committed themselves to realise every individual's right to enjoy, participate, and contribute to the constant development of their well-being. Furthermore, these countries committed to ensuring that an environment is created where people can exercise these rights. The money made from the abundance of natural resources could have been used to improve the livelihoods of people. In all three countries, the government's inability to retain revenue challenges the social development of citizens. Funds lost currently have a detrimental effect on the realisation of basic human rights of its people. It makes it difficult to enforce the socioeconomic rights of people, especially in developing countries that attract corruption. Mineral and oil exploration is known to create a perfect environment for IFFs, due to the fact that these industries are extremely lucrative. Organisations, foundations, and trusts are frequently used as fronts and anonymity makes it difficult to track those accountable. Even in cases where the culprits are identified, the process of recovering assets is a lengthy one and the incurring legal costs are a huge obstacle.

The secretary-general of the UNCTAD, Mukisa Kituyi, made the following statement on the detrimental impact corruption has on human rights:

> Illicit financial flows and corruption are inhibiting African development by draining foreign exchange, reducing domestic resources, stifling trade and macroeconomic stability and worsening poverty and inequality. These illicit flows rob Africa and its people of their prospects, undermining transparency and accountability and eroding trust in African institutions. Faced with high capital flight, tax avoidance and marked dependence on corporate income taxes, African Governance face significant constraint to widen their tax base.[93]

IFFs plague African countries and is detrimental to people's human Right to Development. It undermines democratic values, worsens quality of life, and threatens fundamental human rights. Countries with poor governance create an environment that allows IFFs to thrive, to the detriment of vulnerable and marginalised communities. There is an urgent need to focus on continental mechanism for asset recovery, accountability, and transparency with a view to finding indigenous means to tackle IFFs for Africa's development agenda.

NOTES

1. OECD, *Illicit Financial Flows from Developing Countries: Measuring OECD Responses* (2014) 20.
2. UNCTAD, *Tackling Illicit Financial Flows for Sustainable Development in Africa* (2020) 3.
3. In Nigeria, petroleum contributes 9 per cent to the country's GDP. Statista 'Contribution of oil and natural gas sector to GDP in Nigeria from the 4th quarter of 2018 to the 3rd quarter of 2021' 1 February 2022 https://www.statista.com/statistics/1165865/contribution-of-oil-sector-to-gdp-in-nigeria/ (accessed 18 July 2022).
4. Statista 'Production of diamonds in South Africa from 2004 to 2020' 2 November 2021 https://www.statista.com/statistics/964873/south-africa-diamond-production-volume/ (accessed 18 July 2022).
5. International Trade Administration 'Zimbabwe: Country commercial guide' https://www.trade.gov/country-commercial-guides/zimbabwe-mining-and-minerals (accessed 18 July 2022).
6. S. Kamga and C. C. Ngang 'The natural resource and the right to development dilemma' in Ngang and Kamga (eds.) *Natural Resource Sovereignty and the Right to Development in Africa* (London: Routledge, 2021).
7. United Nations Declaration on the Right to Development: art. 1; A. Sengupta, *The Right to Development: Report of the Independent Expert on the Right to Development* (2000) 8.
8. *Glenister v President of the Republic of South Africa and Others* 2011(3) SA 347(CC): para 166:
9. A Munyai, 'African renaissance: Effects of colonialism on Africa's natural resources and the right to development' (2020) 45 (1), *Journal for Juridical Science* 2.
10. African Charter on Human and People's Rights: art. 22 (1).
11. *Social and Economic Rights Action Center and the Center for Economic and Social Rights v Nigeria* ACHPR, 2001.
12. African Charter on Human and People's Rights: art. 21 (5).
13. S. D. Kamga, *The Right to Development in the African Human Rights System* (2018) 80.
14. African Charter on Human and People's Rights: art.22 (2).

15. *Centre for Minority Rights Development (Kenya) and Minority Rights Group International on behalf of Endorois Welfare Council v. Kenya* 276/2003.

16. UN General Assembly Resolution 41/128:art. 2 (1).

17. UN General Assembly Resolution 41/128:art. 3 (1).

18. UN General Assembly Resolution 41/128:art. 3 (3).

19. The Universal Declaration of Human Rights: art. 1 and 8.

20. UN General Assembly Resolution 41/128:art. 1. The right to self-determination forms an integral part of the RTD, which Serges Kamga describes as the exercise of people's inviolable right to 'full sovereignty' over own natural resources and wealth. See S. D. Kamga, *The Right to Development in the African Human Rights System* (2018) 13.

21. *Centre for Minority Rights v Government of Kenya (Endorois Case).*

22. Igwe, 'Tracking illicit financial flows could support Nigeria's post-pandemic recovery' 6 April 2021, https://blogs.lse.ac.uk/africaatlse/2021/04/06/tracking-illicit-financial-flows-support-nigeria-post-pandemic-recovery-corruption/ (accessed 30 October 2021).

23. Oil contributes 9 per cent to the GDP of Nigeria, mining in South Africa accounts for 8 per cent of the GDP and 12 per cent for Zimbabwe. See 3.1 below.

24. I. Romanova, 'Oil boom in Nigeria and Its Consequences for the Country's Economic Development' https://www.grin.com (accessed 21 July 2022).

25. S. Oyekanmi, 'Crude oil exports fall to an average of $39 billion per annum under Buhari' https://nairametrics.com/2022/04/19 (accessed 21 July 2022).

26. World 'Nigeria Overview' www.worldbank.org/en/country/nigeria/overview (accessed 20 July 2022).

27. World Bank Group, *Nigeria Poverty Assessment* (2022) 20.

28. World Bank Group (n 25 above) 20.

29. The World Bank, 'Nigeria Overview' https://www.worldbank.org/en/country/nigeria/overview (accessed 20 July 2022).

30. Goldhub, 'Gold mine production' 9 June 2022 https://www.gold.org/goldhub/data/historical-mine-production (accessed 18 July 2022).

31. NS Energy, 'Top five diamond mining countries of Africa profiled' 9 March 2020 http://www.nsenergybusiness.com/news/top-five-diamond-mining-africa/ (accessed 10 December 2021).

32. Chamber of Mines of South Africa, *Mine SA 2016 Fact and Figures* (2016) 6.

33. StatsSA 2021, 'Four facts about the mining industry' http://www.statssa.gov.za/?p=14682 (accessed 10 December 2021).

34. Hirschel-Burns, 'Marikana miners strike for better wages, 2012' 4 April 2015 https://nvdatabase.swarthmore.edu/content/marikana-miners-strike-better-wages-2012#case-study-detail (accessed 21 July 2022).

35. Metallon Corporation 'About Zimbawe' https://metcorp.co.uk/about-us/about-zimbabwe.aspx (accessed 10 December 2021).

36. International Trade Administration 2021, 'Zimbabwe: Mining and minerals' https://www.trade.gov/country-commercial-guides/zimbabwe-mining-and-minerals (accessed 13 December 2021).

37. UNECA 2015:10.

38. Financial Action Task Force, *Trade based money laundering* (2006) 4–5.

39. AFRODAD, *Illicit Financial Flows: Towards a More Integrated Approach for Curbing Illicit Flows from Zimbabwe* (2021) 60.

40. M&G Special Report 2021, 'Exploring the role of illicit financial flows in Zimbabwe's political economy' https://mg.co.za/special-reports/2021-05-27-exploring-the-role-of-illicit-financial-flows-in-zimbabwes-political-economy/ (accessed 13 December 2021).

41. AFRODAD (n 38 above) 22.

42. AFRODAD (n 38 above) 23.

43. M. Kwaramba, N. Mahonye and L Mandishara C, 'Capital flight and trade misinvoicing in Zimbabwe' A.

44. Herald.co.zw/foreign-mining-firms-accused-of-under-declaring-exports (13 April 2017) (accessed 20 July 2022).

45. L. Signé, M. Sow and P. Madden, *Illicit Financial Flows in Africa: Drivers, Destinations, and Policy Options. Brookings Institute: Africa Growth Initiative* (2020) 2.

46. UNCTAD, *Tackling Illicit Financial Flows for Sustainable Development in Africa* (2020) 46.

47. Former Governor of Bayelsa State, Mr Diepreye Solomon Alamieyesiagha was detained in September 2005 by the UK's Metropolitan police, he was sentenced to two years and many of his assets in the United Kingdom were ordered to be forfeited to the Bayelsa State government. He later jumped bail. Alamieyesiagha died a decade after his conviction on 10 October 2015.

48. M. Amaza, 'Discretionary Awards of Oil Blocks in Nigeria: A State Capture Culture Passed Down from the Military Government' 21 August 2019, Heinrich Böll Stiftung, Cape Town.

49. J. Stuart, 'Illicit Financial Flows from Africa: South Africa, Nigeria and Zambia' *TRALAC Annual Conference 2019:*2 https://www.tralac.org/documents/events/tralac/2752-tralac-brief-iffs-from-south-africa-nigeria-zambia-march-2019/file.html (accessed 20 November 2021).

50. UNCTAD, *Trade Misinvoicing in Primary Commodities in Developing Countries: The Cases of Chile, Côte D'Ivoire, Nigeria, South Africa and Zambia* (2016) 8; C Okojie, *Illicit Transfers and Tax Reforms in Nigeria: Mapping of the Literature and Synthesis of the Evidence* (2018) 11.

51. Okojie (n 37 above) 11; UNCTAD (n 48 above) 18.

A. O. Adeola *et al.*, 'Crude oil exploration in Africa: socioeconomic implications, environmental impacts, and mitigation strategies' (2021) 42 *Environment Systems and Decisions.*

52. D. Amata, '2022 budget: N3, 453 per capita for the medical care of every Nigerian in 2022' www.dataphyte.com (accessed 21 July 2022).

53. T Ngozo, *OXFAM: Illicit Financial Flows in the Mining Industry in South Africa* (2020) 23.

54. UNCTAD 2016, 'Some countries losing up to 67% of commodity exports to misinvoicing' https://unctad.org/news/some-countries-losing-67-commodity-exports-misinvoicing (accessed 13 December 2021).

55. Ngozo (n 52 above) 26.
56. Ngozo (n 52 above) 24.
57. Ngozo (n 52 above) 24.
58. Ngozo (n 52 above) 26.
59. UNCTAD (n 53 above) 24.
60. UNCTAD (n 53 above) 25.
61. Barbara Curson, 'Trade misinvoicing costs south Africa R325bn a year' 20 December 2021 https://www.moneyweb.co.za/news/economy/trade-misinvoicing-costs-south-africa-r325bn-a-year (accessed 19 October 2022).
62. UNODC 'UNODC supports efforts to combat illicit mining in Southern Africa' https://www.unodc.org/unodc/frontpage/2020/November/unodc-supports-efforts-to-combat-illicit-mining-in-southern-africa.html (accessed 10 December 2021).
63. National Bureau of Statistics, *2019 Poverty and Inequality in Nigeria: Executive Summary* (2020) 6.
64. O. J. Olujobi, 'Nigeria's upstream petroleum industry anti-corruption legal framework: The necessity for overhauling and enrichment' *Journal of Money Laundering Control* (ahead of print) 'Findings'.
65. Petroleum Industry Act of 2021.
66. Nwuke, 'Nigeria's Petroleum Industry Act: Addressing old problems, creating new ones' 24 November 2021 https://www.brookings.edu/blog/africa-in-focus/2021/11/24/nigerias-petroleum-industry-act-addressing-old-problems-creating-new-ones/ (accessed 1 December 2021).
67. Journal of Petroleum Technology, 'Heirs holdings buys 45% of Shell Nigeria's OML 17 Field' 1 March 2021 https://jpt.spe.org/heirs-holdings-buys-45-of-shell-nigerias-oml-17-field (accessed 18 July 2022).
68. Transcorp is Nigeria's largest publicly listed multi-industry company and Heirs Holdings is one of the country's largest conglomerates.
69. Journal of Petroleum Technology, 'Heirs holdings buys 45% of Shell Nigeria's OML 17 Field' 1 March 2021 https://jpt.spe.org/heirs-holdings-buys-45-of-shell-nigerias-oml-17-field (accessed 18 July 2022).
70. The Panama Papers contained 11.1 million documents of offshore companies. Regarding Nigeria, numerous wealthy Nigerians, including politicians, military personnel and businessmen, were exposed for hiding monies and assets in offshore accounts. Most of the wealth was obtained through corruption. ANCIR 'Panama papers' https://panamapapers.investigativecenters.org/ (accessed 18 July 2022).
71. Nwezeh, 'Nigeria: Politicians own 800 assets worth $400m in London, Dubai – report' 28 April 2021 https://allafrica.com/stories/202104280775.html (accessed 18 July 2022).
72. AU/ECA Conference of Ministers of Finance, Planning and Economic Development *Illicit Financial Flow: Report of the High Level Panel on Illicit Financial Flows from Africa* (2021) 93.
73. X Sala-I-Martin and A Subramanian, *Addressing the Natural Resource Curse: An Illustration from Nigeria* (2003) 4.

74. Maluleke, 'Quarterly Labour Force Survey (QLFS) Q2:2021' http://www.statssa.gov.za/publications/P0211/Presentation%20QLFS%20Q2_2021.pdf (accessed 10 December 2021).

75. The Borgen Project, 'What to know about poverty in Zimbabwe' https://borgenproject.org/poverty-in-zimbabwe/ (accessed 14 December 2021). The Borgen Project is an NPO that aims to address poverty and hunger.

76. Muronzi, 'Dollar o'clock: Should Zimbabwe axe its faltering currency again?' 5 May 2022 https://www.aljazeera.com/economy/2022/5/5/dollar-oclock-should-zimbabwe-axe-its-faltering-currency-again (accessed 18 July 2022).

77. M&G Special Report, 'Exploring the role of illicit financial flows in Zimbabwe's political economy' 27 May 2021 https://mg.co.za/special-reports/2021-05-27-exploring-the-role-of-illicit-financial-flows-in-zimbabwes-political-economy/ (accessed 13 December 2021); CNRG *Illicit Financial Flows in Zimbabwe's Artisanal Mining Sector* (2013) 4.

78. Zimbabwe Environmental Law Association, 'Illicit gold trade and smuggling: Vulnerabilities exposed by Rushwaya case' http://www.zela.org/illicit-gold-trade-and-smuggling-vulnerabilities-exposed-by-rushwaya-case/ (accessed 14 December 2021).

79. Muronzi, 'Zimbabwe is haemorrhaging gold. Can a key reform curb smuggling?' 18 December 2020 https://www.aljazeera.com/economy/2020/12/18/zimbabwe-is-hemorrhaging-gold-can-a-key-reform-curb-smuggling (accessed 14 December 2021).

80. UNCTAD/ PRESS/PR/2014/021.

81. L. Gray *et al. Few and Far: The Hard Facts on Stolen Asset Recovery* (2014) 1.

82. Economic and Financial Crimes Commission Act, 2004: sec. 28.

83. Prusa, 'The lost potential of Nigeria's asset recovery: How is the recovery of stolen assets sabotaged by politicians?' 14 October 2021 https://cifar.eu/the-lost-potential-of-nigerias-asset-recovery-how-is-the-recovery-of-stolen-assets-sabotaged-by-politicians/ (accessed 18 July 2022).

84. BellaNaija 'US, other countries have refused to return recovered stolen assets from Nigeria-Dabiri-Erewa, Prof Itse Sagay appeal to Nigerians to lend their voices to campaign' 13 January 2017 www.bellanaija.com/2017/01.us-other-countries-have-refused-to-return-recovered-stolen-assets-from-nigeria-dabiri-erewa-prof-sagay-appeal-to-nigerians-to-lend-their-voices-to-campaign (accessed 22 July 2022).

85. '$300m in Funds Connected to Former Military Leader Abacha' www.aljazeera.com/economy/2020/2/4/nigeria-to-recover-300m-stolen-by-its-former-mlitary-ruler 4, February 2020 (accessed 22 July 2022). 'Nigerian's plan to redistribute Recovered Corruption Money need a Rethink' www.mg.co.za/artixle/2018-07-19-nigerias-plan-to-redistribute-recovered-corruption-money-needs-a-rethink (accessed 22 July 2022).

86. Anti-Corruption Commission Act 13/2002: sec, 11.

87. Murwira, 'Zimbabwe: ZACC Recovers U.S. $100m in Corruption Assets' 18 July 2020 Zimbabwe: ZACC Recovers U.S. $100m in Corruption Assets (accessed 18 July 2022).

88. Kwaramba et al. 'Capital Flight and Trade Misinvoicing in Zimbabwe' 28 (2016) African Development Review 50–64.

89. Civil Forum for Asset Recovery 'South Africa 2021' https://cifar.eu/country-profiles/south-africa-2021/ (accessed 18 July 2022).

90. ENNHRI 'Applying a Human Rights-Based Approach' https://ennhri.org/about-nhris/human-rights-based-approach/ (accessed 15 July 2022).

91. Gray, *et al.* 2014:21.

92. Ulbrich and Bechtel 2021, "5 practices to prevent and disrupt illicit financial flows", https://star.worldbank.org/blog/5-practices-prevent-and-disrupt-illicit-financial-flows (accessed on 14 December 2021).

93. UNCTAD 2020.

BIBLIOGRAPHY

Adeola, AO, Akingboye, AS, Ore OT *et al.* 'Crude oil exploration in Africa: Socio-economic implications, environmental impacts, and mitigation strategies'. *Environment Systems and Decisions* (2021): 42.

AFRODAD, *Illicit Financial Flows: Towards a More Integrated Approach for Curbing Illicit Flows from Zimbabwe* (AFRODAD, Harare 2021).

Barbara Curson, 'Trade misinvoicing costs South Africa R325bn a year'. https:www.moneyweb.co.za/news/economy/trade-misinvoicing-costs-south-africa-r325bn-a-year (accessed 19 October 2022).

Chamber of Mines of South Africa, *Mines SA 2016 Facts and figures* (Chamber of Mines, Johannesburg 2016).

Chamber of Mines of Zimbabwe, 'Mining law'. https://www.chamberofminesofzimbabwe.com/index.php/en/fashion/mining-law (accessed 18 October 2021).

CNRG, *Illicit Financial Flows in Zimbabwe's Artisanal Mining Sector* (Africa Portal, Johannesburg 2013).

Financial Action Task Force, *Trade based money laundering* (FATF/OECD, France 2006).

Goldhub, 'Gold mine production'. https://www.gold.org/goldhub/data/historical-mine-production (accessed 10 December 2021).

Gray, L, Hansen, K, Recica-Kirkbride, P, and Mills L, *Few and Far: The Hard Facts on Stolen Asset Recovery* (The World Bank and the OECD, Washington 2014).

Hirschel-Burns, T, 'Marikana miners strike for better wages, 2012'. 4 April 2015. https://nvdatabase.swarthmore.edu/content/marikana-miners-strike-better-wages-2012#case-study-detail (accessed 21 July 2022).

Igwe, U, 'Tracking illicit financial flows could support Nigeria's post-pandemic recovery'. 6 April 2021. https://blogs.lse.ac.uk/africaatlse/2021/04/06/tracking-illicit-financial-flows-support-nigeria-post-pandemic-recovery-corruption/ (accessed 30 October 2021).

International Trade Administration, 'Zimbabwe: Country commercial guide'. https://www.trade.gov/country-commercial-guides/zimbabwe-mining-and-minerals (accessed 18 July 2022).

Journal of Petroleum Technology, 'Heirs Holdings Buys 45% of Shell Nigeria's OML 17 Field'. 1 March 2021. https://jpt.spe.org/heirs-holdings-buys-45-of-shell-nigerias-oml-17-field (accessed 18 July 2022).

Kamga, S, *The Right to Development in the African Human Rights System* (Routledge, New York 2018).

Magashi, S, 'The Human Right to Development in Nigeria'. LLD Dissertation, Stellenbosch University 2016.

Mail & Guardian Special Report, 'Exploring the Role of Illicit Financial Flows in Zimbabwe's Political Economy'. 27 May 2021. https://mg.co.za/special-reports/2021-05-27-exploring-the-role-of-illicit-financial-flows-in-zimbabwes-political-economy/ (accessed 13 December 2021).

Maluleke, R, 'Quarterly Labour Force Survey (QLFS) Q2:2021'. http://www.statssa.gov.za/publications/P0211/Presentation%20QLFS%20Q2_2021.pdf (accessed 10 December 2021).

Metallon Corporation, 'About Zimbabwe'. https://metcorp.co.uk/about-us/about-zimbabwe.aspx (accessed 10 December 2021).

Muronzi, C, 'Zimbabwe is haemorrhaging gold: Can a key reform curb smuggling?' 18 December 2020. https://www.aljazeera.com/economy/2020/12/18/zimbabwe-is-hemorrhaging-gold-can-a-key-reform-curb-smuggling (accessed 14 December 2021).

Muronzi, C, 'Dollar o'clock: Should Zimbabwe axe its faltering currency again?' 5 May 2022. https://www.aljazeera.com/economy/2022/5/5/dollar-oclock-should-zimbabwe-axe-its-faltering-currency-again (accessed 18 July 2022).

Murwira, Z, 'Zimbabwe: ZACC recovers U.S. $100m in corruption assets'. 18 July 2020 Zimbabwe: ZACC Recovers U.S. $100m in Corruption Assets (accessed 18 July 2022).

National Bureau of Statistics, *2019 Poverty and Inequality in Nigeria: Executive Summary* (2020). https://africacheck.org/sites/default/files/media/documents/2021-06/2019%20POVERY%20AND%20INEQUALITY%20IN%20NIGERIA.pdf.

Ngozo, T, *OXFAM: Illicit Financial Flows in the Mining Industry in South Africa* (OXFAM, South Africa 2020).

NS Energy, 'Top five diamond mining countries of Africa profiled'. http://www.nsenergybusiness.com/news/top-five-diamond-mining-africa/ (accessed 10 December 2021).

Nwezeh, K, 'Nigeria: Politicians own 800 assets worth $400m in London, Dubai report'. 28 April 2021. https://allafrica.com/stories/202104280775.html (accessed 18 July 2022).

OECD, *Illicit Financial Flows from Developing Countries: Measuring OECD Responses* (OECD Publishing 2014).

Okojie C, *Illicit Transfers and Tax Reforms in Nigeria: Mapping of the Literature and Synthesis of the Evidence* (Partnership for African Social and Governance Research, Nairobi 2018).

Pitt M, 'Smuggling and the black market for foreign exchange'. *Journal for International Economics*, 16 (3) (1984): 243–57.

Prusa, V, 'The lost potential of Nigeria's asset recovery: How is the recovery of stolen assets sabotaged by politicians?' 14 October 2021. https://cifar.eu/the-lost

-potential-of-nigerias-asset-recovery-how-is-the-recovery-of-stolen-assets-sabotaged-by-politicians/ (accessed 18 July 2022).

Sala-I-Martin X, and Subramanian A, *Addressing the Natural Resource Curse: An Illustration from Nigeria* (IMF Working Paper 2003).

Sengupta, A, *The Right to Development: Report of the Independent Expert on the Right to Development* (Commission on Human Rights, Geneva 2000).

Signé, L, Sow, M, and Madden, P, *Illicit Financial Flows in Africa: Drivers, Destinations, and Policy Options* (Brookings Institute, Africa Growth Initiative, 2020). https://www.brookings.edu/research/illicit-financial-flows-in-africa-drivers-destinations-and-policy-options/ (accessed 10 December 2021).

Statista, 'Contribution of oil and natural gas sector to GDP in Nigeria from the 4th quarter of 2018 to the 3rd quarter of 2021'. 1 February 2022. https://www.statista.com/statistics/1165865/contribution-of-oil-sector-to-gdp-in-nigeria/ (accessed 18 July 2022).

Statistics SA, 'Four facts about the mining industry'. http://www.statssa.gov.za/?p=14682 (accessed 10 December 2021).

Stuart, J, 'Illicit financial flows from Africa: South Africa, Nigeria and Zambia'. *TRALAC Annual Conference 2019.* https://www.tralac.org/documents/events/tralac/2752-tralac-brief-iffs-from-south-africa-nigeria-zambia-march-2019/file.html (accessed 20 November 2021).

The Borgen Project, 'What to know about poverty in Zimbabwe'. https://borgenproject.org/poverty-in-zimbabwe/ (accessed 14 December 2021).

The World Bank Group, *Nigeria Poverty Assessment* (World Bank, Washington, DC 2022).

The World Bank, 'Nigeria Overview'. https://www.worldbank.org/en/country/nigeria/overview (accessed on 21 July 2022).

Ulbrich, C, and Bechtel, K, '5 practices to prevent and disrupt illicit financial flows'. https://star.worldbank.org/blog/5-practices-prevent-and-disrupt-illicit-financial-flows (accessed 14 December 2021).

UNECA, *Illicit Financial Flows: Report of the High Level Panel on Illicit Financial Flows from Africa* (UNECA, Addis Ababa 2015).

UNCTAD, *Economic Development in Africa 2020 Report: Tackling Illicit Financial Flows for Sustainable Development in Africa* (United Nations Publications, UNCTAD/ALDC/AFRICA 28 September 2020).

UNCTAD, 'Some countries losing up to 67% of commodity exports to misinvoicing'. https://unctad.org/news/some-countries-losing-67-commodity-exports-misinvoicing (accessed 13 December 2021).

UNCTAD, *Trade Misinvoicing in Primary Commodities in Developing Countries: The Cases of Chile, Côte d'Ivoire, Nigeria, South Africa and Zambia* (United Nations, Switzerland 2014).

UNODC, 'UNODC supports efforts to combat illicit mining in Southern Africa'. https://www.unodc.org/unodc/frontpage/2020/November/unodc-supports-efforts-to-combat-illicit-mining-in-southern-africa.html (accessed 10 December 2021).

Zimbabwe Environmental Law Association, 'Illicit gold trade and smuggling: Vulnerabilities exposed by Rushwaya case'. 2021. http://www.zela.org/illicit-gold-trade-and-smuggling-vulnerabilities-exposed-by-rushwaya-case/ (accessed on 14 December 2021).

Chapter 11

Manufacturing Underdevelopment

Coins Trafficking as Illicit Financial Flows in Disguise within the Central Africa Economic and Monetary Cooperation (CEMAC)

Gerard Emmanuel Kamdem Kamga

INTRODUCTION

Our purpose in this chapter is to review a particular kind of scarcity that has been occurring in the CEMAC region in Central Africa for the past few years. It is the phenomenon of coin shortage experienced in this part of the continent that comprises a bloc of nations members of a sub-regional organisation known as the Economic and Monetary Community of Central Africa States (CEMAC). A strange practice consisting of selling coins for banknotes at a higher and more profiting rate has been taking place in some areas of the region. This probably explains why the phenomenon of disappearing coins has become important as time goes on. The year 2019 was a hectic one for businesses in the region owing to one of the greatest shortage of coins that was noticeable particularly in Cameroon.[1] It is worth noting that within the CEMAC, the currency in place is the CFA franc which stands for the Franc des Colonies Francaises d'Afrique. It is on 26 December 1945 that a decree by the then president of the French interim government, Général de Gaulle, instituted a monetary reform and the creation of the Franc des colonies Françaises d'Afrique (CFA) in the region.[2] With regards to the type of currency itself, the region uses banknotes of 500, 1,000, 2,000, 5,000, and 10,000 CFA francs. When it comes to coins, there are 500, 100, 50, 25, 10, 5, 2 et 1 CFA franc. The layers of the economy and development initiatives have been rocked by the disappearance of the later. In other words, economic activities and small businesses have seriously been damaged by this phenomenon.

For example, when purchasing ordinary items of necessities such as groceries, fuel, clothes, and medicines, customers are left with little choice but to complete the transaction by paying with the exact amount whether in coins or banknotes. It happens that most of the time, sellers, and cashiers do not have small change to reimburse their customers. This situation also occurs in the taxi and transport industry where drivers often refrain from providing services because of the lack of petty cash to complete the transactions in an environment where passengers often use banknotes of high value to pay for their trip. Most of the time transactions are cancelled as a result of the fact that neither the customers nor the sellers or service providers have the necessary petty cash. In some instances, the client will proceed with the transaction and give up the change that he or she is entitled to.

A key consequence of the scarcity of coins within CEMAC is that following a mystical process, the nature of coins has shifted from being a mere currency, a tool of financial transaction to becoming a commodity itself subject to trade. On this account, coins can be found for sale in business areas such as petrol stations and some markets among traders in Cameroon. Whenever someone attempts to change a note of 5,000 CFA franc into coins, he or she must bear the cost of up to the 150-franc CFA francs for the transaction to be completed. Nonetheless further investigations show that the scarcity of coins is not a random or accidental phenomenon. The currency is subject to trafficking given that important quantities are purchased, taken out of the country and exported to China where they are melted and turned into jewellery and sold for more profit. On 1 November 2018 members of the gendarmerie in Cameroon arrested a Cameroon national and a Chinese in the city of Douala with 43 bags of coins of 50 and 100 Franc CFA for a value of 2 million franc CFA.[3] The two individuals were suspected to be behind a network of coin trafficking towards Asia.

The phenomenon of coins trafficking has a devastating consequence on the economy and the Right to Development and constitutes in itself an illicit financial flow (IFFs) in disguise. IFFs are defined as 'money illegally earned, transferred or used'.[4] These occur when the funds involved are proceeds from illegal transactions and when the transfer of these funds do not abide with legal prescriptions including transparency, accountability and tax deduction. Put differently, IFFS amount to the fact that 'these flows of money are in violation of laws in their origin, or during their movement or use, and are therefore considered illicit'.[5] This applies to the phenomenon of coins trafficking examined previously and has an impact on the notion of development within CEMAC. The notion of development is broad and refers to sound economic performance and fair distribution of profits. Development amounts to the improvement of the living conditions of citizens through the provision of healthcare, housing, infrastructures, education, and other basic needs. The preamble to the United

Nations Declaration on the Right to Development defines development as a comprehensive economic, social, cultural, and political process, which aims at the constant improvement of the well-being of the entire population and of all individuals, on the basis of their active, free, and meaningful participation in development and in the fair distribution of the benefits resulting therefrom. Following this analysis, the key concern is to know to what extent can coins trafficking contribute to manufacture underdevelopment in Central Africa. What are the consequences on the economies of such region and the impact on the Right to Development? These are the key preoccupations at the heart of the upcoming developments. But prior to further elucidation, it is crucial to introduce the sub-regional organisation known as CEMAC.

INTRODUCING THE CEMAC

The Communauté Economique et Monétaire de l'Afrique Centrale (CEMAC), known in English as the Central Africa Economic and Monetary Cooperation, was established in 1972 following a treaty and later revised in 1994 and 1996. It is a monetary union that comprises countries located in Central Africa including Congo, Gabon, Cameroon, Central African Republic, Chad, and since 1984 Equatorial Guinea. Together with the larger Economic Community of Central African States (ECCAS) CEMAC presents one of the Central African regional Communities established to promote cooperation and exchange among its members. The aim of the treaty is to promote harmonised development in its member states within the framework of a common market. Its key objectives are as follows:

a. to strengthen competitiveness of economic and financial activities by harmonising regulations that govern them;
b. to ensure the convergence towards sustainable economic and financial performance by coordinating economic policies and rendering national budgetary policies consistent with the common monetary policy;
c. to create a common market based on free mobility of persons, goods, capital and services;
d. to assure coordination of national sector policies in the following areas: agriculture, livestock, fishing, industry, commerce, transport, telecommunications, energy, environment, research, education and professional training;
e. to implement common actions and adopt common policies.[6]

CEMAC has a common central bank namely the Banque des Etats de l'Afrique Centrale (BEAC; Bank of Central African States) established in

1972 with the mission to equally issue the CFA Franc as the common currency for member states of the region.

As one can see from this brief introduction, CEMAC along with its central bank, BEAC appears to have been established to boost the development of the region. But this does not seem to be working. In fact, not only this is an institution established by former colonial authorities to perpetuate their interests but more importantly, it was not set up with a genuine will to develop the region and to enhance the Right to Development of the inhabitants of the region. As we have seen the currency does not even belong to the area as it is a device to facilitate exploitation and modern slavery. The fact that such currency is at the heart of trafficking within the region is a pattern that has been consubstantial to its very existence. CEMAC along with its corollary institutions do not have the capacity to control or curb IFFS in disguise that has been occurring in the region for the past decades. The phenomenon of IFFS relies on sophisticated networks and obscure chains of command that aimed essentially at deviating resources from their legitimate aim in this case the development of the region. As a result, member states in CEMAC have been losing a staggering sum of money that would have contributed to poverty alleviation, building of infrastructure and the provision of basic social services.

UNDERSTANDING THE CONCEPT OF IFFS IN DISGUISE

To start this section, it is important to consider a few definitions of IFFs:

IFFs are commonly defined as the transferred monies that is earned, transferred, or utilised through illicit means, into or out of a country. They include legally earned value, money, and monetised instruments that are transferred illicitly or value, money, and monetised instruments that are acquired through illegal activities, such as the proceeds of crimes, including corruption and tax evasion. They can also capture tax avoidance and trade misinvoicing.[7]

A similar definition of IFFs is put forward by the United Nations Office on Drugs and Crime (UNODC) which after pointing out that there is not a single definition of IFFs, consider that they are generated by methods, practices, and crimes aiming to transfer financial capital in contravention of national or international laws.[8] These two definitions point to the fact that IFFs involve if not multiples states but at least more than one state. A key element at the heart of this phenomenon is the notion of borders through which the illicit transaction must be completed. It is further observed that IFFs are characterised by three forms of unrecorded money moving across borders:

- Corrupt: Proceeds of bribery and theft by government officials.

- Criminal: Proceeds of drug trading, human trafficking, counterfeiting, contraband, and myriad forms of additional activities.
- Commercial: Proceeds arising from import and export transactions conducted so as to manipulate customs duties, VAT taxes, income taxes, excise taxes, or other sources of government revenues.[9]

At first glance, a close look at the characterisation of IFFs as analysed above appears not to apply to coins trafficking, which is the purpose of this chapter. Yet, our aim remains the same, that is to show that the scarcity of coins currently experienced within CEMAC is not a random phenomenon but a criminal activity in the hands of obscure networks of chain of command disseminated across the borders of continent. In this particular instance, the nature of coins has shifted from being a currency to become a commodity, a proceed of trafficking transferred from one country to another. It is in this sense that this amounts to IFFs in disguise. The arrest of two coins traffickers with 2 million franc CFA of coins of 50 and 100 franc CFA by Cameroon authorities on 1 November 2018[10] was not an isolated event. In March 2021 a similar operation led by the National Gendarmerie of Cameroon led to the arrest in the city of Yaounde of three people with coins of 100 franc CFA Franc for a value of 150,000 franc CFA.[11] Reports show that their crimes constitute not only coins trafficking but also other fraudulent acts including among other fake banknotes and forged civil documents and other items that members of the law enforcement agencies discovered in their possessions. One of the traffickers confessed that after collecting these coins, they resell them for banknotes at a higher and more profiting rate.[12] The fact is that it could have been a different story if the resell of coins was limited to the local market, but the practice has moved beyond the sphere of what is licit. The disappearing coins occurring in Cameroon and other countries within CEMAC is due to the fact that they are subject to high demand in China. Once the coins enter China, they are melted for jewellery that are sold at a higher rate.[13] As one can see, this situation clearly accounts for IFFs in disguise. First of all, the coins are fraudulently acquired and illegally taken out of a country through trafficking. Second, in the receiving country, such coins are literally destroyed for the purpose of making new items out of them; items that are sold at a value higher than the initial 'raw material' from which they derive. In so doing, the country of origin not only loses a precious asset, that is, its currency but is also deprived of tax income resulting from the sale of the new items made out of that asset.

The smuggling and trafficking of funds (whether banknotes or coins) is prohibited within CEMAC. On 21 December 2018, the Ministerial Committee of this sub-regional organisation adopted Regulation No.02/18/CEMAC/UMAC/CM on exchange control in the CEMAC known as the CEMAC

Regulation. In June 2019, the Bank of Central African States (BEAC) issued a number of directives (instructions) regarding its implementation. This document that entered into force on 1 January 2019 outlines the framework to and the terms and conditions for the realisation of the foreign exchange transactions in the CEMAC member states. A key aspect of this new regulation is that the role of BEAC has been strengthened with its greater involvement in the declaration and authorisation of transactions, the control of the compliance with the foreign exchange regulations and the interpretation of the CEMAC Regulation.[14] Section 4 entitled 'transfer of funds' reads as follows:

> Applications to transfer funds over 1 million CFA Francs (around 1,500 EUR) abroad are subject to the justification of the origin of the funds and to the presentation of supporting documentation required by the exchange control regulation.
>
> Below 1 million CFA Francs per month and per economic agent, transfers abroad only require justifying the origin of the funds and a declaration to the BEAC.[15]

The current coins trafficking that results in disappearing coins within the economies of CEMAC is a practice handled by a network of criminal entrepreneurs for the purpose of making undue profit and advantages by diverting assets crucial to the states of the region. The process strongly affects the structure of the economies in this area. One can understand why through illicit capital flows, vital developmental resources are lost owing to the ease with which stolen assets in this case the coins can flourish in the context of a burgeoning, yet opaque international financial system. It is within this context that IIFs in disguise are considered to be a major disabler of development and the Right to Development.

The Impact on Development

In 2015, a report by the High Level Panel on IFFs from Africa (HLP) revealed that the continent loses an average of USD 50 billion yearly through IFFs. This amount was updated in 2020 during the United Nations Conference on Trade and Development that found that the continent was now losing USD 88.6 billion annually through IFFs. The amount is equivalent to 3.7 per cent of Africa's gross domestic product (GDP).[16] In the same vein, Global Financial Integrity (GFI) estimates that nearly USD 1 trillion of unrecorded money flows out of developing countries annually.[17] This staggering sum of money that Africa has been losing year after year through IFFs are money that would have contributed to development, provide healthcare, education, housing, infrastructure, and other basic needs to the population. The realisation of the Right to Development and socioeconomic is not possible in an environment where public funds are lost to the profit of criminal networks. This explains in part why the African continent despite being the richest in terms of raw materials remains poor. The major section of the population continues to experience extreme poverty, corruption, poor education on a daily basis. The United Nations estimates that from 1990 to 2010, the number of people living on less than $1.25 a day in Africa nearly doubled from 219 million to 414 million.[18] Despite excellent economic performance achieved by the continent, nothing has really changed on the ground in terms of poverty alleviation, provision of social services, and basic needs. It is not only troubling but chocking to see that higher economic performances on a consistent basis contribute nothing in improving people's lives. As already emphasised IFFs are a disabler of development. Similarly, owing to the negative impacts this phenomenon brings on the economic social and cultural life of the populations, it can be said that IFFs enable poverty. The link between the two plagues is noticeable if one pays attention to the guiding principles on extreme poverty and human rights. This document articulates the following:

> States must take deliberate, specific and targeted steps, individually and jointly, to create an international enabling environment conducive to poverty reduction, including in matters relating to bilateral and multilateral trade, investment, taxation, finance, environmental protection and development cooperation. This includes cooperating to mobilize the maximum of available resources for the universal fulfilment of human rights.[19]

It is obvious from the above observation that mobilising the maximum resources is a prerequisite towards the realisation of human rights in general and the Right to Development in particular. It is therefore axiomatic that IFFs remain the greatest threat to this initiative. The indicators of underdevelopment within CEMAC for the past years clearly indicate that the region has been performing poorly. Regarding the Central African Republic for example, according to the 2021/2022 report by the United Nations Development Programme, its Human Development Index stands at 0.404 and remains one of the poorest around the globe. This country ranks 188 out of 191 states in the world and the life expectancy at birth is 53.9 years.[20] Estimates from the World Bank show that the poverty rate in the country is higher than 90 per cent. Similarly, the gross national income per capita stands at USD 966 and has been decreasing as half of the population relies on humanitarian assistance to survive. Another member state of CEMAC is Chad where the situation is not very different from that of Central Africa Republic. According to the 2021–2022 Human Development Report, its index stands at 0.394 and the country ranks 190 out 191 countries globally.[21] Chad's gross national income per capita stands at USD 1,364 with a life expectancy at birth of 52.5 years.[22] To confirm our analysis, we can choose one last country that is member state of CEMAC, Congo. The 2021–2022 Human Development Report for this country indicates that its index stands at 0.571 with a gross national income per capita of USD 2,889. Congo ranks 153 out 191 countries in the world as its life expectancy stands at 63.5.[23] As confirmed by the above developments, IFFs, whether in their traditional form or in disguise, have devastating consequences on the developments of the countries in Central Africa. In Central Africa, countries like Chad and Equatorial Guinea are booming in the area of oil exploration, while the Central African Republic is booming in the extraction of various mineral resources such as gold, diamonds, petroleum, tin, and bauxite. In Gabon, roughly 90 per cent of the territory is covered by forest. Similarly, Congo is host to the largest rainforest on the planet and is at the heart of debate about addressing climate change at the global level. Unfortunately, the wealth and potential of the member states of CEMAC contrast sharply with their state of underdevelopment. The common denominator of such countries is weak state institutions, poor governance structure and their common heritage as 'former' French colonies. The latter is relevant because one must keep in mind that structures inherited from decades of colonialism were never designed to curb IFFs. The whole colonial structure itself owes its very survival to a system of theft, domination, and exploitation embedded that is part of its essence. The consequences extent to human rights in general and the Right to Development in particular that is the object of the next section.

The Impact on the Right to Development

At the beginning of this section, it is crucial to note that the Right to Development is an inalienable human right by virtue of which every human person and all peoples are entitled to participate in, contribute to, and enjoy economic, social, cultural, and political development, in which all human rights and fundamental freedoms can be fully realised. The above quote is the provision of Article 1 of the Declaration on the Right to Development adopted by the United Nations (UN) during its ninety-seventh plenary meeting on 4 December 2006. The inalienable character of the Right to Development (RTD) is highlighted in this provision. There is a clear link between IFFs and human rights in that such flows diminish the resources available to states for investment in programmes that contribute to the realisation of human rights, particularly economic, social, and cultural rights. In essence, the failure to counter IFFs and recover stolen assets is a denial of access to basic healthcare, education, safe water and sanitation, adequate housing and infrastructure, all of which are basic conditions for the enjoyment of human rights. Another way of understanding the link between IFFs and human rights is to examine the link between the availability of resources and the capacity of states to address extreme poverty, which is generally considered a human rights concern. The connection between IFFs and poverty is evident from the guiding principles on extreme poverty and human rights, which state that

> States must take deliberate, specific and targeted steps, individually and jointly, to create an international enabling environment conducive to poverty reduction, including in matters relating to bilateral and multilateral trade, investment, taxation, finance, environmental protection and development cooperation. This includes cooperating to mobilize the maximum of available resources for the universal fulfilment of human rights.[24]

The document further emphasises that ensuring that those living in poverty can enjoy at least minimum essential levels of all economic, social, and cultural rights is not simply a matter of implementing current policies more fully. The eradication of poverty requires policies that specifically address the situation of those living in poverty through a comprehensive and coherent framework covering all domains of public policy and political action.[25]

CURBING IFFS IN DISGUISE

Even though we are dealing with the situation in CEMAC, it is obvious that addressing IFFs will require a concerted effort from various regions or countries. This explains why it is not possible to think about a standalone set of solutions that can apply only to the CEMAC region. While assessing the consequences of IFFs from Africa, the African Economic Outlook issue of 2012 observes that stemming capital flight and encouraging repatriation of finance should be part of African strategies to promote the quality of life of their people. The document further states that it is ironic that poor African countries that are struggling to mobilise resources have vast financial resources that they cannot access as they are hidden abroad.

Addressing IFFs was at the heart of the United Nations Addis Ababa Action Agenda dedicated to the financing for development. This initiative is aimed at promoting peaceful and inclusive societies through good governance, the rule of law, human rights, fundamental freedoms, equal access to fair justice systems and measures to combat corruption and curb IFFs.[26] This is in line with the implementation requirements outlined in the Guiding Principles on Extreme Poverty and Human Rights which states that

> States have obligations relating to the provision of the facilities, goods and services required for the enjoyment of human rights. Even where such facilities, goods and services are provided with the involvement of private sector or civil society entities, States are responsible for ensuring quality, affordability and

coverage and have the duty to protect individuals against abuses committed by private service providers.[27]

The Addis Ababa Agenda further highlights the will to redouble efforts to substantially reduce IFFs by 2030, with a view to eventually eliminating them, including combating tax evasion and corruption through strengthened national regulation and increased international cooperation through the insertion of anti-abuse clauses in all tax treaties.[28] The setting of an organ such as the High Level Panel on Illicit Financial Flows from Africa remains a relevant step towards curbing IFFs from the continent. The purpose of this Panel headed by the former president of South Africa Thabo Mbeki is outlined in the following lines:

- Develop a realistic and accurate assessment of the volumes and sources of these outflows;
- Gain concrete understanding of how these outflows occur in Africa, based on case studies of a sample of African countries and;
- Ensure that we make specific recommendations of practical, realistic, short- to medium-term actions that should be taken both by Africa and by the rest of the world to effectively confront what is in fact a global challenge.[29]

In addition to the Addis Ababa Agenda, there is a key document designed to curb IFFs not only from Africa but at the global level. This document is the United Nations Convention against Corruption (UNCAC) adopted by the United Nations General Assembly in 2003 and entered into force in December 2005. Prior to further elucidation, it is crucial to recall that corruption is one of the most common form and channel of IFFs. As a result, in framing corruption, the UNCAC definitely targets IFFs. It is worth noting as well that IFFs belong to the category of transnational organised crimes. That is why another landmark instrument dealing with this phenomenon is the United Nations Convention against Transnational Organised Crime (UNCTOC) adopted in 2000 and entered into force in 2003. The adoption of two international instruments, one dedicated to corruption, and the other to Transnational Organised Crimes is advantageous in that the struggle against IFFs has gained in efficiency. The UNCAC if properly implemented can indeed contribute to control the scale of IFFs not only from Africa but in other regions of the world. Nonetheless, it is worth noting that Africa and CEMAC remain the most affected victims. According to the provision of section 1 the UNCAC is aimed at the following:

(a) To promote and strengthen measures to prevent and combat corruption more efficiently and effectively;

(b) To promote, facilitate and support international cooperation and technical assistance in the prevention of and fight against corruption, including in asset recovery;
(c) To promote integrity, accountability and proper management of public affairs and public property.

The UNCAC ratified by several countries remain a key anticorruption instrument at the global level. It was designed to curbc IFFs and therefore development issues. The document proposes relevant procedures to fight against corruption. In so doing, its section 3(1) provides as follows:

> This Convention shall apply, in accordance with its terms, to the prevention, investigation and prosecution of corruption and to the freezing, seizure, confiscation and return of the proceeds of offences established in accordance with this Convention.

Despite the above relevant initiatives to curb IFFs, these will be pointless if other states do not come to the party. They can work provided that there is a concerted effort at the international, regional, and sub-regional levels to address the is. One of the problems is that CEMAC, along with the treaty that governs it, remains at the heart of a (new) colonial empire with France at the top. Almost all the resources crucial for the development of this region are controlled by France. For instance, the CFA franc which is the currency used in the region is entirely controlled by France. Within this context, there can no be serious initiative aiming at developing the region. The currency is oriented in France, important quantity of the reserves of are kept in the Bank of France and so on. These account not only for theft but also contribute to aggravate IFFs in the region. It is hardly understandable to see how the role of France can be determinant in fighting IFFs in CEMAC in order to allow for the development of this region.

CONCLUSION

The purpose of this chapter was to review a particular kind of scarcity that has been occurring in the CEMAC region in Central Africa for the past few years. It appears that the scarcity of coins is not a random phenomenon, but something perpetrated on purpose. The trafficking of coins organised by the Chinese counterparts strongly contributes to the phenomenon of IFFs in disguise. But it is relevant to emphasise that this occurs owing to the weak state institutions and poor governance characterising the region. These were inherited from the French colonisation that still occurs following a different format. The region is in need of a proper independence and sovereignty to be at an equal footing with the rest of the world. Already, in the struggle against IFFs, some countries refrain from a serious commitment to deter criminal networks and other multinational corporations from this horrendous practice. It is within this context that in 2006 a report entitled 'The other side of the coin' released by a British parliamentary committee provided detailed information on companies and banks in the United Kingdom that play a key role in corruption and IFFs from Africa. The fact that some areas of activities within the CEMAC region, such as harbours, railways, and farming, are systematically in the hands of French companies attests to the same reality.

Overall, it can be said that when a region is endowed with key natural resources and abundance of raw materials, when such a region is part of a continent that has been achieving the highest global economic performance for the past year and yet remains poor and underdeveloped, then there is a problem. This means that the underdevelopment of such a region is simply manufactured by a plurality of factors, mostly human. The scarcity of coins occurring in the CEMAC region is one of such practices fabricated to prevent any development to take off to the detriment of millions of people. In so doing the RTD has been subject to violation for too long and time has come to look for other alternatives by seeking first a genuine sovereignty and independence.

NOTES

1. Africa News: Could the Coin Shortage in Central Africa be a Thing of the Past? Available at https://www.africanews.com/2019/12/26/efforts-to-stem-coin-shortage-in-central-africa-business-africa//.
2. This was later changed to Franc de la Communauté Financière d'Afrique (CFA).
3. Cameroun: Des jetons pour 2 millions de F saisishttps://www.camer.be/mobile/71260/11:1/cameroun-des-jetons-pour-2-millions-de-f-saisis-cameroon.html.
4. High Level Panel on Illicit Flows from Africa, *Track It! Stop It! Get It! Report of the High Level Panel on Illicit Financial Flows from Africa* (Addis Ababa: Commissioned by the AU/ECA Conference of Ministers of Finance, Planning and Economic Development, 2015), https://www.uneca.org/sites/default/files/PublicationFiles/iff_main_report_26feb_en.pdf.
5. Ibid.
6. Central African Economic and Monetary Community (CEMAC), https://www.devex.com/organizations/central-african-economic-and-monetary-communitycemac-52313.
7. Sustainable Development Goals, Compilation of Metadata for the Proposed Global Indicators for the Review of the 2030 Agenda for Sustainable Development, https://unstats.un.org/sdgs/iaeg-sdgs/metadata-compilation/.
8. Ibid.

9. Ibid.

10. CAMEROUN:: Des jetons pour 2 millions de F saisishttps://www.camer.be/mobile/71260/11:1/cameroun-des-jetons-pour-2-millions-de-f-saisis-cameroon.html.

11. Cameroon: Coins Traffickers Attest Reselling to Traders, Other Business People, https://legideon.org/index.php?page=view/article/3643/Cameroon-Coins-Traffickers-Attest-Reselling-to-Traders-Other-Business-People.

12. Ibid.

13. Voici les raisons de la rareté des pièces de monnaie sur le marché, https://www.camerounweb.com/CameroonHomePage/business/Voici-les-raisons-de-la-raret-des-pi-ces-de-monnaie-sur-le-march-443327.

14. Overview of the CEMAC Regulation of 21 December 2018 on Exchange Control, https://hsfnotes.com/africa/2019/10/10/overview-of-the-cemac-regulation-of-21-december-2018-on-exchange-control/.

15. Ibid.

16. United Nations Conference on Trade and Development, Africa could Gain $89 billion Annually by Curbing Illicit Financial Flows, 28 September 2020, https://unctad.org/news/africa-could-gain-89-billion-annually-curbing-illicit-financial-flows (accessed 20 November 2021).

17. Sustainable Development Goals, Compilation of Metadata for the Proposed Global Indicators for the Review of the 2030 Agenda for Sustainable Development, https://unstats.un.org/sdgs/iaeg-sdgs/metadata-compilation/.

18. Accelerating Poverty and Hunger Reduction in Africa: Progress and Policy Prescriptions, <https://www.undp.org/content/dam/south_africa/docs/mdgs/Accelerating%20Poverty%20 and%20Hunger%20Reduction%20in%20Africa-Progress%20and%20Policy%20Prescriptions.pdf>.

19. Guiding Principles on Extreme Poverty and Human Rights, https://www.ohchr.org/Documents/Publications/OHCHR_ExtremePovertyandHumanRights_EN.pdf.

20. UNDP, Human Development Report 2021–2022, https://hdr.undp.org/content/human-development-report-2021-22.

21. Ibid.

22. Ibid.

23. Ibid.

24. Guiding Principles on Extreme Poverty and Human Rights, https://www.ohchr.org/Documents/Publications/OHCHR_ExtremePovertyandHumanRights_EN.pdf.

25. Ibid.

26. Addis Ababa Action Agenda United Nations General Assembly August 2015, UN document A/RES/69/313 available at https://sustainabledevelopment.un.org/index.php?page=view&type=400&nr=2051&menu=35.

27. Guiding Principles on Extreme Poverty and Human Rights, https://www.ohchr.org/Documents/Publications/OHCHR_ExtremePovertyandHumanRights_EN.pdf.

28. Addis Ababa Action Agenda United Nations General Assembly August 2015, UN document A/RES/69/313 available at https://sustainabledevelopment.un.org/index.php?page=view&type=400&nr=2051&menu=35.

29. African Union (AU) and Economic Commission for Africa (ECA), Illicit Financial Flows: Report of the High Level Panel on Illicit Financial Flows from Africa, AU/ECA, Addis Ababa, 2, 2015.

BIBLIOGRAPHY

Accelerating Poverty and Hunger Reduction in Africa: Progress and Policy Prescriptions. https://www.undp.org/content/dam/south_africa/docs/mdgs/Accelerating%20Poverty%20 and%20Hunger%20Reduction%20in%20Africa-Progress%20 and%20Policy%20Prescriptions.pdf.

Addis Ababa Action Agenda United Nations General Assembly August 2015, UN document A/RES/69/313. https://sustainabledevelopment.un.org/index.php?page =view&type=400&nr=2051&menu=35.

Africa News: Could the Coin Shortage in Central Africa be a Thing of the Past? https://www.africanews.com/2019/12/26/efforts-to-stem-coin-shortage-in-central -africa-business-africa//.

African Union (AU) and Economic Commission for Africa (ECA). (2015). Illicit Financial Flows: Report of the High Level Panel on Illicit Financial Flows from Africa. AU/ECA, Addis Ababa, 2.

Cameroon: Coins Traffickers Attest Reselling to Traders, Other Business People. https://legideon.org/index.php?page=view/article/3643/Cameroon-Coins-Traffickers-Attest-Reselling-to-Traders-Other-Business-People.

CAMEROUN: Des jetons pour 2 millions de F saisis. https://www.camer.be/mobile /71260/11:1/cameroun-des-jetons-pour-2-millions-de-f-saisis-cameroon.html.

Central African Economic and Monetary Community (CEMAC). https://www.devex .com/organizations/central-african-economic-and-monetary-communitycemac -52313.

Guiding Principles on Extreme Poverty and Human Rights. https://www.ohchr.org/ Documents/Publications/OHCHR_ExtremePovertyandHumanRights_EN.pdf.

High Level Panel on Illicit Flows from Africa. *Track It! Stop It! Get It! Report of the High Level Panel on Illicit Financial Flows from Africa.* Addis Ababa: Commissioned by the AU/ECA Conference of Ministers of Finance, Planning and Economic Development, 2015. https://www.uneca.org/sites/default/files/PublicationFiles/iff_main_report_26feb_en.pdf.

Overview of the CEMAC Regulation of 21 December 2018 on Exchange Control. https://hsfnotes.com/africa/2019/10/10/overview-of-the-cemac-regulation-of-21 -december-2018-on-exchange-control/.

Sustainable Development Goals. Compilation of Metadata for the Proposed Global Indicators for the Review of the 2030 Agenda for Sustainable Development. https://unstats.un.org/sdgs/iaeg-sdgs/metadata-compilation/.

UNDP. Human Development Report 2021–2022. https://hdr.undp.org/content/human -development-report-2021-22.

United Nations Conference on Trade and Development. Africa Could Gain $89 Billion Annually by Curbing Illicit Financial Flows. 28 September 2020. https://

unctad.org/news/africa-could-gain-89-billion-annually-curbing-illicit-financial-flows (accessed 20 November 2021).

Voici les raisons de la rareté des pièces de monnaie sur le marché. https://www.cameroun web.com/CameroonHomePage/business/Voici-les-raisons-de-la-raret-des-pi-ces-de-monnaie-sur-le-march-443327.

Chapter 12

Resource Financed Infrastructure under Sicomines Agreement as an Impediment to Achieving the Right to Development in the Democratic Republic of Congo

TD Tumba and Muyamba Mangu

INTRODUCTION

Developing countries have been financing their development projects for the betterment of the livelihoods of their citizens. It is a fact that to achieve the Right to Development (RTD), states need adequate funds. In so doing, they may use their own financial resources or resort to external loans from traditional financial institutions such as the International Monetary Fund (IMF), World Bank and African Bank of Development. In addition to this, states may also choose to rely on alternative methods known as Resource Financed Infrastructure (RFI) to realise their RTD. The RFI is a contractual arrangement that allows states that need infrastructures to lend the proceeds of production rights granted to investors in exchange for natural resource exploitation.[1] Different African countries such as Nigeria, Chad, South Sudan, Angola and the DRC have resorted to RFI as a financing model.[2] Within the context of the DRC, to finance its development projects known as *Cinq Chantiers*, the former president Joseph Kabila approached traditional financial institutions to request financial support in a bid to fulfil its election campaign promises. This was made of a programme to build infrastructures such as roads, railways, bridges, job creation through investment, education (schools and universities), water, electricity, and health. However, these traditional financial institutions were reluctant to fund the realisation of such programme. The reason being that the DRC has become closer to China over the past years. In addition to this, there was an argument according to which the DRC would not be able to repay back the loan given that it was a fragile state weakened by prolonged conflicts inside its borders. In such a situation, the Congolese government returned to China, where it formally signed a memorandum of understanding (MoU) with a group of Chinese companies in 2001 and again in 2007. Following this MoU, the Congolese government entered into a joint-venture agreement to set up a company namely, Sicomines, a mining company where the majority of shares, 68 per cent was held by Chinese companies (Sinohydro, China Railway Engineering Company, Exim Bank) while 32 per cent remains to the DRC (Gecamines).[3] Similarly, the MoU creating Sicomines paved the way for the DRC to rely on the RFI to finance its development projects in exchange of natural resources. The joint-venture company represented in this study is Sicomines, a partner of Chinese enterprises to be involved in the construction of infrastructures in the DRC. At this level of the study, numerous preoccupations arise: What is the regime of this agreement and what are the mechanisms surrounding its implementation? Was this designed in the interest of the people of the DRC? If so, why was China allowed to control more than the major share in this joint venture? This chapter focuses on RFI agreement between the DRC government and Chinese companies to finance socioeconomic infrastructures in a bid to realise the RTD in exchange for mineral resources exploitation. It also looks at the link between the implementation of the RFI agreement as a hidden (soft) form of illicit financial flows (IFFs) and the non-achievement of the RTD within the context of the DRC.

A REVIEW OF RFI AS AN ALTERNATIVE TO TRADITIONAL FINANCE INSTITUTIONS TO REALISE THE RTD

The RFI model is a contractual arrangement that allows governments to lend the proceeds of production rights granted to investors for natural resource exploitation in exchange for a loan for infrastructure construction that is not currently associated.[4] Under RFI as a financing model, a government is allowed to fund its infrastructure development on the basis of future revenues derived from its natural resources. The RFI model requires three major features including government procurement, fiscal regime, and credit facility.[5] Government procurement refers to the process by which the government acquires infrastructure goods and services directly with 100 per cent ownership or through public-private partnership (PPP) transaction. Fiscal regime is the mechanism by which revenues or profits in forms of royalties, taxes, or dividends from the sale of the commodity are paid to government, state-owned resources development partner[6] after the costs of extraction, necessary processing, marketing, and delivery are paid. Credit facility amounts to the way in which the lender or resource developer for the construction and, potentially, the operations and maintenance of the infrastructure provides funds. In addition to these, the RFI includes a provision to ensure that the construction and maintenance of infrastructure adheres to accepted standards and operational requirements.[7] The idea behind using RFI as a financing mode entails that the property owner (the one who pays for the infrastructure) has the financial capacity to keep the property in good condition so as to maximise the property's economic value over time. Each time that a government rely on the RFI model to fulfil its socioeconomics commitments, the payment process should specify the ownership as the state used its own funds to pay to comply with its commitment. In the same vein, the RFI infrastructure assets can operate and be owned under a PPP arrangement.[8] This model of ownership entails both the government and the private partner who have an interest in the RFI to maintain the infrastructure in good shape for future transaction.

The use of RFI allows the state to fulfil its mandate of improving the welfare conditions of its citizens by offering them supplementary infrastructures. In contrast, the execution of the RFI as it was applied in the DRC deprived the Congolese government of necessary funding without which the realisation of human rights to development as provided in the African Charter on Human and Peoples' Rights (ACHPR) and the United Nations Declaration on the RTD (UNDRTD) could not be accomplished. Considered as duty bearers of the RTD, states have the responsibility to finance their socioeconomic projects in order to ensure that their citizens have access to food, housing, drinking water, healthy environment, education, healthcare services, and infrastructures. However, the RFI model consists of the infrastructure financing method in which a government guarantees the repayment of loans taken out to finance the construction of infrastructure with future income from a resource development project.[9] The RFI model enables governments to acquire infrastructures faster than they could have done otherwise should they have waited for resource projects to generate income.[10] In a bid to speed the realisation of infrastructures, effective service delivery and other, the Congolese government concluded on 17 September 2007 and 22 April 2008 a MoU and a Collaboration Agreement respectively with a group of Chinese companies to build public infrastructures such as hospitals, roads, railways, and airports in the DRC. On this account, a Chinese bank named Exim was selected to provide a loan of $6.5 billion to finance these projects. The government of the DRC agreed to reimburse the loan through the creation of a Congolese Chinese joint-venture company named the 'Sino-Congolaise' des Mines (Sicomines) with the view to extract and sell gold, copper and cobalt. With the signing of this agreement, it is noticeable the extent to which the government shift its behaviour in terms of loan. Indeed, in the past it was almost systematic that to comply with its commitments, the government would turn towards the IMF and/or the World Bank for this loan – a loan generally granted in exchanged of exorbitant interests. The advent of RFI marks the beginning of a new multipolar worlds where alternatives and possibilities become available. This does not mean that the RFI is in itself a magic that wants to resolve issues pertaining to the realisation of the RTD in the DRC. As a matter of fact, it is crucial to note that in the abovementioned joint venture (Sicomones), the Chinese possess the majority of shares. If it is submitted that the state as a duty bearer should take all necessary steps to ensure that the people enjoy all facets of the RTD, it is worth noting that in the case of Sicomines, the government may have failed to ensure that any initiative involving public policy takes into account the need to enhance the well-being of all citizens. After this brief assessment of the RFI, it is worth to review the RTD as a human right.

THE RTD AS A HUMAN RIGHT

The discourse surrounding the RTD can be traced back from the Charter of the United Nations[11] which considers in its articles 55, well-being as a centrepiece of friendly cooperation and stability among states to ensure the self-determination of peoples. The concept of human RTD is a newly human right, considered as third generation human right or solidarity right. The RTD is a right linked to the dignity of human being and the existence of humankind. It is a right concerned with promoting and defending individual's ability to participate in, contribute to, and enjoy development whether economic, social, cultural, or political. It is within this framework that the Charter of the United Nations laid down the ground for understanding human dignity as the main substance of the RTD.

The RTD was first mentioned in a speech during the twenty-first session of the United Nations General Assembly (UNGA) on 23 September 1966 by Doudou Thiam, former Senegal's Minister of International Relations when he linked the failure of the United Nations development goals in the newly decolonised states in light of resolving the economic growth imbalance between the developed and developing worlds.[12] At the time the newly liberated African countries were victims of massive human rights violations and plundering of their natural resources. In fact, colonisation had denied them their legitimate right to self-determination and the exercise of national and international sovereignty. Thiam's notion of the RTD took shape twenty years later when the UNGA passed Resolution 41/128 to address political and economic injustices including social disparity between developed and developing worlds brought on by colonisation.

Years later came the Declaration on the RTD that was enshrined in Resolution 41/128 of the UNGA on 4 December 1986.[13] In the same vein, the Senegalese jurist Kéba M'baye is credited for introducing the concept of the RTD into legal discourses in 1972 during a presentation at the International Institute of Human Rights in Strasbourg.[14] Finally, the consecration of the RTD as a human rights was completed by the African Charter in 1981.[15] Years later again, the RTD was reaffirmed as a universal and inalienable human right by numerous instruments including the 1993 Vienna Declaration and Programme of Action, the 2000 Millennium Declaration, and, most recently, the Durban Declaration and Programme of Action in 2001. In addition to such instruments, numerous scholars and thinkers share arguments that clearly posit the RTD as a human right. According to Ibhawoh,[16] the RTD is either a moral and exhortative demand or a legal or quasi-legal demand. In the same vein, a group of eminent figures Karel Vasak, Mohammed Bedjaoui, Georges Abi-Saab, UN Special Rapporteur Philip Alston, and Indian economist and Nobel Prize winner Amartya Sen coined that the RTD should be considered as a human right for individuals and peoples.[17] The background to this claim is that the concept of the RTD is available in the New International Economic Order claim from developing countries, who demand a restructuration of the current international economic order by eliminating global injustice to allow developing countries to achieve their development. The advent of the New International Economic Order emphasised rights-based development discourses to redress the injustices and inequalities of which developing countries have been victims of massive violation of human rights during colonisation. In this regard, the realisation of the RTD in developing countries should not depend on international aid provided by Western countries (former colonisers) but be regarded as a human right. It is within this context that the quest for the restructuring of the International Economic System is likely to bring a new perspective on international aid in considering development as a human right by a decolonial discourse in line with the ACHPR. As put forward by Schrijver, Sengupta and Sen shade light on the holistic aspects of the RTD combining all categories of human rights.[18] This means that the denial of any one of the aforesaid rights will impede the realisation of the RTD. Additionally, the views of the aforementioned scholars concurred with those of developing nations that support a comprehensive understanding of the RTD that prioritises humankind, equity, justice, peace, and liberty as the cornerstones of development.

RTD Under the ACHPR

The African human rights system gives great importance to the RTD. This right seeks to address inequalities in world politics and global institutions that have an impact on the development of African countries. The RTD has been recognised as constitutive of a rights-based approach to development by both human rights and scholarship.[19] Article 22 of the African Charter guarantees the RTD and is the most definitive codification of this right. This article stipulates that all people shall have the right to their economic, social, and cultural development with due regard to their freedom and identity and in the equal enjoyment of the common heritage of mankind. States shall have the duty, individually or collectively, to ensure the exercise of the RTD.

A contextual reading of article 22 of the African Charter portrays different types of development. The first of these is economic development to improve people's economic capabilities. The RTD combines preexisting rights such as the right to a decent standard of living, the right to work, and the right to participate. Second, it is necessary for the state to consider advancing social and cultural rights while taking into account peoples' freedom and identities in order for them to enjoy the common heritage.

Finally, article 22 of the Charter gives the duty to the states to ensure the exercise of the RTD individually or collectively. The RTD encompasses the well-being of societies. The African Charter presents the RTD as a collective right, as people's rights that are grounded also in the United Nations Charter. This collective right does not negate the fact that it is also an individual right and that development is a right for all (individuals and people).[20]

The RTD in the DRC

The scope of the DRC's social policy in fighting poverty and enhancing the well-being of Congolese people, components of the RTD have always been mentioned in the various government initiatives pertaining to its social policy. This is the case of different regulatory frameworks,[21] which highlighted public policies related to education, access to primary health care, clean drinking water and a healthy environment as well as the equitable distribution of the national wealth.

Considering the evolution of the notion of the RTD in the DRC, the constitutional background informs that the 1994 Constitutional Act of Transition provided in its article 12 that 'every Zaïrian has the right to peace, development and to the common heritage of mankind'.[22] In addition, the 2003 constitution made provision of the RTD in its article 55 as follows: 'All Congolese have the right to enjoy national wealth. The State has the duty to redistribute them equitably and to guarantee the RTD.'[23] Besides, the 2006 Congolese constitution provides in its article 58 that 'all Congolese have the right to enjoy the national wealth. The State has the duty to equitably distribute the national wealth and guarantee the RTD'.[24] Although different Congolese constitutions mention the RTD, the various successive governments in the DRC have never shown the political will to realise the RTD for the well-being of the Congolese population. Indeed, the country remains blessed with numerous wealth in terms of a variety of natural resources such as gold, diamond, coltan, and other. But more than the majority of the population living below the poverty line do not have access to infrastructures and basic service delivery.

IFFS AS A BARRIER TO THE REALISATION OF THE RTD IN THE DRC

IFFs coupled with corruption are directly responsible for perpetuating poverty and undermining all initiatives of development to achieve the RTD in developing countries such as the DRC. IFFs prevent developing nations from mobilising and allocating substantial public financial resources necessary for effective and equitable social and economic development. In addition, the loss of potential public funds through IFFs reduces the DRC's capacity to invest in the social sector to improve citizens accessibility to healthcare services, education, housing, safe drinking water, and infrastructures. The situation related to misappropriation of funds resulting from the RFI affecting negatively on the livelihood of Congoleses as expressed by the Human Development Index (HDI)[25] 2022 in which the DRC is ranked 175th out of 189 countries, while the corruption perceptions index[26] places the country 169th out of 180 countries in 2021. The abovementioned information indicates that the Congolese government's ability to ensure the DRC's development is hampered by a lack of funding brought on by the poor design and implementation of RFI agreement, corruption, embezzlement, and IFFs. It can then be observed that IFFs in the country are perpetrated by multiple actors such as government agents, public servants, political actors, and multinational corporations involved in the implementation of the RFI agreement. In the same vein, IFFs can be enabled by factors including inadequate regulation of the financial system and the capital account; trade openness in a context of weak regulation and poor governance, poor institutional quality, and over-reliance on commodity exports.[27] These factors act as channels for the economic, institutional, environmental, and social harm facilitating the occurrence of IFFs within the context of the DRC.[28]

THE IMPLEMENTATION OF RFI MODEL IN THE DRC AS A FORM OF IFF

The development of diplomatic ties between Africa and China is essentially characterised by a typical trade in which African countries systematically export natural resources to China. The literature on China-Africa relations suggests that the relationship is mutually beneficial, while others see it as a new form of imperialism, especially when it comes to the exploitation of African countries' resources.[29] The variety of Chinese political economy has resulted in different modes and structures to support Chinese investments abroad. The Chinese foreign policy pushed Chinese political economy to pay special attention in global natural resource and infrastructure development to have a potential expansion in many African states.[30] This is often mentioned as the sole impetus for the expansion of the Sino-African relations. Although China has not revealed the extent of its loans to Africa, the China Africa Research Initiative team at Johns Hopkins University has tracked some 1,000 loans amounting to $152 billion and extended to 49 African governments and States Owned Enterprises (SOEs) between 2000 and 2018.[31] Recently, the Infrastructure Consortium for Africa (ICA) estimated that infrastructure funding might total $100.8 billion, with China providing roughly a quarter of that amount ($25.7 billion).[32] According to Xu[33], China's SOEs have been deeply engaged in RFI contracts.

As China has propelled RFI as financing approach, there is a growing concern about its nature which intertwined components related to Chinese 'aid', 'trade', and 'Foreign Direct Investment' and resource extraction within the context of RFI.[34] However, China's RFI Model for infrastructure generally favours SOEs and extends China's capacity by creating international opportunities for Chinese firms and employment for Chinese citizens.[35] As discussed earlier, the RFI Model implemented in the DRC under Sicomines Agreement is perceived to be a form of IFFs. This denotes that all the negotiations related to the Sicomines agreement took place in the absence of both the Congolese government and parliament. According to an informal conversation with a member of the DRC parliament, the absence of the disclosure of the Sicomines contract can be perceived as a deliberate act involving some dignitaries of Kabila regime to flee funds outside of the DRC.[36] He also added that the secrecy surrounding the Sicomines contract can be considered as an unethical behaviour (corruption, misinvoicing, falsification convention of collaboration) that constitute a stumbling blocks preventing the DRC from acquiring the needed financial resources to achieve the RTD.[37] Moreover, another worrying aspect of the RFI model as implemented in the DRC is the length of the twenty-five-year contract that established the Sicomines. agreement.[38] Despite the mining code and the investment code recognising tax relief for companies wishing to invest in the DRC, the Code of investments does not allow tax relief for the export of mineral resources. However, the Sicomines contract favoured Chinese firms by allowing them to export mineral resources without paying taxes, causing a financial deficit for the Congolese government.[39] It is important to note that in the event that the DRC government defaults, the sovereign guarantee clause available in the loan agreement provides Chinese companies with the right to recover the loan in any way possible.

The length of the Sicomines agreement is highly perceived by a fraction of Congolese opinion as suspicious because it did not specify the adequate time frame during which the two parties to Sicomines agreement should assess the quantity and determine the content value and financial cost of the extracted mineral resources. It is crucial to point out that the DRC government conceded its mining concessions without knowing their real market value.[40] In addition, neither the Congolese nor the Chinese parties in Sicomines deal have provided a clear explanation of how the minerals will be priced or how much will be spent on infrastructure.[41] This situation shows that the DRC does not possess appropriate technology to assess the monetary value of the extracted and exported raw mineral resources in order to allow the DRC to determine the needed left-over amount of the loan that should be repaid.

Subsequently, the expected investment in the infrastructure sector was estimated to be a total amount of $3 billion; while China disbursed only $825 million so far for building infrastructures according to the President Tshisekedi government.[42] The question here is which direction did the outstanding amount of $2.125 billion take and who benefited from it? In the same vein, the former special adviser to President Kabila named Luzolo Bambi affirms that the DRC loses at least $15 billion of public funds per year through IFFs.[43] In the same vein, Sicomines failed to meet its obligations to build infrastructure, and as a result, this situation is detrimental to the development of the DRC. The following projects, which were agreed to be built under the Sicomines contract, were never completed: construction of 145 healthcare facilities across the country, as well as two modern universities; construction of 2,000 social housing units in Kinshasa and 3,000 in the provinces; construction of 21 hospitals in new provinces; construction of Goma and Bukavu' airports; construction of Katende electrical dam; construction of railway lines Tenke-Kolwezi-Dilolo-Sakanya-Lubumbashi-Kamina-Mwe neditu-Kananga-Ilebo-Kinshasa-Matadi; construction de la Paix and Ndjoku roads in Kinshasa; construction of roads in Butembo and construction of road Bukavu-Kamanyola; the refurbishment of the People's Palace's entrance in Kinshasa.[44] Although Sicomines has access to mines, the reality of the ground shows that certain projects are not being completed as stipulated in the contract. Moreover, the quality of some infrastructures built by Chinese companies is questioned as the quality control was assigned to Chinese companies.[45] The Sicomines contract favoured Chinese companies as it allowed them to export mineral resources without paying taxes which constitutes a shortfall for the Congolese government as some officials from Sicomines are engaged in smuggling activities and illegal exportation of mineral resources from private Chinese companies established in the DRC by abusing the tax exemption given to Sicomines.[46]

In this way, the RFI agreement (Sicomines) was signed in the context of a serious opacity as this raised the question concerning the accountability of the DRC government. There was a great demand from civil society organisations who wanted the Sicomines agreement to be made public. The Sicomines agreement exempts China Mining Companies from paying taxes on the export and profit made from the sale of mineral resources for a period of twenty-five years. The non-payment of taxes as stipulated in the Sicomines agreement denotes the lack of the essential skills in the negotiation from the Congolese experts deprived the DRC of the necessary funds needed for development. In a similar vein, one could contend that because the quantity and quality of minerals exported have never been disclosed, there is a risk that the DRC will be repaying a loan without knowing if the value of the exported mineral resources has already covered the loan to be paid. Although, the RFI agreement acknowledged the construction of socioeconomic infrastructures for a total amount of $3 billion in exchange of mineral resources, in fact, Chinese companies spent only $825 million. Consequently, the DRC still pays for a loan through the exploitation of its minerals for social infrastructures that are either incomplete or non-existent. This suggests that the application of RFI as specified in Sicomines Agreement will not contribute to the development of the DRC because the Congolese government will use its resources to repay the loan (debt) rather than to finance social infrastructures that are crucial for the welfare of its citizens. In this line, the implementation of the Sicomines agreement fell short of Congolese expectations and did not guarantee the improvement of their livelihood.

The above backdrop reveals that the implementation of the RFI under Sicomines in the DRC could be perceived as a soft form of IFFs rather than being a tool for development. In this view, the use of RFI as a financing model paved the way for channelling out billions of dollars that are needed for the improvement of livelihoods in the DRC. The Sicomines agreement also could be considered as a looting machine of mineral resources instead of serving as a vehicle for infrastructure development. Therefore, RFI as operated in the DRC failed to contribute to the achievement of the RTD. In this context the state DRC state will not be able to provide infrastructures, service delivery and improve the lives of the population that remain uneducated, without housing, healthcare, work, and so on. In other words, RFI, instead of being an opportunity to help realising the RTD seems to have been purposedly designed to sabotage this right.

CONCLUSION

The adoption of RFI as a financing model in the context of Sicomines agreement is nothing but a mechanism facilitation the proliferation of IFFs from the DRC. Because it allows the exploitation and exportation of unquantified raw mineral resources with no added value from the DRC to China to the detriment of the Congolese population, it contributes to maintaining poverty, lack of infrastructures, and poor service delivery by the DRC government. The use of RFI model in the DRC raises a question which remain unanswered until the construction of social infrastructures will be complete, but this is not likely to happen given the conceptualisation of the contract from its beginning. It is critical that the Congolese government formulate policies that address all obstacles affecting the implementation of RFI for the promotion of socioeconomic development in the DRC.

In terms of recommendation, the RFI must be substantially revised in terms of not only scope but also the conditions and framework of its implementation. The DRC should strengthen oversight mechanisms to monitor mining contracts signed on behalf of the state to improve the accountability of all companies involved in extractive activities. In so doing, it is strongly recommended that parliament, the civil society, the local communities, and all relevant stakeholders be involved in such a process. This will surely safeguard the country's natural resources and sovereignty that remain the only guarantees and assets to allow for a genuine realisation of the RTD.

NOTES

1. H Halland *et al* 'Resource Financed Infrastructure: A Discussion on a New Form of Infrastructure Financing' (2014) 13 International Bank for Reconstruction and Development / The World Bank, Washington DC.

2. IMF Guide on Resource Revenue Transparency; International Monetary Fund: Washington, DC, USA, 2005, available online: https://www.imf.org/external/pubs/ft/grrt/eng/060705.pdf (accessed 22 July 2022); T Ogwang and F Vanclay 'Resource-Financed Infrastructure: Thoughts on Four Chinese-Financed Projects in Uganda' (2021) 22.

3. Convention de collaboration entre la RDC et le groupement d'entreprises Chinoises: China Railway Group et Sinohydro Corporation relative au development d' un project d'infrastructures en RDC (2008); J Jansson 'The Sicomines Agreement: Challenge and Continuity in the Democratic Republic of Congo's International Relations' South African Institute of International Affairs (2011) 1–31, available at https://media.africaportal.org/documents/saiia_OP_97.pdf (accessed 15 November 2021).

J Malm 'When Chinese Development Finance Met the IMF's Public Debt Norm in DR Congo' PhD dissertation, Department of social sciences and business, Roskilde University, Denmark (2016) 6.

4. H Halland *et al* (n 1 above).

5. H Halland *et al* (as above) 32.

6. In the case under study, Gecamines is a state-owned resource development partner in the project.

7. H Halland *et al* (as above) 61.

8. H Halland *et al* (as above).

9. H Halland *et al* (n 1 as above) 13.

10. DG Landry 'The Risks and Rewards of Resource-for Infrastructure Deals: Lessons from the Congo's Sicomines Agreement' Working Paper No. 2018/16. China-Africa Research Initiative, School of Advanced International Studies, Johns Hopkins University, Washington, DC. Retrieved from http://www.sais-cari.org/ publications.

11. The Charter of the United Nations, available at http://www.un.org/en/charter-united-nations/.

12. United Nations General Assembly, Official Records, Twenty-first Session, 1414th Plenary Meeting, 23 September 1966.

13. A/RES/41/128 (Declaration on the Right to Development), available at http://www.un.org/documents/ga/res/41/a41r128.htm.

14. I Bunn 'The Right to Development: Implications for International Economic Law' (2000) 15 American University International Law Review 1433.

15. The African Charter, adopted on 27/07/1981 and entered into force on 21/10/1986.

16. B Ibhawoh 'The Right to Development: The Politics and Polemics of Powers and Resistance' (2011) 87 Human Rights Quarterly 91.

17. N Schrijver 'A New Convention on the Human Right to Development: Putting the Cart before the Horse?' (2020) 38(2) Netherlands Quarterly of Human Rights 84–93.

18. N Schrijver (n 21 as above); A Sengupta 'Realising the Right to Development' (2002) 31(3) Development and Change 566; AK Sen 'Development as Freedom'. The First Presidential Lecture. Washington, DC: The World Bank.

19. S Kindornay *et al* 'Rights-based Approaches to Development: Implications for NGOs' (2012) 34(2) Human Rights Quarterly 472–506.

20. K M'baye 'Le droit au développement comme un droit de l'homme' (1972) 5 Revue des Droits de l'Homme 515.

21. DRC Constitution 2006, DRC Mining Code 2918.

22. DRC Constitution 1994, article 12.

23. DRC Constitution 2003, article 55.

24. DRC Constitution 2006, article 58.

25. The United Nations Development Programme (UNDP) compiles the Human Development Index (HDI) of 189 nations in the annual Human Development Report, https://hdr.undp.org/data-center/human-development-index#/indicies/HDI.

26. Transparency International Index 2021, available at https://www.transparency.org/en/cpi/2021/index/cod.

27. L Ndikumana 'Capital Flight: Measurement and Drivers' (2014) Political Economy Research Institute 1–62.

28. United Nations (as above) 24.

29. I Kolstad and A Wiig 'Better the Devil You Know? Chinese Foreign Direct Investment in Africa' (2011) 12(1) Journal of African Business 31–50.

30. J Xu 'Chinese Resource-for-Infrastructure (RFI) Investments in Sub-Saharan Africa and the Future of the "Rules-Based" Framework for Sovereign Finance: The Sicomines Case Study' (2020) 41(3) Michigan Journal of International Law 615.

31. V Furness 'China's Belt and Road Initiative: Can Africa Escape a Debt Trap?' (2020), available at https://www.euromoney.com/article/b1lwrkkwwpxs0x/chinas-belt-and-road-initiative-can-africa-escape-a-debt-trap.

32. Infrastructure Consortium for Africa 'Infrastructure Financing Trends in Africa 2018 Abidjan Infrastructure Consortium in Africa' (2018) 7–8, available at https://www.icafrica.org/fileadmin/documents/IFT_2018/ICA_Infrastructure_Financing_Trends_in_Africa_-_2018_Final_En.pdf.

33. J Xu (as above).

34. J Xu (as above).

35. Y Sun 'China's Aid to Africa: Monster or Messiah?', Brookings Institution, 7 February 2014, available at https://www.brookings.edu/opinions/chinas-aid-to-africa-monster-or-messiah/ (accessed 19 December 2021).

36. Informal conversation with a member of DRC Parliament in Kinshasa, 20 May 2022.

37. Informal conversation (as above).

38. Convention de collaboration entre la RDC et le groupement d'entreprises Chinoises (n 3 as above).

39. C Kabemba 'China-Democratic Republic of Congo Relations: From a Beneficial to a Development Cooperation' (2016) 16(3–4) African Studies Quarterly.

40. A Nguh 'Corruption and Infrastructure Megaprojects in the DR Congo: A Recipe for Failure?' International Rivers (2013) 15.

41. Global Witness 'China and Congo: Friends in Need' (2011) 16.

42. M J Kavanagh and W Clowes 'China Cash Flowed Through Congo Bank to Former President's Cronies A Leak of 3.5 million Documents Shows How a Chinese-run Company Moved millions of Dollars to Former Congo President Joseph Kabila's Family and Allies' Bloomberg (2021), available at https://www.bloomberg.com/news/features/2021-11-28/africa-s-biggest-data-leak-reveals-china-money-role-in-kabila-s-congo-looting.

43. Radio Okapi 'La RDC perd chaque année 15 milliards USD dans les détournements des fonds publics' Publie le 21/6/2018 Available at https://www.radiookapi.net/2018/06/21/actualite/societe/la-rdc-perd-chaque-annee-15-milliards-usd-dans-les-detournements-des (accessed 14 December 2021).

44. Convention de collaboration entre la RDC et le groupement d'entreprises Chinoises (n 3 as above) Appendix c.

45. H Halland *et al* (n 1 as above) 14.

46. Informal conversation with a member civil society in Kinshasa 20 May 2022.

BIBLIOGRAPHY

A/RES/41/128 (Declaration on the Right to Development). http://www.un.org/documents/ga/res/41/a41r128.htm.

Bhusal, Tara Prasad. "Corruption and Illicit Financial Flows in Nepal." *Tribhuvan University Journal* 30, no. 2 (2016): 211–24.

Bunn, Isabella D. "The Right to Development: Implications for International Economic Law." *American University International Law Review* 15 (1999): 1425.

Convention de collaboration entre la RDC et le groupement d'entreprises Chinoises: China Railway Group et Sinohydro Corporation relative au développement d'un projet d'infrastructures en RDC (2008).

Donnelly, Jack. "In Search of the Unicorn: The Jurisprudence and Politics of the Right to Development." *California Western International Law Journal* 15 (1985): 473.

DRC Constitution 2006.

DRC Mining Code 2918.

Financial, Measuring OECD Responses to Illicit. "Illicit Financial Flows from Developing Countries: Measuring OECD Responses." (2014). https://www.superbancos.gob.pa/superbancos/documentos/prevencion_op_il/mejores_practicas_2014/Illicit_FF.pdf.

Furness, Virgina. "China's Belt and Road Initiative: Can Africa Escape a Debt Trap?" (2020). https://www.euromoney.com/article/b1lwrkkwwpxs0x/chinas-belt-and-road-initiative-can-africa-escape-a-debt-trap.

Global Integrity Foundation. "Illicit Financial Flows." (2021). http://www.gfntegrity.org/issue/illicit-fnancial flows.

Global Witness. "China and Congo: Friends in Need." (2011). https://cdn.globalwitness.org/archive/files/library/friends_in_need_en_lr.pdf.

Halland, Håvard, John Beardsworth, Bryan Land, and James Schmidt. *Resource Financed Infrastructure: A Discussion on a New Form of Infrastructure Financing*. World Bank Publications, 2014.

Ibhawoh, Bonny. "The Right to Development: The Politics and Polemics of Power and Resistance." *Human Rights Quarterly* 33 (2011): 76.

International Monetary Fund. "Guide on Resource Revenue Transparency." (2005). https://www.imf.org/external/pubs/ft/grrt/eng/060705.pdf.

Informal Conversation with a Member of DRC Parliament in Kinshasa, 20 May 2022.

Infrastructure Consortium for Africa. "Infrastructure Financing Trends in Africa 2018." https://www.icafrica.org/fileadmin/documents/IFT_2018/ICA_Infrastructure_Financing_Trends_in_Africa_-_2018_Final_En.pdf.

International Monetary Funds. "The IMF and the Fight against Illicit and Tax Avoidance Related Financial Flows." 2021. https://www.imf.org/en/About/Factsheets/Sheets/2018/10/07/imf-and-the-fight-against-illicit-financial-flows access.

Jansson, Johanna. "The Sicomines Agreement: Change and Continuity in the Democratic Republic of Congo's International Relations." (2011). https://media.africaportal.org/documents/saiia_OP_97.pdf.

Kabemba, Claude. "China-Democratic Republic of Congo Relations: From a Beneficial to a Developmental Cooperation." *African Studies Quarterly* 16, no 3–4 (2016): 73–88.

Kamga, Serges Djoyou. *The Right to Development in the African Human Rights System.* Routledge, 2018.

Kavanagh, Michael J., and William Clowes. "China Cash Flowed Through Congo Bank to Former President's Cronies A Leak of 3.5 Million Documents Shows How a Chinese-Run Company Moved Millions of Dollars to Former Congo President Joseph Kabila's Family and Allies." *Bloomberg* (2021). https://www.bloomberg.com/news/features/2021-11-28/africa-s-biggest-data-leak-reveals-china-money-role-in-kabila-s-congo-looting.

Kindornay, Shannon, James Ron, and Charli Carpenter. "Rights-Based Approaches to Development: Implications for NGOs." *Human Rights Quarterly* 34, no. 12 (2012): 472–506.

Kolstad, Ivar, and Arne Wiig. "Better the Devil You Know? Chinese Foreign Direct Investment in Africa." *Journal of African Business* 12, no. 1 (2011): 31–50.

Landry, David. "The Risks and Rewards of Resource-for-Infrastructure Deals: Lessons from the Congo's Sicomines Agreement." *Resources Policy* 58 (2018): 165–174.

M'baye, Kéba. "Le droit au développement comme un droit de l'homme." *Revue des Droits de l'Homme* 5, no. 1 (1972): 503–534.

Malm, Johanna. "When Chinese Development Finance Met the IMF's Public Debt Norm in DR Congo." PhD Dissertation, Roskilde University (2016).

Ndikumana, L., J. Boyce, and A. Ndyiaye. "Capital Flight: Measurement and Drivers, University of Massachusetts/Amherst Political Economy Research Institute." *Working Paper Series*, no 363 (2014).

Nguh, Augustin, and Rudo Sanyanga. *Corruption and Infrastructure Megaprojects in the DR Congo.* Oakland: International Rivers, 2013.

Ngwenya Lindelwa. "The Spill-Over of Illicit Financial Flows." In *Inter-Agency Cooperation and Tax Governance in Africa*, edited by Owens J. Jeffrey and McDonell Rick, 43–60. Pretoria University Law Press, 2017.

Ogwang, Tom, and Frank Vanclay. "Resource-Financed Infrastructure: Thoughts on Four Chinese-Financed Projects in Uganda." *Sustainability* 13, no. 6 (2021): 3259.

Radio Okapi. " La RDC perd chaque année 15 milliards USD dans les détournements des fonds publics." (2021). https://www.radiookapi.net/2018/06/21/actualite/societe/la-rdc-perd-chaque-annee-15-milliards-usd-dans-les-detournements-des.

Schrijver, Nico. "A New Convention on the Human Right to Development: Putting the Cart Before the Horse?" *Netherlands Quarterly of Human Rights* 38, no. 2 (2020): 84–93.

Sen Armatya. *Development as Freedom.* New York: Oxford University Press, 1999.

Sengupta, Arjun Kumar. "Realising the Right to Development." *Development and Change* 31, no. 3 (2002): 553–78.

Sun, Y. "China's Aid to Africa: Monster or Messiah? Brookings." (2014). https://www.brookings.edu/opinions/chinas-aid-to-africa-monster-or-messiah.

The African Charter, adopted on 27/07/1981 and entered into force on 21 /10/1986.

The Charter of the United Nations. http://www.un.org/en/charter-united-nations/.

The United Nations Development Programme (UNDP) Compiles the Human Development Index (HDI) of 189 Nations in the Annual Human Development Report. https://hdr.undp.org/data-center/human-development-index#/indicies/HDI.

Transparency International Index 2021. https://www.transparency.org/en/cpi/2021/index/cod.

United Nations "Resolution adopted by General Assembly on 27 July 2015" 69/313 Addis Ababa Action Agenda of the Third International Conference on Financing for Development (Addis Ababa Action Agenda) A/RES/69/313 (2015) Paragraph 26.

United Nations General Assembly, Official Records, Twenty-first Session, 1414th Plenary Meeting, 23 September 1966.

Xu, Jingwei. "Chinese Resource-for-Infrastructure (RFI) Investment in Sub-Saharan Africa and the Future of the 'Rules-Based' Framework for Sovereign Finance: The Sicomines Case Study." *Michigan Journal of International Law* 41 (2020): 615.

Chapter 13

Taxation, Tax Injustice, and the Right to Development in Africa

Serges Djoyou Kamga

INTRODUCTION

While controversial at the global level, the Right to Development (RTD) is binding in the African human rights system. This means that African states are obliged to deliver this right to their people. For this to happen taxation is critical as it is imperative to ensure that tax revenue reaches the national treasury and the money invested for the achievement of the RTD made of civil and political rights as well and socio-economic rights. However, this does not happen as most of the money is diverted from the treasuries through illicit financial flows (IFFs) in the form of tax evasion and tax avoidance and other forms of tax injustices.

Tax abuses are elements of IFFs, which deprive governments and population from key resources needed for their empowerment.[1] The aim of this chapter is to examine the extent to which tax injustice hinders the realisation of the RTD in Africa. To this end, the chapter will examine the theory of taxation and tax injustice and explore whether there is a directly link between tax injustice and poverty or the failure to realise the RTD in Africa. In this exercise, among others, the chapter will rely on data on tax avoidance and explore whether there is direct correlation between a poor standard of living and tax injustice. It argues that although the link is difficult to make, the failure to achieve the RTD in Africa has something to do with tax injustice. It shows that tax justice is a human right issue and therefore maps out the way forward to provide remedies to the problem of tax injustice to ensure the realisation of human rights and the RTD in particular.

In terms of structure, the chapter is divided into five parts including this introduction. The second part of the chapter explores the theory of taxation and tax injustices. The third part of the chapter examines the nexus between tax injustice and the violation of the RTD. The fourth part of the chapter suggests a road map to ensure tax justice for the realisation of the RTD and the final part provides concluding remarks.

THE THEORY OF TAXATION AND TAX INJUSTICE

According to the Oxford English Dictionary, 'tax' is 'A compulsory contribution to the support of government, levied on persons, property, income, commodities, transactions, etc'. In the Australian case of *R v Barger*,[2] the court held that 'the primary meaning of "taxation" is raising money for the purposes of government by means of contributions from individual persons'. In other words, taxation is the vehicle used by the government to raise money to finance services and achieve human rights. Taxpayers, whether individuals or companies are obliged by law to pay taxes as to enable the government to provide human rights to citizens.

Tax injustice occurs when the taxpayer refuses to pay taxes through tax evasion or tax avoidance.[3] On the one hand, tax evasion is a violation of the law of taxation with the aim of not paying taxes.[4] It evades taxes. It happens in the form of trade misinvoicing.[5] The latter consists of distorting the quality or price of imports or exports to hide or amass money in other jurisdictions.[6] This is often done to evade taxes, sidestep customs duties, pay kickbacks, or money laundry.[7] A case of trade misinvoicing took place in Mozambique, where export records displayed 260,385 cubic metres of logs and sawn timber to the world, yet records from China alone showed that 450,000 cubic metres of the same products originating from Mozambique.[8] This is a clear evidence that trade documents were falsified to benefit tax fraudsters.

Other forms of trade misinvoicing take place in the form of 're-invoicing', which happens 'when goods are exported under one invoice, the invoice is then sent to another jurisdiction, such as a tax haven, where the price is altered, and finally, the revised invoice is sent to the importing country for clearing and payment'.[9] This technique of tax evasion is extremely costing to developing countries that lost $98 billion to $106 billion per year between 2002 and 2006.[10] On the other hand, tax avoidance consists of using numerous techniques to avoid paying taxes. Culprits of tax avoidance generally confuse tax authorities in using the loopholes in the law of taxation. They often rely on tax experts to commit the offence.[11] As correctly observed by the UN Special Rapporteur, 'the overall effect of those practices is to reduce the corporate tax base of many countries in a way not intended by domestic policy'.[12] The practice of tax avoidance often perform by transnational companies 'harms society by avoiding a "fair share" of the tax burden'.[13] In their criminal activities, international corporations avoid tax through 'profit-shifting', where they 'take advantage of tax rate differentials across jurisdictions and shift taxable income and assets away from source countries, where economic activity takes place, and into associated companies in tax havens, sometimes with no real staff or business activities'.[14] Not only this practice divert revenues from the state, it also foster inequalities because it enriches a minority while the majority of the population carries the tax burden. Tax Justice Network is unequivocal in arguing that tax injustice 'fuels inequality, fosters corruption and undermines democracy'.[15] In terms of number, research shows that the global annual tax abuse is estimated between US$100 billion and US$500 billion.[16]

THE NEXUS BETWEEN TAX INJUSTICE AND THE VIOLATION OF THE RTD

The RTD financing necessitates financial resources assembled by the state through taxation. In other words, to build schools, hospitals, roads, provide water, social security, employment, and foster the protection of all other human rights, elements of the RTD, the state needs money. The Independent Expert on the effects of foreign debt and other related international financial obligations of states on the full enjoyment of all human rights, particularly economic, social, and cultural rights writes:[17]

> illicit financial flows, . . . divert resources away from activities that are critical for poverty eradication and sustainable economic and social development, as well as for realizing economic, social, cultural, civil and political rights and *the right to development.*

Taxes helps the state to foster the peoples' standard of living and reduce inequality by closing the gap between the rich and poor as requested the RTD discourse informed by the need to secure equity and fairness.[18] This is to say that tax injustices constraint the enjoyment of the RTD. They disable the state which *par ricochet* unwillingly violates the RTD of the people. In other word, for the RTD to become a reality, it is imperative to comply with taxation and pay the taxes appropriately. This will also advance the accountability of the government who will be obliged to take responsibility for its achievement or failure to fulfil the RTD.

Furthermore, complying with tax justice not only empowers the citizens but also frees the state from depending on development assistance for the RTD financing.[19] This is important because development assistance often comes with strong consequences such as high interest rates for repayment.[20] It increases the debt burden of the state and as such constraints its ability to be effective in delivering services to the needy.[21] The International Bar

Association's Human Rights Institute Task Force on Illicit Financial Flows, Poverty and Human Rights is of the opinion that Tax abuse is 'a very significant part of illicit financial flows . . . depriving governments, communities and citizens of substantial resources'.[22] In a similar vein, the Independent Expert on the effects of foreign debt and other related international financial obligations of states on the full enjoyment of all human rights, particularly economic, social, and cultural rights, explains as follows:

> Illicit financial flows also contribute to the build-up of unsustainable debt as Governments lacking domestic revenue may resort to external borrowing.[23]

However, while at the first sight, it could be argued that taxes would translate into better standard of living for all, it could also be claimed that there is a lack of evidence to prove that assumption. In *Architecture of Australia's Tax and Transfer System*, the Australian Treasury writes:

> A core characteristic of a tax is that *there is no clear and direct link between the payment of the tax and the provision of goods and services to the taxpayer.* The funds that the government raises from taxes may be used to provide goods or services to the community as a whole, and this may provide a benefit to the taxpayer, *but the payment will still be considered a tax if there is no direct relationship between the amount of the payment and the benefit to the taxpayer.*[24]

Similarly, the Australian Bureau of Statistics in Australian System of Government Finance Statistics: Concepts, Sources and Methods observes that even though 'taxpayers expect provision of government services in return for the taxes they pay', there is 'usually no direct link between taxes paid by an individual taxpayer and the government services consumed by that taxpayer'.[25]

In other words, it could be incorrect to claim that tax justice will lead to the enjoyment of the RTD, because human rights are and ideal that cannot be achieved, they are unrealistic, not practical and cannot be costed.[26] Nonetheless, this argument is extremely problematic because nowadays, human rights are practical quantifiable, measurable, and can be costed.[27] For example, the building of infrastructures such as school for the right to education, hospital for the right to health, and houses for the right to housing should be budgeted for. To this end the state needs money gathered through taxation. Even if tax justice may not translate into access to rights, the latter cannot be realised if everyone refuses to pay taxes. In other words, paying taxes is the most critical way to enable the state to comply with its obligations under international human rights law.[28] The Tax Justice Network explains as follows:

> Tax provides the critical underpinning to ensure that states are able to meet their obligations, including through funding public services and curtailing economic and social inequalities. It also enables a robust process of representation within society so that political inequalities can be overcome.[29]

If the state's representatives siphoned off the money, this is a crime which also violates the RTD.[30] In fact, the stolen money is often sent to safe haven countries. This act is also an illicit financial outflow of resources from the treasury.[31] This criminal act fosters economic inequality as the wealthy takes everything while the poor are stranded in poverty.[32] Sharing this view[33] Echoing Balakrishnan, the Independent Expert on the effects of foreign debt and other related international financial obligations of states on the full enjoyment of all human rights, particularly economic, social, and cultural rights, writes:

> While human rights law does not necessarily imply a perfectly equal distribution of income and wealth, it does require that resources in a society are distributed such that individuals are guaranteed equal enjoyment of their basic rights without discriminatory outcomes.[34] When economic inequality results in such discriminatory outcomes, it becomes a human rights issue.[35]

Put differently, tax injustice violates social justice because it frustrates the empowerment of the poor and weaken human rights as it hinders the ability of many to enjoy a better standard of living. It weakens taxpayers' moral who can become reluctant to pay taxes as they don't see their impact on the society.[36]

The effect of tax abuses on the RTD cannot be overemphasised because as demonstrated by Cobham *et al*, 'people who move their wealth offshore short-change their governments out of $182 billion in tax every year'.[37] This is scary in a context where states have the duty to realise human rights for their citizen. Under article 8 (1) of the UN Declaration on the RTD,[38]

> States should undertake, at a national level, all necessary measures for the realisation of the right to development and shall ensure . . . equality of opportunity for all in their access to basic resources, education, health services, food, housing, employment and fair distribution of income.

Siphoning financial resources to be allocated to the RTD financing will frustrate and hinder the state in its role of duty bearer of human rights. As the duty bearer of human rights, the state can only deliver if resources are available to that effect. Hence, if resources are taken away through tax abuses, the state simply loses its primary function which is to provide for its citizens. In fact, to be able to be responsive to people's demands, the state should endeavour to stop tax abuses, while businesses take their responsibility in terms avoiding tax activities that violate human rights.[39] Shubert writes:

> Curbing tax-related illicit financial flows . . . has the potential to make the largest fiscal impact on States' abilities to realize human rights, especially social, economic and cultural rights [*and the RTD*].[40]

In the same perspective, the Tax Justice Network argues that 'the tax and financial systems are [the] most powerful tool' to establish a just and an equalitarian society.[41]

After observing that tax abuse is problematic for the enjoyment of the RTD, it is therefore imperative to address these hindrances to this right. The next section therefore explores the roadmap to addressing tax injustices as to improve the prospects of the realisation of the RTD in Africa.

THE ROAD MAP TO ENSURE TAX JUSTICE FOR THE REALISATION OF THE RTD

To advance tax justice or address tax injustice, the state and the international community have roles to play.

The Role of the State at the National Level

At the national level, the state should enforce constitutionalism characterised by a separation of powers, respect for rule of law. This constitutionalism should be supported by good governance with strong institutions through which civil servants and other members of the society can be held accountable for tax abuses as well as other criminal activities.[42] This is critical to develop 'trust between citizens and state'[43] and empower the state in discharging its responsibilities in terms of providing human rights.[44]

This calls for the adoption of adequate laws and legislation to enforce tax justice in African countries. In this perspective, 'good tax governance and strong collaboration between law enforcement agencies and tax authorities, anti-money laundering agencies', are critical to address corruption, 'IFFs and foster tax justice.'[45]In this vein, 'good tax governance and strong collaboration between law enforcement agencies and tax authorities, anti-money laundering agencies', are critical to address corruption, IFFs and foster tax justice.[46]

In the same perspective, it is imperative to train tax and custom agencies or improve their capacity in taxation, tackling tax-related crimes and update their knowledge in taxation and connected activities. Tax and custom agencies should be trained on how to detect and prevent tax crimes, understand how their committed and what are the sites and roles of secrecy jurisdictions and safe havens. As correctly explained by Gordon, this capacity-building exercise 'has a significant impact on the fiscal capabilities of governments and their ability to improve their economies and standards of living of their citizens'.[47] It is indeed imperative to stop secrecy jurisdictions which 'provides a haven for unearned income, untaxed or lightly taxed wealth, and for criminal proceeds to escape regulatory authorities' to use the words of Tax Justice Network.[48] In spite of the might of some multinational companies, governments should regulate the playing field and get these companies to comply with their taxes obligations, get their commitment to tax codes, and force them to pay their fair portion of taxes within the countries where they operate and generate benefits.[49]

The sustainability of state's activities in strengthening tax justice will increase its legitimacy and get all actors including taxpayers to comply with their obligation to pay taxes. This is to say, states need to be aggressive and visible in fostering taxes justice which increases its legitimacy.[50] In this regard, states should display a strong political will not only to convince taxpayers to pay their taxes but also to punish or force the recalcitrant to comply with their tax obligations. This approach will be an illustration of state's effectiveness in establishing a fair tax system without which the RTD cannot be achieved.[51]

The Role of the International Community

Given the transnational nature of IFFs in which tax evaders or avoiders operate, it is important to have the international community commitment for a successful fight against tax abuses. In this respect, state members of the international community should exchange tax-related information and apply similar standards in dealing with tax abuses across the board. In addition, they should work together to destroy secrecy jurisdictions and tax havens wherever they are established.[52] International cooperation in dealing with tax injustice should also be characterised by the need to trace stolen money and send its back to where it originated. The bridge to this activity should be an aggressive tax cooperation between states. In fact, the obligation to cooperate in addressing tax abuse should be associated with sanctions in case of noncompliance. Failure to cooperate should amount to a violation of human rights. In this perspective, Cohen *et al* explain as follows:

> [States] that encourage or facilitate tax abuses, or that deliberately frustrate the efforts of other States to counter tax abuses, could constitute a violation of their

> international human rights obligations, particularly with respect to economic, social and cultural rights [and *the RTD*].[53]

In other words, African countries will not be able to win the battle against tax abuses if the international community does not join them in this fight. One entry point could be the implementation of the UN Convention against corruption which urge member states to jointly '(a) promote and strengthen measures to prevent and combat corruption more efficiently and effectively; (b) To promote, facilitate and support international cooperation and technical assistance in the prevention of and fight against corruption, including in asset recovery' among other objectives. In a similar vein, African states in particular should give effect to the African Union Convention on Preventing and Combating Corruption.[54]

In fighting tax abuses, it is important to implement the recommendations of the High-Level Panel on Illicit Financial Flows from Africa. The High-Level Panel urged the international community to take all measures possible to close down secrecy jurisdictions, introduce transparency in financial transfers, deal with money laundering and foster a greater transparency in the international banking system.[55] In a similar vein, it is necessary to implement the recommendations of the High-Level Panel on International Financial Accountability, Transparency and Integrity for Achieving the 2030 Agenda (known as the FACTI Panel). The FACTI Panel urged the international community to request the accountability of all stakeholders in the business sector (e.g. the executive, staff, and board members) who fail to address, or advance IFFs in order to grow their own business. It also urges the international community to foster transparency, fairness, disempower enablers, collect and data, and improve capacity in needy countries.[56] More importantly, it also calls for the adoption of a UN Tax Convention. Using the principles of equity and fairness the UN Tax Convention 'would provide for taxing multinationals and capital gains fairly. It would develop a mechanism for fair and impartial dispute resolution'.[57] Furthermore, it would 'provide the basis for legitimate action against any jurisdiction that is undermining global norms and damaging the legitimate tax base of any country'.[58]

Very importantly, the UN Tax Convention will establish an intergovernmental tax body controlled by the UN to supervise the future negotiations of international rules. In addition, the Convention would adopt measures to penalise or hold accountable any countries whose action is prejudicial to other countries in terms of tax revenues, 'through the proposed Centre for Monitoring Taxing Rights'.[59] Ultimately, addressing tax injustices goes through a strong commitment of the state at national level, on the one hand, and of serious devotion of the international community, on the other hand.

CONCLUDING REMARKS

The aim of this chapter was to explore the significance of tax injustices or tax abuses on the enjoyment of the RTD in Africa. The chapter unveiled that tax injustice takes place in the form of tax evasion and tax avoidance with the ultimate objective to siphon funds away from the national treasury. This act deprives the state of resources for the RTD financing. Put differently, tax injustice is detrimental for the enjoyment of the RTD as it violates the right to equality of citizens, destabilises social justice, and hinders the state's ability to finance the RTD.

It was also found that to remedy the situation, states should embark on extraordinary governance. The latter should be characterised by the adoption of appropriate laws and related institutions to hold all culprits of IFFs and tax justice accountable. The states should demonstrate a serious political will to address the issue of tax injustice characterised by the empowerment of tax officers and institutions as well as collaboration among tax agencies and law enforcement units in the countries.

An optimistic view, enshrined in the FACTI panel's recommendations, calls for our collective efforts to put national governments under pressure and to secure their political will, resource and coherence for a central and urgent change in the global governance of tax. It was equally found that the role of the international community is critical. It should cooperate in tax matters by exchanging information, hold tax haven countries responsible for the activities which facilitate IFFs, and importantly respect the right to sovereign equality of each country. It should comply with the recommendations of the AU/ECA Panel on Illicit Financial Flows that calls on national governments to demonstrate a political will and on the international community to cooperate in addressing tax injustice. It should also comply with the FACTI Panel's recommendations, with special attention on the need to adopt a UN Tax Convention considered as 'the pivotal instrument that will reverse the international failures of the global tax system'.[60] Ultimately, the chapter found that while tax injustice frustrates the realisation of the RTD in Africa, the situation can be reversed if the state on the one hand shows a political will, and if the international community on the other hand adopts and implements global measures to address tax injustice.

NOTES

1. Ilias Bantekas and Cephas Lumina (eds) *Illicit Financial Flows, Sovereign Debt, and Human Rights* (Oxford: Oxford University Press, 2018).
2. *R v Barger* (1908) 6 CLR 41 (at para 68).

3. Global Financial Integrity 'Trade Misinvoicing' https://gfintegrity.org/issue/trade-misinvoicing/ (accessed 29 October 2022).

4. Global Financial Integrity 'Trade Misinvoicing.'

5. Global Financial Integrity 'Trade Misinvoicing.'

6. AU/ United Nations Economic Commission for Africa 'Report of the High Level Panel on Illicit Financial Flows from Africa' (2015) https://repository.uneca.org/handle/10855/22695 (accessed 29 October 2022).

7. AU/ United Nations Economic Commission for Africa 'Report of the High Level Panel on Illicit Financial Flows from Africa.'

8. AU/ United Nations Economic Commission for Africa 'Report of the High Level Panel on Illicit Financial Flows from Africa.'

9. Final study on illicit financial flows, human rights, and the 2030 Agenda for Sustainable Development of the Independent Expert on the effects of foreign debt and other related international financial obligations of States on the full enjoyment of all human rights, particularly economic, social and cultural rights, /HRC/31/61, para 14.

10. A. Hollingshead 'The Implied Tax Revenue Loss from Trade Mispricing,' Global Financial Integrity (2010), 1.

11. 'The Enablers, the Tools and Secrecy' *Minority & Majority Staff Report Permanent Subcommittee on Investigations*, 2006, https://www.hsgac.senate.gov/imo/media/doc/tax%20haven%20abuses%20report%20(8-1-06)(final%201-07)1.pdf (accessed 29 November 2022).

12. 'Final Study on Illicit Financial Flows,' para 17.

13. 'Final Study on Illicit Financial Flows,' para 17 UN.

14. 'Final Study on Illicit Financial Flows,' para 18.

15. Tax Justice Network 'Let's Take Back Control of Our Tax System,' https://taxjustice.net/ (accessed 21 October 2022).

16. Tax Justice Network 'Tax Justice & Human Rights: The 4 Rs and the Realisation of Rights—Tax Justice and Human Report' (2021) 12, https://taxjustice.net/wpcontent/uploads/2021/12/Tax-Justice-Human-Rights-Report_July_2021.pdf (accessed 12 October 2022).

17. 'Final Study on Illicit Financial Flows' para 2. My emphasis.

18. Serges Djoyou Kamga *The Right to Development in the African Human Rights System* (Abingdon: Routledge, 2018).

19. William Hynes and Simon Scott 'The Evolution of Official Development Assistance- Achievements, Criticisms and a Way Forward,' OECD Development Co-operation Working Papers, No. 12, OECD Publishing, http://dx.doi.org/10.1787/5k3v1dv3f024-en (accessed 29 October 2022).

20. William Hynes and Simon Scott 'The Evolution of Official Development Assistance.'

21. 'Final Study on Illicit Financial Flows' para 2.

22. International Bar Association's Human Rights Institute Task Force on Illicit Financial Flows, Poverty and Human Rights, *Tax Abuses, Poverty and Human Rights: A Report of the International Bar Association's Human Rights Institute Task Force on Illicit Financial Flows, Poverty and Human Rights* (London: International Bar Association, 2013).

23. 'Final Study on Illicit Financial Flows' para 2.

24. Commonwealth of Australia 'Architecture of Australia's Tax and Transfer System' (2008) 11, my emphasis, https://treasury.gov.au/sites/default/files/2019-10/afts_architecture_of_australias_tax_and_transfer_system_revised.pdf (accessed 20 September 2022).

25. Australian Bureau of Statistics 'Australian System of Government Finance Statistics: Concepts, Sources and Methods' (2015), https://www.abs.gov.au/statistics/detailed-methodology-information/concepts-sources-methods/australian-system-government-finance-statistics-concepts-sources-and-methods/2015 (accessed 20 September 2022).

26. Patricia Brander, Laure De Witte, Nazila Ghanea, Rui Gomes, Ellie Keen, Anastasia Nikitina, and Justina Pinkeviciute (eds) *Compass, Manual for Human Rights, Education with Young People* (Council of Europe, 2020).

27. Serges Djoyou Kamga 'Illicit Financial Flows, Asset Recovery, the Power Game and the Right to Development in Africa' *CILSA* 52, no. 2 (2019): 193–214.

28. Tax Justice Network 'Tax Justice & Human Rights: The 4 Rs and the Realisation of Rights,' 10.

29. Tax Justice Network 'Tax Justice & Human Rights: The 4 Rs and the Realisation of Rights,' 10.

30. Khulekani Moyo 'An Analysis of the Impact of Corruption on the Realisation of the Right to Development,' *South African Journal on Human Rights* (2017) 18.

31. Serges Djoyou Kamga 'Illicit Financial Flows, Asset Recovery, the Power Game and the Right to Development.'

32. Serges Djoyou Kamga 'Illicit Financial Flows, Asset Recovery, the Power Game and the Right to Development.'

33. 'Final Study on Illicit Financial Flows' para 28; R. Balakrishnan, J. Heintz and D. Elson 'What Does Inequality Have to Do With Human Rights?', Political Economy Research Institute, Working Paper Series No. 392 (2015).

34. R. Balakrishnan et al. 'What Does Inequality Have to do with Human Rights; also 'Final Study on Illicit Financial Flows' para 28.

35. 'Final Study on Illicit Financial Flows' para 27.

36. 'Final Study on Illicit Financial Flows' para 29.

37. Tax Justice Network 'The State of Tax Justice 2020: Tax Justice in the Time of COVID-19' (report 2020) 14, https://www.taxobservatory.eu/repository/the-state-of-tax-justice-2020/ (accessed 29 October 2022).

38. A.G 41/128.Declaration on the Right to Development.

39. Adrienne Margolis 'Tax Justice and Human Rights: The Beginning of a Beautiful Friendship?' *Tax Justice Focus* 9, no. 2 (2014): 2.

40. Esther Shubert 'Illicit Financial Flows, Tax and Human Rights' Background paper (9 October 2015) 4 my emphasis, https://www.ohchr.org/sites/default/files/Documents/Issues/IEDebt/IllicitFinancialFlowsConsultation/BackgroundPaperFinal.pdf (accessed 29 September 2022).

41. Tax Justice Network 'Let's Take Back Control of Our Tax System,' https://taxjustice.net/ (accessed 29 September 2022).

42. Q Reed and A Fontana 'Corruption and Illicit Financial Flows: The Limits and Possibilities of Current Approaches' *U4 Issue Anticorruption Resource*, 2011, https://www.u4.no/publications/corruption-and-illicit-financial-flows-the-limits-and-possibilities-of-current-approaches-2 (accessed 29 October 2022).

43. Tax Justice Network 'Tax Justice & Human Rights: The 4 Rs and the Realisation of Rights,' 22.

44. FACTI Panel 'Financial Integrity for Sustainable Development' Report of the High Level Panel on International Financial Accountability, Transparency and Integrity for Achieving the 2030 Agenda (2021) 8, https://www.factipanel.org/ (accessed 29 October 2022).

45. Pravin Gordhan 'High Level Conference on Illicit Financial Flows: Inter-Agency Cooperation and Good Tax Governance in Africa Organized In Cooperation with United Nations Office on Drugs and Crime' Address by Minister of Finance, Mr Pravin Gordhan 14 July (2016) 2&6, http://www.treasury.gov.za/comm_media/speeches/2016/2016071501%20-%20Speech%20by%20Minister%20of%20Finance%20on%20Illicit%20Financial%20Flows.pdf (accessed 31 October 2022).

46. Gordhan 'High Level Conference on Illicit Financial Flows,' 2 & 6.

47. Gordhan 'High Level Conference on Illicit Financial Flows,' 4.

48. Tax Justice Network 'Tax Justice & Human Rights: The 4 Rs and the Realisation of Rights,' 10.

49. Gordhan 'High Level Conference on Illicit Financial Flows,' 8.

50. World Bank World Bank *Doing Business Measuring Regulatory Quality and Efficiency* (Washington, DC, 2016), 5.

51. M Everest-Phillips 'The Political Economy of Controlling Tax Evasion and Illicit Flows' in P Reuter (ed) *Draining Development? Controlling Flows of Illicit Funds from Developing Countries* (Washington DC: World Bank, 2012), 74.

52. Gordhan 'High Level Conference on Illicit Financial Flows,' 8.

53. International Bar Association *Tax Abuses, Poverty and Human Rights* (London: International Bar Association, 2013), 2. My emphasis.

54. The African Union Convention on Preventing and Combating Corruption adopted on July 01, 2003.

55. AU/ United Nations Economic Commission for Africa 'Report of the High-Level Panel on Illicit Financial Flows from Africa.'

56. AU/ United Nations Economic Commission for Africa 'Report of the High Level Panel on Illicit Financial Flows from Africa.'

57. FACTI Panel 'Financing for Sustainable Development Office Department of Economic and Social Affairs United Nations,' https://www.factipanel.org/about (accessed 29 October 2022).

58. FACTI Panel 'Financing for Sustainable Development Office Department of Economic and Social Affairs United Nations.'

59. Tax Justice Network 'Tax Justice & Human Rights: The 4 Rs and the Realisation of Rights,' 32.

60. Tax Justice Network 'Tax Justice & Human Rights: The 4 Rs and the Realisation of Rights,' 39.

BIBLIOGRAPHY

AU/United Nations Economic Commission for Africa. 'Report of the High Level Panel on Illicit Financial Flows from Africa.' (2015). Accessed 29 October 2022. https://repository.uneca.org/handle/10855/22695.

Australian Bureau of Statistics. 'Australian System of Government Finance Statistics: Concepts, Sources and Methods.' (2015). Accessed 20 September 2022. https://www.abs.gov.au/statistics/detailed-methodology-information/concepts-sources-methods/australian-system-government-finance-statistics-concepts-sources-and-methods/2015.

Balakrishnan, R., Heintz, J., and Elson, D., 'What Does Inequality Have To Do with Human Rights?' Political Economy Research Institute, Working Paper Series No. 392 (2015): 1–33.

Bantekas, I., and Lumina, C. (Eds.). *Illicit Financial Flows, Sovereign Debt, and Human Rights*. Oxford: Oxford University Press, 2018.

Brander, P., De Witte, L., Ghanea, N., Gomes, R., Keen, E., Nikitina, A., and Pinkeviciute, J. (Eds.). *Compass, Manual for Human Rights, Education with Young People*. Council of Europe, 2020.

Commonwealth of Australia. 'Architecture of Australia's Tax and Transfer System.' (2008) 11. Accessed 20 September 2022. https://treasury.gov.au/sites/default/files/2019-10/afts_architecture_of_australias_tax_and_transfer_system_revised.pdf.

Everest-Phillips, M. 'The Political Economy of Controlling Tax Evasion and Illicit Flows.' In P. Reuter (Ed.), *Draining Development? Controlling Flows of Illicit Funds from Developing Countries*. Washington DC: World Bank, 2012, 69–108.

FACTI Panel. 'Financial Integrity for Sustainable Development.' Report of the High Level Panel on International Financial Accountability, Transparency and Integrity for Achieving the 2030 Agenda (2021). Accessed 29 October 2022. https://www.factipanel.org/.

Final study on illicit financial flows, human rights and the 2030 Agenda for Sustainable Development of the Independent Expert on the effects of foreign debt and other related international financial obligations of States on the full enjoyment of all human rights, particularly economic, social and cultural rights, /HRC/31/61.

Global Financial Integrity. 'Trade Misinvoicing.' Accessed 29 October 2022. https://gfintegrity.org/issue/trade-misinvoicing/.

Gordhan, P. 'High Level Conference on Illicit Financial Flows: Inter-Agency Cooperation and Good Tax Governance in Africa Organized In Cooperation with United Nations Office on Drugs and Crime.' Address by Minister of Finance, Mr Pravin Gordhan 14 July 2016, 2&6. Accessed 31 October 2022. http://www.treasury.gov.za/comm_media/speeches/2016/2016071501%20-%20Speech%20by%20Minister%20of%20Finance%20on%20Illicit%20Financial%20Flows.pdf.

Hollingshead, A. 'The Implied Tax Revenue Loss from Trade Mispricing.' *Global Financial Integrity* (2010). Available at https://www.gfintegrity.org/wp-content/uploads/2014/05/implied-tax-revenue-loss-report_final.pdf.

International Bar Association's Human Rights Institute Task Force on Illicit Financial Flows, Poverty and Human Rights. *Tax Abuses, Poverty and Human Rights: A Report of the International Bar Association's Human Rights Institute Task Force on Illicit Financial Flows, Poverty and Human Rights*. London: International Bar Association, 2013.

Kamga, Djoyou Serges. 'Illicit Financial Flows, Asset Recovery, the Power Game and the Right to Development in Africa.' *CILSA* 52, no. 2 (2019): 193–214.

Kamga, Djoyou Serges. *The Right to Development in the African Human Rights System*. Abingdon: Routledge, 2018.

Margolis, Adrienne. 'Tax Justice and Human Rights: The Beginning of a Beautiful Friendship?' *Tax Justice Focus* 9, no. 2 (2014). Accessed 20 October 2022. https://www.business-humanrights.org/en/latest-news/pdf-tax-justice-and-human-rights-the-beginning-of-a-beautiful-friendship-2/.

Moyo, Khulekani. 'An Analysis of the Impact of Corruption on the Realisation of the Right to Development.' *South African Journal on Human Rights* 33 (2017) : 193–213.

R v Barger (1908) 6 CLR 41.

Reed, Q., and Fontana, A. 'Corruption and Illicit Financial Flows: The Limits and Possibilities of Current Approaches.' *U4 Issue* Anticorruption Resource, 2011. Accessed 29 October 2022. https://www.u4.no/publications/corruption-and-illicit-financial-flows-the-limits-and-possibilities-of-current-approaches-2.

Shubert, Esther. 'Illicit Financial Flows, Tax and Human Rights.' Background paper, 9 October 2015. Accessed 29 September 2022. https://www.ohchr.org/sites/default/files/Documents/Issues/IEDebt/IllicitFinancialFlowsConsultation/BackgroundPaperFinal.pdf.

Tax Justice Network. 'Let's Take Back Control of Our Tax System.' Accessed 29 September 2022. https://taxjustice.net/.

Tax Justice Network. 'Tax Justice & Human Rights: The 4 Rs and the Realisation of Rights—Tax Justice and Human Report.' (2021). Accessed 12 October 2022. https://taxjustice.net/wpcontent/uploads/2021/12/Tax-Justice-Human-Rights-Report_July_2021.pdf.

Tax Justice Network. 'The State of Tax Justice 2020: Tax Justice in the time of COVID-19.' (report 2020) 14. Accessed 29 October 2022. https://www.taxobservatory.eu/repository/the-state-of-tax-justice-2020/.

The African Union Convention on Preventing and Combating Corruption adopted on 1 July 2003.

'The Enablers, the Tools and Secrecy' *Minority & Majority Staff Report Permanent Subcommittee on Investigations*, 2006. Accessed 29 November 2022. https://www.hsgac.senate.gov/imo/media/doc/tax%20haven%20abuses%20report%20(8-1-06)(final%201-07)1.pdf.

World Bank. *Doing Business Measuring Regulatory Quality and Efficiency*. Washington, DC: World Bank, 2016.

Chapter 14

Haemorrhaging

The Impacts of Illicit Financial Flows on the Realisation of the Right to Development in Africa: A Case for Uganda

Nampwera Chrispus and Kirunga Joyce

INTRODUCTION

The Right to Development is a multifaceted right that encompasses all the other human rights. It has been defined as 'an inalienable human right where every human person and all people are entitled to participate in, contribute to, and enjoy economic, social, cultural, and political development, and in which all human rights and fundamental freedoms can be fully realized'.[1] The Right to Development is thus intrinsically linked to other human rights, and thus enshrines the basic principles of equality, non-discrimination, participation, accountability and transparency, and whose elements and principles apply both locally and globally.[2]

This therefore gives the right a multidimensional outlook having both a positive expectation to achieve its entitlement, and a negative duty to protect it from derogation. It is therefore a right in itself, and a means through which development and universally recognised human rights may simultaneously be achieved. It thus imposes a duty on the state to ensure that this right is achieved through equal and adequate access to essential resources; through formulating appropriate national development policies that aim at the constant improvement of the well-being of the entire population and of all individuals;[3] the creation of national and international conditions favourable to the realisation of the Right to Development;[4] and to co-operate with each other in ensuring development and eliminating obstacles to development.

This has further been buttressed by the African Charter on Human and Peoples Rights which requires states parties to make it possible for the peoples of Africa to exercise their Right to Development, to create an enabling environment, and to provide the opportunity to put the Right to Development effectively into practice.

The intrinsic linkage between the Right to Development and other human rights means that it is fundamental in the realisation of those other rights, and thus, grossly influences their realisation. With the robust legal framework and the positive economic growth indicators in Africa, one would think that the right is being fully realised or at least minimally realised. However, most countries on the continent lag behind in development. The available data shows that there is a wide chasm between development reality and theory in Africa. For instance, the rule of law is declining while gender and social inequality is constantly increasing. Similarly, the continent is bedevilled with poor infrastructure, bad governance, inefficient public and social services systems, and abject poverty. This has been majorly as a reason of insufficient public funds which can be attributed to the increasing levels of huge amounts revenue lost to illicit financial flows (IFFs).

The Independent Expert on the effects of foreign debt and other related international financial obligations of states on the full enjoyment of all human rights, particularly economic, social and cultural rights has noted; 'there is a clear link between IFFs in that such flows diminish the resources available to states for investment in programmes that contribute to the realisation of human rights, particularly economic, social, and cultural rights. In essence, the failure to counter IFFs and recover stolen assets is a denial of access to basic health care, education, safe water and sanitation, adequate housing and infrastructure, all of which are basic conditions for the enjoyment of human rights'.[5]

DEFINING IFFS

Different authors and reports have tried coming up with a definition, and Epstein defines IFFs as 'capital taken abroad in a hidden form, perhaps because it is illegal, or perhaps because it goes against social norms, or perhaps because it might be vulnerable to the economic or political threat'.[6]

The Advisory Committee of the Human Rights Council report offers a two-tiered interpretation of the word 'illicit'. In the first, 'illicit' would refer to funds which are illegally earned, transferred, or utilised and include all unrecorded private financial outflows that drive the accumulation of foreign assets by residents in breach of relevant national or international legal frameworks.[7] In its second sense, 'illicit' would refer to funds from legitimate economic activity that become illicit due to the subsequent contravention or circumvention of laws in how those funds are handled or dealt with. This includes all arrangements designed to circumvent the law or its spirit such as tax evasion, forms of tax avoidance, forms of tax optimisation schemes, as well as profit shifting by multinational corporations, trade misinvoicing, and transfer mispricing.[8]

On its part, Global Financial Integrity defines IFFs refer to movement of money and value from one country to another that is illegitimately earned, transferred, and/or utilised,[9] while the Economic Development in Africa Report 2020, IFFs have been defined as movements of money and assets across borders which are illegal in source, transfer or use, and sometimes, as flows that are in violation of laws in their origin, or during their movement or use, and are therefore considered illicit, that is, money that is illegally earned, transferred, or utilised.[10]

IFFS AND AFRICA

Over the last fifty years, it is estimated that Africa has lost in excess of 1 trillion dollars in IFFs.[11] This sum is roughly equivalent to all of the official development assistance received by Africa during the same timeframe. Annually, an estimated $88.6 billion which is an equivalent of 3.7 per cent of Africa's gross domestic product leaves the continent of Africa as illicit capital flight.[12]

To put this into context, countries are losing a total of $483 billion in tax a year to global tax abuse committed by multinational corporations and wealthy individuals, an amount enough to fully vaccinate the global population against COVID-19 more than three times over.[13] A small club of rich countries with de facto control over global tax rules is responsible for the majority of tax losses suffered by the rest of the world, with lower-income countries hit the hardest by global tax abuse. The findings are further galvanising calls to move rule-making on international tax from the Organisation for Economic Cooperation and Development (OECD) to the United Nations.[14] OECD members are responsible for facilitating 78 per cent of the tax losses countries suffer a year, and the handing over of $378 billion a year from public purses around the world to the wealthiest multinational corporations and individuals.

In the context of IFFs, when a state party chooses to enact laws and regulations. The right to dispose of the wealth and natural resources in the exclusive interests of the people meanwhile creates three very specific obligations for state parties, as provided in the African Charter; to promote international economic co-operation based on mutual respect, equitable exchange, and principles of international law; for state parties, acting individually and collectively to strengthen African unity and solidarity; and, to eliminate all forms of foreign economic exploitation, particularly as practised by international monopolies. The obligation to protect entails enacting and enforcing laws and regulations that regulate non-state actors and that empower the state to undertake investigations into the activities of all the entities within the extractive industries supply chain, prosecute if necessary and take other proactive steps to ensure that revenues that are due to the state, in fact reach the state.

The state obligation to fulfill entails ensuring that the revenue is spent in the interests of the people. Moreover, under this article the state has a duty to act in solidarity with other states to combat IFFs. Hence a state is in breach of this obligation if it enters into agreements that compromise the ability of other state parties to harness revenues due to it. Non-state actors have both positive and negative obligations under this right; positive obligations particularly regarding fiscal transparency while its negative obligation entails that it does no harm and takes appropriate steps to rectify harm done. This obligation cuts across the supply chain and includes proper fiscal management and compliance. These flows are therefore in violation of laws in their origin, or during their movement or use, and are therefore considered illicit. According to the Tax Justice Network of the $483 billion in tax that countries lose a year, $312 billion is lost to cross-border corporate tax abuse by multinational corporations, and $171 billion is lost to offshore tax evasion by wealthy individuals.[15]

That the $483 billion loss consists of only direct tax losses: that is, tax losses that can be observed from analysing data self-reported by multinational corporations and from banking data collected by governments. Uncounted in the estimate are the indirect losses: the chain-reaction losses that arise from tax abuses accelerating the race to the bottom and driving tax rates down globally. The worst side of this is the fact that the International Monetary Fund estimates that indirect losses from global tax abuse by multinational corporations are at least three times larger than direct losses. The network further reports that the $483 billion lost to tax havens a year is the tip of the iceberg. That what we can see above the surface is thanks to some recent progress on tax transparency, but there's a lot more tax abuse below the surface costing magnitudes more in tax losses. And that an adjustment of the State of Tax Justice 2021's estimates of direct tax losses would see overall losses well beyond $1 trillion.

The worst culprit among OECD members is the United Kingdom, which is responsible for over a third (39 per cent) of the world's tax loss. It is by far the world's greatest enabler of global tax abuse, which it facilitates through a network made up of British Overseas Territories like the Cayman Islands, Crown Dependencies like Jersey and the City of London. Together with OECD members Netherlands, Luxembourg, and Switzerland, they are responsible for over half of the tax losses the world suffers (55 per cent), which is why the countries are often collectively referred to as the 'axis of tax avoidance'. The axis cost the world over $268 billion in tax losses a year, equivalent to more than eighteen times the amount of money expected to have been spent globally on facemasks in 2020 and 2021.

LEGAL REGIME

The Right to Development can be traced in the provisions of the Universal Declaration on Human Rights and a few other International Human Rights Covenants.[16] Through the United Nations Charter, member states undertook to 'promote social progress and better standards of life in larger freedom', and 'to achieve international cooperation in solving international problems of an economic, social, cultural, or humanitarian character, and in promoting and encouraging respect for human rights and for fundamental freedoms for all without distinction as to race, sex, language or religion'. It therefore recognises the promotion of social progress and better standards of life and the right to non-discrimination, the right to participate in public affairs and the right to an adequate standard of living. It also contains everyone's entitlement to a social and international order in which the rights and freedoms set forth in the Declaration can be fully realised.

In 1957, the United Nations General Assembly passed resolution (number 1161 (XII)) where it expressed the view that a balanced and integrated economic and social development would contribute towards the promotion and maintenance of peace and security, social progress and better standards of living, and the observance of and respect for human rights and fundamental freedoms. While in 1969, it adopted the Declaration on social progress and development in its resolution 2542 (XXIV). There were other subsequent resolutions passed thereafter, all of which directly or indirectly recognize the right to development including; resolutions number 4 (XXXIII) of 21 February 1977, 36 (XXXVII) of 11 March 1981, among others.

The Right to Development was eventually expressly and categorically proclaimed by the United Nations in 1986 in the declaration on the Right to Development, adopted via General Assembly resolution number 41of 128. The declaration in article 1 defines the right as an inalienable human right by virtue of which every human person and all peoples are entitled to participate in, contribute to, and enjoy economic, social, cultural, and political development, in which all human rights and fundamental freedoms can be fully realised. The right is therefore defined to include; the full sovereignty over natural resources; self-determination; popular participation in development, equality of opportunity, and the creation of favourable conditions for the enjoyment of other civil, political, economic, social, and cultural rights.

In the declaration, the human person is identified as the beneficiary of the Right to Development, as of all human rights, and, the right can be invoked both by individuals and by peoples, and imposes obligations both on individual states to ensure equal and adequate access to essential resources and on the international community to promote fair development policies and effective international co-operation.

The world conference on human rights held in Vienna in 1993 dealt extensively with the Right to Development where it was recognised that democracy, development, and respect for human rights and fundamental freedoms are interdependent and mutually reinforcing.[17] The conference also reaffirmed the Right to Development as a universal and inalienable right and an integral part of fundamental human rights. It further stated that while development facilitates the enjoyment of all human rights, lack of development may not be invoked to justify the abridgement of internationally recognised human rights.

The Millennium Declaration of 2000 that set out the international agenda to tackle peace and security, development, human rights, and the environment also had an element of the Right to Development. Besides development goals on poverty, water, and education, commitments were also made to promote democracy and respect for all human rights. This included the Right to Development and relevant economic, social, and cultural rights. In 2001, these development goals were amended and published in a single list called the Millennium Development Goals. Relatedly, in 2015, world leaders adopted the 2030 Agenda and set of seventeen goals known as sustainable development goals, and 167 targets that serve as the overall framework to guide global and national development action for the next fifteen years.

The Right to Development is also enshrined in Article 1 of the International Covenant on Economic, Social and Cultural Rights (CESCR),[18] Article 23 of the Declaration on the Rights of Indigenous Peoples,[19] Articles 1 and 2 of the Vienna Declaration and Programme of Action,[20] Principle 3 of the Rio Declaration on Environment and Development,[21] among others. Regionally, the right can be traced in Article 22 of the African Charter on Human and People's Rights.[22]

Nationally, the Constitution does not expressly provide for the Right to Development in its Articles; however, it has provided for it under the National Objectives and Directive Principles of State Policy under objective IX, X, and XI.[23]

THE UGANDAN EXPERIENCE

In Uganda IFFs are mainly propagated by a number of factors and actors such as the legal and institutional gaps in domestic and financial systems which encourage malpractices in the form of IFFs such as corruption, trade invoicing. Tax Justice Network estimates that in 2021, Uganda lost 382,831,205 million dollars to global tax abuse.[24] That amount culminates into $365 million that has been lost to global tax abuse committed by multinational corporations, while $17 million has been lost to global tax evasion committed by private individuals.[25] The report further interestingly notes that these tax losses are enough to fully vaccinate 22,257,628 million people against COVID-19 which is 55.81 per cent of the total population, and is equivalent to 110.06 per cent of health budget.[26] Uganda's trading partners that are apparently most responsible for this vulnerability include Kenya, Rwanda, and the Netherlands.

Also, the United Nations Conference on Trade and Development's (UNCTAD) Economic Development in Africa Report 2020, estimated that Uganda loses at least 1.5 trillion Uganda shillings every year to illegal activities perpetrated by multinational companies, which is almost four times the budget allocated for agriculture 2020/21 financial year. Another report puts the figure at more than 2 trillion Uganda shillings, which is about three-quarters of the general national budget support by development partners for the 2020/2021 financial year, amounting to 2.9 trillion Uganda shillings.[27]

While, according to Advocates Coalition for Development and Environment (ACODE), this situation could get worse with the commencement of commercial oil production.[28] A study by the civil society coalition on oil and gas revealed that in a period spanning 2006 to 2015, the country lost in excess of 7 billion dollars in trade misinvoicing alone.[29] Oil is one of the high-stake economic sectors that is extremely susceptible to IFFs manoeuvres and this is well exemplified in several studies including one by the UNCTAD which noted that IFFs related to the export of extractive commodities (amounting to $40 billion in 2015, which is about Shs147trillion) remains the largest component of illicit capital flight from Africa.[30]

A report by ACODE notes that factors like base erosion, profit shifting, unequal production sharing agreements, and double taxation agreement treaties are the main commercial drivers of IFFs in Uganda in the extractives sector. In the other sectors such as government, IFFs in Uganda also manifest themselves through tax evasion, money laundering, false declarations, overpricing, transfer pricing, money laundering, corruption, and false declarations, all largely responsible for denying the government the resources it needs to deliver much needed social service to the country.

The report further points out that major international oil companies currently involved in Uganda's oil sector are registered in tax havens, and some have concealed ownership structures which pose a high IFFs risk. It also notes that production-sharing agreements give international oil companies undue advantage over the state to the extent that they contain stabilisation clauses aimed at restricting the state's capacity to task the companies and, although the country has comprehensive transfer pricing rules aimed at reducing incidences of tax avoidance, there is too much secrecy and information unavailability.[31]

In 2019, the *Daily Monitor* reported Uganda Revenue Authority's (URA) findings that 72 per cent of total profit from foreign bank businesses and specifically those from South Africa, India, and the United Kingdom after tax was at risk of repatriation.[32] It further reported that Uganda loses Uganda shillings1.3 trillion (2 per cent of the Budget) annually in tax holidays.[33]

Uganda also loses a share of her revenue through tax avoidance. This being the legal practice of seeking to minimise a tax bill by taking advantage of a loophole or exception to tax regulations or adopting an unintended interpretation of the tax code. Seeking to minimise a tax bill by taking advantage of a loophole or exception to tax regulations or adopting an unintended interpretation of the tax code.

Another form Uganda's financial resources get drained is through tax evasion. These are actions by a taxpayer to escape a tax liability by concealing from the revenue authority the income on which the tax liability has arisen. Taxpayer concealing from the revenue authority the income on which the tax liability has arisen. In 2019, Uganda's ministry of finance declared that 30 per cent of eligible value-added tax in Uganda which is 4 per cent of the country's total gross domestic product is lost annually.[34] Also, in 2019, the URA not only recovered Shillings 62 billion in its operations but also noted that the country loses so much revenue in false declarations and specifically, through fake invoices.[35]

Money laundering has also been a big loophole through which illicit financial resources outflow. The international consortium of investigative journalists this year released the now famous pandora papers where it reviewed more than 11 million documents from fourteen organisations that help powerful people across the globe hide properties overseas in offshore accounts away from the intriguing eyes of the public and tax collectors.[36] According to the papers, the then Ugandan security minister Jim Muhwezi owned and held shares in two shell companies. It is reported that in February 2015, Muhwezi who was then the minister of information and national guidance became one of three shareholders of the British Virgin Islands company Audley Holdings Ltd. The company's directors authorised it to manage bank accounts in Europe, and that in the same year, an Israeli businessman sued Muhwezi's co-shareholders in a Ugandan court disputing the transfer of shares in a similarly named company, Audley Limited, which owns two unnamed casinos in Uganda. The lawsuit did not name Muhwezi, but the court later ruled to stop the share transfer. Audley Holding Ltd. is the holding company of Audley Ltd in Uganda.[37]

Related to the above are tax havens, shell companies, and secrecy jurisdiction. Tax Havens are jurisdictions whose legal regime is exploited by non-residents to avoid or evade taxes. A tax haven usually has low or zero tax rates on accounts held or transactions by foreign persons or corporations. This is in combination with one or more other factors, including the lack of effective exchange of tax information with other countries, lack of transparency in the tax system and no requirement to have substantial activities in the jurisdiction to qualify for tax residence. Tax havens are the main channel for laundering the proceeds of tax evasion and routing funds to avoid taxes. In 2016, Oxfam International exposed Mauritius as one of the world's worst corporate tax havens. According to ACODE companies operating in Uganda register in tax havens where it is possible to avoid the taxes that would otherwise be payable.[38]

Extensive research has documented the ways in which the United Kingdom's network of jurisdictions operates as a web of tax havens facilitating corporate and private tax abuse, at the centre of which sits the City of London. The UK spider's web consists of the following British Overseas Territories and Crown Dependencies: Cayman Islands, British Virgin Islands, Guernsey, Jersey, Gibraltar, Bermuda, Isle of Man, Anguilla, Turks and Caicos Islands, and Montserrat. The Global Face Mask Market size was estimated at USD 6,867.82 million in 2020, and expected to reach USD 7,808.64 million in 2021.[39] The European Union blacklist, last updated on 5 October 2021, is composed of American Samoa, Fiji, Guam, Palau, Panama, Samoa, Trinidad and Tobago, US Virgin Islands, and Vanuatu. Collectively, the jurisdictions facilitated 0.51 per cent of global tax abuse, costing the world $2.47 billion in lost tax a year.[40]

Secrecy jurisdictions, on the other hand, are cities, states, or countries whose laws allow banking or financial information to be kept private under all or all but few circumstances. Such jurisdictions may create a legal structure specifically for the use of non-residents. The originators of IFFs may need to prevent the authorities in the country of origin from identifying them (e.g. if the money is the proceeds of tax evasion), in which case the flow will be directed to a secrecy jurisdiction. Because those directing IFFs seek out low taxes and secrecy, many tax havens are also secrecy jurisdictions, but the concepts are not identical.

Shell banks/corporations are banks and/or corporations without any physical presence or employees in the jurisdiction in which it is incorporated. These allegations and how they are used can, for instance, be seen in the pandora papers where it was reported that Jim Muhwezi owned and held shares in two shell companies, as one of three shareholders of the British Virgin Islands company Audley Holdings Ltd.[41] ACODE reports that major international oil companies currently involved in Uganda's oil sector are registered in tax havens, and some have concealed ownership structures which pose a high IFFs risk.[42]

Double taxation. This happens where a company or individual incurs a tax liability in more than one country, the two countries' claims on the taxing rights can overlap, resulting in double taxation of the same declared income. Hence Double tax avoidance agreement /Double Taxation Treaty (DTT or Tax Treaties), which are usually in form of bilateral treaties, also known as tax conventions. They are designed to prevent an individual from being taxed on the same income or any other form of wealth including such things as gifts, estates by two different countries. Some tax avoidance strategies, if not all exploit international tax instruments in ways that were not intended, for example by ensuring that the right to tax a transaction is allocated to a country that levies no or low taxation on it. The OECD suggests that countries often suffer from 'double non-taxation' as a result of abuse of these treaties.

By concluding them, countries reach a negotiated settlement that restricts their source and residence taxation rights in a compatible manner, alleviating double taxation, and allocating taxing rights between the parties. Treaties also harmonise the definitions in countries' tax codes, provide mutual agreement procedures that can be invoked if there are outstanding instances of double taxation and establish a framework for mutual assistance in enforcement. A treaty between a developing country and a country from which it receives investment will shift the balance of taxing rights away from the developing country. Such treaty provisions create opportunities for treaty shopping by foreign investors. Uganda has multiple double taxation agreements with countries including Denmark, India, Italy, Mauritius, the Netherlands, Norway, South Africa, the United Kingdom, and Zambia.

It therefore becomes almost impossible to curb IFFs with such agreements with detrimental clauses. The DTAs have oftentimes been relied on to restrict or stop countries from levying withholding taxes, and this gives a bad deal to Uganda.[43] In May 2017, Tax Justice Network reported that Uganda's former energy minister, Syda Bhumba, had confirmed that she signed a tax waiver agreement with a United Kingdom company, Tullow Oil, without reading the document.[44] The waiver, which exempted both income and capital gains from tax, was later disputed by the URA on the grounds that the minister had no authority to sign such a waiver since such authority in that area lied with the finance minister. She confessed that she signed the waiver on the advice of the solicitor general, and was unaware at the time that the agreement with Tullow included tax exemptions while appearing before a special parliamentary committee.

The report further noted that oil and mineral-rich African countries have been overtime skinned alive by rapacious mining and oil companies who extract huge tax reliefs, exemptions, and holidays from hapless and/or corrupt politicians. In Uganda, as elsewhere, tax treaties have always been surrounded by an investment promotion discourse in political debate, yet there is little convincing evidence that they have had a positive effect on investment flows into low-income countries.

Production Sharing Agreements. With the discovery of oil and planned exploration, Uganda has entered production sharing agreements with different international corporations. It should be noted that these agreements give international companies undue advantage over the state to the extent that they contain stabilisation clauses which restrict the government from generating revenues.

Corruption has also been one of the most pronounced ways IFFs occur in Uganda. According to the 2018 African Union (AU) high-level report on IFFs, corruption is described as a cross-cutting issue that drives and fuels IFFs at every stage. This includes payments made, job opportunities offered to customs officers, judges, police and other civil servants, bribes, embezzlement of state fund among others.[45]

A 2010 World Bank report ranked Uganda a corrupt state estimating that the nation loses about USD 300 million annually through corruption and procurement malpractices. Uganda was also ranked 142nd out of 180 countries on the corruption perception index, 2020.[46] Corruption also extends to the use of political influence to stop officials from doing their jobs, such as forbidding the vetting of mineral exports, or searching planes or 'cutting off political deals to frustrate prosecution of crimes relating to IFFs'.

According to a 2014 OECD report, states that have high levels of corruption combined with weak institutions are drivers of illicit flows and these are often symptoms of deeper governance failures.[47] For Uganda, the situation is worse. Former foreign affairs minister Sam Kutesa was accused of conniving with a Chinese businessman and taking bribes, and was even declared persona non-grata by the United States.[48] In addition to this, ministers like Kabafunzaki, Alice Kaboyo, Jim Muhwezi, Mike Mukula, Kamugisha have repeatedly been implicated in corruption scandal after another, but they somehow manage to get reappointed to public offices every other time. The office of the prime minister has arguably seen the most corruption scandals, from swindling Katosi road funds worth billions, to procurement scandals, temangalo land saga, accounting fraud and his cohort, among others.

It is therefore not surprising that former Ugandan social security fund minister Ms Zoe Bakoko in an interview with SAHARA Live TV noted that while in office, USD 5 million of the national social security fund money was being stolen monthly and diverted to Channel Islands behind her back.[49]

The gold trade. The precious metal has overtaken coffee to become Uganda's most important commodity in recent years with gold exports totalling $1.7 billion shillings between November 2019 and December 2020, making 44 per cent of its total exports.[50] Much of this gold however comes from neighbouring countries, spirited across the border by shadowy smuggling networks. Uganda's central bank estimated in 2019 that only about 10 per cent of the gold flowing out of Uganda was actually mined in the country.[51]This bustling illegal market and the challenges related to properly regulating it have been a source of both fascination and frustration for years, within Uganda and internationally.

Uganda's situation is worsened by public office appointments. A case in point is Alice Kaboyo who was convicted on her own plea of guilty to charges of abuse of office after she got involved in the misuse of funds from the Global Alliance for Vaccines and Immunization (GAVI) in 2012.[52] It is relevant and important to note that she was charged alongside other three former health minister Jim Muhwezi, Dr Kamugisha, and Mike Mukula. Appointing particular individuals to take up leadership positions despite their past questionable record on performance like having been implicated and some even convicted on corruption charges could undermine the well-thought-out move to weed out corruption and IFFs from the country.[53]

Though the three were acquitted and discharged after being accused of mismanaging Shillings 1.6 billion, Ms Kaboyo was sentenced to a fine of Shillings 20 million or be jailed for eight years but decided to pay the fine. Mr Mukula was also found guilty of embezzling shillings 210 million. Mr Muhwezi was even after that appointed the minister of information and national guidance, and currently serves as the minister of security. Ms Kaboyo's appointment was on the other hand refused by Parliament basing on the above plea, but was nevertheless confirmed days later, having even received backing from the country's top corruption watchdog, the inspectorate of government.[54]

Trade misinvoicing. This is the most significant area of IFFs in Uganda that can be estimated using publicly available data. From 2006 to 2015, the latest years for which the necessary data are available, potential trade misinvoicing amounted to roughly 18 per cent of total Ugandan trade over the ten-year period. The figure for possible outflows is some 10 per cent of total trade, and for possible inflows, it is estimated to be around 8 per cent of total trade (2006–2015). The potential over- and under-invoicing of imports from 2006 to 2015 was approximately US$4.9 billion, and over- and under-invoicing of exports may have reached US$1.7 billion.[55]

HIGHLIGHTED EFFECTS

These IFFs have grossly affected the realisation of the Right to Development which in turn has affected the realisation of other human rights because of the inadequate resources: human, financial, and material. They affect the amount of revenue that a government has to spend on social and economic development. Secondly, IFFs also damage important institutions of governance and affects the resilience of a state. Thus, IFFs can be termed as both a cause and a consequence of conflict. The outflow of financial resources undermines the ability of the state to sustain and boost public expenditure and investment for sustainable development, intrinsically linked to its ability to ensure the realisation of rights, most notably the Right to Development, and economic, social, and cultural rights including to food, water and sanitation, health, education, and social security.

Some portion of illicit financial outflows from a developing country may correspond to tax revenues lost by that country which would then be unavailable for use by the government towards reducing inequality, eliminating poverty, raising the quality of life for people and for sustainable development. At the same time, a vital means by which the SDGs are to be financed is encapsulated in target 17.1, which calls for mobilising additional financial resources for developing countries from multiple sources and call for the combustion of IFFs.

Uganda has had a fair share of the problem with Gross development Product (GDP) constraints which has affected the most critical sectors of the economy such as education, health, infrastructure, and also increased the debt burden. Uganda's laws and regulations on financial transparency and anti-money laundering have the strongest influence on IFFs, and there are notable gaps in the framework the Government of Uganda has in place to address the sources, transfer methods, and motivations of IFFs in the country. In particular, laws governing corporations in Uganda are generally weak in so far as they do not require the official identification of the beneficial owners of companies or the complete identity of all shareholders in a company. The government's anti-money laundering regime mostly exists on paper and could do with strengthening.

The Financial Intelligence Authority, which was only recently established, acknowledges this shortcoming and is working to enhance its performance in helping to prevent, track, and prosecute money laundering in the country. Uganda's extractive sector and the presence of numerous transnational crime markets add to the importance of both financial transparency and anti-money laundering. An October 2018 report noted that insufficient levels of financial transparency globally and domestically and government accountability in Uganda, coupled with a regulatory system that can incentivise financial crimes, are helping to drive high levels of illicit financial inflow and outflows in the country, which are undermining development efforts.

Uganda will struggle to meet its goal of rising to middle-income status and reducing its reliance on foreign debt unless it increases efforts to combat the commercial tax evasion, corruption, and money laundering of criminal proceeds and terrorist financing.[56] It was further noted that the central government has a decent capacity to combat these opportunities for IFFs on paper, but its willingness or capacity to act to curtail IFFs is lagging.

SPECIFIC SECTORS

The right to education is one of the many rights grossly affected by the IFFs. Education has faced chronic underfunding by the government. The Committee on Economic, Social, and Cultural rights in its concluding observations noted the insufficient resources allocated to the education sector.[57] In the last financial year, the education sector was allocated about 10.1 per cent of the National Budget and yet Uganda's education sector still faces poor infrastructure, underpaid teachers, high levels of school dropouts, widening gap in access to quality education and the limited inclusion of children with disabilities.

Tax Privatisation and Rights to Education: Influencing Education Financing and Policy to Transform Children's report estimates that the annual revenue foregone from tax incentives is 272 million dollars of which 20 per cent of it could pay for a place on a primary school for about 477,000 out of school children and qualified teachers and cater school meals for about 412,047 children from one year. This therefore means that the amount of resources lost in the form of IFFs could uplift the quality of education in Uganda.

The right to health has also been grossly affected. IFFs reduce the state revenue and impacts directly upon the number of hospitals available to treat poor and vulnerable groups, the quality of the facilities, the number of patients that could have received life-saving medication, the number of doctors that could have been trained and employed and, it directly impacts upon whether a person dies with dignity or in misery. In addition, as stated earlier, IFFs increase inequality. Consequently, those with the means and are able to afford private health care enjoy high quality services and facilities and are treated with dignity. While this is often not the case in under-resourced public healthcare facilities. The $483 billion lost to tax havens a year is enough to cover the cost of purchasing and delivering two COVID-19 vaccine doses for the global population three times over.[58] This is equivalent to vaccinating 1,000 people against COVID-19 every second. The taxes that lower-income countries lose to tax havens in a year would be enough to vaccinate 60 per cent of their populations, bridging the gap in vaccination rates between lower-income and higher income countries.

With their vaccination rates far lower, global tax abuse deals a double blow to lower-income countries by robbing them of the funding to protect their populations against COVID-19 and, consequentially, exposing them to an even greater human and economic toll. Analysis for the State of Tax Justice

2021 reveals that if OECD countries had not pledged any money to COVAX but simply stopped facilitating global tax abuse instead, countries around the world could have collected enough tax revenue to vaccinate the global population against the COVID-19 virus 2.9 times over.[59]

Comparatively, IFFs have led to a wide chasm in the providence of health budgets. While higher income countries lose more tax in absolute terms, $443 billion a year, their tax losses represent a smaller share of their revenues – 9.7 per cent of their collective public health budgets. Lower-income countries in comparison lose less tax in absolute terms, $39.7 billion a year, but their losses account for a much higher share of their current tax revenues and spending. Collectively, lower-income countries lose the equivalent of nearly half (48 per cent) of their public health budgets and unlike OECD members, they have little or no say on the international rules that continue to allow these abuses.[60] This affects their ability to deal with crises.

For example, in a study on financing universal health coverage of eighty-nine low- and middle-income countries researchers found that a 10 per cent increase in tax revenue leads to a 17 per cent increase in public health spending in low-income countries, and increasing public health spending by 1 per cent decreases under-five mortality by 0.86 per cent.[61] They concluded that increasing domestic tax revenues is integral to achieving universal health coverage, particularly in countries with low tax bases.

Also, IFFs have affected the realisation of the rule of law, democracy, and the strides made therein in Uganda. These are being affected by the widespread tax evasion and avoidance by individuals, particularly politically exposed people and by corporations.[62] The United Nations Independent Expert on the effects of foreign debt concluded that 'a weakened tax base leads to poor social services and unequal treatment.' The widespread occurrence of IFFs in Africa also points to a governance problem in the sense of weak institutions and inadequate regulatory environments. IFFs accordingly contribute to undermining state capacity.

To achieve their purposes, the people and corporations behind IFFs often compromise state officials and institutions. Left unchecked, these activities lead to entrenched impunity and the institutionalisation of corruption. Corruption is both a source and enabler of IFFs. The transfer of the proceeds of bribery and abuse of power are one thing, but the role of corruption in enabling IFFs across the board is another. The negative impact of corruption on development is well known, including the debasement of values needed in the development process, misdirection of energies on 'rent-seeking' activities and the misalignment of incentives such that private gain, no matter how acquired becomes the leitmotif of all economic activity.

In addition to other governance and development consequences, IFFs strain the capacities of African governments in various ways. While a good deal of

IFFs take place because of weak regulatory and law enforcement capacities, the effort to stem such outflows strains these already weak capacities. Drawing on the example of global negotiations in development, trade, and climate change, for instance, the ability of African countries to negotiate and obtain fair outcomes is always a matter of concern. This is also the case with regard to the negotiation of agreements and contracts that sometimes enable IFFs. The already haemorrhaging countries therefore have to resort to investing the little of their remaining resources to curbing the scourge that's IFFs.

IFFs promote and encourage regressive forms of taxation. As multinational companies cruise, domestic or local small and medium enterprises and vulnerable groups such as the poor, women, and youth bear the greatest brunt of the tax burden as government increasingly relies on such things as pay-as-you-earn tax which is imposed on income of employees and value-added tax where the final consumer pays the tax. The latter drives most of the citizens into theatrics of tax evasion, misinvoicing, and false declarations costing the country more revenue as a result.

Relatedly, IFFs undermine the legitimacy of the originating country's tax system and in some cases, the ruling regime especially where elements of state capture are evident.

RECOMMENDATIONS

If IFFs in Africa are successfully combated, it could go a long way in enhancing development, UNCTAD's Economic Development in Africa Report 2020 affirms the positive impact stopping illicit capital flight would have. It could almost cut in half the annual financing gap of $200 billion (about Shs733 trillion) that the continent of Africa faces to achieve the Sustainable Development Goals (SDGs).[63] It is therefore imperative that IFFs are minimised to enhance development through.

Renegotiating DTA's to include clauses that guards against reducing the country's tax threshold and undermining the domestic tax regime.

Ultimately, the fight to control illicit outflows from the developing world must focus on building responsive, effective institutions that deliver services to their population.

States also need to have fiscal strength and autonomy, political will and adequate resources, robust government institutions that are accountable, impartial, transparent, and fair and that operate within a strong set of equitable rules should manage and implement the plans of such a state. The ECA emphasises that a state's ability to fulfil its developmental role depends largely on its relative autonomy from the interest of powerful interest groups such as big business, large accounting and audit firms, mining companies.[64]

CONCLUSION

IFFs have significantly led to inadequate growth, contributed to and ensured high levels of poverty, and they also affect the amount of revenue that a government has to spend on social and economic development. Increasing domestic tax revenues is integral to achieving such things as universal health coverage, health insurance, an improved standard of living, improving infrastructure, and providing other social services like education, water, housing, among others particularly in countries with low tax bases. It is therefore imperative that there be a global concerted effort in fighting IFFs to enhance equitable development in all countries.

NOTES

1. United Nations General Assembly 'The Right to Development Resolution / Adopted by the General Assembly,' A/RES/72/164 / 19 December, 2017, available at https://www.ohchr.org/en/professionalinterest/pages/righttodevelopment.aspx.
2. Bhumika Muchhala 'The Right to Development and Illicit Financial Flows: Realising the Sustainable Development Goals and Financing for Development' A/HRC/WG.2/19/CRP.
3. 1United Nations General Assembly, 'The Right to Development Resolution,' Article 3.
4. Ibid.
5. Cephas Lumina. Final Report of the Independent Expert on Effects of foreign Debt: The negative impact of non-repatriation of funds of illicit origin on the enjoyment of human rights (United Nations Human Rights Commission) A/HRC/25/52, 7 March 2014.
6. Epstein A Gerald *Capital Flight and Capital Controls in Developing Countries*, Cheltenham, UK.
7. UN Human Rights Advisory Committee Draft progress report on the research-based study on the impact of flow of funds of illicit origin and the non-repatriation thereof to the countries of origin on the enjoyment of human rights, A/HRC/AC/18/CRP.3, 13 February 2017, available at http://www.ohchr.org/Documents/HRBodies/HRCouncil/AdvisoryCom/Session18/A_HRC_AC_18_CRP_3.docx, para 7.
8. Ibid.
9. Illicit Financial Flows. Accessed at https://gfintegrity.org/issue/illicit-financial-flows/ on 17 June 2022.
10. Ibid.
11. Kar *Devon* (2010). Illicit Financial Flows from Africa: Hidden Resource for Development. Washington, DC: Global Financial Integrity. Accessed at https://gfintegrity.org/report/briefing-paper-illicit-flows-from-africa/.
12. UNCTAD (2020). Economic Development Report in Africa: Tackling Illicit Financial Flows for Sustainable development in Africa. Geneva.

13. Global Tax Alliance for Justice and Tax justice Network (2021) 'The State of Tax Justice.'

14. Ibid.

15. Global Alliance for Tax Justice, Loses to OECD Tax havens could vaccinate global population three times over, 16 November 2021.

16. Milestone events in the right to development. Accessed at https://www.ohchr.org/EN/Issues/Development/Pages/Backgroundrtd.aspx on 15th November 2021.

17. 'Vienna Declaration and Programme of Action.' Accessed at https://www.ohchr.org/en/instruments-mechanisms/instruments/vienna-declaration-and-programme-action.

18. International Covenant on Economic Social and Cultural Rights. Accessed at https://www.ohchr.org/sites/default/files/cescr.pdf.

19. Declaration on the Rights of Indigenous Persons. Accessed at https://www.un.org/development/desa/indigenouspeoples/declaration-on-the-rights-of-indigenous-peoples.html.

20. Milestone Events in the Right to Development.

21. Rio Declaration on Environment and Development. Accessed at https://www.un.org/en/development/desa/population/migration/generalassembly/docs/globalcompact/A_CONF.151_26_Vol.I_Declaration.pdf.

22. African Charter on Human and Peoples Rights https://www.achpr.org/legalinstruments/detail?id=49.

23. Constitution of the Republic of Uganda, 1995.

24. Tax Justice Network <The State of Tax Justice 2021– published by the Tax Justice Network, the Global Alliance for Tax Justice and the global union federation Public Services International. Accessed 16 November 2021 on https://taxjustice.net/events/the-state-of-tax-justice-2021/.

25. Tax Justice Network Country Profiles. Accessed at https://taxjustice.net/country-profiles/uganda/ on 17 November 2021.

26. Losses to OECD tax havens could vaccinate global population three times over, study reveals https://taxjustice.net/2021/11/16/losses-to-oecd-tax-havens-could-vaccinate-global-population-three-times-over-study-reveals/.

27. Kar *Devon* (2010). Illicit Financial Flows from Africa: Hidden Resource for Development.

28. D Ngabirano, J Muhindo, P Lumunu, and O James 'Illicit Financial Flows Risk Factors in Uganda Oil and Gas Sector,' Kampala, CSCO, info sheet. Accessed at http://www.acode-u.org/uploadedFiles/IFFs_info_Final.pdf.

29. Ibid.

30. Kar *Devon* (2010). Illicit Financial Flows from Africa: Hidden Resource for Development.

31. Ladu M Ismail 'The Extractive Sector: Why the Country should Care about the Illicit Financial Flows' *The Daily Monitor* 13 March 2021. Accessed at https://www.monitor.co.ug/uganda/business/finance/extractive-sector-why-the-country-should-care-about-illicit-financial-flows-3322054.

32. Kasemire Christine 'Shs 528 billion in Banking Exposed to Profit Repatriation Report' *Daily Monitor* 31 August 2020. https://www.monitor.co.ug/uganda/business

/finance/shs528b-in-banking-exposed-to-profit-repatriation-report-1924674?view=htmlamp.

33. Ladu M Ismail 'Uganda Loses shs 1,3 trillion in Tax Holidays' *Daily Monitor* 26 March 2019. Accessed at https://www.monitor.co.ug/uganda/news/national/uganda-loses-shs1-3t-annually-in-tax-holidays-1844770.

34. Samilu Busein 'URA Unveils Plans to Curb Illicit Financial Flows' *Chimp Reports* 17 July 2021. Accessed at https://chimpreports.com/ura-unveils-plan-to-curb-illicit-financial-flows/.

35. Ibid.

36. Uganda Radio Network 'Jim Muhwezi is Ugandan Named in Pandora Papers' *The Independent* 6 October 2021. Accessed at https://www.independent.co.ug/jim-muhwezi-is-ugandan-named-in-pandora-papers/.

37. Ibid.

38. Advocates Coalition for Development and Environment 'Illicit Financial Flows in Uganda Fact Sheets'. Accessed http://www.acode-u.org/uploadedFiles/IFFs_info_Final.pdf.

39. Research and Markets, Face Mask Market Research Report by Type (Dental Mask, Hospital Mask, and Industrial Mask), Distribution Channel, Region (Americas, Asia-Pacific, and Europe, Middle East & Africa)—Global Forecast to 2027—Cumulative Impact of COVID-19. Accessed on https://www.researchandmarkets.com/reports/5337646/face-mask-market-research-report-by-type.

40. https://taxjustice.net/2021/11/16/losses-to-oecd-tax-havens-could-vaccinate-global-population-three-times-over-study-reveals/. Accessed 16th November 2021.

41. N 38.

42. N 25.

43. N 40.

44. Nixon Segawa 'Bbumba: I Signed $157 Tax Waiver to Tullow without Reading Agreement' ChimpReports. Accessed at https://chimpreports.com/bbumba-i-signed-157m-tax-waiver-to-tullow-without-reading-agreement/ on 17th June 2022.

45. Illicit Financial Flows: Report of the High-Level Panel on Illicit Financial Flows from Africa. Accessed at https://au.int/en/documents/20210708/report-high-level-panel-illicit-financial-flows-africa.

46. Kisa Isaac 'Gold Surpasses Tourism, Coffee as Uganda's Biggest Foreign Exchange Earner' *The Independent* 2 March 2021. Accessed at https://www.independent.co.ug/gold-surpass-tourism-coffee-as-ugandas-biggest-foreign-exchange-earner/; OECD Foreign Bribery Report. An Analysis of the Crime of Bribery of Foreign Public Officials. Accessed at https://www.oecd.org/corruption/oecd-foreign-bribery-report-9789264226616-en.htm.

47. Ibid.

48. Ian Katusiime 'Cover Story: Visa Denied' *The Independent* 14 October 2019. Accessed at https://www.independent.co.ug/cover-story-visa-denied/ on 21st December 2021.

49. Frederick Musisi 'Katosi Road: The Fraud that Lifted Lid off Politics of Patronage in Government' 20 July 2021. Accessed at https://www.monitor.co.ug/

uganda/magazines/people-power/katosi-road-the-fraud-that-lifted-lid-off-politics-of-patronage-in-government-1598034?view=htmlamp.

50. Neiman Sophie 'Uganda's Illegal Gold Market Is Bustling' 8 October 2021. Accessed at https://www.worldpoliticsreview.com/articles/30024/uganda-s-illegal-gold-market-is-bustling.

51. Ibid.

52. Lubwama Siraje 'Ex-State House Aide Kaboyo Pleads Guilty, Pays 20m Fine' *The Observer* 12 June 2012. Accessed at https://www.observer.ug/index.php?option=com_content&view=article&id=19238&catid=34&Itemid=114.

53. Ambrose Musasizi 'Will Museveni Walk his Talk against Corruption, Illicit Financial Flows through His Sixth Term?' *Daily Monitor* 6 August 2021. Accessed at https://www.monitor.co.ug/uganda/news/national/will-museveni-walk-his-talk-against-corruption-illicit-financial-flows-through-his-sixth-term--3501982.

54. A Scoping Study of Illicit Financial Flows Impacting Uganda accessed at https://gfintegrity.org/report/a-scoping-study-of-illicit-financial-flows-impacting-uganda/.

55. CPIA transparency, accountability, and corruption in the public sector rating (1=low to 6=high). Accessed at https://data.worldbank.org/indicator/IQ.CPA.TRAN.XQ?locations=UG on 22 December 2021.

56. A Scoping Study of Illicit Financial Flows Impacting 1.

57. Concluding observations on the initial report on Uganda, ESCR Committee, 24 June 2015 E/C.12/UGA/CO/1 (2015).

58. As below.

59. Ibid.

60. Tax justice networks countries profiled.

61. Ibid.

62. A human Rights based approach to addressing illicit financial flows from Africa A (draft) study of the African Commission on Human and Peoples' Rights.

63. Kar *Devon* (2010). Illicit Financial Flows from Africa: Hidden Resource for Development.

64. Ibid.

BIBLIOGRAPHY

Advocates Coalition for Development and Environment. 'Illicit Financial Flows in Uganda'. Fact Sheets. http://www.acode-u.org/uploadedFiles/IFFs_info_Final.pdf.

African Charter on Human and Peoples Rights. https://www.achpr.org/legalinstruments/detail?id=49.

'A Scoping Study of Illicit Financial Flows Impacting Uganda'. https://gfintegrity.org/report/a-scoping-study-of-illicit-financial-flows-impacting-uganda/.

Christine Kasemire. 'Shs 528 Billion in Banking Exposed to Profit Repatriation Report'. *Daily Monitor*, 31 August 2020. https://www.monitor.co.ug/uganda/business/finance/shs528b-in-banking-exposed-to-profit-repatriation-report-1924674?view=htmlamp.

'CPIA Transparency, Accountability, and Corruption in the Public Sector Rating (1=low to 6=high)'. https://data.worldbank.org/indicator/IQ.CPA.TRAN.XQ?locations=UG.

D. Ngabirano, O. Mugyenyi, J. Muhindo, and P. Lamunu (2021). 'Illicit Financial Flows Risk Factors in Uganda's Oil and Gas Sector, Kampala'. CSCO, Infosheet. http://www.acode-u.org/uploadedFiles/IFFs_info_Final.pdf

Declaration on the Rights of Indigenous Peoples.

Dev Kar, and Devon Cartwright-Smith (2010). *Illicit Financial Flows from Africa: Hidden Resource for Development*. Washington, DC: Global Financial Integrity.

'Draft Progress Report on the Research-Based Study on the Impact of Flow of Funds of Illicit Origin and the Non-Repatriation Thereof to the Countries of Origin on the Enjoyment of Human Rights, A/HRC/AC/18/CRP'. http://www.ohchr.org/Documents/HRBodies/HRCouncil/AdvisoryCom/Session18/A_HRC_AC_18_CRP_3.docx.

Economic Commission for Africa. (2015). 'Illicit Financial Flows: Report of the High-Level Panel on Illicit Financial Flows from Africa; 2015 IIS 3190-M27'.

Frederick Musisi. 'Katosi Road: The Fraud that Lifted Lid Off Politics of Patronage in Government'. 20 July 2021. https://www.monitor.co.ug/uganda/magazines/people-power/katosi-road-the-fraud-that-lifted-lid-off-politics-of-patronage-in-government-1598034?view=htmlamp.

Global Finance Integrity. (2018). *A Scoping Study of Illicit Financial Flows Impacting Uganda*. Available https://www.gfintegrity.org/wp-content/uploads/2018/10/Uganda-Report-2018_12.20.18.pdf.

'Gold Surpasses Tourism, Coffee as Uganda's Biggest Foreign Exchange Earner'. https://www.independent.co.ug/gold-surpass-tourism-coffee-as-ugandas-biggest-foreign-exchange-earner/.

Ian Katusiime. 'Cover Story: Visa Denied'. https://www.independent.co.ug/cover-story-visa-denied/.

'International Covenant on Economic, Social and Cultural Rights'. Available at https://www.ohchr.org/sites/default/files/cescr.pdf.

Ismail M. Ladu. 'The Extractive Sector: Why the Country Should Care About the Illicit Financial Flows'. *The Daily Monitor*, 13 March 2021. https://www.monitor.co.ug/uganda/business/finance/extractive-sector-why-the-country-should-care-about-illicit-financial-flows-3322054.

Ismail M. Ladu. 'Uganda Loses shs 1,3 Trillion in Tax Holidays'. *Daily Monitor*, 26 March 2019. https://www.monitor.co.ug/uganda/news/national/uganda-loses-shs1-3t-annually-in-tax-holidays-1844770.

'Illicit Financial Flows'. https://gfintegrity.org/issue/illicit-financial-flows/.

'Illicit Financial Flows: Report of the High-Level Panel on Illicit Financial Flows from Africa'. https://au.int/en/documents/20210708/report-high-level-panel-illicit-financial-flows-africa.

'Losses to OECD Tax Havens Could Vaccinate Global Population Three Times Over, Study Reveals'. https://taxjustice.net/2021/11/16/losses-to-oecd-tax-havens-could-vaccinate-global-population-three-times-over-study-reveals/.

'Milestone Events in the Right to Development'. 15 November 2021. https://www.ohchr.org/EN/Issues/Development/Pages/Backgroundrtd.aspx.

Musasizi Ambrose. 'Will Museveni Walk his Talk Against Corruption, Illicit Financial Flows Through his Sixth Term?' *Daily Monitor*, 6 August 2021. https://www.monitor.co.ug/uganda/news/national/will-museveni-walk-his-talk-against-corruption-illicit-financial-flows-through-his-sixth-term--3501982.

Nixon Segawa. 'Bbumba: I Signed $157 Tax Waiver to Tullow Without Reading Agreement'. *ChimpReports*. 17 June 2022. https://chimpreports.com/bbumba-i-signed-157m-tax-waiver-to-tullow-without-reading-agreement/.

Organization of Economic Cooperation and Development (OECD). (2014). 'Illicit Financial Flows from Developing Countries: Measuring OECD Responses'. Available at https://www.oecd.org/corruption/illicit_financial_flows_from_developing_countries.pdf.

Rio Declaration on Environment and Development.

Samilu Busein. 'URA Unveils Plans to Curb Illicit Financial Flows'. *Chimp Reports*, 17 July 2021. https://chimpreports.com/ura-unveils-plan-to-curb-illicit-financial-flows/.

SEATINI. (2017). 'Taxation in Uganda: Review and Analysis of National and Local Government Performance, Opportunities and Challenges'. Southern and East African Trade Information and Negotiation Institute (SEATINI).

Siraje Lubwama. 'Ex-State House Aide Kaboyo Pleads Guilty, Pays 20m Fine'. 21 December 2021. https://www.observer.ug/index.php?option=com_content&view=article&id=19238&catid=34&Itemid=114.

Sophie Neiman. 'Uganda's Illegal Gold Market Is Bustling'. Accessed 22 December 2021. https://www.worldpoliticsreview.com/articles/30024/uganda-s-illegal-gold-market-is-bustling.

Tax Justice Network Country Profiles. https://taxjustice.net/country-profiles/uganda/.

The State of Tax Justice 2021—'Published by the Tax Justice Network, the Global Alliance for Tax Justice and the Global Union Federation Public Services International'. Accessed 16 November 2021. https://taxjustice.net/events/the-state-of-tax-justice-2021/.

UNCTAD. (2020). *Economic Development Report in Africa: Tackling Illicit Financial Flows for Sustainable development in Africa*. Geneva.

Vienna Declaration and Programme of Action. Available at https://unctad.org/system/files/official-document/aldcafrica2020_en.pdf.

Index

About the Contributors

Olayinka Oluwakemi Adeniyi is a researcher, an advocate, and barrister of the Supreme Court of Nigeria, resident in South Africa. She is presently a research fellow with the Institute for Social and Economic Research (ISER) Rhodes University, South Africa. She has a doctoral degree in Law (LLD) from the University of Pretoria, South Africa, and obtained her master's and first degree from the Obafemi Awolowo University, Osun State, Nigeria. She is a 2018/2019 Research Fellow of the International Centre for Women's Research of Coady International Institute, Antigonish, Nova Scotia, Canada. She has authored book chapters and papers in accredited journals in the area of women and children's rights and development issues and has presented papers in local and international conferences and workshops. Olayinka is the CEO and Founder of Women on the Watch (WOW) Society Initiative, a not-for-profit registered in South Africa. Her present research interest is the rights of vulnerable persons, women, children, and persons with disabilities in the emergence of developed technology.

Linah Aduda is an advocate of the High Court of Kenya with four years of experience working on human rights, sexual, and gender issues. She is currently practising as an independent legal and human rights consultant. Linah holds an LLM in East Africa Community Law and Regional Integration Law (University of Dar es Salaam, Tanzania), a bachelor of laws degree (University of Nairobi), and a postgraduate diploma in Law (Kenya School of Law). Further to this, she holds a postgraduate certificate in Sustainable Development and Global Justice (University of Antwerp, Belgium), and a certificate on the Communications Procedures and the Jurisprudence of the

Africa Committee of Experts on Rights and Welfare of the Child (Dullah Omar Institute, South Africa).

Marie-Louise F. Aren is an international economic lawyer. Her research interests include International Economic Laws, Business & Human Rights, Sovereign Debt, African/International Development. Marie-Louise adopts a transdisciplinary approach to knowledge and problem solving leading her to serve in various research and drafting teams such as the Petroleum Industry Governance Laws Draft Team; the development team for the Nigerian Justice Policy and the National Law Review Team responsible for reviewing the Laws of the Federation of Nigeria 2018. Marie-Louise is currently a doctoral candidate of International Tax Law at the University of Pretoria, South Africa.

Nampwera Chrispus is an advocate of the Courts of Judicature of Uganda, State Attorney Ministry of Justice and Constitutional Affairs, member of the Network of Public Interest Lawyers in Uganda, and a fellow of the East Africa Emerging Public Interest Advocates Programme. Chrispus holds a postgraduate bar course diploma in Legal Practice and an ordinary diploma in law both from the Law Development Centre, and an upper-second class bachelor's degree in Law with honours from Makerere University. He holds two Advanced Human Rights certificate respectively on the Right to Development, and on Civil Society Law in Africa, both from the Centre for Human Rights, University of Pretoria. He also holds a certificate on the Political Economy of Land Governance in Africa from the Institute for Poverty, Land and Agrarian Studies, the Network of Excellence on Land Governance in Africa, and the University of the Western Cape. The author has published on a range of areas including the right to health, right to land and development, social insurance, and the right to a fair hearing. He is passionate about human rights, public international law, TMT among others.

Annelie de Man holds a BCom LLB (University of the Free State (UFS)), LLB (UFS), LLM (UFS), European master's degree in Human Rights and Democratisation (EIUC) and LLD (UFS). She has worked as an intern at Human Rights Watch, Brussels; a legal researcher at the Supreme Court of Appeal, South Africa; and coordinator of the Human Rights Desk of the Institute for Reconciliation and Social Justice, UFS. Since 2016 she has been the coordinator of the Advocacy Division of the Free State Centre for Human Rights and was appointed as a senior lecturer in 2019. Her research focus is human rights and development; corruption; the rights-based approach to development; economic, social, and cultural rights and intergenerational rights. She is also the coordinator of a master`s module in human rights and development and supervisor to master's and doctoral students.

Tumba Tuseku Dieudonné is a research fellow at the Thabo Mbeki African School of Public and International Affairs, University of South Africa. He obtained his doctorate degree in Political Sciences at the University of South Africa. Tumba has served as a facilitator in the Pan-African Programme on Managing Democratic Elections in Africa, at the University of South Africa. He previously worked as a junior lecturer at the University of Kinshasa and a project coordinator at the Humana People to People and MEDICUS MUNDI. He was involved in election observation missions in Lesotho, South Africa, Congo Brazzaville, and DR Congo. Tumba's research interests include Comparative politics, E-governance, Policy capacity, Political trust, Election-related violence, Election quality, and Political participation. Currently, he is conducting two research projects focusing on 'Contrasting Trends in Election-related violence in Africa' and 'Determinants of Public Trust and its Relationship to Youth Political Participation in the SADC region'.

Felix Dube is a Senior Lecturer in the Department of Public Law, Faculty of Law, University of Pretoria. He completed a Bachelor of Laws from the University of Venda, after which he successfully pursued a Master of Laws and Doctor of Laws from the North-West University. During his doctoral studies, he taught constitutional law and legal history at North-West University. His research interests include constitutional hermeneutics, human rights theory, and selected aspects of public and private law that link to constitutional law.

Toyin Falola is a renowned scholar of African history and African studies. He holds the Jacob and Frances Sanger Mossiker Chair in the Humanities at the University of Texas, Austin. He has published, as author or editor, more than 100 scholarly books on topics ranging from diaspora, migration, and globalisation to intellectual history, international relations, religion, and culture. He has been awarded thirteen honorary doctorates and has received, among many other awards, the Distinguished Africanist Award from the African Studies Association, the Ibadan Foundation Award for Professional Excellence in Scholarship and the Cheikh Anta Diop Award for Excellence in African Studies. He served as vice president of UNESCO's International Scientific Committee, Slave Route Project from 2011 to 2015 and currently is a member of the Carnegie African Diaspora Fellows Programme and the International Committee of the Thabo Mbeki African Leadership Institute at UNISA. He is also an extraordinary professor at the Free State Centre for Human Rights.

Chané Henney is a research assistant at the Free State Centre for Human Rights. She obtained her LLB and master's degrees in law (LLM) from the University of the Free State (UFS). She is enrolled currently for a doctorate in law at the UFS. Her research interests include International Law, Criminal Law, and Legal Philosophy. Chané is also an academic tutor for Criminal Law: Specific Crimes at the University of South Africa, as well as a freelance content writer. She previously worked as a research assistant in the Department of Public Law, at the University of the Free State.

Serges Djoyou Kamga is a professor of law and dean of the Faculty of Law, the University of the Free State. He is a member of the 'building committee' of the Cross-cultural Human Rights Centre, a consortium of one European University, ten Chinese and four African universities aimed at bringing Southern concepts and ideas in the area of human rights to Northern audiences. His areas of interest include Leadership and African renaissance, Development and human rights, human rights from a cross-cultural perspective, and Disability rights. He publishes in these areas.

Gerard Emmanuel Kamdem Kamga is a senior lecturer and coordinator, research and postgraduate division at the Free State Centre for Human Rights, programme director research and postgraduate studies, faculty of law, University of the Free State. He has a multidisciplinary background including in law, human rights, political science, critical theory, and gender analysis. He holds a master's and doctor of laws degrees from the University of Pretoria. His current projects essentially revolve around the problem of the exception, democracy, and the mechanics of violence and question the existing global, regional, and domestic systems of governance and policies as well as their effects on the human condition, social justice, human rights, and the rule of law. He is the author of various publications in these areas.

T. K. Seife has held executive positions in the governmental, private, not-for-profit, international, and academic sectors. He has served in national, regional, and international capacities. He formerly worked with the Ministry of Youth, Sport, and Culture as a senior government advisor for policy strategies. He also worked as a public diplomat for more than fifteen years, rising to the rank of chief commissioner. He served as chief executive officer of Africa Connect Addis Ababa and chief operating officer of Africa Technology Holdings in South Africa in the private sector. He was a lecturer at private colleges and universities in Addis Ababa, Ethiopia, and an e-tutor at the University of Pretoria. Former Pan African Youth Movement (PYU), president and African Youth Peace Council (AYPC), vice president of World Federation Democratic Youth (WFDY), Africa Speaks and Great Run Africa. He has also served at the African Union and the United Nations ECOSOC. Education: BSc in Business Administration and Computer Science, Honours in Development Studies, Master's in Political Science, and PhD in International Relations. At UNISA/TMALI, he also studied political economy and thought leadership. Currently, he is working at the Institute of Pan African Thought and Conversation (IPATC), the University of Johannesburg, as a senior research Fellow.

Kirunga Joyce is a human rights lawyer with a passion in intellectual property, data protection, and business and human rights. She has a keen interest in social, economic, and political inclusion of young people and women in different societies. She holds a bachelor of laws from Uganda Christian University Mukono, a postgraduate from Kenya School of Law and a master of laws from the University of Nairobi. She currently works with the Uganda Association of Women lawyers (FIDA-Uganda) where she works as an Advocacy officer. Her work focuses on developing advocacy strategies for the advancement of women's rights in the social and political arena.

Arnold Kwesiga is a human rights advocate and academic with over twelve years of experience working on forced migration issues, gender and sexuality, transitional justice, economic, social, and cultural rights, business and human rights, and corporate accountability. He currently manages the Business and Human Rights Unit at the Centre for Human Rights, University of Pretoria, South Africa, and also oversees the work of the African Coalition for Corporate Accountability (ACCA), a 132-membership coalition, whose secretariat is hosted at the Centre for Human Rights. Arnold holds an LLM in International Human Rights Law (University of Notre Dame, USA), a bachelor of laws degree (Makerere University, Uganda), and a diploma in law (Law Development Centre, Uganda). He also holds a number of advanced human rights certifications around sustainable development and global justice (University of Antwerp, Belgium), strategic litigation (Central European University), and business and human rights and the right to development (University of Pretoria, South Africa).

Muyamba Mangu has served as the Belgium Technical Cooperation (Enable) where he occupied various positions such as programme officer, National Director and Provincial Coordinator. He also formerly served as acting director of the Department of Development at the Council of Christian Churches in the Democratic Republic of Congo (DRC). Currently, he is deputy coordinator in charge of administration and finances at Office des Routes in the DRC, and he is a member of Institute for Democracy, Governance, Peace and Development in Africa (IDGPA). He holds a master of laws (LLM) in Multidisciplinary Human Rights from the Centre for Human Rights, University of Pretoria. He is currently a doctoral candidate in Law at the University of South Africa. His field of expertise comprises gender, community development, right to development, corporate social responsibility, and human rights. He also published book and articles in accredited journal.

John Olawuyi is a graduate of law from the University of South Africa (UNISA), and a law school graduate from the University of Pretoria. Presently, he is working as a legal assistant in a law firm in Nigeria whose principal is the first female chairperson of the Nigerian Bar Association. His research interests are human rights and corporate law. He is involved in a lot of practical things with technology and development while he looks forward to his LLM program in the nearest future.

Rita Ozoemena is currently an Associate Professor in the Department of Public, Constitutional, and International Law, College of Law, University of South Africa. She was appointed senior lecturer and coordinator, Legal Division Free State Centre for Human Rights, University of the Free State, South Africa in 2020. She is an advocate of the High Court of South Africa and was a member of the Johannesburg Society of Advocates (Johannesburg Bar). She is a multidisciplinary researcher. The specialist field of focus for her is exploring the gender dimensions of right to development and the contested area of culture and human rights in Africa. In these areas, she has traversed the social, cultural, and economic development particularly as it relates to the female gender. Her experience in the right to development scholarship has been the role and impact of culture, socioeconomic development and developing appropriate responses to Sustainable Development Goals. She has published several articles on gender justice and development in peer reviewed international journals.

Marianne Séverin is a researcher in at the Center for African studies, Les Afriques dans le Monde (LAM)/Science Po Bordeaux (France), as specialist of South African political context. She completed her PhD on the ANC and still works on the South African political and socioeconomic contexts. Her research focuses on the South African political landscape as well as the Rith to Development in South Africa, the protection of human rights including women's rights and disability rights in Africa, the struggle against corruption/ Illicit Financial Flows. She has presented numerous papers in international conferences, has published many articles and book chapters to address these questions. Currently her scientific interests focus on the concept of Ubuntu and the fight against corruption/illicit financial flows in South Africa.

Isaac Shai is an associate professor of law in the Department of Public, Constitutional and International Law at the University of South Africa. He earned his LLD from the University of Pretoria focusing on legal philosophy, constitutional theory, and the systems theoretical approach to law. His research interests include post-apartheid jurisprudence, post-apartheid constitutionalism, South African legal culture and postcolonial and decolonial approaches to law. His current projects include modernity, colonialism and constitutionalism, legal culture and legal reasoning in South Africa, law and development, constitutionalism, and radical transformation in South Africa. He is also an advocate of the High Court of South Africa and a member of the National Bar Council of South Africa.

www.ingramcontent.com/pod-product-compliance
Ingram Content Group UK Ltd.
Pitfield, Milton Keynes, MK11 3LW, UK
UKHW041832031026
15587UKWH00002B/718

9 781666 932300